The Kids' Complete Baseball Catalogue

Eric Weiner

JULIAN MESSNER

We have attempted to trace the ownership of all copyrighted material and to secure permission from copyright holders when required. In the event of any question arising as to the use of any material, we will be pleased to make corrections in future printings.

Acknowledgments

In compiling the information for this book, I had to make over a thousand phone calls. Almost without exception, the people I spoke with were happy to help and generous with their time. I thank them all.

Special thanks to: my editor, Bob McCord, who pitched in and helped out whenever my bases were loaded; Tom Heitz, Pat Kelly and the staff of the National Baseball Hall of Fame Library; the library's photo research department, who not only gave us endless hours of help, but who also gave us access to the xerox machine; and most of all, my girl friend Cherie, whose support never wavered despite her deepseated hatred of our national pastime.

The publishers of *Baseball America, Sports Market Place, Baseball Market Place,* and *Everything Baseball* by James Mote kindly gave us permission to use their reference books as a background for sections of this catalogue. I would also have been lost without: *Baseball Anecdotes* by Daniel Okrent and Steve Wulf; *The Baseball Catalog* by Dan Schlossberg; *Great Baseball Feats, Facts & Firsts* by David Nemec; *How to Watch Baseball* by Steve Fiffer; *The Sporting News Baseball Trivia Book;* and *Total Baseball.* Special thanks to Pat Fogarty.—Eric Weiner.

Library of Congress Cataloging-in-Publication Data

Weiner, Eric
    The kids' complete baseball catalogue / by Eric Weiner
    p. 256 cm.
    Includes bibliographical references and index.
    Summary: A guide for locating information, services, products, and other materials relating to baseball.
    1. Baseball—Juvenile literature.   [1. Baseball—Miscellanea.]
    I. Title.
    GV867.5.M43   1990
    796.357—dc20
    ISBN 0-671-70196-7
    ISBN 0-671-70197-5 (pbk.)
                                      90-45155
                                      CIP
                                      AC

Cover Photo Credits
© Topps Baseball Cards Inc.; Jose Canseco, TV Sports Mailbag; Little League Photo, Putsee Vannucci; Childbatting, Jack Goldstein; Press Pins, National Baseball Library

Photo Credits
p2 TV Sports Mailbag; p4 National Baseball Library, Cooperstown, NY (NBL); p6 NBL; p7 NBL; p9 UPI Bettmann; p10 TV Sports Mailbag, UPI Bettmann; p13 NBL; p15 UPI Bettmann; p17 UPI Bettmann; p19 UPI Bettmann; p21 NBL; p22 NBL; p28 Yale University; p31 NBL; p33 Yale; p35 USC; p36 University of Georgia; p37 UCLA; p38 University of Notre Dame; p39 USC; p41 Wide World; p42 NBL; p43 NBL; p44 UPI Bettmann; p46 NBL; p49 AP; p50 NBL; p52 AP; p54 NBL; p55 NBL; p56 TV Sports Mailbag; p57 AP; p58 UPI Bettmann; p59 NBL; p60 NBL; p61 NBL; p62 James Cavanaugh; p63 James P. McCoy; p65 NBL; p67 AP; p69 Bruce Endries, Oneonta Daily Star; p70 American Legion Baseball; p71 AP; p73 Valdosta State College; p74 Kathy Mecklenburg; p76 Putsee Vannucci; p84 George Biron; p87 George Biron; p88 Vannucci; p91 NBL; p92 NBL; p93 UPI Bettmann; p94 TV Sports Mailbag; p96 NBL; p97 NBL; AP; p99 NBL; p100 NBL; p101 NBL; p105 Stan Diamond/Pony Baseball, American Amateur Baseball Congress; p107 NBL; p108 NBL; p109 TV Sports Mailbag, Elizabeth Karnazes; p111 Elizabeth Karnazes; p113 NBL; p114 NBL; p116 NBL; p119 Sports Illustrated; p120 AP; p123 NBL; p124 TV Sports Mailbag; p126-7 AP; p128 Elizabeth Karnazes; p129 NBL; p130 Paramount Picture Corp; p133 NBL; p135 NBL; p137 NBL; p138 NBL; p139 Orion Pictures; p140 NBL; p141 Elizabeth Karnazes; p143 NBL; p147 NBL; p151 Vannucci; p155 NBL; p159 Marc Okkonen, NBL; p168 Newsday; p177 NBL; p178 UPI Bettmann; p182 Marc Okkonen, NBL; p190 NBL; p191 AP; p193 NBL; p195 TV Sports Mailbag; p198 NBL; p200 NBL; p201 NBL; p203 NBL; p204 NBL; p205 AP; p207 AP; p209 NBL; p210 NBL; p211 NBL, Grand Slam, Inc.; p214-15 Grand Slam, Inc.; p217 NBL; p218 NBL; p222 NBL; p223 NBL; p224 NBL; p226-7 NBL; p228 NBL; p229 AP; p231 Detroit Tigers; p234 UPI Bettmann; p235 USC; p236 TV Sports Mailbag; p237 NBL; p238 Oakland Tribune; p239 NBL; p240 UPI; p241 TV Sports Mailbag; p242 NBL; p242 NBL; p244 NBL; p245 UPI Bettmann; p246 NBL.

INTRODUCTION

"It's a long fly ball ... it's going back ... way back!"

That sounds like an announcer describing a home run. But it also describes baseball itself.

The game of baseball goes back, way back. Who knows? Maybe even the cave people used to club rocks around now and then. (See the articles in this chapter on baseball history.)

Needless to say, baseball has changed a lot over the years. And every year it seems that baseball's popularity in the United States grows even larger. It's not called the national pastime for nothing. By 1986, every major league team had an annual attendance of more than a million fans!

And that's just the major leagues. Then there are the minor leagues, college leagues, amateur leagues, youth leagues, softball leagues, and leagues in foreign countries. If you counted up all these fans, who knows how high a number you'd get?

With so many baseball lovers out there, the field of baseball has expanded wildly. There are baseball museums, libraries, games, camps ... the list goes on and on.

And that's the purpose of this book, to try to bring all these various services and products together in one place—one central information source. It's a kids' baseball "yellow pages."

There's so much information out there that one catalogue cannot contain it all. Often this catalogue will refer you to other catalogues (many of which you can send for, for free). And those catalogues will probably mention other catalogues. And so on.

Superstar Bo Jackson gets set to clobber the ball.

2

The truth is, once you get involved with baseball, there's no limit to how involved you can get. At the very least, this book will get you to first base. And, if the baseball bug bites you, you'll soon be rounding second, then third, and heading for home.

HOW TO USE THIS BOOK

No one likes to read instructions. People usually read a new toy's instructions after they've broken the toy. Then they read the instructions to find out why!

But you should read the notes in this introduction before you read any other part of the book. From then on, you can jump around from chapter to chapter, page to page, or go straight through.

If you're looking for something specific, first check the table of

contents. The chapter headings should guide you to the right chapter. It may help to read the introduction to each chapter before reading the chapter itself. These have more instructions and tell you what's included. Or if you're looking for something even more specialized, look it up in the index.

Some information falls into several chapters. For instance, for many baseball-related activities, you'll want to get in touch with the office of a team. These team addresses and telephone numbers are listed in Chapter 1 and are not repeated. But whenever you need that information for a suggested activity, there's a note that says, "See Chapter 1 for the addresses and phone numbers of team offices."

No matter how you use this book, you're sure to "slide into" baseball jokes, trivia, questions, quizzes, mysteries, and puzzles along the way. This catalogue is loaded with them!

SENDING AWAY FOR THINGS AND OTHER LETTER-WRITING INSTRUCTIONS

The prices of baseball

material listed in this catalogue vary widely. For instance, if you want to buy a coin-operated batting cage for your backyard, you'll need to spend $100,000 (Chapter 9). But getting your glove repaired by the American Glove Company (also Chapter 9) could cost you as little as $3 plus postage.

A $3 expense is within most kids' budgets. But if you're sending away for something—even if it's very cheap—you shouldn't send cash or coins in the mail. (Someone could open up the letter and steal the money. At the very least, coins will weigh the letter down and add to the postage costs.)

You'll need to ask your parents to make out a check or money order to the company. The check should be for the price of the item plus postage and handling (handling means they charge you a little for the time it takes them to "handle" your order). If you're ordering a product from your own state, you'll also need to pay sales tax. Check with the company first to find out the exact amount.

Whenever you write to a company (to make an order, to get a catalogue, or to ask a question), be sure to *write your return address*—neatly—on the envelope and on the letter itself.

FREE MATERIAL AND SASE's

Talk about cheap ... many of the items listed in this catalogue are *free!* There's even a special chapter on free material (Chapter 5).

In many cases, when you're sending for something free, such as a catalogue, you'll need to include a SASE (pronounced "sassy"). That's a self-addressed stamped envelope.

When you send a SASE, all that the company has to do is stick the material into your envelope, seal it up, and drop it in the mail. That's easy for them to do, and because it's so easy they're much more likely to do it.

Your SASE should be big enough to hold whatever it is you're asking for (at least business size, 9½ inches long). And you should put the correct amount of postage on it. Otherwise it won't get to you.

When you're addressing a SASE, you should always put the proper return address on it as well. The return address

on a SASE is the address of the company you're writing to!

This next tip goes for all letters to companies, but it's especially important if you're requesting something free: Be sure to state in your letter exactly which item or piece of information you want.

It helps to <u>underline</u> what you're asking for. It also helps if you don't ask for more than one thing at a time. If you write to a team office and ask them

to do nine different favors for you at once, they're liable to do you the favor of tossing your letter in the trash.

HOLD THE PHONE

This catalogue lists hundreds of phone numbers. Warning: Unless your family keeps moving—and always moves to the state you want to call just at the right moment—almost all of these calls will be *long distance* calls for you.

THE DOUBLEDAY MYTH
BASEBALL THROUGH THE AGES

Quick! Who invented baseball? Abner Doubleday? Thomas Alva Edison? Or Alexander Graham Ball, uh, Bell?

Most people would answer Doubleday. But it's a trick question. Because most sports historians feel that the correct answer is "none of the above." They say that Doubleday's invention of baseball is pure myth.

First of all, there are records of people playing with a ball and stick since ... well, since the time that people started keeping records!

Some of the games that may have led to modern-day baseball include lapta (a Russian ball-and-stick game), rounders (a British children's game played in the 1600s with stakes for bases), cricket (the British game that gave us umpires and innings), and one old cat (an American version of rounders with only one

base and three players.

There are various records of these forms of baseball being played in America way before Doubleday came on the scene. For example, an army surgeon by the name of Albigence Waldo wrote about George Washington's soldiers playing a form of baseball at Valley Forge, as they tried to unwind during the Revolutionary War.

Doubleday supposedly invented the game in Cooperstown, New York, one summer in 1839. As it turns out, records show that Doubleday wasn't even in Cooperstown that summer. And he probably only made a few slight changes in the game as it was already being played.

Nevertheless, the magnificent Baseball Hall of Fame and Museum chose Cooperstown as its home, in Doubleday's honor.

That means that they will be EXPENSIVE. Your parents will not appreciate it if any of these calls show up on their bill without their permission.

Even calls to the Information operator (to find out other phone numbers) will show up on the monthly bill. And making a lot of local calls (calls to your own area code) can add up to extra money on the bill as well. *So remember: Before making any calls, be sure to check* *with your parents first.*

One exception, and a happy one, is the 800 number. Any number with an 800 area code (the area code is the first three digits listed in parentheses) is FREE, no matter where you call it from. (This applies only to the 800 area code—not the 900 area code. And not to any other area code.)

Companies pay for 800 numbers as a courtesy to their customers and as a way to help drum up business. If you only call 800 numbers, you can browse by phone for free—add your name to mailing lists, check to see if certain products are still available, ask for free catalogues, etc.

(Sometimes companies have two 800 numbers. One is for the people who live in the same state or city as the company, the other is for everyone else. Be sure to call the right number or you won't get through.)

DIALING INSTRUCTIONS

To dial a local number (one that's in your area code), you don't have to dial the area code. For all other numbers, you'll need to dial 1 first. (Otherwise you'll hear a recording that says, "Dial 1 first!")

Then dial the area code and number. Sometimes numbers are spelled out with letters or words. For instance, H&B, the makers of Louisville Slugger bats, list their toll-free number as (800) 282-BATS!

That's just an easy way for you to remember the number. If you look on the phone, you'll see that the letters stand for numbers. (Take a look at the letters that match up with your own phone number. You may be able to make up a word or phrase for your own number as well.)

I GOT YOUR NUMBER! (ADDRESS CHANGES)

Phone numbers change. So do addresses. Companies go out of business, and new ones start up. Even as you read this, some of the information in this book is slowly becoming (gasp!) out of date.

Hopefully, everyone you contact will still be where this book says they are. But, with a little detective

1988 Cy Young winner, Frank Viola.

work on your part, you can also track down some of the companies who've moved.

When a company changes its phone number, it usually leaves a recorded message at the old number telling you where you can reach it now. If the recording just says that the number has been disconnected, it may be a sign that the company has gone out of business.

If you really need to reach them, though, you can check with Information. To do this, dial 1, the three-digit area code of the original number, then 555-1212. (Remember: This is not a free call!) Ask for the city listed in the company's address. If the company has a new number in the same city, Information can give it to you.

YOUR THOUGHTS?

Do you have ideas for baseball items to be added to future editions of this catalogue? Are there things about the book that you'd like to see changed? Or maybe you'd just like us to know that the book is absolutely 100 percent perfect in each and every way and thank you very much.

No matter what kind of comment you'd like to make, we'd love to hear from you. We won't be able to answer all the letters, but we *can* respond to your comments in future editions.

Write to:

THE KIDS' COMPLETE
BASEBALL CATALOGUE
Robert McCord
c/o Homerun Publications
382 Central Park West,
Suite 12R
New York, NY 10025

ALEXANDER CARTWRIGHT
THE REAL FATHER OF MODERN BASEBALL

In the 1840s there were still a number of different types of baseball being played in the United States. In fact, if it wasn't for Alexander Cartwright, people today might still be playing Massachusetts' version.

That would mean that if you fielded a grounder on the first bounce, the runner would be out. Or you could get the runner out by throwing the ball at the runner and hitting him!

Cartwright organized a team, the New York Knickerbocker Club. Just as importantly, he wrote down his version of baseball rules, so that everyone would be playing the same game.

Those rules have changed drastically over the years. But many feel that the Knickerbockers' first game against the New York Nine in Hoboken, New Jersey, was the true beginning of modern baseball.

What thanks did Cartwright get for organizing such an important event? His team had the honor of losing, 23–1.

JOIN THE CLUB!
FAN CLUBS AND OTHER GROUPS

HOORAYYYYYYYYYYYY!!!!!!

What's all the cheering about? No reason, just for the fun of yelling and rooting. Of course, it's more fun to cheer at a baseball game—when you're yelling and rooting for the home team to win!

Baseball fans, like fans in most sports, tend to feel very close to their team. A victory by their team can make their day, and a loss can ruin it.

Whether your team wins or loses, you don't have to suffer (or rejoice) alone. Most major league teams have fan, or booster, clubs. Booster clubs are usually for grownups, but you might be able to join with a parent. And some, such as the Oakland A's Booster Club, welcome young members with or without parents.

Information about some of the major league booster clubs is listed below. You can also contact your favorite team's office (see Chapter 1).

Many of the major league teams also run junior fan clubs. Most of these clubs involve special ticket discounts and come with a membership card and special gifts. More specific information is listed below for each team.

The prices and gifts in these clubs vary widely from year to year. You'll have to check with the team in question (using the addresses in Chapter 1) to find out the current status of the club.

If you want to write a letter to a major league player, coach, or manager, you should write to him in care of the team. (Again, get the address from Chapter 1.)

For instance, if you wanted to write to Wally Joyner, you would address the letter like this:

Mr. Wally Joyner
c/o The California Angels
P.O. Box 2000
Anaheim, CA 92803

Some star players, such as Cal Ripken, Jr., of the Baltimore Orioles, have a fan club all their own. A few of these individual fan clubs are mentioned on page 11, under the team that the player plays for.

But many times the team office isn't aware that the player has a fan club of his own. The best way to find out is to write to the player in care of his team.

STARTING YOUR OWN FAN CLUB

If your favorite player doesn't have a fan club, and you're feeling very ambitious, you might even be able to start your own!

Fans are always starting fan clubs. What's involved? It's really up to

The gloves are white. So what team are these kids rooting for?

you. If you want to have an informal club, you and a small bunch of friends can form the club, sit together at games, make banners that announce your club, etc.

If you're going to charge a membership fee, or give away any souvenirs such as photos of the player, then you're going to need special permission. *You'll need that permission both from the player himself, and from the community services department of the player's team.*

The community services department may be able to help you with some general advice, and tell you about other player fan clubs that have sprung up recently.

Among other things, this department helps to arrange for players to make public appearances. If your fan club gets big enough, you may be able to get your star to come speak to the club.

But to get that many members, you'll have to find a way to advertise your club. Ms. Ruth Burnette, who runs the Cal Ripken, Jr., Fan Club in Baltimore, gives all her members special T-shirts that advertise the club. When members wear the T-shirts at games, it helps promote her club.

She has also gotten some free advertising by calling local TV and radio stations (see Chapter 7) and telling them about her club. Announcers have mentioned her fan club on the air—that's free publicity.

And news stations have filmed her special Cal Ripken Room, a room in her house that she's devoted to Ripken souvenirs and paraphernalia.

If you write a letter to your local paper about your club, explaining why you think your player deserves a fan club, you might get yourself some more free advertising (that is, if they print the letter).

You could also start your own newsletter. For this, you'll probably need access to a copy machine—at school, say, or at your mom's or dad's office. In your newsletter you could print letters from members of your club, special

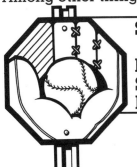

SHORTSTOPS
At first, fans stood up for the "7th inning stretch" because the number 7 was thought to be lucky. Standing up in the 7th, fans hoped, would bring good luck to their team.

9

information about the player—anything you want!

How long will your fan club last? Some fan clubs have lasted for years and years. The St. Louis Browns have been defunct for thirty years. But in 1984, diehard fans started a new fan club for their beloved team!

Many Brooklyn Dodgers fans still suffer over their team's departure for Los Angeles in 1957. These fans have a tradition that's still alive today. They don't mention the name of the man who moved the team without also uttering an oath.

The name? Walter O'Malley.

Drat on him!

Any Oriole fan could name these three. From left to right: Billy Ripkin, Cal Ripkin, Sr., and Cal Ripkin, Jr.

BAT BOYS AND BAT GIRLS

If joining a fan club still doesn't make you feel close enough to your favorite team, there is a way to spend every day with them: Be a bat boy or bat girl.

These are hard jobs to get, since lots of kids cherish the idea of hanging around the players or being on the field during game time.

It's harder for girls. Few teams use full-time bat or ball girls, since a large part of the work involved takes place in the players' locker room. But many teams have honorary bat boys and bat girls who perform duties just during the game.

Usually for pay, full-time bat boys help clean up the clubhouse—vacuuming, washing the uniforms, polishing players' shoes.

During the game, bat boys and girls retrieve foul balls, run a new bat out to batters who've broken their bat, keep the umpire supplied with fresh baseballs, and retrieve the dropped bats of players who have gotten on base.

In general, teams look

Some extra chores for a bat boy: This Yankee bat boy umps in neighborhood games.

for kids 16 and up with good grades—to be sure that they can handle the long hours at the stadium without falling behind at school. (Some clubhouse jobs may need you for as many as five hours a day.)

To apply, write to the team in care of the Clubhouse Manager or Equipment Manager. For information about what a specific team is looking for in a bat boy or bat girl, check in this chapter in the section under that team's name.

OTHER BASEBALL GROUPS

Beginning on page 24, you'll find a listing of other baseball-related groups. They're not fan clubs, and almost all of them are not clubs you can join. But they are baseball groups that may be of use to you, providing you with everything from minor league statistics to answers to questions about obscure baseball history.

THE AMERICAN LEAGUE

BALTIMORE ORIOLES

Each year a local paper, the *Baltimore Sun,* sponsors the Fantastic Fans club.

For a $13 membership fee, fans get single tickets to eight Orioles home games, plus a chance to purchase eight additional reserved tickets for any or all of those games at 50 percent off the normal price.

Fantastic Fans also receive a club membership card, a special cap, and other discounts on merchandise and food. Better still, you can attend the Orioles' annual baseball clinic at the stadium, with players coaching you on your hitting.

And you get a chance to win a bat boy/bat girl contest. If you win, you'll attend batting practice and meet all the players.

Fantastic Fans might also end up in the press box as a guest during the broadcast, if they win a special contest.

Cal Ripken, Jr., has his very own fan club. Members get a membership card, T-shirt, photos of Ripken, and an invitation to the annual banquet. The Ripkens attend.

Membership is $20 for the first year, $15 a year thereafter. To join, write to:

The Cal Ripken, Jr., Fan Club
c/o Ms. Ruth Burnette
826 Lynn Lee Drive
Aberdeen, MD 21001

If you're interested in being a bat boy or bat girl all season long, write to the Equipment Manager. Right now that's Mr. Jim Tyler. He gets lot of applicants, and bat boys and bat girls like to hold onto their jobs from the previous season. But it's worth a try. To be eligible, you can be any age right up through high school.

MASCOT. The Orioles' Bird is a large orange-breasted Oriole who walks through the stadium every game, stirring up the fans. The person inside the bird suit changes from year to year.

UNUSUAL PROMOTION DAYS. In addition to many other special days, the Orioles often offer a "Shirt Off Our Backs Day" at the end of the season.

Fans enter a raffle contest. Winners receive an Orioles jersey right off the player's back, as a souvenir.

SPECIAL FAN CUSTOMS. If you're not from Baltimore and you attend an Orioles home game, you may come away thinking that the fans here are terrible singers.

Since the Orioles are known as the O's, fans have taken to screaming out the "O" during the national anthem. So "O say does that star-spangled banner..." becomes "OOOOOOOOOOOOOO!!! say does that star-spangled banner..."

"It kind of ruins the song," says a spokesman for the team, "but it's fun."

THE BULL PEN
Q: Why was it so breezy at the stadium?
A: Because of all the fans.

BOSTON RED SOX

There isn't a kids' fan club. Kids can join the BoSox Club, a booster club, but you'll need to join with a parent.

The annual fee is $40. You'll need to get an application and be sponsored by a member. (The club recommends paying for admission to one of their luncheons as a way of meeting other members and being sponsored.)

The boosters do volunteer work for the Sox. They go to spring training to see their team warm up. They hold special booster luncheons. And, most popular of all, on special family nights they get free tickets to Sox games and attend an autograph session with the players.

The club also sponsors an annual essay-writing contest for kids. The winner gets to go to baseball camp for free.

For information about the contest or joining the club, write to:

BoSox Club
P.O. Box 582
Needham, MA 02194
(617) 449-0989

MASCOT. None.
UNUSUAL PROMOTION DAYS. On Father, Son, and Daughter Day, the children of the players play a special pregame exhibition game. (A number of other teams have this tradition as well.)

SPECIAL FAN CUSTOMS. Not thinking highly of the New York Yankees.

CALIFORNIA ANGELS

The Angels Booster Club is mainly for adults, but you might be able to join with your parents.

The avid fans in this club go to the games as a group. They also meet between games for special lectures by guest speakers, and to root for their team. For information, contact:

Angels Booster Club
P.O. Box 3820
Anaheim, CA 92803
President: Mr. Rich Kanger

The Angels themselves run what they call their Junior Angels Club. For a low price, kids 15 and under get tickets to five different Angels games. Those games usually include a number of giveaway games—such as Bat Day—when every kid who comes to the stadium gets a special baseball gift.

Members of the club also get a membership card, an Angels decal, and their name printed on their tickets.

The specific details of the Junior Angels Club vary from year to year, so contact the team office for more information (see Chapter 1).

MASCOT. None.
UNUSUAL PROMOTION DAYS. Like many teams, the Angels have a Fan Appreciation Day. On theirs, a team photo is given to every fan who comes to the stadium.

They also have Neon Sunglasses Day. Every fan gets a pair for that cool, California look.

SPECIAL FAN CUSTOMS. The Angels have begun giving away rally bells on promotion days, to be rung whenever the players start a rally.

CHICAGO WHITE SOX

Fans of all ages are welcome to join the Chisox Club. For a $10 membership fee, you get an official membership card, two free tickets to a home game, baseball cards, and a quarterly publication known as *The Comiskey Columns*, with lots of information on the team.

MASCOT. Ribbie and

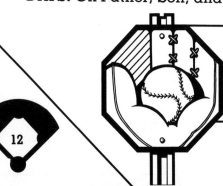

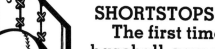

SHORTSTOPS
The first time admission was charged for a baseball game was in 1858. The price was 50 cents.

Rhubarb, two bearlike creatures, used to be the mascots. But currently the team is mascotless.

UNUSUAL PROMOTION DAYS. In addition to about 50 different giveaway days, the Chisox boast of fireworks every Saturday night. Not only that, every time the home team hits a homer, the scoreboard explodes—literally. It shoots off a brief fireworks display of its own.

CLEVELAND INDIANS

The Indians have the Little Indians Club. A $6 membership fee gets you a fan club gift (such as a sports bag), a membership card, a picture of your favorite Indians player, tickets to four games for $1 each, a game schedule, a team decal, a discount card for souvenirs, and a birthday card sent to you from the team on the

appropriate date.

At the end of the season, all Little Indians are invited to an autograph session with all the players. Membership forms can be picked up at certain area stores, depending on which store is sponsoring the program that year. Or you can write to the team for an application card.

MASCOT. None.

UNUSUAL PROMOTION DAYS. Kids Opening Weekend. This is a new custom. The Indians will be offering special prizes for kids right from the start of the season.

DETROIT TIGERS

They don't have any official fan clubs as such.

If you're interested in being a bat boy (the Tigers don't have bat girls), write to the Clubhouse Manager. The job of bat boy is a full-time, paid position with the Tigers.

If you're a Tigers bat boy, you're known as a clubhouse boy. You arrive at 12:00 noon each day to do the laundry and help out with other chores before game time. The job lasts from April through September. What are they looking for in their applicants? They'll only consider 16- to 18-year-olds

THE OLDEN TIMES

In 1902, Charlie Smith lived out every fan's greatest dream. That year, Smith was in the stands for a Cleveland-Philadelphia game. Cleveland needed a pitcher. A ticket taker told the Cleveland manager that there was a fan in the stands who was talented.

Smith was given a brief tryout on the spot. He signed a contract, came in to pitch, and won the game! He went on to play pro ball for the next ten years.

with straight A's!

MASCOT. None. But one avid fan, Joe Diroff, could almost be said to fill the role for all of Detroit sports. He attends every single Tiger home game. He also goes to all the Redwings and Pistons games.

When teams return from road trips at 2:00, 3:00, and 4:00 in the morning, he's there to greet them. In his white shirt, golf cap, and Tiger tie, he's always marching around the stadium during Tiger games, leading Tiger cheers.

UNUSUAL PROMOTION DAYS. Each year the Tigers honor the Millionth Fan to come to a game. The winner gets a color TV, two season passes for the next season, and is honored during the game.

They also give a Two Millionth Fan award, if attendance gets that high.

On Fan Appreciation Weekend, big prizes such as trips to Disney World are given away. Winners are selected in a random drawing of ticket stubs from the weekend games.

KANSAS CITY ROYALS

According to the team office, there are no fan clubs for the teams and no fan clubs for individual players. Take it away, Royals fans!

MASCOT. None.
UNUSUAL PROMOTION DAYS. Famous Chicken Day. A clown in a chicken suit roams around the stadium and on the field, squawking at the umpires.

MILWAUKEE BREWERS

If you're under 16 you're eligible to join the Brewers' Ticket Fan Club. You get tickets to six games at a reduced price ($14.95 for the whole season). You also get a fan club T-shirt, a team photo, a membership card, and a one-year subscription (nine issues) to *What's Brewing?*, the Brewers' official magazine.

Bat boys (they don't have bat girls) must be at least 16 years of age and have good grades at school. To apply, write to Mr. Jimmy Bank, the team's traveling secretary.

Bat boy is an all-season job and hard to get. You must be willing to be at the stadium for long hours during the season.

MASCOT. None.
SPECIAL FAN CUSTOMS. During the 7th inning stretch, Brewers fans sing "Roll Out the Barrel" in honor of their namesake, the beer industry along with the traditional "Take Me Out to the Ball Game."

Abbyland Brats, a popular local sausage, are served at the stadium along with hot dogs. (Brat

WHEN FANS GET ROWDY

Expressing disapproval is part of being a baseball fan. For instance, there's the Bronx Cheer. It's named after Yankee fans (Yankee Stadium is in the Bronx). The Bronx Cheer isn't a cheer at all. It's an expression of disgust made by blowing hard past one's loose lips. (It's also known as a raspberry.)

Of course, the more universal fan disapproval method is the boo. Fans boo the umps when they don't like their calls. They boo the manager when they don't like his decisions. They razz and boo the opposing players to try to throw them off their game. They even boo their own players—when they don't get a hit for a long time, say, or make a key error.

How do players feel about being booed? Los Angeles pitcher Bo Belinsky once said,

is short for bratwurst.)

MINNESOTA TWINS

Here's another team that seems to be currently short on fan clubs. Dan Gladden does have his own fan club, however. There's both a Minnesota chapter and a California chapter (in his home town). Members receive a newsletter, a birthday card from Dan, a visor, and invitations to special pregame tailgate parties attended by Dan.

The cost is $12 per year. To join, your parents would need to send a check (made payable to the Dan Gladden Fan Club) to:

The Dan Gladden Fan Club
33178 Lake Superior Place
Fremont, CA 94555

MASCOT. None.
UNUSUAL PROMOTION DAYS. It's against the rules for a fan in a baseball stadium to throw "Some day I would like to go up in the stands and boo some fans."

Booing may hurt a player's feelings, but it's part of baseball. Unfortunately, some fans don't leave it at that.

Rowdy fans also throw things, and they have since the beginnings of baseball. In 1907, fans stopped a game by throwing snowballs!

Snowballs thrown from great heights can be very dangerous. But fans have thrown more lethal objects. One umpire was nearly killed by a soft drink bottle thrown by a fan.

To try to protect the players' lives, major league teams have taken to prohibiting certain items from being brought into the stadium. They forbid any items that a fan is likely to toss.

They've also passed rules that forbid beer sales in the late innings. These rules have kept fans more sober, and a little less rowdy.

Rowdy fans have caused other major problems, such as fighting in the stands. Baseball teams have had to increase the police security at ballparks to try to combat the fisticuffs.

Hopefully, in the future fans will spend more and more of their time watching the game!

anything. Other fans and players could be terribly injured by almost anything thrown from high up in the stands.

So the Twins have a special Paper Airplane Day to help their fans get it out of their systems. Throughout the game, fans can purchase paper airplanes for 50 cents each. After the game, prize cars are parked in the middle of their field with their windows rolled down.

Fans sign and throw their paper airplanes, aiming for the cars. The winner of each car is randomly selected from the airplanes that have glided inside that car's open windows.

SPECIAL FAN CUSTOMS. Hankie-waving has gone out of fashion here since the last time the Twins made it to the World Series. So far no new fad has replaced it.

NEW YORK YANKEES

For $6 you can join the Yankee Juniors. You'll get a T-shirt, ticket and souvenir discounts, a pocket schedule, decals, and other material. You'll also be invited to attend baseball clinics with the Yankee players (there'll be at least two during the

season).

Don Mattingly has his own fan club. So does Steve Sax. For more information, write to them in care of the team.

The Yankees don't have bat girls. Bat boy candidates should apply to the stadium manager, Bill Squires, sometime in January. Applicants must be 16 and have good grades. It's a big job requiring lots of hours at the stadium.

MASCOT. None.

OAKLAND ATHLETICS

The A's have one of the biggest and most successful booster clubs in the nation. Its 1,900 members get together regularly to attend games and pregame tailgate parties. They hold fund-raising luncheons and help the A's in any way they can.

They organize trips—to spring training, to Modesto to see the A's minor league team, and to root for the A's when they're away from home.

They also do charity work. The club raises funds to sponsor a trip for a handicapped group to every Saturday home game.

Kids are welcome to join the booster club, with or without their parents.

Membership is $7.50 a year (luncheons and other outings cost extra). Members get an embroidered jacket patch, a decal, a monthly newsletter, and good seats at the stadium (sometimes at discounted prices).

For an application card, contact:

Oakland A's Booster Club
P.O. Box 491
San Leandro, CA 94577
(415) 351-3097

Mark McGwire has his own fan club, which is run by his brother. For information, write to Mark in care of the A's.

As with most teams, the A's bat boys are hired through the Clubhouse Manager. Honorary bat boys and bat girls are selected through contests.

MASCOT. None.

UNUSUAL PROMOTION DAYS. They have Airplane Toss Day. To win the prizes, fans try to get their paper airplanes to land in hoops on the field.

SEATTLE MARINERS

They've had official fan clubs and booster clubs in the past, but as of the writing of this book, their

SHORTSTOPS
During the Civil War, Union Army soldiers sometimes played exhibition baseball games. This helped spread the game all over the country.

fan club has folded.

According to a team spokesman, it's up to the fans to start clubs for individual players. So for all you Mariners fans out there: They need you!

MASCOT. A special contest was held to elect an animal as mascot. The moose won. Starting in 1990, a man in a large moose costume should be a standard sight at home games, leading cheers.

Umps Billy Williams (left) and Tom Gorman (right) rode to this game in style.

TEXAS RANGERS

Kids 13 and under are eligible to join the Dr. Pepper Junior Rangers Club. You can join by getting an application from the back of a two-liter Dr. Pepper bottle bought in a local supermarket.

If you're not from the area, contact the team directly for an application.

For $12, you get a membership card, a picture of your favorite Ranger, general admission tickets to eight different games, a T-shirt, a decal, and a coupon for a free two-liter bottle of Dr. Pepper.

On Junior Ranger Night, the Junior Rangers all sit together in the outfield. One Junior Ranger is selected to throw out the game ball.

If you want to apply for full-time bat boy work, write to the General Manager. Honorary bat boy and bat girl positions are auctioned off during the season and are selected in other ways. The winners perform game duties for one game.

MASCOT. None.

UNUSUAL PROMOTION DAYS. Kids 13 and under are eligible for giveaways on special days. If you go to all of them, you can assemble an entire Rangers uniform during the course of a season, with cap, shirt, pants, bat, ball, glove, wrist bands, socks, and equipment bag.

SPECIAL FAN CUSTOMS. Fans used to wave a Beat the Yankee Hankie, but it's gone out of fashion.

TORONTO BLUE JAYS

There isn't a kids' fan club. But they do have Junior Jay Days—on a couple of days during the year kids get in for a much cheaper price.

MASCOT. B. J. Birdy. The B. J. stands for Blue Jay, of course.

UNUSUAL PROMOTION DAYS. Fans in attendance on Radio Day receive a numbered sticker to put on their gift radio. If they're listening to the radio during the game and hear their number called, they win a prize.

SPECIAL FAN CUSTOMS. During the 7th inning stretch, local fitness instructors get on the dugout roofs and lead fans in a series of exercises. Also, "Take Me Out to the Ball Game" is *not* sung. Since 1982, "O.K. Blue Jays" has been the vastly more popular selection.

THE NATIONAL LEAGUE

ATLANTA BRAVES

The Braves booster club, known as the 400 Club, is mainly for senior citizens. At present there are no formally organized kids' fan clubs.

MASCOT. The Braves have three—count 'em, three—mascots. Homer the Brave, a big Indian, dresses up for the games in a funny outfit and huge head (like a giant Mr. Potato Head). His head weighs 80 pounds, and he's eight feet tall.

Rally—a big, red furry thing—is known as a great dancer. Furskin Bear, a five-foot-tall teddy bear, runs around in a Braves uniform, clowning throughout the game.

In addition to stirring up the fans, from the fourth through the eighth innings the mascots are available in the kids' corner at Gate Q's picnic tent. During these innings you can get the mascots' autographs and have your picture taken with them.

You might also meet one of the Braves' mascots around town. Through what's called the Grandslam Program,

Braves mascots have been making trips to schools and hospitals. "They're more popular than the players!" says a team spokesman.

The mascots are encouraging Atlanta schoolkids to stay in school, stay off drugs, stay informed about current events by reading, and stay fit.

UNUSUAL PROMOTION DAYS. In the 1970s, the Braves' stadium was the sight of some pretty strange and funky events to promote fan excitement. They even held ostrich races!

Since then, the Braves have returned to a more standard schedule of giveaway days. Postgame concerts by big groups such as the Beach Boys have become very popular.

So has the new Sunday Autograph Program. Every Sunday during the season, four players are available for 30 minutes before the game. The autograph sessions are open to the public. And free baseball cards for the four players are distributed, so you have something for the player to sign.

SPECIAL FAN CUS-TOMS. In 1990, TV's Ernest makes his first appearance on the Diamond Vision

scoreboard. Among other duties, Ernest will lead fans in singing 7th inning stretch songs. The Braves hope Ernest will catch on and become a full-fledged tradition.

CHICAGO CUBS

Believe it or not, the Cubs Diehard Fan Club has died! That leaves the Cubs without an official fan club.

The Cubs use two full-time bat boys. Applicants must be on the honor roll at school and enter an essay-writing contest on "what it means to you to be a bat boy for the Cubs." Contact Tom Cooper, Director of Stadium Operations.

They also have honorary bat boys and bat girls who serve one game each. These positions are awarded through contests.

MASCOT. None.

UNUSUAL PROMOTION DAYS. On Youth Clinic Day, the first 5,000 kids to arrive get to participate in an on-field pregame baseball clinic with the players.

SPECIAL FAN CUS-TOMS. Baseballs hit into the stands are much-sought-after souvenirs in every other park. But when an opposing team player hits a ball into the stands

SHORTSTOPS
The length of a baseball game—nine innings —was set in 1857.

here, it is customary among Cubs fans to throw the ball back onto the field.

It's as if the fans are saying, "Your baseball isn't good enough for us." Or, "If we fans have anything to do with it, you can't hit the ball into our stands. Not for long anyway!"

CINCINNATI REDS

The Reds booster club is for adult women. They're called the Rosy Reds, and they help out the team with their fund-raising activities.

MASCOT. None.

HOUSTON ASTROS

The Astros fan club for kids is known as the Buddies Club. For $6 you receive six free game coupons, an Astros backpack, a sticker sheet, a subscription to the Astros magazine, and a schedule of games.

There's also a booster club known as the Astro Orbiters, but it's mainly for adults.

MASCOT. Its name is Orbit. It's a creature seven feet tall, green and furry. Orbit wears an Astros' uniform and batting helmet. The helmet has two antennae, with a

baseball wobbling at the end of each one. Orbit entertains at games and goes to schools as part of a program sponsored by the F.B.I. for helping kids stay off drugs.

UNUSUAL PROMOTION DAYS. On Instant Vacation Day, fans who come to the park with their bags packed are eligible to win a free vacation. The winners leave directly from the stadium.

SPECIAL FAN CUSTOMS. Fans ring cow bells.

FAMOUS PROMOTIONS

Owners of baseball teams will do almost anything to get the fans to come to the ballpark in large numbers. One of the wackiest promoters was Cleveland Indians owner Bill Veeck.

In 1948, the Indians won the pennant. The following year, they didn't repeat as pennant winners. When they were officially out of the race, Veeck held a mock funeral out beyond center field. They put the pennant in a coffin and buried it!

On another occasion, Veeck let some of the fans manage the game. On August 24, 1951, 1,115 fans got to sit behind the dugout and hold up large YES or NO cards when the coaches held up cards with questions printed on them, such as STEAL? The fans did well. The home team won 5–3.

When Charlie Finley owned the often-losing Kansas City Athletics, he too tried all sorts of gimmicks to liven things up. He even put a flock of sheep out beyond the right-field wall with a shepherd to tend them. He got a mule named Charlie O. for a mascot. In one game the Kansas City starting lineup all rode in on mules.

LOS ANGELES DODGERS

The Dodgers have two booster clubs for grown-ups. At the moment they don't have a fan club for kids.

MASCOT. None.

UNUSUAL PROMOTION DAYS. What else for a Los Angeles team? The Dodgers have Hollywood Stars Night. A pregame exhibition game is played by movie celebrities.

MONTREAL EXPOS

Joining the Expos Fan Club costs $10 for kids and $20 for adults. As of 1990, they also require that your parents have a bank account at the Bank of Montreal. (Your checks will say Expo Fan Club on them, if you like.)

With a year's membership you get bulletins, letters from the players, an Expos pin, two gift certificates to attend a game during the season, a fan club bumper sticker, and a badge that you can sew onto your clothes.

MASCOT. He's called Youppi, and he looks kind of like a teddy bear.

UNUSUAL PROMOTION DAYS. On Saturdays and Sundays the players are available for autographs before the game, near the dugout.

NEW YORK METS

Kids 14 and under can join the Tropicana Team Mets Club. Among other items, members receive: a Team Mets fanny pack, baseball cards, discount ticket offers, and entry into a Mets baseball clinic.

To join, send $7 or $6 plus *two* Tropicana pure premium or pure premium homestyle 64 oz. carton proofs-of-purchase (UPC symbols) to:

Tropicana Team Mets Club
P.O. Box 4777
Trenton, NJ 08650

Include your name, address, and telephone number. Allow six to eight weeks for delivery.

MASCOT. None.

SPECIAL FAN CUSTOMS. Fans hang a row of K's to mark their pitchers' strikeouts. This started with Dwight Gooden, whose strikeout power earned him the nickname "Dr. K." ("K" is the symbol for a strikeout on a scorecard.)

PHILADELPHIA PHILLIES

There are plans for a Junior Phillies Phan Clan in the works. Contact the team office to see if the club has begun accepting members.

In the meantime, they have the Phan Clan for grownups and kids. For $20 you get a lifetime membership. That comes with a membership card and certificate, a Phan Clan lapel pin and window decal, a Phillies yearbook, a box seat ticket voucher for the year you join, a six-month subscription to the *Phillies Report* (a newspaper), and discounts on souvenirs, special Phillies trips, etc.

Members of the Phan Clan are also invited to the Holiday Fair in December. That's a big sale of Phillies souvenirs and merchandise at cost.

Honorary bat boys and bat girls are selected for a game at a time through a contest sponsored by the Leaf Candy Company. The winners get to hang out in the dugout before the game, and have their picture taken with the players.

The full-time bat boys are usually about 20 years old.

TRIVIA QUIZ

What baseball brothers have the highest total number of career home runs?

A) The Alou brothers (Matty, Jesus, and Felipe)
B) Hank and Tommie Aaron
C) The three DiMaggios (Joe, Dom, and Vince).

Answer: B, by a long shot. Hank's 755 easily make up for Tommie knocking out only 13.

fans go down onto the field and take pictures of the players up close.

PITTSBURGH PIRATES

The Pirates offer two different clubs for kids. The Knothole Gang is for kids 14 and under. With membership you get to go to two Pirates games. You take your pick from 10 different games. You also get a membership button, a painter's cap, a vinyl 6" x 8" baseball card holder, a wooden bat pen, and two issues of the Pirates newsletter.

It's all free, except for a $1 handling charge per membership. You can pick up a registration form at any of the 29 participating Hills Department Stores in Pennsylvania and nearby states. Or write or call the team office.

By the way, the idea of a "knothole" club goes way back. A manager named Abner Power invented it in 1889. That was two years after he founded the first rain-check system, allowing fans to see a game for the rained-out game they missed.

He noticed that there were always kids outside the stadium, looking in through knotholes in the

MASCOT. The Phillies Phanatic is big and green and very popular. In the fifth inning of every home game, he puts on a show. First he rides out from left field on his four-wheeler motorcycle. His act changes from game to game.

He's fond of lining up a few of the batting helmets of the opposing team and crushing them with a sledgehammer.

During the 7th inning stretch, he dances on the roof of the dugout. During the off season, you can hire the Phanatic to entertain at birthday parties, bar mitzvahs, and other special occasions. Contact Ms. Christine Legault in the Promotion Department.

UNUSUAL PROMOTION DAYS. On Camera Night

On bat day, every fan gets his or her very own "fan club"!

wooden fences. They didn't have the money to pay to get in, and Power decided to let them in free. Various major league teams have had knothole clubs ever since.

The other Pirates kids club is called the Straight-A Achievement Program. It's for students in grades 6–12.

In this program, there are two ways for students to earn free Pirates tickets: (1) by getting straight A's or an A average or (2) by improving your grade by two letters in any one subject or by one letter grade in two different

subjects while at the same time not getting a D, F, or incomplete in any subject.

The program is run by the schools. More than 400 schools participate in 35 Pennsylvania counties. Students receive two free tickets to two games out of a selection of eight.

MASCOT. If you write to the Pirate Parrot in care of the team, he may send you a postcard with his picture.

The card lists the following biographical data. *Hatched:* April 6, 1979. *Height:* Big. *Weight:* Feather. *How Acquired:* Born before a crowd of 36,141 in Three Rivers

Stadium on opening day, 1979.

UNUSUAL PROMOTION DAYS. On Halloween Night, held on Friday the 13th, fans come to the game dressed up in costume. All fans in costumes come out onto the field for costume judging. Best kids' costume and best adult costume each win a prize.

The Pirates also offer a weekly pizza pop-up. In their version of this event, a fan comes out onto the field and tries to catch three pop flies flung by a pitching machine. If he or she catches one pop-up, everybody in the park gets a free soft drink. If the fan catches two pop-ups, everybody in the park gets a free pitcher of soft drink.

And ... if the fan catches all three pop-ups, every fan in the park gets a small pizza. As you can imagine, the fans in the stands scream for the fan on the field to catch the ball.

SAN DIEGO PADRES

Padre fans 14 and under can join the Junior Padres. You sign up at 7-11's in and around San Diego, or you can write to the team.

For a $6 membership fee, Junior Padres can go to 11 free Padres games.

THE BULL PEN
Q: How is a pitcher like a yo-yo?
A: He starts each play with a wind-up.

You also get a set of Padres baseball cards and, on your birthday, a birthday card from the Padres themselves.

If you have a grandparent who takes you to the game, they might be interested in joining the Senior Padre Club. Seniors 55 and over get six free games for $6, a free meal, and $1 off their public transit ride to the stadium.

MASCOT. None.

UNUSUAL PROMOTION DAYS. Every Sunday that there's a home game, the Padres have Allie's Pop Fly Payoff. If the fan selected to do the honors catches any of three pop-ups, he or she earns some free food prizes from Allie's Restaurant.

Every Tuesday home game is also Denny's Trivia Tuesday. Fans receive a scratch-off card with Padres trivia questions. Scratch off the right answers and you'll win a free breakfast at Denny's.

Here's a sample trivia question that was asked in 1989:
The all-time Padre strikeout leader is:
A) Eric Show.
B) Sandy Jones.
C) Clay Kirby.
The correct answer is Eric Show.

SPECIAL FAN CUS-TOMS. Every stadium does the wave. But on Beach Towel Night here, Padres fans do the beach towel wave.

SAN FRANCISCO GIANTS

The official kids' fan club is known as the Little Giants. It's for kids 14 and under. The membership fee is $14.

Members receive coupons for the best available seats to five Giants games. Little Giants also get a digital wristwatch with the team logo, a Giants logo sticker sheet, and a membership card that's good for discounts at Giants Dugout stores (local stores that sell Giants souvenirs).

During the season, there are two special Little Giants games. At one, there is a Little Giants parade during the pregame show. Members make signs and carry them around the field.

At the other Little Giants event, the team's manager, Roger Craig, hosts a baseball clinic where Little Giants get batting instruction from the stars. They also get free hot dogs and other refreshments at the

hour-long tailgate party.

MASCOT. None.

UNUSUAL PROMOTION DAYS. Once a season the Giants hold a five-kilometer Run to Homeplate. Most of the race takes place outside the stadium. But the finish line is at home plate.

Anyone of any age can enter (the entry fee is $14). The first man and first woman to reach home plate get prizes. Everyone who enters gets a T-shirt, a free ticket to the game, and a chance at the grand prize raffle.

So you can run the race slowly and still be eligible for a prize. But you can't run too slowly. You'll miss the game!

On Save a Life Saturday, the Giants offer free CPR classes for kids and adults. Anyone who attends the class gets a coupon good for one free ticket to a Giants home game the following season.

SPECIAL FAN CUS-TOMS. Two local papers, the *San Francisco Examiner* and the *San Francisco Chronicle*, regularly include large orange cardboard cards in their editions during baseball season. The cards have simple messages such as "I FEEL

GOOD." Giants fans wave them at games, usually while chanting "Beat L.A.!"

ST. LOUIS CARDINALS

Another team that could use some fan clubs. There are no official ones at present.

MASCOT. The ever-popular Fred Bird (as opposed to red bird).

OTHER GROUPS RELATED TO BASEBALL

Associated Sports Fans (ASF)
1501 Lee Highway, Suite 205
Arlington, VA 22209
(703) 243-9101

The hope of this group is that if fans band together they'll have some say in what happens in sports. If enough fans join, maybe someday a group such as this could stop a baseball players' strike. (That's when all the players refuse to play until the team owners meet their salary demands.)

Association of Professional Ball Players of America
12062 Valley View Street, Suite 211
Garden Grove, CA 92645
(714) 892-9900

Not all baseball players get rich by any means. And some get sick, can't play, or run into hard times after they retire. This group works to help such needy players.

Baseball Alumni Team
350 Park Avenue
New York, NY 10022
(212) 371-7800

Like the Association of Professional Ball Players, this group works to help needy athletes after retirement.

Baseball Commissioner's Office
350 Park Avenue
New York, NY 10022
(212) 371-7800

The commissioner runs major league baseball, handing down many important rulings during each season. If you have a comment on one of those rulings, this is where to write.

Major League Baseball Players Association
805 Third Avenue
New York, NY 10022
(212) 826-0808

This is the players' union. The union negotiates with team owners trying to get better deals for players. It's the union that decides if the players will refuse to play

(go on strike). If you don't like the decision, this is where to write.

National Association of Professional Baseball Leagues
P.O. Box A
201 Bayshore Drive Southeast
St. Petersburg, FL 33731
(813) 822-6937

This group covers all the minor leagues. They keep minor league statistics, which could be useful to fantasy baseball players and other fans.

U.S. Baseball Federation
2160 Greenwood Avenue
Trenton, NJ 08609
(609) 586-2381

This group oversees all the different amateur leagues and athletes across the country.

They oversee the U.S. team which competes internationally. The Federation is also in charge of the U.S.A. Junior Team, 16- to 18-year-olds who compete for the U.S. against foreign teams.

BASEBALL FOR THE HANDICAPPED

If you want to play ball and you've got a handicap, here are some organizations to contact for more information about a team for you in your area.

American Athletic Association for the Deaf
1134 Davenport Drive
Burton, MI 48529
(313) 239-3972

National Wheelchair Softball Association
1616 Todd Court
Hastings, MN 55033
(612) 437-1792

Special Olympics
1350 New York Avenue N.W.
Suite 500
Washington, DC 20005
(202) 628-3630
Organized softball for kids with mental retardation and other disabilities.

BASEBALL RESEARCH ORGANIZATIONS

If you get fanatical about baseball history and lore, you could be on your way to a hobby (or career) as a baseball researcher and historian. If you've got a research question, this society can help you. (For more information, see Chapter 6.)

Society for American Baseball Research
Administrative offices:
P.O. Box 10033
Kansas City, MO 64111
(816) 561-1320
Research inquiries:

P.O. Box 1010
Cooperstown, NY 13326

BASEBALL WRITERS

Baseball Writers Association of America
36 Brookfield Road
Fort Salonga, NY 11768
(516) 757-0562

If you want to write to a baseball writer with questions or comments, the best place to write is probably care of a magazine or paper that published the writer's work recently, or that publishes the writer's work regularly. This association organizes the annual Hall of Fame voting by sports writers. Fans can't vote, but if you've got a comment on previous ballots and a wish for future votes, this is where to write.

COLLEGE BASEBALL ORGANIZATIONS

American South Conference
3501 North Causeway Boulevard, Suite 205
Metairie, LA 70002
(504) 834-6600
FAX: (504) 834-6806
Mailing Address:
Box 4348
New Orleans, LA 70178

Member schools: Arkansas State U., Lamar U., Louisiana Tech U., U. of New Orleans, Pan American U., U. of Southwestern Louisiana.

Arkansas Intercollegiate Conference
P.O. Box 15725 (GMF)
N. Little Rock, AR 72231-5725
(501) 758-6688
Member schools: Arkansas Col., Arkansas Tech., Col. of the Ozarks, Harding U., Henderson State U., Hendrix, Quachita Baptist U., Southern Arkansas U., U. of Arkansas (Monticello), U. of Arkansas (Pine Bluff), U. of Central Arkansas.

Association of Mid-Continent Universities
310 South Peoria, Suite 210
Chicago, IL 60607
(312) 829-9122
FAX: (312) 829-1270
Member schools: Cleveland State U., Eastern Illinois U., U. of Illinois-Chicago, U. of Northern Iowa, Southwest Missouri State U., Valparaiso U., Western Illinois U., U. of Wisconsin-Green Bay.

Atlantic Coast Conference
P.O. Box 29169
Greensboro, NC 27429-9169
(919) 282-8800
FAX: (919) 282-5039
Member schools: Clemson U., Duke U., Georgia Institute of Technology (Georgia Tech), U. of Maryland, U. of North Carolina, North Carolina State U., U. of Virginia, Wake Forest U.

Atlantic 10 Conference
10 Woodbridge Center Drive
Woodbridge, NJ 07095

SHORTSTOPS
Legend has it that in 1883, Ted Sullivan invented the word "fan." Sullivan was the manager of the St. Louis Browns. People think his new word was short for either fanatic or fancier (meaning someone who fancies, or likes, baseball).

(201) 634-6900
FAX: (201) 634-6923
Member schools: Duquesne U.,
George Washington U., U. of
Massachusetts, Penn State U., U. of
Rhode Island, Rutgers U., St.
Bonaventure U., St. Joseph's,
Temple U., West Virginia U.

Big East Conference
321 S. Main Street
Heritage Building,
Penthouse
Providence, RI 02903
(401) 272-9108, 9109
FAX: (401) 751-8540
Member schools: Boston College, U.
of Connecticut, Georgetown U., U.
of Pittsburgh, Providence College,
St. Johns U., Seton Hall U.,
Syracuse U., Villanova U.

Big Eight Conference
104 West Ninth Street
Baltimore Place, Suite 408
Kansas City, MO 64105-
1713
(816) 471-5088
FAX: (816) 471-4061
Member schools: U. of Colorado,
Iowa State U., Kansas State U., U.
of Kansas, U. of Missouri, U. of
Nebraska, Oklahoma State U., U. of
Oklahoma.

Big South Conference
201 Main Street
Conway, SC 29526
(803) 248-9693
Mailing Address:
P.O. Box 2099
Conway, SC 29526
Member schools: Armstrong State
Col., Augusta Col., Baptist Col.,
Campbell U., Radford U.,
UNC-Asheville, UNC-Coastal,
Winthrop Col.

Big State Intercollegiate Conference
c/o Dr. Tex Kassen,
Commissioner
809 Country Club Road
Georgetown, TX 78626
(512) 863-5276
Member schools: East Texas Baptist
U., Huston-Tillotson Col., U. of
Mary Hardin-Baylor, St. Edward's
U., St. Mary's U., Texas Lutheran
Col.

Big Ten Athletic Conference
1111 Plaza Drive, Suite 600
Schaumburg, IL 60173-4990
(312) 605-8933
FAX: (312) 517-2955
Member schools: U. of Illinois,
Indiana U., U. of Iowa, U. of
Michigan, Michigan State U., U. of
Minnesota, Northwestern U., Ohio
State U., Purdue U., U. of Wisconsin.

Big West Conference
1700 East Dyer Road, Suite
140
Santa Ana, CA 92705
(714) 261-2525
FAX: (714) 261-2528
Member schools: Cal State U. at
Fullerton, Cal State U. at Long
Beach, Fresno State U., New Mexico
State U., San Diego State U., San
Jose State U., U. of California at
Irvine, U. of California at Santa
Barbara, U. of Hawaii, U. of Nevada
at Las Vegas, U. of the Pacific, Utah
State U.

California Collegiate Athletic Association
40 Via di Roma Walk
Long Beach, CA 90803

(213) 498-4051
Member schools: Cal State U.
Bakersfield, California U. at
Riverside, California Polytechnic
State U. at San Luis Obispo,
California State Polytechnic U. at
Pomona, Chapman College, Cal
State U. Dominguez Hills, Cal State
U. Los Angeles, Cal State U.
Northridge.

Canadian Colleges Athletic Association
1600 James Naismith Drive
Gloucester, Ontario
Canada K1B 5N4
(613) 748-5626

Canadian Interuniversity Athletic Union
1600 James Naismith Drive
Gloucester, Ontario
Canada K1B 5N4
(613) 748-5619
FAX: (613) 748-5706
Membership includes 46
institutions coast to coast.

Carolina's Intercollegiate Athletic Conference
26 Cub Drive
Thomasville, NC 27360
(919) 884-1488
Member schools: Atlantic Christian
Col., Catawba Col., Elon Col.,
Guilford Col., High Point Col.,
Lenoir Rhyne Col., Pembroke State
U., Pfeiffer Col., Wingate Col.

Central Atlantic College Conference
c/o Alfred Restaino,
Commissioner
Bloomfield College

TRIVIA QUIZ
   What number does famous baseball clown Max Patkin wear on his uniform?
   A) 1   B) 1,000   C) ?

Answer: C. He doesn't have a number. He has a question mark instead. He's clowned around the minor leagues since 1946, and was in the baseball movie Bull Durham.

Bloomfield, NJ 07003
(201) 748-9000
Member schools: Bard Col., Bloomfield Col., Dominican Col., King's Col., Mount St. Mary Col., Nyack Col., Col. of St. Rose, St. Thomas Aquinas Col.

Central Intercollegiate Athletic Association
2013 Cunningham Drive, Suite 230
Hampton, VA 23666
(804) 838-8801
FAX: (804) 838-6459
Member schools: Bowie State Col., Elizabeth City State U., Fayetteville State U., Hampton Institute, Livingstone Col., Norfolk State U., North Carolina Central U., St. Augustine's Col., St. Paul's Col., Shaw U., Johnson C. Smith U., Virginia State U., Virginia Union U., Winston-Salem State U.

Central States Intercollegiate Conference
3426 Craig Lane
St. Joseph, MO 64506
(816) 279-8050
Member schools: Emporia State U., Fort Hays State U., Kearney State Col., Missouri Southern State Col., Missouri Western State Col., Pittsburg State U., Washburn U., Wayne State Col.

Chicagoland Intercollegiate Athletic Conference
c/o Pat Sullivan, Commissioner
College of St. Francis
500 Wilcox Street
Joliet, IL 60435
(815) 740-3464

College Athletic Business Management Association

c/o Jon Burianek, President
University of Colorado
Stadium 126, Box 372
Boulder, CO 80309
(303) 492-8337

College Athletic Conference
c/o Walter D. Bryant, Commissioner
2327 Bonnieview Drive
Ormond Beach, FL 32074
(904) 441-7343
Member schools: Centre Col., Earlham Col., Fisk U., Rose Hulman Institute, Rhodes Col., The U. of the South.

College Sports Information Directors of America (COSIDA)
Campus Box 114
Kingsville, TX 78363
(512) 595-3908

Colonial Athletic Association
c/o Thomas E. Yeager, Commissioner
2550 Professional Road, Suite 200
Richmond, VA 23235
(804) 272-1616
FAX: (804) 272-1688
Member schools: American U., East Carolina U., George Mason U., James Madison U., U. of North Carolina-Wilmington, U. of Richmond, U.S. Naval Academy, College of William & Mary.

CUNY Baseball Conference
715 Ocean Terrace
Staten Island, NY 10301
(718) 390-7607
Member schools: Baruch Col., City

Col. of NY, Hunter Col., John Jay Col., Lehman Col., Col. of Staten Island.

Diamond Baseball Conference
c/o Vin Salomone, Commissioner
LIU-C.W. Post College
Greenvale, NY 11548
(516) 299-2289
Member schools: Brooklyn Col., Long Island U.-C.W. Post Col., New York Institute of Tech., Pace U., West Chester U.

Dixie Intercollegiate Athletic Conference
c/o Dr. Milton Reece, President
Greensboro College
Greensboro, NC 27401
(919) 271-2235
Member schools: Averett Col., Ferum Col., Greensboro Col., Methodist Col., Christopher Newport Col., North Carolina Wesleyan Col., Virginia Wesleyan Col.

East Coast Conference
Athletic Dept. Bldg. 14
Drexel University
Philadelphia, PA 19104
(215) 222-2700
Member schools: Bucknell, U. of Delaware, Drexel U., Hofstra U., Lafayette Col., Lehigh U., Rider Col., Towson State U.

Eastern College Athletic Conference
1311 Craigville Beach Road
Centerville, MA 02632
(508) 771-5060
FAX: (508) 771-9481
Mailing Address:

P.O. Box 3
Centerville, MA 02632
Member schools: Adelphi, Albany, Albright, Alfred, American, American International Col., Amherst, Assumption, Babson, Baruch, Bates, Bentley, Binghamton State, Bloomsburg, Boston College, Boston U., Bowdoin, Brandeis, Bridgeport, Bridgewater, Brockport, Brooklyn, Brown, Bryant, Bucknell, Buffalo, Buffalo State, C.W. Post, California State (PA), Canisius, Castleton, Catholic, Central Connecticut, Cheyney, City Col. of New York, Clarion State, Clark, Clarkson, Colby, Colgate, Columbia, Concordia, Connecticut, Connecticut Col., Cornell, Cortland, Curry, Dartmouth, Davidson, Delaware, Delaware Valley, Dowling, Drew, Drexel, East Carolina, East Stroudsburg State, Eastern Connecticut State, Elmira, Emerson, Emmanuel, Medgar Evers, Fairfield, Fairleigh Dickinson, Fairleigh Dickinson (Madison), Fitchburg, Fordham, Framingham State, Franklin & Marshall, Franklin Pierce, Fredonia, Frostburg, Gannon, Geneseo, George Mason, Georgetown, Gettysburg, Glassboro State, Hamilton, Hartford, Hartwick, Harvard, Haverford, Hawthorne, Hellenic, Herbert Lehman, Hobart, Hofstra, Holy Cross, Hunter, Indiana U. (PA), Iona, Ithaca, James Madison, Jersey City, John Jay, Kean, Keene State, King's, Kutztown, Lafayette, LaSalle, Lebanon Valley, Lehigh, LeMoyne, Lincoln, Lock Haven State, Long Island U., Lowell, Loyola, Maine, Maine Maritime Academy, Manhattan, Manhattanville, Marist, Maritime Col. (SUNY), Mary Washington, Maryland (Baltimore County), M.I.T., U. Mass-Amherst, Massachusetts-Boston, Mass. Maritime, Mercy, Mercyhurst, Merrimack, Middlebury, Millersville State, Molloy, Monmouth State, Montclair State, Moravian, Morgan State,

Mount Holyoke Col., Mount St. Mary's, Muhlenberg, Nazareth, New England, New Hampshire, New Hampshire Col., New Haven, New Jersey Institute of Technology, New Paltz, New York Institute of Technology, New York U., Niagara, Nichols, North Adams, North

Mets star Ron Darling first starred at Yale.

Carolina (Wilmington), Northeastern, Norwich, Old Westbury, Oneonta, Oswego, Pace, Pennsylvania, Philadelphia Textile, Plattsburgh, Plymouth State, Polytechnic Institute (NY), Potsdam, Pratt, Princeton, Providence, Queens, Quinnnipiac, Ramapo, R.P.I., Rhode Island Col., U. of Rhode Island, Richmond, Rider, Robert Morris, Rochester, Rochester Institute of Tech., Roger Williams, Rutgers-Camden, Rutgers-Newark, Sacred Heart, St. Anselm's, St. Francis (NY), St. Francis (PA), St. John Fisher, St. John's, St. Joseph's, St. Lawrence, St. Michael's, St. Peter's, Salem, Salisbury State, Scranton, Seton Hall, Shippensburg, Siena, Simmons, Skidmore, Slippery Rock, Smith, Southampton, Southeastern Massachusetts, Southern Connecticut, Springfield, Staten Island, Stevens Institute of Technology, Stockton State,

Stonehill, Stony Brook, Suffolk, Susquehanna, Syracuse, Temple, Thomas, Towson State, Trenton State, Trinity, Tufts, Union, U.S. Coast Guard Academy, U.S. Merchant Marine Academy, U.S. Military Academy, U.S. Naval Academy, U. of District of Columbia, Upsala, Ursinus, Utica, Vassar, Vermont, Villanova, Wagner, Wentworth Institute, Wesleyan, West Chester State, Western Connecticut State, Western New England, Westfield State, Wheaton (MA), Widener, Wilkes, William & Mary, William Paterson, Williams, Worcester Polytechnic Institute, Worcester State, Yale, Yeshiva, York (NY).

Eastern Intercollegiate Baseball League
70 Washington Road
Princeton, NJ 08540
(609) 452-6426
FAX: (609) 683-9091
Member schools: Army, Brown, Columbia, Cornell, Dartmouth, Harvard, Navy, Pennsylvania, Princeton, Yale.

Empire State Conference
c/o Director of Athletics
Molloy College
Rockville Centre, NY 11570
(516) 678-5000
Member schools: Adelphi U., Long Island U.-C.W. Post Campus, Mercy Col., Molloy Col., New York Inst. of Technology, Pace U., U.S. Military Academy

Georgia Intercollegiate Athletic Conference
c/o Bill Ensley, Commissioner
North Georgia College
Dahlonega, GA 30533
(404) 864-3391
Member schools: Berry Col., Georgia Col., Georgia Southwestern

Col., Kennesaw Col., LaGrange Col., North Georgia Col., Piedmont Col., Shorter Col., Southern Tech.

Golden State Athletic Conference
Point Loma Nazarene Col.
c/o Dr. Carroll Land
3900 Lomaland Drive
San Diego, CA 92106
(619) 221-2200
Member schools: Azusa Pacific U., California Lutheran U., Fresno Pacific Col., Point Loma Nazarene Col., Southern California Col., Westmont Col.

Great Lakes Intercollegiate Athletic Conference
5015 Tressa Drive
Lansing, MI 48910
(517) 394-5015
Member schools: Ferris State U., Grand Valley State U., Hillsdale Col., Lake Superior State U., Northern Michigan U., Michigan Technological U., Oakland U., Saginaw Valley State U., Wayne State U.

Great Lakes Valley Conference
P.O. Box 1012, College Station
Rensselaer, IN 47978
(219) 866-5217
Member schools: Ashland Col., Bellarmine Col., Indiana Purdue-Fort Wayne, U. of Indianapolis, Kentucky Wesleyan Col., Lewis U., Northern Kentucky U., Saint Joseph Col., U. of Southern Indiana.

Great Northwest Conference
P.O. Box 2002
Billings, MT 59103

(406) 656-4369
Member schools: U. of Alaska-Anchorage, U. of Alaska-Fairbanks, Eastern Montana Col., Metropolitan State Col., U. of Puget Sound, Seattle Pacific U.

Greater Boston League
c/o Athletic Department
Brandeis University
415 South Street
Waltham, MA 02254
(617) 736-3630
Member schools: Boston Col., Boston U., Brandeis U., Harvard U., M.I.T., Northeastern U., Tufts U.

Gulf Coast Athletic Conference
c/o Thomas Howell, Commissioner
216 Myrtle Street
Pineville, LA 71360
(318) 487-7102
Member schools: Belhaven Col., Dillard U., Louisiana Col., Mobile Col., Southern U.-New Orleans, Spring Hill Col., Tougaloo Col., William Carey Col., Xavier Col.

Gulf South Conference
4 Office Park Circle, Suite 218
Birmingham, AL 35223
(205) 870-9750
FAX: (205) 870-9751
Member schools: Delta State U., Jacksonville State U., Livingston U., Mississippi Col., Troy State U., U. of North Alabama, U. of Tennessee at Martin, Valdosta State Col., West Georgia Col.

Heart of America Athletic Conference
c/o Charlie Burri, Commissioner
3426 Craig Lane

St. Joseph, MO 64506
(816) 279-1948
Member schools: Baker U., Central Methodist Col., Culver-Stockton Col., Graceland Col., Missouri Valley Col., Mid-America Nazarene Col., Tarkio Col., William Jewell Col.

Independent College Athletic Conference
c/o Robert F. Ducatte, Commissioner
Rensselaer Polytechnic Institute
Troy, NY 12181
(518) 276-6685
Member schools: Alfred U., Clarkson U., Hobart Col., Ithaca Col., Rensselaer Polytechnic Inst., Rochester Inst. of Technology, St. Lawrence U., Wm. Smith Col.

Iowa Intercollegiate Athletic Conference
1615 West Schrock Road
Waterloo, IA 50701
(319) 296-2227
Member schools: Buena Vista Col., Central Col., U. of Dubuque, Loras Col., Luther Col., Simpson Col., Upper Iowa U., Wartburg Col., William Penn Col.

Ivy League
70 Washington Road
Princeton, NJ 08540
(609) 452-6426
FAX: (609) 683-9091
Member schools: Brown U., Columbia U., Cornell U., Dartmouth Col., Harvard U., U. of Pennsylvania, Princeton U., Yale U.

Knickerbocker Baseball Conference
c/o Robert Greenburg
2865 Ocean Ave., Apt 5E

SHORTSTOPS
Jack Norworth wrote the lyrics to the famous baseball song "Take Me Out to the Ball Game." But his wish didn't come true for more than 30 years. It took that long for him to go to a stadium and watch his first big league game!

Brooklyn, NY 11235
(718) 891-8163
Member schools: Adelphi, CCNY, Concordia, Dowling, John Jay, Lehman, Manhattanville, Mercy, Queens, Staten Island, Stony Brook.

Lone Star Conference
Box 7795
Abilene, TX 79699-7795
(915) 674-2693
FAX: (915) 674-2202
Member schools: Abilene Christian U., Angelo State U., Cameron U., Central State U., East Texas State U., Eastern New Mexico U., Texas A & I, West Texas State.

Mason-Dixon Athletic Conference
c/o C. Edward Sherlock, President
Univ. of Pittsburgh-Johnstown
Johnstown, PA 15904
(814) 266-9661, Ext. 275
Member schools: Liberty U., Longwood Col., Mt. St. Mary's Col., U. of Pittsburgh-Johnstown, Randolph-Macon Col.

Massachusetts State College Athletic Conference
c/o F. Paul Bogan, Commissioner
Westfield State College
Westfield, MA 01085
(413) 568-3311, Ext. 405
Member schools: Bridgewater State, Fitchburg State, Framingham State, Mass. Maritime Academy, North Adams, Salem State, Westfield State, Worcester State.

Mayflower Conference
c/o Darrell Pound, Commissioner

Lyndon State College
Lyndonville, VT 05851
(802) 626-9371
Member schools: Castleton State Col., Franklin Pierce Col., Green Mountain Col., Hawthorne Col., Johnson State Col., Lyndon State Col., College of St. Joseph the Provider, Southern Vermont Col., Trinity Col.

Metro Atlantic Athletic Conference
1 Lafayette Circle
Bridgeport, CT 06604
(203) 368-6969
(203) 384-8170
Member schools: Army, Canisius Col., Fairfield, Fordham, Holy Cross, Iona, LaSalle, Loyola (Md.), Manhattan, Niagara Col., St. Peter's, Siena Col.

Metro Collegiate Athletic Conference
One Ravinia Drive, Suite 1120
Atlanta, GA 30346
(404) 395-6444
FAX: (404) 395-6423
Member schools: U. of Cincinnati, Florida State U., U. of Louisville, Memphis State U., U. of South Carolina, U. of Southern Mississippi, Tulane U., Virginia Tech.

Metropolitan Collegiate Baseball Conference
Paul Fernandez, Commissioner
C.W. Post College
Greenvale, NY 11548
(516) 299-2289
Member schools: C.W. Post Col., Fairleigh Dickinson U., Fordham U., Iona Col., Long Island U., Manhattan Col., St. Francis Col., Seton Hall U., Wagner Col.

Michigan Intercollegiate Athletic Conference
P.O. Box 63
Spring Lake, MI 49456
(616) 842-7865
Member schools: Adrian Col., Albion Col., Alma Col., Calvin Col., Hope Col., Kalamazoo Col., Olivet Col.

Mid-American Athletic Conference
Four SeaGate, Suite 501
Toledo, OH 43604
(419) 249-7177
Member schools: Ball State U., Bowling Green State U., Central Michigan U., Eastern Michigan U., Kent State U., Miami U., Ohio U., U. of Toledo, Western Michigan U.

Middle Atlantic States Collegiate Athletic Conference
c/o Nathan N. Salant, Commissioner
Schwartz Center
Widener University
Chester, PA 19013
(215) 499-4525
Member schools: Albright Col., Delaware Valley Col., Dickinson Col., Drew U., Elizabethtown Col., Fairleigh Dickinson U. (Madison), Franklin & Marshall Col., Gettysburg Col., Haverford Col., Johns Hopkins U., Juanita Col., King's Col. (PA), Lebanon Valley Col., Lycoming Col., Messiah Col., Moravian Col., Muhlenberg Col., U. of Scranton, Susquehanna U., Swarthmore Col., Upsala Col., Ursinus Col., Washington Col. (MD), Western Maryland Col., Widener Col., Wilkes Col.

Mid-Eastern Athletic Conference
102 North Elm Street

Famous Fans

In baseball, players on the field aren't the only ones who've gotten famous. Through the years, a number of fans have managed to stand out of the crowd and make something of a name for themselves. Here's a look at some of the most famous baseball fans throughout baseball history:

The All-American Earache: Patsy O'Toole, a Detroit fan. In the 1930's, his screaming was so loud and frequent that he became famous.

The Bleacher Bums: Nickname for the crazy fans in the bleachers at Chicago's Wrigley Field, in the 1960's, known for their intense razzing of the other team's outfielders.

The Flagpole Sitter: Starting on May 31, 1949, for 117 straight days the devout Cleveland Indians fan sat on a platform on top of a flagpole. Charley Lupica said he wouldn't come down until his team made it into first place.

The team began to do better, but couldn't make it past third place. When they were officially eliminated from the pennant race, Lupica finally came down.

Giant Killer: A Dodger fan once got into such a violent argument with a Giant fan that he shot and killed him. He was sentenced to death and made headlines again with his last words. He asked if the Dodgers had beaten the Giants that day.

Good Old Joe Earley: In 1948, this fan wrote a letter to a newspaper complaining that the players got all the attention. He, an ordinary fan, should get some awards, too, just for rooting, argued Earley. He signed the letter "Good Old Joe Earley."

In response, Cleveland Indians owner Bill Veeck held a "Good Old Joe Earley" night. Earley was presented with all sorts of awards and prizes, including a car and a cow!

Hilda Chester: In the 1940s, this famous Brooklyn Dodger fan used to bring two loud cowbells to the game and wave a banner that read "Hilda Is Here." Thanks to her efforts, everyone always knew when she was at the game.

Mary Ott: A famous St. Louis Cardinal fan from the 1940s who always sat in the bleachers. She made a name for herself with her loud laugh that everyone thought sounded like a horse's whinny. Legend has it that Ott's whinny was piercing enough to make enemy outfielders miss fly balls.

The Royal Rooters: A group of Boston fans from the early 1900s. The Rooters used to taunt the opposing teams by changing the lyrics to songs that were then famous.

To razz the great Honus Wagner, for example, the Rooters changed the lyrics to "Tessie, Why Do I Love You Madly?" Instead, the Rooters sang, "Honus, Why Do You Hit So Badly?"

Opposing teams said the Rooters' songs threw them off at key moments.

The Rooters leader was a man nicknamed "Nuf Ced." He got the name because of his vast baseball knowledge. What he said on baseball matters was taken to be the last word—"enough said."

401 Southeastern Building
Greensboro, NC 27401
(919) 275-9961
Telecopier: (919) 275-9964
Mailing Address:
P.O. Box 21205
Greensboro, NC 27420-1205
Member schools: Bethune-Cookman
Col., Coppin State Col., Delaware
State Col., Florida A&M U., Howard
U., U. of Maryland Eastern Shore,
Morgan State U., North Carolina
A&T State U., South Carolina State
Col.

Midwest Collegiate Athletic Conference

c/o Ralph L. Shively,
Commissioner
Lake Forest College
Lake Forest, IL 60045
(312) 234-3100
Member schools: Beloit, U. of
Chicago, Coe, Cornell, Grinnell,
Illinois Col., Knox, Lawrence, Lake
Forest, Monmouth, Ripon, St.
Norbert.

Midwestern Collegiate Conference

Pan American Plaza, Suite
500
201 S. Capitol Street
Indianapolis, IN 46225
(317) 237-5622
Member schools: Butler U., U. of
Dayton, U. of Detroit, U. of
Evansville, Loyola U. of Chicago,
Marquette U., U. of Notre Dame, St.
Louis U., Xavier U.

Minnesota Intercollegiate Athletic Conference

405 Laurie Lane
Stillwater, MN 55082
(612) 439-7768
Member schools: Augsburg Col.,
Bethel Col., Carlton Col.,
Concordia Col., Gustavus
Adolphus Col., Hamline U.,
Macalester Col., St. John's U., St.
Mary's Col., St. Olaf Col., Col. of St.
Thomas.

Missouri Intercollegiate Athletic Association

430 West Lincoln Street
P.O. Box 508
Maryville, MO 64468
(816) 582-5655
Member schools: Central Missouri
State U., Lincoln U., Northeast
Missouri State U., Northwest
Missouri State U., Southeast
Missouri State U., Southwest
Baptist U., U. of Missouri (Rolla), U.
of Missouri (St. Louis).

Missouri Valley Conference

200 North Broadway
Suite 1905
St. Louis, MO 63102
(314) 421-0339
Member schools: Bradley U.,
Creighton U., Drake U., Indiana
State U., Illinois State U., Southern
Illinois U., U. of Tulsa, Wichita
State.

National Association of Academic Advisors for Athletics (NAAAA)

c/o Steve Milburn,
President
University of Louisville
Louisville, KY 40292
(502) 588-5555

National Association of Collegiate Directors of Athletics (NACDA)

24651 Detroit Road
Westlake, OH 44145
(216) 892-4000
FAX: (216) 892-4007

Mailing Address:
P.O. Box 16428
Cleveland, OH 44116

National Association of Intercollegiate Athletics (NAIA)

1221 Baltimore Avenue
Kansas City, MO 64105
(816) 842-5050
FAX: (816) 421-4471

National Christian College Athletic Association

P.O. Box 80454
Chattanooga, TN 37411
(615) 899-7980

National Collegiate Athletic Association (NCAA)

Nall Avenue at 63rd Street
P.O. Box 1906
Mission, KS 66201
(913) 384-3220
FAX: (913) 384-3220 (Ask for
recipient of FAX)

National Collegiate Baseball Writers Association

c/o Mark Brand,
Secretary-Treasurer
Arizona State U., Activity
Center
Tempe, AZ 85287
(602) 965-6592

National Junior College Athletic Association (NJCAA)

Suite 100
1825 Austin Bluff Parkway

Colorado Springs, CO
80907
(719) 590-9788
FAX: (719) 590-9788, Ext. 17
Mailing Address:
P.O. Box 7305
Colorado Springs, CO
80933-7305

**New England College
Athletic Conference**
c/o Athletic Department
Attn: Dick Lipe
Bentley College
Waltham, MA 02254
(617) 891-2256
FAX: (617) 891-2648
Member schools: American
International Col., Amherst Col.,
Anna Maria Col., Assumption Col.,
Babson Col., Bates Col., Bentley
Col., Boston Col., Boston U.,
Bowdoin Col., Brandeis U.,
Bridgeport U., Bridgewater State
Col., Brown U., Bryant Col.,
Castleton State Col., Central
Connecticut State Col., Clark U.,
Colby Col., U. of Connecticut,
Connecticut Col., Curry Col.,
Dartmouth Col., Eastern
Connecticut State U., Fitchburg
State Col., Framingham State Col.,
U. of Hartford, Harvard U., Holy
Cross Col., Keene State Col., U. of
Lowell, U. of Maine (Orono),
Massachusetts Maritime, U. of
Massachusetts (Amherst), U. of
Massachusetts (Boston),
Massachusetts Institute of
Technology, Merrimack Col.,
Middlebury Col., New England
Col., U. of New Hampshire, New
Hampshire Col., U. of New Haven,
Nichols Col., North Adams State
Col., Northeastern U., Norwich U.,
Plymouth State Col., Providence

This Yale baseball player went on to star in other fields. It's George Bush, and he's being congratulated by Babe Ruth.

Col., Quinnipiac Col., U. of Rhode
Island, Rhode Island Col., Roger
Williams Col., Sacred Heart U., St.
Anselm's Col., St. Joseph's Col., St.
Michael's Col., Salem State Col.,
Salve Regina Col., Simmons Col.,
Smith Col., Southeastern
Massachusetts U., Southern
Connecticut State U., U. of Southern
Maine, Springfield Col., Stonehill
Col., Suffolk U., Thomas Col.,
Trinity Col., Tufts U., U.S. Coast
Guard Academy, U. of Vermont,

Wentworth Institute, Wesleyan U.,
Western Connecticut State U.,
Western New England Col.,
Westfield State Col., Williams Col.,
Worcester Polytechnic Institute,
Worcester State Col., Yale U.

**New England Collegiate
Conference**
University of New Haven
300 Orange Avenue

TRIVIA QUIZ
   During a recent season, angry Yankee fans felt that Dave "Rags"
Righetti was the only good pitcher on the team. So they nicknamed
the pitching crew:

A) Righetti and Meatballs
B) Righetti and Forgetti the Rest
C) The New York Righetties
D) The Ragamuffins

Answer: A

33

West Haven, CT 06516
(203) 932-7022
FAX: (617) 891-2648
Member schools: U. of Bridgeport, Keene State, U. of Lowell, New Hampshire Col., U. of New Haven, Quinnipiac Col., Sacred Heart U., Southern Connecticut State U.

New Jersey Athletic Conference
c/o Susan Newcomb, President
Stockton State College
Pomona, NJ 08240
(609) 652-4217
Member schools: Glassboro State, Jersey City State, Kean, Montclair State, William Paterson, Ramapo, Rutgers U.-Camden, Rutgers U.-Newark, Stockton, Trenton State.

North Atlantic Christian Conference
c/o Tom Figart, Jr.
Lancaster Bible College
901 Eden Road
Lancaster, PA 17601
(717) 569-7071
Member schools: Baptist Bible Col. (PA), Lancaster Bible Col., Northeastern Bible Col., Philadelphia Col. of Bible, United Wesleyan Col., Valley Forge Christian Col., Washington Bible Col.

North Central Intercollegiate Athletic Conference
Ramkota Inn
2400 North Louise
Sioux Falls, SD 57107
(605) 338-0907
Member schools: Augusta Col., Morningside Col., U. of Northern Colorado, U. of Nebraska-Omaha, U. of South Dakota, South Dakota State U., U. of North Dakota, North Dakota State U., St. Cloud State U.,

Mankato State U.

North Dakota College Athletic Conference
LaVerne Jessen, Executive Secretary
Box 290
Dickinson State U.
Dickinson, ND 58601
(701) 227-2371
Member schools: Dickinson State U., Jamestown Col., U. of Mary, Mayville State U., Minot State U., Valley City State U.

Northeast Conference
900 Route 9
Woodbridge, NJ 07095
(201) 636-9119
FAX: (201) 636-6496
Formerly ECAC Metro Conference.
Member schools: Fairleigh Dickinson U., Long Island U.-Brooklyn Center, Loyola Col. (MD), Marist Col., Monmouth Col., Robert Morris Col., St. Francis Col. (NY), St. Francis Col. (PA), Wagner Col.

Northeast-10 Conference
c/o Bentley College
Waltham, MA 02154
(617) 891-2330
Member schools: American International Col., Assumption Col., Bentley Col., Bryant Col., Merrimack Col., Quinnipiac Col., St. Michael's Col., Springfield Col., Stonehill Col., St. Anselm Col.

Northern California Athletic Conference
3415 Nathan Court
Rocklin, CA 95677
(916) 624-1181
Member schools: California State U.-Chico, California State U.-Hayward, California State

U.-Stanislaus, Humboldt State U., Col. of Notre Dame, San Francisco State U., Sonoma State U., U. of California-Davis.

Northern California Baseball Assocation
51 Oak Knoll Loop
Walnut Creek, CA 94596
(415) 731-2283
Member schools: Fresno, California State U., U. of Nevada (Reno), U. of the Pacific, St. Mary's Col., U. of San Francico, San Jose State U., U. of Santa Clara.

Northern California Christian College Athletic Conference
800 Bethany Drive
Scotts Valley, CA 95066
(408) 438-3800
Member schools: Bethany Bible Col., Col. of Notre Dame, San Jose Bible Col., Simpson Bible Col., West Coast Bible Col.

Northern Illinois Intercollegiate Conference
c/o Sam Bedrosian, President
Aurora University
Aurora, IL 60506
(312) 844-5112
Member schools: Aurora Col., Concordia Col., Illinois Benedictine Col., Judson Col., Olivet Nazarene Col., Rockford Col., Trinity Col.

Northern Intercollegiate Christian Conference
Bud Pierce, Commissioner
St. Paul Bible College
Bible College, MN 55375
(612) 446-1411
Member schools: Faith Baptist Bible Col., Minnesota Bible Col., North Central Bible Col., Pillsbury Baptist Bible Col., St. Paul Bible Col.,

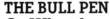

THE BULL PEN
Q: What baseball cards did Minnie want?
A: Minnie-sought-da Twins!

Trinity Bible Institute.

Northern Intercollegiate Conference
Dr. David J. Rislove,
Executive. Secretary
Winona State University
Winona, MN 55987
(507) 457-5295
Mailing address:
Moorhead State U.
Moorhead, MN 56560
(218) 236-2113
Member schools: Bemidji State U.,
Moorhead State U., Northern State
Col., Southwest State U., U. of
Minnesota (Duluth), U. of Minnesota
(Morris), Winona State U.

Northwest Conference of Independent Colleges
Dr. Jerry Lerum, President
Pacific Lutheran College
Tacoma, WA 98447
(503) 535-7561
Member schools: Lewis & Clark
Col., Linfield Col., Pacific U.,
Pacific Lutheran U., Whitman Col.,
Willamette U.

Ohio Athletic Conference
Four SeaGate, Suite 501
Toledo, OH 43604
(419) 249-7179
Member schools: Baldwin-Wallace
Col., Capital U., Heidelberg Col.,
Marietta Col., Mount Union Col.,
Muskingum Col., Ohio Northern U.,
Otterbein Col., Wittenberg U.

Ohio Valley Conference
50 Music Square West,
Suite 203
Nashville, TN 37203
(615) 327-2557
FAX: (615) 327-2558
Member schools: Austin Peay State

U., Eastern Kentucky U., Middle
Tennessee State U., Morehead State
U., Murray State U., Tennessee
State U., Tennessee Technological U.

Old Dominion Athletic Conference
P.O. Box 971
Salem, VA 24153
(703) 389-7373
Member schools: Bridgewater,
Eastern Mennonite, Emory & Henry,
Hampden-Sydney, Hollins,
Lynchburg, Mary Baldwin,
Randolph-Macon, Randolph-Macon
Women's Col., Roanoke, Sweet
Briar, Washington & Lee.

Pacific-10 Conference
800 South Broadway, Suite 400
Walnut Creek, CA 94596
(415) 932-4411
FAX: (415) 932-4601
Member schools: Arizona State U.,
U. of Arizona, U. of California-Ber-
keley, UCLA, U. of Oregon, Oregon
State U., U. of Southern California,
Stanford U., U. of Washington,
Washington State U.

Pennsylvania State Athletic Conference
c/o Rod C. Kelchner,
Chairman
Alumni Hall, Room 118
Mansfield University
Mansfield, PA 16933
(717) 662-4046
Member schools: Bloomsburg U.,
California U., Cheyney U., Clarion
U., East Stroudsburg U., Edinboro
U., Indiana U., Kutztown U., Lock
Haven U., Mansfield U., Millersville
U., Shippensburg U., Slippery Rock
U., West Chester U.

President's Athletic Conference

c/o R. Jack Behringer,
Commissioner
Grove City, PA 16127
(412) 458-6600
Member schools: Bethany Col.,
Carnegie-Mellon U., Grove City
College, Hiram Col., John Carroll
U., Thiel Col., Washington and
Jefferson Col.

Rocky Mountain Athletic Conference
2940 East Bates Avenue
Denver, CO 80210
(303) 753-0600
Member schools: Adams State Col.,
Colorado School of Mines, Fort
Lewis Col., Mesa Col., U. of
Southern Colorado, Western New
Mexico State U., Western State Col.

**John Jackson, USC
outfielder, slides in safely.**

University of Georgia's Roger Miller is the all-time hit leader in his conference.

Show-Me Collegiate Conference
c/o Lee O'Donnell, Commissioner
6800 Wydown Street
St. Louis, MO 63105
(314) 889-1432
Member schools: Columbia Col., Fontbonne Col., Hannibal La Grange Col., Harris-Stowe State Col., Lindenwood Col., Missouri Baptist Col.

South Atlantic Conference
c/o Monte Dutton, Publicity Director
Presbyterian College
Clinton, SC 29325
(803) 833-2936

Member schools: Carson Newman Col., Catawba Col., Elon Col., Gardner Webb Col., Lenoir Rhyne Col., Mars Hill Col., Newberry Col., Presbyterian Col.

Southeastern Conference
3000 Galleria Tower, Suite 990
Birmingham, AL 35244
(205) 985-3686
FAX: (205) 985-3685
Member schools: U. of Alabama, Auburn U., U. of Florida, U. of Georgia, U. of Kentucky, Louisiana State U., U. of Mississippi, Mississippi State U., U. of Tennessee, Vanderbilt U.

Southern California Intercollegiate Athletic Conference
c/o Grayle Howlett, Publicity Director
Claremont McKenna College
Ducey Gym
Claremont, CA 91711
(714) 621-8000
Member schools: California Institute of Tech., Claremont McKenna-Harvey Mudd-Scripps Col., U. of La Verne, Pomona-Pitzer, Occidental, U. of Redlands, Whittier.

Southern Conference
10 Woodfin Street, Suite 206
Asheville, NC 28801
(704) 255-7872
FAX: (704) 251-5006
Member schools: Appalachian State U., The Citadel, East Tennessee State U., Furman U., Marshall U., U. of Tennessee-Chattanooga, Virginia Military Institute, Western Carolina U.

Southern Intercollegiate Athletic Conference
c/o J.E. Hawkins, Commissioner
Box 4186
Fort Valley State College
Fort Valley, GA 31030
(912) 825-8460
Member schools: Alabama A&M U., Albany State Col., Benedict Col., Clark Col., Fort Valley State Col., Knoxville Col., Lane Col., LeMoyne-Owen Col., Miles Col., Morehouse Col., Morris Brown Col., Paine Col., Rust Col., Savannah State Col., Stillman Col., Tuskegee Institute.

Southland Conference
P.O. Box 863579
Plano, TX 75086-3579
(214) 424-4833
FAX: (214) 424-4099
Member schools: McNeese State U., U. of North Texas, Northeast Louisiana U., Northwestern Louisiana U., Sam Houston State U., Southwest Texas State U., Stephen F. Austin U., U. of Texas (Arlington).

Southland Christian Athletic Conference
William Parsons, Commissioner
6900 Wilkinson Blvd.
Charlotte, NC 28214
Member schools: Appalachian Bible Col., East Coast Bible Col., John Wesley Mid-South Bible Col., Piedmont Bible Col., Southeastern Baptist Col., Wesley Col.

Southwest Athletic Conference
1300 West Mockingbird, Suite 444
P.O. Box 569420
Dallas, TX 75356-9420
(214) 634-7353
FAX: (214) 638-5482

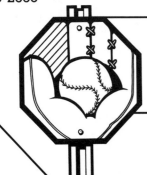

SHORTSTOPS
In the first days of baseball, fans weren't known as "fans." They were called "kranks" or "bugs"!

Member schools: U. of Arkansas, Baylor U., U. of Houston, Rice U., Southern Methodist U., U. of Texas, Texas A&M, Texas Christian U., Texas Tech U.

Southwestern Athletic Conference

c/o James Frank, Commissioner
6400 Press Drive
New Orleans, LA 70126
(504) 283-0791
Member schools: Alabama State (Montgomery), Alcorn State, Grambling State U., Jackson State U., Mississippi Valley State U., Prairie View A&M U., Southern U. (Baton Rouge), Texas Southern U.

State University of New York Athletic Conference

c/o Dr. Patrick R. Damore, Commissioner
Fredonia State
Fredonia, NY 14063
(716) 673-3105
Member schools: SUNY (Binghamton), Brockport State, Buffalo State, Cortland State, Fredonia State, Geneseo State, New Paltz State, Oneonta State, Oswego State, Plattsburgh State, Potsdam State.

Sun Belt Conference

1408 North Westshore Blvd., Suite 1010
Tampa, FL 33607
(813) 872-1511
FAX: (813) 873-7751
Member schools: U. of Alabama-Birmingham, Jacksonville U., U. of North Carolina-Charlotte, Old Dominion U., U. of South Alabama, U. of South Florida, Virginia Commonwealth U., Western Kentucky U.

Sunshine State Conference

500 Ocean Trail Way, No. 306
Jupiter, FL 33477
(407) 575-7702
Member schools: Barry U., Eckerd Col., Florida Institute of Technology, Florida Southern Col., Rollins Col., St. Leo Col., U. of Tampa.

Tennessee Collegiate Athletic Conference

c/o E. L. Hutton, Commissioner
150 Timbercreek Drive, No. 92
Cordova, TN 38018
(901) 756-4030
Member schools: Belmont Col., Bethel Col., Blue Mountain Col., Christian Brothers Col., Cumberland U., David Lipscomb Col., Freed-Hardeman Col., Lambuth Col., Trevecca Nazarene Col., Union U.

Tennessee Valley Athletic Conference

c/o Dr. Earl D. Brooks, President
Lincoln Memorial College
Harrogate, TN 37752
(615) 869-3611
Member schools: Carson-Newman Col., King Col., Lee Col., Lincoln Memorial Col., Milligan Col., Tennessee Wesleyan Col., Tusculum Col.

Texas Intercollegiate Athletic Association

c/o Reed Richmond
Box T-309
Stephenville, TX 76402
(817) 968-9077
Member schools: Austin Col.,

Howard Payne U., McMurry Col., Midwestern State U., Sul Ross State U., Tarleton State U.

Trans America Athletic Conference

337 S. Milledge Avenue, Suite 200
Athens, GA 30605
(404) 548-3369
FAX: (404) 548-0674
Member schools: U. of Arkansas-Little Rock, Centenary Col., Georgia Southern Col., Georgia State U., Hardin-Simmons U., Houston Baptist U., Mercer U., Samford U., Stetson U., U. of Texas-San Antonio.

University Sport, Federation International Du

Correspondence:
Secretariat F.I.S.U.
Rue General Thys 12

UCLA on defense: Mannie Adams (#18) and Mike Hawkins.

1050 Bruxelles
Belgique
+ 32 + 2/6406873
Telex: 64557 FISU B

U.S. Collegiate Sports Council
Blatt PE Center
University of South
Carolina

Columbia, SC 29208

West Coast Athletic Conference
400 Oyster Point Blvd.,
Suite 221
South San Francisco, CA
94080
(415) 873-8622
Member schools: Gonzaga U., U. of
Portland, U. of San Francisco, St.

Mary's Col., U. of Santa Clara,
Pepperdine U., Loyola Marymount,
U. of San Diego.

West Virginia Intercollegiate Athletic Conference
701 Mercer Street, Suite 108
Princeton, WV 24740
(304) 487-6298
FAX: (304) 487-6299
Member schools: Alderson Broadus,
Bluefield State, Concord, Davis &
Elkins, Fairmont State, Glenville
State, U. of Charleston, Salem,
Shepherd State, West Liberty State,
West Virginia Tech, West Virginia
State, Wheeling Jesuit.

Western Athletic Conference
14 West Dry Creek Circle
Littleton, CO 80120
(303) 795-1962
FAX: (303) 795-1960
Member schools: Air Force
Academy, Brigham Young U.,
Colorado State U., Hawaii U., U. of
New Mexico, San Diego State U., U.
of Texas-El Paso, U. of Utah, U. of
Wyoming.

Wisconsin State University Conference
P.O. Box 8010
Madison, WI 53708
(608) 263-4402
Member schools: the University of
Wisconsin at the following
locations: Eau Claire, La Crosse,
Oshkosh, Platteville, River Falls,
Stevens Point, Stout, Superior,
Whitewater.

HIGH SCHOOL BASEBALL

National Federation of

Notre Dame takes third.

USC coach Rod Dedeaux with some of his former players—all 1979 major league all-Stars: (left to right) Steve Kemp, Roy Smalley, Fred Lynn, and David Kingman.

State High School Associations
P.O. Box 20626
11724 Plaza Circle
Kansas City, MO 64195
(816) 464-5400

This group oversees more than 20,000 high schools and writes the rules for high school sports. If you want information on interstate and international high school baseball competition, this is the group in charge.

SOFTBALL
The name "softball" suggests a lazy sport. But softball is played very *hard* all over the U.S. in thousands of competitive leagues. In fast pitch, the ball can be thrown faster than it is in major league hardball! Here are some of softball's governing bodies, which can provide you with more information about the sport as it's played in your area.

Amateur Softball Organization
2801 Northeast 50th Street
Oklahoma City, OK 73111
(405) 424-5267

International Softball Congress
(Men's fast pitch)
6007 East Hillcrest Circle
Anaheim Hills, CA 92807

U.S. Slow Pitch Softball Association
3935 S. Crater Road
Petersburg, VA 23805
(804) 732-4099

HALLS OF FAME

THE BASEBALL MUSEUMS

Here's a simple question for you: Who is the greatest baseball player of all time?

Babe Ruth? Ty Cobb? Lou Gehrig? Hank Aaron?

Of course, it's not a simple question! In fact, baseball fans love to debate such questions for hours. (In the 1960s, sports writers voted on just this question and gave the award to Ruth.)

Every year all over the United States and Canada, people are nominating and selecting baseball heroes. The winners are inducted into sports halls of fame.

With plaques and other exhibits, these museums honor baseball's immortal stars. Many of the museums are open to the public. Here you can see all sorts of baseball memorabilia, from Cy Young's old shaving razor to benches from Ebbets Field. In some of the bigger museums there are also computer games, baseball films, and other entertainment.

Some of the smaller halls of fame don't have museums you can visit. But almost all the halls accept nominations. So by using this guide, you can nominate your own favorite players!

This chapter also has a list of sports libraries. If you've got a baseball question or simply want to read up on baseball history, these are the places to go. Here you'll find everything from 200-year-old stats to recent baseball videos.

SPORTS MUSEUMS AND HALLS OF FAME

Australian Gallery of Sport and Olympic Museum
P.O. Box 175
East Melbourne
Victoria 3002
Australia
Telephone (03) 650-5682

Cricket is much more popular here than baseball. But Australians do play, and baseball is represented in this museum. Among other artifacts, they have Australian baseball uniforms dating back to the 1930s.

Admission is $3.00 for adults, $1.50 for kids. (Of course, airfare to Australia will cost you quite a bit more than that!). The museum is open every day except Monday, from 10:00 A.M. to 4:00 P.M.

The Babe Ruth Museum
216 Emory Street
Baltimore, MD 21230
(301) 727-1539

Baltimore was Babe Ruth's birthplace. In fact, he was in reform school here until the Orioles spotted his incredible baseball talent.

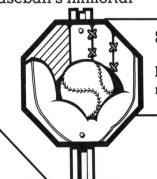

SHORTSTOPS
Hall-of-Famer Hank Greenberg holds the record for most homers hit in one stadium in a single season. In 1938, he whacked 39 round-trippers out of Briggs Stadium in Detroit.

The museum that bears his name honors the great "Bambino," and the Orioles as well. There's memorabilia to see, baseball videos to watch, and a 25-minute documentary on Ruth that is shown on request.

The concession shop sells all kinds of Oriole and Babe Ruth souvenirs. There's even a bust of the Babe available for $250.

Museum hours are 10:00 A.M. to 4:00 P.M. seven days a week during the off season, and 10:00 A.M. to 5:00 P.M. during baseball season. Admission is $3.00 for adults, $2.00 for senior citizens, and $1.50 for kids ages 5–12.

Canada's Sports Hall of Fame
Exhibition Palace
Toronto, Ontario
Canada M6K 3C3
(416) 595-1046

Founded in 1955, this large museum gets about a quarter of million visitors a year. There are three floors to see. The main floor has the Hall of Fame proper. As of 1989, 358 Canadian sports heroes have been inducted and honored here.

This exhibit is in eight different sections. In each section, interactive computers with touch screens allow you to find out extra information about the players. The computers also give sports quizzes and play high-lights from Hall of Fame action.

So far, only three baseball players have made it into the Team Sports Division. There's Phil Marshaldon, a pitcher for the old Philadelphia Athletics; George Gibson, an All-Star catcher for the Pirates, Giants, and Cubs; and Ferguson Jenkins, a pitcher for the Phillies, Cubs, Rangers, and Red Sox.

**Hall of Famer
Joltin' Joe DiMaggio**

Anyone can nominate a player, simply by writing a letter to the museum. All these nominations are passed along to the selection committee, which votes each year.

You don't have to be Canadian to nominate someone, but the player either must be Canadian or must have played most of his or her career in Canada.

In the basement of the museum is the Heritage Gallery, with exhibits from the history of Canadian sports. On the third floor are exhibits of Canada's newer sports. For instance, they have an exhibit on Ringette, a new sport invented by a Canadian, Samuel Jacks.

The museum is open seven days a week all year round except for major holidays, from 10:00 A.M. to 4:30 P.M. It's free. While you're there, you can also visit the Hockey Hall of Fame in the same building (they charge admission).

Canadian Baseball Hall of Fame and Museum
P.O. Box 4008, Station A
Toronto, Ontario
Canada M5W 2R1
(416) 477-0014

Started in 1982, this museum now gets about

Four recent visitors to the Baseball Hall of Fame pose in front of the very first inductees.

400,000 visitors a year. It honors players and others who've made great contributions to baseball in Canada. Among the honorees is George Selkirk, the Yankee right-fielder who so ably replaced Babe Ruth. And that was a tough act to follow!

In addition to an exhibit of Canadian baseball artifacts, this museum owes a lot of its popularity to its baseball amusement center. Here are batting cages, pitcher's mounds, and all sorts of baseball games.

One game lets you test your arm against the major leaguers. You see a film of Montreal base-stealing star Tim Raines streaking toward second. (The film is projected against a long wall.) You've got a real baseball. Can you throw to second fast enough to pick Raines off?

Like many halls of fame, this museum accepts written nominations for new members. If you're planning a visit, admission is $2.00, and the museum is open from 9:00 A.M. to 9:00 P.M., seven days a week, year-round.

Delaware Sports Hall of Fame
c/o Mr. Tom Dew,
Executive Director

21 Molly Lane
Chadds Ford, PA 19317

This Hall of Fame was begun by Delaware's bicentennial commission in 1976. You can't visit it yet, because it's still looking for a permanent home. But so far 101 athletes from Delaware (or athletes famous for playing in Delaware) have been inducted.

These 101 include a number of baseball players, such as Chris Short of the Phillies. Bob Carpenter and his son Ruley are also in the Hall. They were the longtime owners of the Phillies.

You can nominate a

THE BULL PEN
Q: Why did the cows go to Cooperstown?
A: To see the MOO-seum.

player by writing to the above address.

Georgia Sports Hall of Fame
1455 Tullie Circle, Suite 117
Atlanta, GA 30329
(404) 634-9138

There are about 200 athletes in Georgia's Hall of Fame, and that includes some very famous ball players indeed—names such as Hank Aaron, Ty Cobb, and Phil Niekro.

They don't have a museum here as yet, but they hope to build one in the near future. In the meantime, nominations, balloting, and an induction banquet go on each year.

To participate, you need to be a member, which costs $10 a year. Any member can nominate a player who meets the following requirements:

The player has to have been born in the state of Georgia or played in it. A player who was born in Georgia but *never* played there is *not* eligible. The player must be out of his or her sport for at least five years, or in it for 20 years and still participating.

If you have a question about Georgia baseball history, Joe Gerson, the Hall's executive director, is a storehouse of anecdotes and baseball lore. For instance, Gerson remembers the only time anyone ever smacked the ball clean out of Atlanta's old Cracker Stadium. It turned into one of the longest home runs ever.

"The ball landed in the coal car of a passing train," recalls Gerson. "The train went 100 miles to Chattanooga before they found the ball!"

International Jewish Sports Hall of Fame
Alan Sherman, Chairman
7400 Berra Drive
Bethesda, MD 20817
(301) 229-7733

Founded in 1979, this museum honors Jewish athletes who were tops in their sport. So far, 108 athletes have been inducted, including four baseball players.

The players are Sandy Koufax, the former Dodgers ace; Hank Greenberg of the Tigers and Pirates; Al Rosen of the Cleveland Indians; and Litman Pike. (Koufax and Greenberg are both members of the Coopers-town Hall of Fame as well.)

Pike was the very first professional baseball player. In 1866, he was hired by the Philadelphia Athletics to play third base for $20 a week, thus becoming baseball's first player to earn a salary.

Young Hank Aaron as a Milwaukee Brave. He is beginning one of the most famous careers in baseball.

Major league salaries have gone up a little since then!

In addition to those four players, three baseball figures have been honored by the museum with Pillars of Achievement awards. These awards are for players and people who contributed greatly to baseball—but not on the field.

In baseball, the Pillar winners are Moe Berg (see page 51), Mel Allen, the famous baseball announcer, and Barney Dreyfuss. Dreyfuss was the first owner of the Pittsburgh Pirates (from 1900 to 1933). The World Series was Dreyfuss's idea! Dreyfuss also built the first steel-reinforced stadium with decks.

To see the International Jewish Sports Hall of Fame, you have to go to Israel. It's located at the Wingate Institute of Physical Education in South Netanya, just north of Tel Aviv. Admission is free.

The museum also invites nominations. To nominate a player, simply write to the address on previous page, saying why you think the player should be inducted.

Kingdome Sports Museum
201 South King Street
Seattle, WA 98104
(206) 296-3663

This sports memorabilia collection is located right in the Kingdome Stadium, and it's free anytime you go to a Kingdome sporting event. It's also part of the stadium tour (see page 91).

Jewish Hall-of-Famer Al Rosen in 1950.

There's lots of Babe Ruth memorabilia to see, plus a special tribute to Jackie Robinson. Hall of Fame athletes from the Pacific Northwest are honored here.

Manitoba Sports Hall of Fame
1700 Ellice Avenue
Winnipeg, Manitoba
Canada R3H 0B1
(204) 985-4180

Manitoba province isn't all that big on baseball, and most of the athletes honored here made their mark on snow or ice!

But there are some ball players who have made it—Eddie Cass, for instance, who played baseball in Manitoba from 1919 to 1926 and was known here as Mr. Baseball. He was a first baseman, an All-Star, and later a famous coach.

There isn't a museum you can visit, but if you live in Manitoba the museum may visit you! Its mobile display units travel to shopping malls and schools. The exhibits contain pictures and biographies of the 109 inductees.

There's also memorabilia, such as Donald Beane's turn-of-the-century mitt. It's a huge, well-stuffed mitt. Says Lois Howard of the museum, "It'll make you wonder how they ever caught the ball!"

If you want to nominate an athlete (any player who's from Manitoba or who played his or her glory years in the province is eligible), write to Ms. Howard for a nomination form.

Muskegon Area Sports Hall of Fame
Muskegon County Museum
430 West Clay Avenue
Muskegon, MI 49443
(616) 722-0278

In its fourth year, this Hall of Fame honors local athletes as well as local people who excel in other aspects of sports, such as coaching. Jack Tighe, who managed the Detroit Tigers, is one inductee. Frank Secory, a ball player who spent his last 17 years as an umpire, is another.

The exhibit includes Secory's umpire's uniform. They also have Earl Morrall's Super Bowl jersey.

Admission is free, and the museum is open from 9:00 A.M. to 5:00 P.M., seven days a week.

National Baseball Hall of Fame and Museum
Box 590
Cooperstown, NY 13326
(607) 547-9988

Not everyone agrees that Abner Doubleday was the original inventor of baseball (see article on page 4). But in 1930, when baseball set out to celebrate its 100th year, the powers that be decided to give Doubleday full credit.

So they founded the National Baseball Hall of Fame in Doubleday's hometown, Cooperstown, New York.

Each year, a few of the all-time greats from baseball history are inducted into the hall. After the induction ceremony, the museum adds the player's bronze

plaque to its gallery.

The plaque lists the player's notable achievements and his records and stats, and it has a bronze profile of the player himself. As of 1989, there were 204 players inducted.

The Cooperstown museum has become a very popular tourist attraction, with more than 400,000 visitors a year.

Among other things, fans come to see the exhibits of famous baseball paraphernalia. Here you can see artifacts such as the first baseball ever used. Or the bat Bobby Thompson used to hit the shot heard 'round the world (see page 228). Or Babe Ruth's and Lou Gehrig's old lockers from Yankee Stadium.

There are also interactive computer exhibits. The computers flash the faces of all the Hall of Famers. Touch a button and you can access that player's bio, stats, records, and see how that Hall of Famer stacks up against the other players.

During the season, the

WANT TO START A HALL OF FAME?

What better way to make it into a Hall of Fame? Start your own!

But seriously ... does your state have a Hall of Fame? Your town? Your school? If you have an idea for a Hall of Fame

and genuinely want advice on starting one, contact:
Association of Sports Museums and Halls of Fame
c/o Al Cartwright
101 West Sutton Place

Wilmington, DE 19810
(302) 475-7068

This group keeps sports museums informed about what other sports museums are doing. They

encourage their member museums to swap exhibits. And for $15 they'll send you a pamphlet with advice for people starting a Hall of Fame.

The National Baseball Hall of Fame and Museum in Cooperstown, N.Y.

Great Moments Room plays highlights from that week's major league games. A videotape of Abbott and Costello doing their famous "Who's on First?" routine (see page 133) plays here constantly.

The museum's theater has a multimedia presentation on baseball history. Slides and film are used for a nostalgic look at the greats of yesterday. There are three or four shows daily.

In back of the museum is this country's only baseball library. Along with a vast collection of baseball books, the library keeps a file on every player who ever appeared—even for a single game—in pro ball.

Last but not least, the museum has a gift shop (see page 100) where you can buy everything from baseball caps to expensive collectibles such as crystal Hall of Fame baseballs ($300).

The museum is open year-round, seven days a week. Its hours are 9:00 A.M. to 9:00 P.M. during baseball season and 9:00 A.M. to 5:00 P.M. in the winter. In fact, the museum is closed only three days a year: Thanksgiving, Christmas, and New Year's Day.

Admission is $6.00 for adults and $2.50 for kids ages 7–15.

National High School Sports Hall of Fame
11724 Plaza Circle
P.O. Box 20626
Kansas City, MO 64195
(816) 464-5400

Formed in 1982, this Hall of Fame has so far inducted 107 members. As yet, there isn't an exhibit for the public to see, but the Hall has plaques for a number of baseball players. And some of them are players well known for their major league play as well.

For instance, Johnny Bench—who played high school ball in Binger, Oklahoma—is honored not only for his catching but also for his high school pitching!

Don Sutton is another well-known major leaguer whose standout high school play has been honored. Sutton was a star hurler at Tate High School in Gonzalez, Florida.

Anyone can nominate a high school player for the Hall. To do it, you'll need an official nomination form, which you can get

SHORTSTOPS
William A. "Candy" Cummings started throwing baseball's first curveballs in 1864. Few believed the ball was truly curving.

WHO'S IN BASEBALL'S HALL OF FAME?

(The year next to each player's name tells when he was inducted into the National Baseball Hall of Fame at Cooperstown.)

First Basemen
Anson, Cap, 1939
Beckley, Jake, 1971
Bottomley, Jim, 1974
Brouthers, Dan, 1945
Chance, Frank, 1946
Connor, Roger, 1976
Foxx, Jimmie, 1951
Gehrig, Lou, 1939
Greenberg, Hank, 1956
Kelly, George, 1973
Killebrew, Harmon, 1984
McCovey, Willie, 1986
Mize, Johnny, 1981
Sisler, George, 1939
Stargell, Willie, 1988
Terry, Bill, 1954

Second Basemen
Collins, Eddie, 1939
Doerr, Bobby, 1986
Evers, Johnny, 1946
Frisch, Frankie, 1947
Gehringer, Charlie, 1949
Herman, Billy, 1975
Hornsby, Rogers, 1942
Lajoie, Nap, 1937
Morgan, Joe, 1990
Robinson, Jackie, 1962
Schoendienst, Red, 1989

Shortstops
Aparicio, Luis, 1984
Appling, Luke, 1964
Bancroft, Dave, 1971
Banks, Ernie, 1977
Boudreau, Lou, 1970
Cronin, Joe, 1956
Jackson, Travis, 1982
Jennings, Hugh, 1945
Maranville, Rabbit, 1954
Reese, Pee Wee, 1984
Sewell, Joe, 1977
Tinker, Joe, 1946

Vaughan, Arky, 1985
Wagner, Honus, 1936
Wallace, Bobby, 1953
Ward, Monte, 1964

Third Basemen
Baker, Frank, 1955
Collins, Jimmy, 1945
Kell, George, 1983
Lindstrom, Fred, 1976
Mathews, Eddie, 1978
Robinson, Brooks, 1983
Traynor, Pie, 1948

Left-Fielders
Brock, Lou, 1985
Burkett, Jesse, 1946
Clarke, Fred, 1945
Delahanty, Ed, 1945
Goslin, Goose, 1968
Hafey, Chick, 1971
Kelley, Jose, 1971
Kiner, Ralph, 1975
Manush, Heinie, 1964
Medwick, Joe, 1968
Musial, Stan, 1969
O'Rourke, Jim, 1945
Simmons, Al, 1953
Wheat, Zack, 1959
Williams, Billy, 1987
Williams, Ted, 1966
Yastrzemski, Carl, 1989

Center-Fielders
Averill, Earl, 1975
Carey, Max, 1961
Cobb, Ty, 1936
Combs, Earle, 1970
DiMaggio, Joe, 1955
Duffy, Hugh, 1945
Hamilton, Billy, 1961
Mantle, Mickey, 1974
Mays, Willie, 1979
Roush, Edd, 1962
Snider, Duke, 1980
Speaker, Tris, 1937
Waner, Lloyd, 1967
Wilson, Hack, 1979

Right-Fielders
Aaron, Hank, 1982
Clemente, Roberto, 1973
Crawford, Sam, 1957
Cuyler, Kiki, 1968
Flick, Elmer, 1963
Heilmann, Harry, 1952
Hooper, Harry, 1971
Kaline, Al, 1980
Keeler, Willie, 1939
Kelly, King, 1945
Klein, Chuck, 1980
McCarthy, Tommy, 1946
Ott, Mel, 1951
Rice, Sam, 1963
Robinson, Frank, 1982
Ruth, Babe, 1936
Slaughter, Enos, 1985
Thompson, Sam, 1974
Waner, Paul, 1952
Youngs, Ross, 1972

Catchers
Bench, Johnny, 1989
Berra, Yogi, 1972
Bresnahan, Roger, 1945
Campanella, Roy, 1969
Cochrane, Mickey, 1947
Dickey, Bill, 1954
Ewing, Buck, 1939
Ferrell, Rick, 1984
Hartnett, Gabby, 1955
Lombardi, Ernie, 1986
Schalk, Ray, 1955

Pitchers
Alexander, Grover, 1938
Bender, Chief, 1953
Brown, Mordecai, 1949
Chesbro, Jack, 1946
Clarkson, John, 1963
Coveleski, Stan, 1969
Dean, Dizzy, 1953
Drysdale, Don, 1984
Faber, Red, 1964
Feller, Bob, 1962
Ford, Whitey, 1974
Galvin, Pud, 1965
Gibson, Bob, 1981
Gomez, Lefty, 1972

Grimes, Burleigh, 1964
Grove, Lefty, 1947
Haines, Jess, 1970
Hoyt, Waite, 1969
Hubbell, Carl, 1947
Hunter, Catfish, 1987
Johnson, Walter, 1936
Joss, Addie, 1978
Keefe, Tim, 1964
Koufax, Sandy, 1972
Lemon, Bob, 1976
Lyons, Ted, 1955
Marichal, Juan, 1983
Marquard, Rube, 1971
Mathewson, Christy, 1936
McGinnity, Joe, 1946
Nichols, Kid, 1949
Palmer, Jim, 1990
Pennock, Herb, 1948
Plank, Eddie, 1946
Radbourne, Old Hoss, 1939
Rixey, Eppa, 1963
Roberts, Robin, 1976
Ruffing, Red, 1967
Rusie, Amos, 1977
Spahn, Warren, 1973
Vance, Dazzy, 1955
Waddell, Rube, 1946
Walsh, Ed, 1946
Welch, Mickey, 1973
Wilhelm, Hoyt, 1985
Wynn, Early, 1972
Young, Cy, 1937

From Negro Leagues
Bell, Cool Papa (OF), 1974
Charleston, Oscar (1B-OF), 1976
Dandridge, Ray (3B), 1987
Dihigo, Martin (P-OF), 1977
Foster, Rube (P-Mgr), 1981
Gibson, Josh (C), 1972

Irvin, Monte (OF), 1973
Johnson, Judy (3B), 1975
Leonard, Buck (1B), 1972
Lloyd, Pop (SS), 1977
Paige, Satchel (P), 1971

Managers
Alston, Walter, 1983
Harris, Bucky, 1975
Huggins, Miller, 1964
Lopez, Al, 1977
Mack, Connie, 1937
McCarthy, Joe, 1957
McGraw, John, 1937
McKechnie, Bill, 1962
Robinson, Wilbert, 1945
Stengel, Casey, 1966

Umpires
Barlick, Al, 1989
Conlan, Jocko, 1974
Connolly, Tom, 1953
Evans, Billy, 1973
Hubbard, Cal, 1976
Klem, Bill, 1953

Pioneers and Executives
Barrow, Ed, 1953
Bulkeley, Morgan, 1937
Cartwright, Alexander, 1938
Chadwick, Henry, 1939
Chandler, Happy, 1982
Comiskey, Charles, 1939
Cummings, Candy, 1939
Frick, Ford, 1970
Giles, Warren, 1979
Griffith, Clark, 1946
Harridge, Will, 1972
Johnson, Ban, 1937
Landis, Kenesaw, 1944
MacPhail, Larry, 1978
Rickey, Branch, 1967
Spalding, Al, 1939
Weiss, George, 1971
Wright, George, 1937
Wright, Harry, 1953
Yawkey, Tom, 1980

from the office at the above address. Submit this nomination by the second week of December of each year in order to have your nominee considered for induction the following year.

National Museum of American History
10th Street & Constitution Avenue, N.W.
Washington, DC 20560
(202) 357-1300

They have a huge sports memorabilia collection that includes some 3,000 baseball items. About 2,000 of these are baseball cards. In addition, there are lots of autographed baseballs, going back to the 1880s, and some of baseball's earliest uniforms.

The museum is open from 10:00 A.M. to 5:30 P.M. daily, and from 10:00 A.M. to 7:30 P.M. in the summer. Admission is free.

National Softball Hall of Fame and Museum
2801 Northeast 50th Street
Oklahoma City, OK 73111
(405) 424-5267

Established in 1957, the Softball Hall of Fame now has 108 inductees, such as Joan Joyce, the legendary pitcher from Stratford, Connecticut.

In her 17-year career with the Orange Lionettes and the Raybestos Brakettes, Joyce's 75-m.p.h. delivery helped her collect 427 wins, against only 27 losses. She also pitched an astounding 5,677 strikeouts, 105 no-hitters, and 33 perfect games.

In the men's division there are players such as Herb Dudley, who played softball until he was 61. A pitcher, he won more than 1,000 games. He struck out 14,000 batters and had over 100 no-hitters, including 13 in 1948. He holds the national softball record for most strikeouts in one game, with 55, a record he set in 1949.

At the museum there are also exhibits based on the history of softball. Among many other things, you'll learn how a softball is made (with 88 stitches, as opposed to 108 for the smaller hardball).

The annual induction ceremony is held in Oklahoma City in June or July and is open to the public. From March to October the museum itself is open from 8:00 A.M. to 5:00 P.M. weekdays, 10:00 A.M. to 4:00 P.M. on Saturday, and 1:00 P.M. to 4:00 P.M. on Sunday. The museum is closed during the winter months. Admission is $1.00.

New Brunswick Sports Hall of Fame
P.O. Box 6000, Queen Street
Fredericton, New Brunswick
Canada E3B 5H1
(506) 453-3747

Founded in 1970, but without a home until 1977, this Hall of Fame now has 100 inductees. Players must come from the province of New Brunswick. From Labor Day until the end of April, the museum is open from 12:00 noon to 4:30 P.M. on weekdays, Saturday from 10:00 A.M. to 5:00 P.M., and Sunday from 1:00 P.M. to 5:00 P.M. From the first of May until Labor Day, it's open from 10:00 A.M. to 5:00 P.M. daily and Friday until 9:00 P.M. Admission is free.

New England Museum of Sport
1175 Soldiers Field Road
Boston, MA 02134
(617) 787-7678

In addition to general baseball exhibits, this museum has permanent exhibits on the history of the Red Sox and the old Boston Braves.

Admission is $3.50 for adults and $2.50 for 6- to 17-year-olds. Senior citizens and children five and under get in free.

The hours of the museum—and its location—will be changing sometime in 1990, so call first. (They also have a sports library; see page 57).

The great Ted Williams watches another long hit sail off into the outfield.

North Carolina Sports Hall of Fame

3316 Julian Drive
Raleigh, NC 27604
(919) 872-9289

Anyone can nominate players for North Carolina's Hall. Players must have played at least part of their career in North Carolina to be eligible.

The athletes already inducted include some of baseball's greatest, such as Catfish Hunter and the immortal Enos Slaughter.

Right-fielder Slaughter is also in the Cooperstown Hall of Fame. One of his many feats was to score the Cardinals' winning run in the 1946 World Series. He was on first when Harry Walker hit a single. Enos made what came to be known as Slaughter's "Mad Dash Home"—he scored all the way from first!

A museum is being built for this Hall of Fame, to be ready for visitors in 1991. It will include all the memorabilia donated by the inductees, plus computerized games and exhibits. There will also be a sports library and archives.

Olympic Museum

18, Avenue Ruchonnet
1003 Lausanne
Switzerland 20 93 31

Baseball is on its way to becoming an Olympic event, and this museum already has medals for ballplayers who've competed in Olympic demonstration games. Mostly, though, this museum is devoted to the official Olympic sports. There's a 6,000-book library open to kids, and a

Famed Cardinals outfielder, Enos "Country" Slaughter.

35-seat movie theater for viewing Olympic films.

Oregon Sports Hall of Fame

900 S.W. Fifth Avenue, Suite C80
P.O. Box 4381
Portland, OR 97208-4381
(503) 227-7466

This 10-year-old museum has all sorts of memorabilia, including a large collection of famous bats and balls. One of the many famous ball players in this Hall of Fame is Larry Jansen. Jansen pitched and won the famous Giants-Dodgers game that ended with Bobby Thompson's late homer (see chapter 12).

Johnny Pesky is another inductee. Pesky is the Red Sox shortstop often blamed for holding the ball too long during Enos Slaughter's "Mad Dash Home" (see the listing above for North Carolina's Hall of Fame).

It wasn't plays like that that landed Pesky in this Hall of Fame!

Nomination for this Hall of Fame are by members only. Admission is free. The hours are 9:00 A.M. to 3:00 P.M., Monday to Friday.

Peter J. McGovern Little

League Museum

Route 15
P.O. Box 3485
South Williamsport, PA 17701
(717) 326-3607

There are nine different theme rooms in this hands-on museum, showing different aspects of Little League baseball. Throughout the museum there are lots of exhibits you can touch and play with. For example, the Play Ball Room lets you hit and pitch. Then you watch a videotape of your form.

Admission is $4.00 for adults, $2.00 for seniors, and $1.00 for children.

Rome Sports Museum and Hall of Fame

City Hall Building
Rome, NY 13440
(315) 336-6000

This young local Hall of Fame has only about 20 inductees so far, but the Hall is only three years old. It accepts nominations from the public for "Romans" who have brought athletic fame to their community.

The Hall also has a display of Roman sports memorabilia, which includes program books and scrapbooks of the old Rome Colonels, a team that used to play in Rome.

Ball players inducted so far include Jerry Burlison, who played with the Dodgers. The museum is open from 10:00 A.M. to 4:00 P.M. during baseball season. Special arrangements can be made for group visits.

MOE BERG
BASEBALL'S SPY HERO

Moe Berg wasn't much of a batter. In fact, Joe Siegman, who founded the International Jewish Sports Hall of Fame, says Berg was the inspiration for the phrase, "Good field, no hit."

A scholar trained at Princeton and Columbia universities, Berg knew many languages, including Sanskrit. According to the sports writers, though, he couldn't hit in any of them!

But Berg had a job off the field as well. He was a spy for the United States government. Added to a team of All-Stars touring Japan in 1934, Berg, who spoke Japanese, snuck off to take secret reconnaissance photos of Tokyo. The photos proved very valuable to the United States during World War II.

After retiring from baseball, Berg continued to work as a U.S. spy. Working for the Office of Strategic Services, he helped keep track of how the Germans were doing in their efforts to build an atom bomb.

St. Louis Sports Hall of Fame, Inc.
100 Stadium Plaza
St. Louis, MO 63102
(314) 421-6790

This museum honors St. Louis stars from various sports, including hockey, soccer, golf, and the Olympics. Honored in baseball are many famous players, such as Lou Brock and Stan Musial.

Musial, a nationwide star, piled up 3,630 hits, enough to rank him fourth in career hits, behind Hank Aaron, Ty Cobb, and Pete Rose.

The museum's exhibit for Musial and the other honored ball players consists of a baseball locker with a plaque, stats, uniform, and other memorabilia inside.

There is also a model of Busch Memorial Stadium and St. Louis's World Series trophies. A 25-minute movie, shown daily, covers 109 years of St. Louis sports history.

In addition, there's a sports trivia game in the lobby where you can test your knowledge of St. Louis sports. For example, who was the first player to hit the ball out of Busch Stadium? (Answer: Mike Shannon.)

The museum and gift

shop are open 10:00 A.M. to 5:00 P.M. weekdays during the off season and seven days a week during baseball season. Admission is $2.00 for adults and $1.50 for people aged 15 and under.

(The museum also sponsors a daily stadium tour—see chapter 4.)

In 22 seasons with the Cardinals, Stan Musial rounded a record number of bases: 6,134.

San Diego Hall of Champions, Inc.
1649 El Prado—Balboa Park
San Diego, CA 92101-1689
(619) 234-2544

This Hall honors San Diego athletes in all sports, but its baseball exhibit is large. So is the number of San Diego Padres inducted here, baseball greats such as Tony Gwynn.

The most famous ball player in this Hall of Fame is Ted Williams. Known for his amazing years with the Red Sox, Williams began his career with the Padres in 1936.

In the museum's exhibit are old uniforms, photos, old baseballs and bats, and video games and films of the inducted players. Other permanent exhibits take you behind the scenes to learn such things as how baseball bats are made.

The Hall of Champions accepts nominations. The usual eligibility rules apply. The player must be from San Diego or have played part of his or her career there.

The museum hours are 10:00 A.M. to 4:30 P.M. weekdays, Sunday 12:00 noon to 5:00 P.M. Admission is $2.00 for adults, $1.00 for students and seniors over 65, and 50¢ for kids ages 6–17.

Saskatchewan Sports Hall of Fame
2205 Victoria Avenue
Regina, Saskatchewan
Canada S4P OS4
(306) 780-9200

Right now, there are only a handful of baseball players inducted into this Hall of Fame. Daisy Junor and Arleene Noga, Saskatchewan players who made names for themselves in American softball, are among the few honored.

This museum does accept nominations, however. So maybe you can add to the baseball list! If you know a worthy candidate who meets the usual eligibility requirements (must be from Saskatchewan or have played there), write for a nomination form.

The museum is open to the public and has exhibits honoring all its inductees, plus exhibits of Saskatchewan sports such as hockey, football, riding, curling, track and field, swimming, and diving.

The museum is open weekdays from 9:00 A.M. to 5:00 P.M., and on weekends and holidays from 1:00 P.M. to 5:00 P.M. year-round, although from September through May the museum is not open on holidays. Admission is free.

State of Michigan Sports Hall of Fame
Cobo Hall Convention Center
1 Washington Boulevard
Detroit, MI 48226
(313) 224-1010

To date, there are 154 inductees in this Hall. Leading the baseball players is the amazing Ty Cobb.

Cobb won 12 batting championships! For 57 years—from 1928 until

HARDBALL AND SOFTBALL
WHICH IS "HARDER"?

If you compare the records of softball Hall-of-Famers with hardballers', the softballers seem to win hands down. Joan Joyce has 5,677 career strikeouts, for example, dwarfing Nolan Ryan's record-breaking 4,277.

But softball players have some advantages. For one thing, softball pitchers stand closer to the batter—46 feet away instead of 60. For another thing, softball pitchers throw faster!

Why? It seems it's easier to put extra zip on an underhand "windmill" pitch than it is on an overhand "slingshot" throw.

Joan Joyce's fastball was clocked at 116 m.p.h. By contrast, Nolan Ryan, perhaps the fastest hardball pitcher, has been timed at a mere 100.9 m.p.h.

Historically, hardball hitters haven't had much luck trying to get hits off the top softball pitchers. In a special exhibition game, Joan Joyce once struck out batting champ Ted Williams.

In another exhibition game, Babe Ruth once faced a softball pitcher and missed 12 straight softball pitches!

1985—he held the career record for hits (Pete Rose was the man who finally outdid him). He was also the longtime leader in career stolen bases, with 892. (Lou Brock "stole" that record from him with 938.)

Cobb was infamous as well as famous—off the field he was known for being a troubled, violent man. But his achievements on the field were glorious. And they are honored at Cooperstown and here at the Michigan Hall of Fame. It's a small exhibit located in Cobo Hall, a large convention center.

The exhibit has plaques and pictures of the inductees. It's free and can be seen anytime the convention center is open (almost all the time, year-round).

Nominations for new players are *not* accepted from the general public.

Michigan sports writers vote on inductees.

Texas Sports Hall of Champions and Tennis Museum
Charles R. McCleary, Executive Director
P.O. Box 3475
Waco, TX 76707
(817) 756-2307

With this museum you get many Halls of Fame in one. It started out as a

A common sight during Ty Cobb's career. The Tiger and Athletic star is second in career steals with 892.

tennis museum, but today almost every Texan sport is honored here, from baseball to golf.

Not only that, kids are honored here as well as pros, as the museum keeps records of young athletes' achievements.

In some cases, whole teams have been honored. One semi-pro baseball team made it in after the team batted around three times in one inning!

The museum accepts nominations for new Hall of Famers. To be inducted, players must be from Texas and be at least 10 years out of high school. Six new players are chosen each year.

Along with its Halls of Fame, the museum has a large collection of Texas sports memorabilia. For example, you can see four old bases that Babe Ruth and Ty Cobb once rounded. There are also many photos, posters, trophies, and other sports items.

The museum is free and it's open year-round except for Thanksgiving, Christmas, and New Year's Day. Sunday through Friday, the hours are 1:00 P.M. to 5:00 P.M. Saturdays, it's open 10:00 A.M. to 5:00 P.M.

The World Baseball Hall of Fame and Museum, Inc.
P.O. Box 418
Saugerties, NY 12477
(914) 246-9287

According to Jim Thorn, one of the founders of this new Hall of Fame, baseball is spreading so rapidly that "the staging of a true 'World Series' cannot be far off."

Right now baseball is being played in 79 countries, from Australia to Sri Lanka. And this Hall plans to honor ball players from all over the world.

There's no building to visit yet (first they have to pick a country and a city in which to build!), but there are plans for both a museum and a library. The election of players may be done by polling fans in every country where baseball is played.

LAST BUT NOT LEAST...

You've just read about museums, halls of fame, and libraries. Last but not least, there's the *Sports Hall of Shame.* It's not a museum you can go visit (though there are plans to start one). And it's a museum no one wants to be inducted into! It's a series of books by Bruce Nash and Allan Zullo that chronicles the worst blunders in sports history.

If you'd like to nominate anybody—and you have the newspaper or magazine clippings to back up your story—write to:

The Sports Hall of Shame
P.O. Box 6218
West Palm Beach, FL 33405

With this swing, Babe Ruth set many records, such as highest World Series batting average, .625 in 1928.

SPORTS LIBRARIES AND ARCHIVES

Almost any public library will have a sports collection. If you're working on a school paper or just want to read more about baseball, your local library may very well have what you need.

But if you're looking for more specialized information—such as box scores from the 1880s—you're probably going to have to check a more specialized library.

There are only a few libraries devoted entirely to sports. Some of them are listed below.

In addition, some university libraries have great sport archives. Ohio State's sports collection is one of the best known.

Athletic Foundation Paul Ziffren Sports Resource Center
2141 West Adams Boulevard
Los Angeles, CA 90018
(213) 730-9696

This library owns about 25,000 books, 1,000 videos, and 50,000 photos, and subscribes to 200 magazines—all about sports!

Its large baseball collection includes every *Sporting News* magazine ever published, as well as *Spalding Annuals* from the late 1800s. Put out by the sporting goods company, these magazines review each year's season and are full of historical information.

The library is open weekdays from 10:00 A.M. to 5:00 P.M., and on alternate Saturdays from 10:00 A.M. to 3:00 P.M. There

Chicago Cub shortstop Ernie Banks, who was league MVP in 1958.

is no fee for using the library, but elementary school kids need to go with a parent.

You can't take out the books or videos, but there are reading rooms and viewing rooms for watching the tapes in the library.

If you can't get to the library itself, the librarians can answer some baseball questions for you over the phone or, for a small fee, they will send you a copy of the information you need.

National Baseball Hall of Fame Library
Box 590
Cooperstown, NY 13326
(607) 547-9988

Located in a building just behind the Hall of Fame is the Hall of Fame's baseball library. It's the only library in the country devoted entirely to baseball.

The Library's archives have box scores on every pro game ever played and much, much more. A special photo collection contains more than 150,000 baseball pictures.

The Library isn't a lending library, though. It's a research library. That means you can't take books out. You also need

an appointment.

Appointments are easy to make, but you'll need to let them know what research project you're working on. The librarians say that the purpose of this rule is to make sure that the library isn't over-crowded on any given day. The library is open from 9:00 A.M. to 5:00 P.M., Monday through Friday.

National Museum of American History
10th Street and Constitu-tion Avenue N.W.
Washington, DC 20560
(202) 357-1300

In addition to free exhibits, the museum has large sports archives for private research. The library is open from 10:00 A.M. to 5:30 P.M., seven days a week.

New England Museum of Sport Library
1175 Soldiers Field Road
Boston, MA
(617) 787-7678

If you're looking for information about the Red Sox or the old Boston Braves (they moved out of Boston in 1953), this research library can help you. They have a large collection of baseball books, magazines, videos,

and other historical material, such as old programs.

You have to make an appointment to visit the Library. And you can't take books out. The library's hours are 10:00 A.M. to 6:00 P.M. on Wednesday through Saturday, and from 12 noon to 6:00 P.M. on Sunday.

Cardinals ace Dizzy Dean is the last National Leaguer to win 30 games.

GIANTS, TIGERS, AND PIRATES?
—A LEAGUE ROUNDUP

Do you want to write a letter to Bo Jackson? The best way is to write to him in care of his team, the Kansas City Royals. You'll find the address, and the addresses for all the other major league teams, in this chapter.

These addresses will come in handy if you want to check on a team's schedule, find out about tickets, or see if the players will be making personal appearances in your area.

Or maybe you'd like information about your favorite team's spring training plans, so you can pay them a visit. (See the article on page 71 about the Grapefruit and Cactus leagues.)

If you get to be a fantasy league fanatic (see the article page 68) these addresses will help you get the inside scoop on your "own" team's players. And if your player is sent down to the minors, the minor league addresses are here as well.

Minor league teams get less publicity, and they tend to be easier for fans to contact. From the Memphis Chicks to the Toledo Mud Hens, you can find out about the team in your area and start getting involved. Or maybe you'd like to start following a team in Japan! Like the Yokohama Whales.

Here's another reason to get in touch with a team. Many teams—major and minor—run baseball clinics for kids. At clinics, the players are on hand to give pointers—and

autographs. The team's office can let you know the details.

And after all these hours spent being a fan and watching the pros play ball, you'll probably be itching to swing the bat and crack some homers of your own.

At the end of this chapter is a listing of all the major national leagues for kids. By contacting these offices, you can find out about teams that you can join in your area. And, remember, most of the players you watch in the major leagues started out in the kids' leagues, just like you!

Baltimore pitching great Jim Palmer won the Cy Young award two years straight, 1975 and 1976!

MAJOR LEAGUES
AMERICAN LEAGUE

American League
350 Park Avenue
New York, NY 10022
(212) 371-7600

Baltimore Orioles
Memorial Stadium
Baltimore, MD 21218
(301) 243-9800

Boston Red Sox
Fenway Park
Boston, MA 02215
(617) 267-9440

California Angels
P.O. Box 2000
Anaheim, CA 92803
(714) 937-6700

Chicago White Sox
324 West 35th Street
Chicago, IL 60616
(312) 924-1000

Cleveland Indians
Cleveland Stadium
Cleveland, OH 44114
(216) 961-1200

Detroit Tigers
2121 Trumbull Avenue
Detroit, MI 48216
(313) 962-4000

Kansas City Royals
P.O. Box 419969
Kansas City, MO 64141
(816) 921-2200

Milwaukee Brewers
Milwaukee County
Stadium
Milwaukee, WI 53214
(414) 933-4114

Minnesota Twins
501 Chicago Avenue, South
Minneapolis, MN 55415
(612) 375-1366

Old Shibe Park, home to the Philadelphia Phillies until 1970, and one of the first stadiums to provide the visiting team with a dressing room.

New York Yankees
Yankee Stadium
Bronx, NY 10451
(212) 293-4300

Oakland Athletics
Oakland Alameda County
Coliseum
Oakland, CA 94621
(415) 638-4900

Seattle Mariners
P.O. Box 4100
Seattle, WA 98104
(206) 628-3555

Texas Rangers
P.O. Box 1111
Arlington, TX 76010
(816) 273-5222

Toronto Blue Jays
Box 7777, Adelaide Street
PO
Toronto, Ontario
Canada M5C 2K7
(416) 595-0077

59

NATIONAL LEAGUE

National League
350 Park Avenue
New York, NY 10022
(212) 371-7300

Atlanta Braves
P.O. Box 4064
Atlanta, GA 30302
(404) 522-7630

Chicago Cubs
1060 West Addison Street
Chicago, IL 60613
(312) 281-5050

Cincinnati Reds
Riverfront Stadium
Cincinnati, OH 45202
(513) 421-4510

Houston Astros
P.O. Box 288
Houston, TX 77001
(713) 799-9500

Los Angeles Dodgers
1000 Elysian Park Avenue
Los Angeles, CA 90012
(213) 224-1500

Montreal Expos
P.O. Box 500, Station M
Montreal, Quebec
Canada H1V 3P2
(514) 253-3434

New York Mets
Shea Stadium
Flushing, NY 11368
(718) 507-6387

Philadelphia Phillies
P.O. Box 7575
Philadelphia, PA 19101
(215) 463-6000

Pittsburgh Pirates
Three Rivers Stadium
Pittsburgh, PA 15212
(412) 323-5000

Forbes Field, Pittsburgh. The Pirates played here through 1970.

St. Louis Cardinals
250 Stadium Plaza
St. Louis, MO 63102
(314) 421-3060

San Diego Padres
P.O. Box 2000
San Diego, CA 92102
(619) 283-7294

San Francisco Giants
Candlestick Park
San Francisco, CA 94124
(415) 468-3700

MINOR LEAGUES

Major League teams have what are known as "farm clubs." Like farms, these minor league teams grow new crops of great players for the majors.

The minor league teams are in different divisions, from AAA to A. Triple A is the best. It's the last stop

THE BULL PEN
Q: Why did the Los Angeles players always get hit by the ball?
A: They weren't good Dodgers!

before beginning a career in the big leagues.

American Association (AAA)

3860 Broadway
Grove City, OH 43123
(614) 871-0800

Buffalo Bisons
Affiliated with: Pittsburgh
Pirates
275 Washington Street
P.O. Box 450
Buffalo, NY 14203
(716) 846-2000

Denver Zephyrs
Aff: Milwaukee Brewers
2850 West 20th Avenue
Denver, CO 80211
(303) 433-8645

Indianapolis Indians
Aff: Montreal Expos
Owen J. Bush Stadium
1501 West 16th Street
Indianapolis, IN 46202-2063
(317) 632-5371

Iowa Cubs
Aff: Chicago Cubs
Sec Taylor Stadium
Second & Riverside Drive
Des Moines, IA 50265
(515) 243-6111

Louisville Redbirds
Aff: St. Louis Cardinals
Cardinal Stadium
P.O. Box 36407
Louisville, KY 40233
(502) 367-9121

Nashville Sounds
Aff: Detroit Tigers
Herschel Greer Stadium
P.O. Box 23290
Nashville, TN 37202
(615) 242-4371

Oklahoma City Rangers
Aff: Texas Rangers
All Sports Stadium
P.O. Box 75089
Oklahoma City, OK 73147
(405) 946-8989

Omaha Royals
Aff: Kansas City Royals
Rosenblatt Stadium
P.O. Box 3665
Omaha, NE 68103
(402) 734-2550

THE OLDEN TIMES

The great Satchell Paige takes a mighty windup.

In 1920, America was still segregated. African-Americans were kept separate from whites—in schools, restaurants, buses, and in baseball. Nonwhites were simply not allowed to play in the major leagues. And so the Negro leagues were formed.

Many amazing players became famous in these leagues. One of the greatest was Satchel Paige. He pitched 2,500 games. He hurled more than 100 no-hitters!

By the time African-Americans were allowed into the regular leagues, Paige was 40 years old. But he kept on pitching, and winning games, until he was 62!

How did he do it! Paige gave this famous advice for staying young: "If you're over six years of age," he said, "follow these rules closely.
1. Avoid fried meats, which anger up the blood.
2. If your stomach disputes you, lie down and pacify it with cool thoughts.
3. Keep the juices flowing by jangling around gently as you move.
4. Go very lightly on the vices, such as carrying on in society—the social ramble ain't restful.
5. Avoid running at all times.
6. And don't look back. Something might be gaining on you."

International League (AAA)
P.O. Box 608
Grove City, OH 43123
(614) 871-1300

Columbia Clippers
Aff: New York Yankees
1155 West Mound Street
Columbus, OH 43223
(614) 462-5250

Pawtucket Red Sox
Aff: Boston Red Sox
McCoy Stadium
P.O. Box 2365
Pawtucket, RI 02861
(401) 724-7300

Richmond Braves
Aff: Atlanta Braves
The Diamond
P.O. Box 6667
Richmond, VA 23230
(804) 359-4444

Rochester Red Wings
Aff: Baltimore Orioles
Silver Stadium
500 Norton Street
Rochester, NY 14621
(716) 467-3000

Scranton/Wilkes-Barre
Red Barons
Aff: Philadelphia Phillies
P.O. Box 3449
Scranton, PA 18505
(717) 969-2255

Syracuse Chiefs
Aff: Toronto Blue Jays
MacArthur Stadium
Syracuse, NY 13208
(315) 474-7833

Tidewater Tides
Aff: New York Mets
P.O. Box 12111
Norfolk, VA 23502
(804) 461-5600

Toledo Mud Hens
Aff: Detroit Tigers
P.O. Box 6212
Toledo, OH 43614
(419) 893-9483

Pacific Coast League (AAA)
2101 East Broadway Road,
Suite 35
Tempe, AZ 85282
(602) 967-7679

Albuquerque Dukes
Aff: Los Angeles Dodgers
P.O. Box 26267
Albuquerque, NM 87125
(505) 243-1791

Calgary Cannons
Aff: Seattle Mariners
P.O. Box 2690, Station B
Calgary, Alberta
Canada T2M 4M4
(403) 284-1111

Edmonton Trappers
Aff: California Angels
10233 96th Avenue
Edmonton, Alberta
Canada T5K 0A5
(403) 429-2934

Las Vegas Stars
Aff: San Diego Padres
850 Las Vegas Boulevard
North
Las Vegas, NV 89101
(702) 386-7200

Phoenix Firebirds
Aff: San Francisco Giants
5999 East Van Buren Street
Phoenix, AZ 85008
(602) 275-0500

**Pilot Field in Buffalo,
home to the Buffalo Bisons.**

SHORTSTOPS
The longest game ever played was a minor league game between the Pawtucket Red Sox and the Rochester Red Wings. Pawtucket won, 3–2, in a mere 33 innings!

Portland Beavers
Aff: Minnesota Twins
P.O. Box 1659
Portland, OR 97207
(503) 223-2837

Tacoma Tigers
Aff: Oakland A's
P.O. Box 11087
Tacoma, WA 98411
(206) 752-7707

Tucson Toros
Aff: Houston Astros
P.O. Box 27045
Tucson, AZ 85726
(602) 325-2621

Vancouver Canadians
Aff: Chicago White Sox
Baseball Stadium
4601 Ontario Street
Vancouver, British
Columbia
Canada V5V 3H4
(604) 872-5232

Eastern League (AA)
P.O. Box 716
Plainville, CT 06062
(203) 747-9332

Albany-Colonie Yankees
Aff: New York Yankees
Albany-Shaker Road
Albany, NY 12211
(518) 869-9236

Canton-Akron Indians
Aff: Cleveland Indians
Thurman Munson
Memorial Stadium
Canton, OH 44707
(216) 456-5100

Orlando Mered covers first for the Buffalo Bisons.

Hagerstown Suns
Aff: Baltimore Orioles
P.O. Box 230
Hagerstown, MD 21740
(301) 791-6266

Harrisburg Senators
Aff: Pittsburgh Pirates
P.O. Box 15757
Harrisburg, PA 17105
(717) 231-4444

London Tigers
Aff: Detroit Tigers
89 Wharncliffe Road
London, Ontario
Canada N6H 2A7
(519) 645-2255

New Britain Red Sox
Aff: Boston Red Sox
P.O. Box 1718
New Britain, CT 06050
(203) 224-8383

Pittsfield Cubs
Aff: Chicago Cubs
P.O. Box 2246
Pittsburgh, MA 01201
(413) 499-0077

Reading Phillies
Aff: Philadelphia Phillies
P.O. Box 15050
Reading, PA 19612
(215) 375-8469

Williamsport Bills
Aff: Seattle Mariners
P.O. Box 474
Williamsport, PA 17703
(717) 321-1210

Southern League (AA)
235 Main Street, Suite 103
Trussville, AL 35173
(205) 655-7062

Birmingham Barons
Aff: Chicago White Sox
P.O. Box 360007
Birmingham, AL 35236
(205) 781-1117

Charlotte Knights
Aff: Chicago Cubs
2280 Deerfield Drive
Fort Mill, SC 29715
(704) 332-3746

Chattanooga Lookouts
Aff: Cincinnati Reds
P.O. Box 11002
Fifth & O'Neal
Chattanooga, TN 37401
(615) 267-2208

Columbus Mudcats
Aff: Houston Astros
Golden Park
Fourth Street
P.O. Box 2425
Columbus, GA 31902
(404) 324-3594

Greenville Braves
Aff: Atlanta Braves
1 Braves Avenue
P.O. Box 16683
Greenville, SC 29606
(803) 299-3456

Huntsville Stars
Aff: Oakland A's
P.O. Box 14099
Huntsville, AL 35815
(205) 882-2562

Jacksonville Expos
Aff: Montreal Expos
Wolfson Stadium
1201 East Duval Street
P.O. Box 4756
Jacksonville, FL 32201
(904) 358-2846

Knoxville Blue Jays
Aff: Toronto Blue Jays
Meyer Stadium
633 Jessamine Street
Knoxville, TN 37917
(615) 525-3809

Memphis Chicks
Aff: Kansas City Royals
McCarver Stadium
800 Home Run Lane
Memphis, TN 38104
(901) 272-1687

Orlando Twins
Aff: Minnesota Twins
Tinker Field
287 South Tampa Avenue
P.O. Box 5645
Orlando, FL 32805
(407) 849-6346

Texas Baseball League (AA)
10201 West Markham
Street, Suite 214
Little Rock, AR 72205
(501) 227-7703

Arkansas Travelers
Aff: St. Louis Cardinals
P.O. Box 5599
Little Rock, AR 72215
(501) 664-1555

El Paso Diablos
Aff: Milwaukee Brewers
P.O. Box 9337
El Paso, TX 79984
(915) 544-1950

Jackson Mets
Aff: New York Mets
P.O. Box 4209
Jackson, MS 39216
(601) 981-4664

Midland Angels
Aff: California Angels
P.O. Box 12
Midland, TX 79702
(915) 683-4251

San Antonio Missions
Aff: Los Angeles Dodgers
P.O. Box 28268
San Antonio, TX 78228
(512) 434-9311

Shreveport Captains
Aff: San Francisco Giants
P.O. Box 3448
Shreveport, LA 71133
(318) 636-5555

Tulsa Drillers
Aff: Texas Rangers
P.O. Box 4448
Tulsa, OK 74159
(918) 744-5901

Wichita Wranglers
Aff: San Diego Padres
P.O. Box 1420
Wichita, KS 67201
(316) 267-3372

California League (A)
1060 Willow, Suite 6
San Jose, CA 95125
(408) 977-1977

Carolina League (A)
P.O. Box 9503
Greensboro, NC 27429
(919) 273-7911

Florida State League (A)
P.O. Box 6455
Lakeland, FL 33807
(813) 644-2909

TRIVIA QUIZ
    Many major leaguers have played in the Japanese league. Only
one has made the Japanese All-Star team. Can you name him?
    A) Mickey Mantle B) Vince Coleman C) Eric Davis D) Davey Johnson
                                                        Answer: D

64

Midwest League (A)
P.O. Box 936
Beloit, WI 53511
(608) 364-1188

New York-Pennsylvania League (A)
P.O. Box 1313
Auburn, NY 13021
(315) 253-2957

Northwest League (A)
P.O. Box 30025
Portland, OR 97230
(503) 256-0085

South Atlantic League (A)
P.O. Box 38
Kings Mountain, NC 28086
(704) 739-3466

INTERNATIONAL LEAGUES

In the United States, baseball is known as the national pastime. But the U.S. isn't the only country that plays the game. Sixty-five different countries now belong to the International Baseball Association (IBA). People are rounding the bases everywhere from the Soviet Union to Guam!

Here are some addresses that will help you get in touch with foreign teams. For info about baseball in countries not listed here, contact the IBA.

International Baseball Association (IBA)
Pan American Plaza, Suite 490
201 South Capitol Avenue
Indianapolis, IN 46225
(317) 237-5757

AUSTRALIA
Australia Baseball Federation
3/98 Burbridge Road
Holton, SA 5033
Australia

OH, WHAT A HITTER!

His name is Oh, but opposing pitchers would probably call him "Uh Oh." Sadaharu Oh, the most famous name in Japanese baseball, has hit more home runs than Hank Aaron!

On the other hand, Hank Aaron fans say that Japanese hitters have it easier. For one thing, the stadiums are smaller, usually only 300 feet to the foul poles, compared with about 330 feet in major league parks. For another thing, the pitchers don't throw as hard.

FRANCE
Federation Francaise de
Base-Ball et Soft Ball
23 rue d'Anjou
75008 Paris
France

CARIBBEAN
Caribbean Baseball
Conferation
Apartado 1852
Hato Rey, Puerto Rico 00919

DOMINICAN REPUBLIC
Dominican Winter League
Apartado 1246
Santo Domingo
Dominican Republic

JAPAN
Japan Pro Baseball
Imperial Tower
1-1-1 Uchisaiwaicho
Chiyoda-ku, Tokyo 100
Japan

Japan Central League
Asahi Building, 5F
6-6-7 Ginza
Chuo-ku, Tokyo 104
Japan

Chunichi Dragons
4-1-1 Sakae
Naka-ku, Nagoya-shi
Aichi-ken
Japan

Hanshin Tigers
Chiyoda Building
2-5-8 Umeida
Kita-ku, Osaka-shi
Japan

Hiroshima Toyo Carp
5-25 Motomachi
Hiroshima-shi, Hiroshima-
ken
Japan

Yakult Swallows
1-1-19 Shimbashi
Minato-ku
Japan

Yokohama Taiyo Whales
4-43 Masagocho
Naka-ku, Yokohama-shi
Japan

Yomiurui Giants
1-7-1 Otemachi
Chiyoda-ku
Japan

Japan Pacific League
Asahi Building, 9F
6-6-7 Ginza
Cho-ku, Tokyo 104
Japan

Hankyu Braves
Hankyu Grand Building
8-47 Kakutamachi
Kita-ku, Osaka-shi
Japan

Lotte Orions
2-2-33 Hyakunincho
Shinjuku-ku
Japan

Nankai Hawks
2-8-110 Namba Naka
Naniwa-ku, Osaka-shi
Japan

Nippon Ham Fighters
Roppongi Denki Building
6-1-20 Roppongi
Minato-ku
Japan

Seibu Lions
Sunshine Building
3-1-1 Higashi-Ikebukuro
Toshima-ku
Japan

MEXICO
Mexican League
Angel Pola 16
Col. Periodista
CP 11220 Mexico, D.F.
Mexico

Mexican Pacific League
Presqueria No. 613-B Sur
Navojoa, Sonora
Mexico

PUERTO RICO
Puerto Rican Winter
League
Avenida Munoz Rivera 1056
Apartado 1852
Hato Rey, Puerto Rico 00919

UNITED KINGDOM
Baseball Association of
Great Britain
78 Connaught Road
Barnet, Herts
England EN5 2PY

British Amateur Baseball
and Softball Federation
197 Newbridge Road
Hull
England HU9 2LR

Welsh Baseball Union
42 Heol Hir
Llanishen, Cardiff
Wales (0222) 759474

THE BULL PEN
Q: What kids work for the Chicago Cubs?
A: Cub scouts.

VENEZUELA
Venezuelan Winter League
Avenida Sorbona
Edif. Marta-2do. Piso, No. 25
Colinas de Bello Monte
Caracas, Venezuela

LEAGUES FOR KIDS

So you want to play in a world series? You're only seven years old? Don't despair! There are hundreds of thousands of kids playing league ball in this country. There are teams for kids of all ages, and almost every league has a world series.

Most leagues also have many famous graduates. For instance, Ken Griffey, Jr., is now making a name for himself in the majors. As a kid he played for years in the American Amateur leagues (see listing below).

Of course, most players in the kid leagues don't go on to the big leagues. But they probably do have a lot of fun. To find out about a league team in your area, contact one of these groups:

All American Amateur Baseball Association
Tom J. Checkush, Secretary
340 Walker Drive
Zanesville, OH 43701
(614) 453-7349

This little leaguer blows major league bubbles.

Started in 1944, the Association now includes about 2,500 teenagers playing in 22 leagues in the eastern United States. Boys under 20 are eligible. Most of the players are 18 and 19, though some are as young as 16. Orel Hershiser is one of many famous grads.

FANTASY LEAGUES

In January 1980, a small group of diehard baseball fans held a special meeting at La Rotisserie restaurant in New York City. They were meeting to set up what they called a "Rotisserie®" or fantasy league.

They each picked players from the current major league teams. Each "manager" picked an entire roster, with players coming from all different teams. Then they managed their fantasy team all season, making trades with other players.

At the end of the season they added up the statistics to see whose team had done the best and won the pennant. Fantasy league baseball was born.

Since then, fantasy leagues have spread across the United States, and to some other countries as well. It's been estimated that there are now hundreds of thousands playing fantasy baseball each year!

Fantasy players say the game provides extra excitement and pleasure throughout the entire baseball season. Each player has an added reason to study the box scores in the newspaper each morning. Like many fans, they want to see how the real teams are doing. But also they have important decisions to make about their fantasy team.

STARTING YOUR OWN FANTASY LEAGUE

Whole books have been written about playing fantasy baseball and setting up your own league.

But you can start a league of your own pretty simply. You need about six to ten players. One of you will be the commissioner. In addition to playing the game, the commissioner draws up the rules and supervises play.

Before opening day of the real baseball season, hold a draft day. Flip a coin to see who goes first.

Then, using either the American or the National league, take turns selecting one player each.

You each pick a 24-man roster made up of nine pitchers, five outfielders, two catchers, and seven infielders. Your players don't have to come from any one team. You can choose your players from every team in the league.

When the season starts, it's time to start watching the box scores. These are the statistics printed in the newspaper each day, telling you how each player did. You need to see how each of your players did in the following areas:

HITTING
Batting average
Hits
Homers
Runs batted in (RBIs)
Stolen bases

PITCHING
Wins
Losses
Earned-run average (ERA)
Strikeouts
Saves

If a player is doing badly in a lot of these areas, you can try to trade him to another manager in your league. At the end of the season, all the managers compare stats. You see how each player on your team ranks in your league in each of the scoring areas.

For instance, let's say there are 10 teams in your league. and you have Don Mattingly on your team. Probably Mattingly will have one of the highest batting averages in the league. If he comes in first, he scores 10 points for you in that category.

The player whose batting average ranks second in the league is worth 9 points. The third player is worth 8 points, and so on.

The lowest score any player can get is 1. So the worst a nonpitching player could score is a 1 in all five hitting areas, bringing you only 5 points. Let's hope you traded that player long ago—or were smart enough not to pick him!

If a player gets injured or is sent down to the minors, you can pick another player from the remaining pool of unpicked people. If your original player returns, though, you have to take him back and discard his replacement.

You'll probably need a few more rules, but you can make them up yourself as you go along. You'll also want to make a pennant to be kept by each year's first-place winner, and decide on a prize, if any.

Fantasy players say that the game makes them feel like real managers. They also say it makes watching baseball on TV much more exciting. Your favorite team could be losing by 20 runs. But you'll still be screaming for your fantasy team player to get a hit!

If you want to get more serious and play against grownups, check your local bookstore for a book on Fantasy League strategy. It should list several leagues for you to contact. The trouble is, these leagues charge hefty admission prices each year. "Buying a team" could cost you as much as $200. Also, these leagues discourage kids from joining, warning that the competition is rough indeed. If you want to join, it's probably a good idea to join with your mom and dad—as long as they really know their baseball!

For more information, write to:
**Rotisserie League Baseball Association
41 Union Square West, Suite 936
New York, NY 10003
(212) 691-7846**

American Amateur Baseball Congress

Joseph R. Cooper, President
118 Redfield Plaza
Marshall, MI 49068
(616) 781-2002

Founded in 1935, this group oversees 9,400 teams of kids playing in 40 U.S. states, Mexico, Puerto Rico, and Canada! Ozzie Smith and Frank Viola are a couple of names from the long list of this league's famous graduates.

The age groups break down this way:
Ages 8 and under—the Roberto Clemente League
10 and under—the Willy Mays League
12 and under—the Pee Wee Reese League
14 and under—the Sandy Koufax League
16 and under—the Mickey Mantle League
18 and under—the Connie Mack League
Unlimited—the Stan Musial League

American Legion Baseball

P.O. Box 1055
Indianapolis, IN 46206
(317) 635-8411

Founded in 1925 for teenage boys 16 to 19 years old, this organization has about 76,000 players on teams throughout the states. Major league scouts regularly attend the Legion's annual world series.

Babe Ruth Baseball & Softball

P.O. Box 5000
1770 Brunswick Avenue
Trenton, NJ 08638
(609) 695-1434

No, Babe Ruth didn't play in this league. But today there are more than 600,000 kids in the United States and Canada who do! The age breakdown of the league is:
6 to 12—Bambino League
13—Prep League
13 to 15—Babe Ruth League
16 to 18—Babe Ruth 16-to-18-year-old league

Baseball Canada/Canadian Federation of Amateur Baseball

1600 James Naismith Drive
Gloucester, Ontario
Canada K1B 5N4
(613) 748-5706

This group helps keep about 400,000 Canadian kids running around the diamond in youth leagues. It also organizes tryouts for the national team. If you

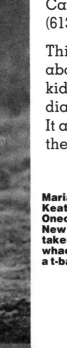

Maria Keating of Oneonta, New York, takes a whack at a t-ball.

live in Canada, contact Tom Valcke, technical director, to find out about the teams nearest you.

Dixie Baseball, Inc.
215 Watauga Lane
P.O. Box 222
Lookout Mountain, TN 37350
(615) 821-6811

This group runs the largest youth baseball league in the southern United States. About 260,000 kids play in Dixie leagues in 11 southern states.

The George Khoury Association of Baseball Leagues, Inc.
5400 Meramec Bottom Road
St. Louis, MO 63128
(314) 849-8900

These leagues began in 1936 when Mr. and Mrs. Khoury saw that their three sons always ended up playing baseball against much older kids. There are now Khoury Leagues in Florida, Kentucky, Illinois, California, and Missouri. There are softball leagues for girls. Ages for both the boys' and girls' teams are:
Atom—7 to 9
Bantam—9 to 11
Midget—11 to 13
Juvenile—11 to 15
Juniors—15 to 17

Little League Baseball Incorporated
P.O. Box 3485
Williamsport, PA 17701
(717) 326-1921

In 1939, Carl Stotz saw that his young nephews never got to play in the neighborhood sandlot baseball games. The older kids wouldn't let them in the game. So Stotz and two others founded the Little League.

Today there are about 2.5 million kids playing in the Little League, in 33 different countries! In addition to the United States, there are Little League teams in places such as Poland, China, and Jordan. Eight teams, including four from the U.S., meet for the international world series each year. Recently, two ex-Little Leaguers made the Hall of Fame—Jim Palmer and the great Yaz, Carl Yazstremski.

Boys and girls six to 18 are eligible.

Pony Baseball, Inc.
P.O. Box 225
Washington, PA 15301
(412) 225-1060

The American Legion in action.

There are 20,000 Pony league teams in the United States and seven foreign countries, including Korea and Australia. Bronco, Pony, Colt, and Palomino leagues each play their own annual international world series.

One of the largest youth baseball leagues in the world, Pony Baseball prides itself on having many different leagues for the different age groups. This way, kids don't have to compete with anyone who's more than one year older.

They also use different size fields, so that younger kids play on smaller diamonds. Girls and boys are eligible for hardball, or girls can choose softball if they prefer. The age breakdowns are:
Shetland—5 and 6 year olds
Pinto—7 and 8 years olds
Mustang—9 and 10 year olds
Bronco—11 and 12 year olds
Pony—13 and 14 year olds
Colt—15 and 16 year olds
Palomino—17 and 18 year olds

United States Stickball League (USSBL)
P.O. Box 363
East Rockaway, NY 11518
(516) 764-6307

Let's say you're a city kid, and you're used to playing street games of stickball (bash the rubber ball past three manhole covers for a homer!). There are stickball leagues and major stickball competitions.

AND DON'T FORGET... THE GRAPEFRUIT AND CACTUS LEAGUES!

In 1986, two millions fans went to see major league games—before the season even started! How? They visited spring training. These are the weeks before each season when the major league and minor league players "warm up" in two very warm sites, Florida and Arizona.

Florida's spring training stadiums are known as the Grapefruit League (since Florida farmers grow lots of grapefruits). Arizona hosts what is known as the Cactus League (with its hot, dry climate, the state is filled with cacti).

About 70 percent of the fans who come to spring training journey from other states. Why do so many fans make the long trip?

Spring training for the Braves. This is not a heads-up play!

The relaxed atmosphere—and tiny stadiums—let fans get close to the players. Practice sessions are open to the public, so you can meet the players in person.

For the players, it's not all fun and games, though. They're trying to make the team. So in addition to seeing the stars, you'll get a firsthand look at the some of the hot minor league players in action. If they play well enough in spring training, you'll see them in the majors, too.

If you decide to visit the Twins, Astros, and Royals, you can visit Disney World and Sea World at the same time. These teams all play near Orlando, home of many amusement parks.

For more information on spring training and addresses for the spring training stadiums, see Chapter 12.)

GOING! GOING! GONE!

CAMPS, SCHOOLS, AND TOURS

Ah ... Summer! Summer doesn't just mean baseball season. It's also camp season.

If you're lucky enough to go to summer camp, you'll find that almost any camp will include some baseball in its weekly schedule of events.

But if you're a baseball lover and a more serious player, there are special camps and schools that play nothing but baseball. *All day.* With breaks for baseball movies!

At baseball camp, you'll get to work on your skills with coaches, who in some cases are famous players. At the more expensive camps, you'll be using all sorts of fancy training equipment, such as video cameras so that you can tape your play and study and improve your baseball form.

Practice may not make perfect, but after a week or longer at baseball camp your game is sure to improve. And there are not only summer camps, there are even some winter camps as well. Many camps have single-week sessions. But if you have the time and money, you can go to baseball camp for months at a time!

If you're looking for a day camp, use the guide below to find a camp close by. You'll want more information in choosing the right camp for you. Almost all of these camps will gladly send you a free brochure if you write or call.

And after you've played several weeks of nonstop baseball at camp, you'll probably be in the mood to do something more relaxing, such as watch others play.

The second half of this chapter has information on tours of stadiums, a bat-making factory, tours that take you to major league games in other cities, cruises with star players, and other more relaxing ways to *see* baseball, rather than play it!

CAMPS AND SCHOOLS

ALABAMA

Birmingham

Sleep-over and day camp for boys 8–18
Contact:
Birmingham-Southern Baseball Schools
Birmingham-Southern College
800 8th Avenue West
Box A-35
Birmingham, AL 35254
(205) 226-4600

Dothan

Day camp for boys and girls 6–16
Contact:
Sam Frichter, Director
Baseball Camp
George C. Wallace State Community College—

THE BULL PEN
Q: Why are there always birds and insects at a ballpark?
A: How else could players hit flies and fouls?

Dothan
Dothan, AL 36303
(205) 983-3521

Florence

Sleep-over and day camp
for 8- to 17-year-olds
Contact:
North Alabama Baseball
Camp, Baseball Office/
Flowers Hall Annex
University of North
Alabama
Florence, AL 35632-0001
(205) 760-4397

Tuscaloosa

Sleep-over and day camp
for boys 10–17
Contact:
Barry Shollenberger
Baseball Camp
Baseball Office
University of Alabama
P.O. Box K
University, AL 35486
(205) 348-6161

ARIZONA

Flagstaff

Sleep-over and day camp
for boys 9–17
Contact:
NAU Baseball Camp
Northern Arizona
University
Box 15400
Flagstaff, AZ 86011-5400
(602) 523-3550

Glendale

Sleep-over and day camp
for athletes ages 7 through
23
Doyle Baseball Arizona
P.O. Box 10007
Glendale, AZ 85318
(800) 443-5536
(602) 978-5096 or (in Arizona
only) (800) 423-1661

ARKANSAS

Little Rock

Day camp for boys and
girls 6–17
Contact:
The Gary Hogan Baseball
Camp
University of Arkansas
–Little Rock
2801 S. University Avenue
Little Rock, AR 72204
(501) 569-3306

CALIFORNIA

Berkeley

Day camp for boys and
girls 8–12

Contact:
Cal Baseball Summer
Camp
61 Harmon Gym
Berkeley, CA 94720
(415) 642-0383

Davis

Sleep-over and day camp
for athletes 10–14 and 14–17
Contact:
Baseball Camp, University
Extension
University of California–
Davis
Davis, CA 95616-8727
(916) 757-8889

Fresno

Day camp for boys and
girls going into grades 6
through 12
Contact:
Baseball Camp
Department of Athletics
California State University
at Fresno
Fresno, CA 93740
(209) 278-4240

**Valdosta State College's
summer camp, as kids
learn the basics of fielding.**

Irvine

Day camp for boys 8 and older
Contact:
Anteater Baseball
P.O. Box 4601
Irvine, CA 92716-4601
(714) 856-7600

Larkspur

Day camp for boys and girls 8–15
Contact:
Orlando Cepeda Baseball Camp
5764 Paradise Drive
Suite 7
Corte Madera, CA 94925
(415) 924-8725 or (in California only) (800) 542-6005

Long Beach

Day camp for boys and girls 8–13
Contact:

Recreation Department
Men's Gym, Room 116
Long Beach City College
4901 East Carson Street
Long Beach, CA 90808
(213) 420-4248

Moraga

Sleep-over and day camp for boys 8–17
Contact:
St. Mary's College
Summer Athletic Camps
P.O. Box 5100
Moraga, CA 94575
(415) 376-4411, ext. 386

Northridge

Day camp for boys in grades 3–12
Contact:
CSUN Sports Camp
18111 Nordhoff Street
Northridge, CA 91330
(818) 885-3215

Riverside

Day camp for boys 7–17
Contact:
Jack Smitheran
Department of Physical Education
University of California–Riverside
Riverside, CA 92521
(714) 787-5441

Sacramento

Day camp for boys and girls 9–20
Contact:

One-on-one training at Rockford College's Runnin' Regents Baseball Camp.

Paul Carmazzi
Athletic Department
Sacramento City College
3835 Freeport Boulevard
Sacramento, CA 95822
(916) 449-7329

Santa Barbara

Day camp for boys and
girls in grades 3 through 9
Contact:
Chet Kammerer
Westmont College
955 La Paz Road
Santa Barbara, CA
93108-1099
(805) 565-6010

Santa Clara

Day camp for boys and
girls 8–17
Contact:
Mission College
3000 Mission College
Boulevard
Santa Clara, CA 95054
Attention: Mike Sanchez
(408) 988-2200, ext. 1537

Day camp for boys 10–16
Contact:
Athletic Department
Santa Clara University
Santa Clara, CA 95053
(408) 554-4680

Van Nuys

Day camp for boys and
girls 9–16
Contact:
Community Services

Los Angeles Valley College
5800 Fulton Avenue
Van Nuys, CA 91401
(818) 781-1200

COLORADO

Colorado Springs

Sleep-over and day camp
for boys 8–17
Contact:
Jim Hanley, USAFA
Falcon Sport Camps
Sports Ticket Office
Colorado Springs, CO
80840-5461
(719) 472-1895

Denver

Day camp for boys
Contact:
Jack Rose
University of Denver
Baseball Camp
Denver, CO 80208-0321
(303) 871-3904

Grand Junction

Sleep-over and day camp
for boys in grades 3–12
Contact:
Byron Wiehe, Director
Mesa College Baseball
School
391 Evergreen Road
Grand Junction, CO 81501
(303) 242-5228 or (303)
248-1369

CONNECTICUT

New Haven

Day camp for boys 9–17
Contact:
Yale Sports Camps
402A Yale Station
New Haven, CT 06520
(203) 432-2488

Simsbury

Sleep-over and day camp
for boys 8–10 and 10–16
Contact:
Baseball U.S.A. Camps
P.O. Box 1134
Mountainside, NJ 07092
(201) 277-3715
Ask for information on the
Westminster School Boys'
Baseball Camp in
Simsbury, Connecticut.

West Haven

For young men 17–28 who
just missed making it into
the majors
Contact:
Connecticut Professional
Baseball School
2546 Cropsey Avenue
Brooklyn, NY 11214
If you're calling from New
York, call (718) 946-9827. If
you're calling from
Connecticut, call (203)
754-9055.

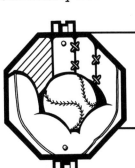

SHORTSTOPS
The very first ballpark was the Union Grounds in Brooklyn, where games were played in 1862. The price of admission? Ten cents.

DISTRICT OF COLUMBIA

Washington, D.C.

Day camp for boys 10–14
Contact:
St. Albans Summer
Programs
Mount Saint Alban
Washington, DC 20016
(202) 537-6450

FLORIDA

Bradenton

Day camp for 8- to
16-year-olds
Contact:
Manatee Community
College
Baseball Office
5840 26th Street West
Bradenton, FL 33507
(813) 755-1511, ext. 4261

Coral Gables

Day camp for boys 6–17
Contact:
Ron Fraser's Sports Camp
University of Miami
P.O. Box 248167
Coral Gables, FL 33124
(305) 284-4171

Fort Lauderdale

Sleep-over and day camp
for boys and girls 8–23
"Play Ball" Baseball
Academy
P.O. Box 4855
Fort Lauderdale, FL 33338
(305) 776-6217

Victoria Bucker takes her cuts.

Miami

Day camp for boys 7–17
Contact:
St. Thomas University
16400 32nd Avenue, N.W.
Miami, FL 33054
(305) 625-6000

Orlando

Sleep-over and day camp
for boys 8–13
Contact:
Jay Bergman
UCF Summer Baseball
Camps
Athletic Department
University of Central
Florida
Orlando, FL 32816-0555
(407) 275-2256

Panama City

Day camp for boys 8 and
over
Contact:
Gulf Coast Community
College
5230 West Highway 98
Panama City, FL 32401
(904) 769-1551

Pensacola

Baseball camp for boys
8–12
Contact:
Dr. Donn Peery
Director of Athletics
Pensacola Junior College
1000 College Boulevard
Pensacola, FL 32504
(904) 484-1690

St. Petersburg Beach

Sleep-over or day camp for boys and girls of all ages
Contact:
The Jim Rice Pro-Baseball School
400 Corey Avenue
Suite 250
St. Petersburg Beach, FL 33706
(800) 552-HITS (outside Florida)
(813) 360-2900 (in Florida and from Canada)

Sarasota

Sleep-over camp for boys 12–18
Contact:
Baseball U.S.A. Camps
P.O. Box 1134
Mountainside, NJ 07092
(201) 277-3715

Winter Haven

Sleep-over or day camp for boys and girls 8–21
Contact:
Doyle Baseball
P.O. Box 9156
Winter Haven, FL 33883
(813) 293-8994
(800) 443-5536

Winter Park

Day camp for boys 9–17
Contact:
Center for Lifelong Education
Rollins College
Campus Box 2728
Winter Park, FL 32789
(407) 646-2604

GEORGIA

Atlanta

Day camps for boys 8–12 and 13–18, and a sleep-over session for boys 13–18
Contact:
Georgia Tech/Jim Morris Baseball Camp
Georgia Tech Athletic Association
150 Bobby Dodd Way, N.W.
Atlanta, GA 30332
(404) 894-5400

Barnesville

Sleep-over and day camp for boys 8–15
Contact:
Baseball Camp
Gordon Junior College
103 College Drive
Barnesville, GA 30204
(404) 358-5082

Clarkston

Day camp for boys 6–14
Contact:
Greg Ward or Doug Casey
DeKalb College–Central
555 North Indian Creek Drive
Clarkston, GA 30021-2396
(404) 244-5050

Statesboro

Sleep-over and day camp for boys 10–17
Contact:
Jack Stallings
Georgia Southern University Baseball Camp
Landrum Box 8115
Georgia Southern University
Statesboro, GA 30460
(912) 681-5376

Valdosta

Sleep-over and day camp for boys 6–18
Contact:
Blazer Baseball Camp
Valdosta State College
Valdosta, GA 31698
(912) 333-5890

ILLINOIS

Belleville

Day camp for boys in grades 4–9
Contact:
BAC Boys Summer Baseball Camp
Belleville Area College
2500 Carlyle Road
Belleville, IL 62221
(618) 235-2700, ext. 271

Champaign

Sleep-over and day camp for boys 9–18
Contact:
Fighting Illini Summer Camps
113 Assembly Hall
1800 South First Street
Champaign, IL 61820
(217) 333-1102

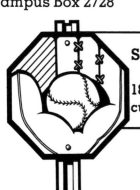

SHORTSTOPS
  "Candy" Cummings is said to have invented the curveball in the 1860s. He got the idea as a kid, throwing a clamshell. The clamshell curved, so he later tried it with a baseball.

Edwardsville

Day camp for boys 8–16
Contact:
Summer Baseball Camp
Conferences and Institutes
Box 1036
Edwardsville, IL 62026-1036
(618) 692-2660

Normal

Sleep-over and day camps
for boys from age 10
through senior year in high
school
Contact:
Redbird Specialty
Baseball Camp
College of Continuing
Education and Public
Service
Illinois State University
Normal, IL 61761
(309) 438-5151

Rockford

Day camp for boys of all
ages
Contact:
Bill Langston
Athletic Director/Baseball
Coach
Rockford College
5050 E. State
Rockford, IL 61109
(815) 226-4000

INDIANA

Terre Haute

Sleep-over and day camp
for boys 7–17
Contact:

Bob Warn's Camp of
Champions
4th and Chestnut Street
Terre Haute, IN 47809
(812) 237-4051

Winona Lake

Christian sleep-over and
day camp for boys 14–18
Contact:
Jeff Kowatch
Grace College
200 Seminary Drive
Winona Lake, IN 46590
(219) 372-5217

IOWA

Ames

Sleep-over and day camp
for boys 9–17
Contact:
Midwest Baseball School
Iowa State University
2018 State Gym
Ames, IA 50011
(515) 294-4132

Iowa City

Sleep-over and day camps
for boys 10–17
Contact:
The University of Iowa
Sports Camps
E216 Field House,
University of Iowa
Iowa City, IA 52242
(319) 335-9714

KANSAS

Emporia

Sleep-over and day camp
for boys in grades 9–12
Contact:
Brian Embery
Emporia State University
Summer Baseball Camp
Physical Education
Department, Box 20
1200 Commercial
Emporia, KS 66801-5087
(316) 343-5354

Lawrence

Day camp for boys 9–12
and sleep-over camp for
boys 13–17
Contact:
Kansas Jayhawk Baseball
Camp
Allen Field House, Room
217
University of Kansas
Lawrence, KS 66045
(913) 864-7907

Wichita

Sleep-over and day camp
for boys
Contact:
Loren Hibbs
Wichita State University
Box 18
Wichita, KS 67208
(316) 689-8142

KENTUCKY

Lexington

Sleep-over and day camp
for boys
Contact:
Wildcat Baseball Camp
University of Kentucky
Memorial Coliseum
Lexington, KY 40506-0019
(606) 257-8829

Morehead

Sleep-over and day camp
for boys and girls of all
ages, run by Denny Doyle
Contact:
Doyle Baseball School
c/o Dr. Frank Spaniol
Morehead State University
Morehead, KY 40351
(606) 783-2881

LOUISIANA

Baton Rouge

Sleep-over and day camp
for boys in grades 2–11
Contact:
Skip Bertman Baseball
Camp
Louisiana State University
P.O. Box 16355
Baton Rouge, LA 70893
(504) 388-4148

New Orleans

Day camp for boys 8–12
and 13–17
Contact:
UNO Summer Baseball
Camp
Athletic Department
Lakefront Arena, Room 139
University of New Orleans
New Orleans, LA 70148
(504) 286-6239

MAINE

Summer day and sleep-
over camp for boys 9–18
Contact:
Summer Sports Clinic
Memorial Gymnasium
University of Maine at
Orono
Orono, ME 04469-0143
(207) 581-1073

MARYLAND

Frederick

Baseball camp for boys
Contact:
Rhett Ross
11505 Warbler Lane
Ijamsville, MD 21754
(301) 831-3967

La Plata

Day camp for boys 10–17
Contact:
Boys' Baseball Camp
c/o Rob Chamberlain
Physical Education Office
Charles County Commu-
nity College
P.O. Box 910
La Plata, MD 20646
(301) 934-2251, ext. 206

McDonough

Day camp for boys 8–16
Contact:
Mike McMillan, Director
Elrod Hendricks' Baseball
Camp
McDonough School, Box
380
Owings Mills, MD 21217
(301) 581-4751

Towson

Day camp for boys 9–16
Contact:
Mr. Bill Hunter, Director
Boys' Baseball Camp
Towson State University
Towson, MD 21204
(301) 830-2759

MASSACHUSETTS

Amherst

Sleep-over and day camp
for boys 8–17
Contact:
Summer Camps Program
Boyden Building,
Room 248A
University of Massa-
chusetts
Amherst, MA 01003
(413) 545-3522

Brockton

Day camp for boys and
girls 8–17
Contact:
Massasoit Community
College
One Massasoit Boulevard

TRIVIA QUIZ
Babe Ruth named his bat:
A) Wonderboy
B) Thunderbolt
C) Black Beauty
D) The Swat Stick
E) The Sultan

Answer: C

79

Brockton, MA 02402
Attention: Athletic
Department
(508) 588-9100

Gardner

Day camp for boys 8–18
directed by Phillies scout
George Biron
Contact:
Mount Wachusett
Community College
Division of Continuing
Education
Green Street
Gardner, MA 01440
(508) 597-2543

Springfield

Day camp for boys 8–12
and 13–17
Contact:
Springfield College
Baseball Camp
Box 1793, 253 Alden Street
Springfield College
Springfield, MA 01109
(413) 788-3274
(413) 788-3111

Wellesley

Sleep-over and day camp
for boys 8–18
Contact:
Bob Horan, Director
Rich Gedman All-American
Baseball Camp
6 Ridge Road
Milford, MA 01757
(508) 478-0514

West Peabody

Sleep-over and day camp
for campers 9–18
Contact:
Mike Andrews Baseball
Camp
P.O. Box 2157
West Peabody, MA 01960
(508) 535-1718

MICHIGAN

Allendale

Sleep-over and day camp
for boys 8–18
Contact:
Andy Chopp
Baseball Office
Grand Valley State
University
Allendale, MI 49401
(616) 895-3584

Ann Arbor

Sleep-over and day camp
for boys 9–17
Contact:
Michigan Camps of
Champions
1000 South State Street
Ann Arbor, MI 48109
(313) 747-1218

Birmingham

Day camp for boys and
girls 10–13
Contact:
Frank Orlando, Director
Department of Athletics
Detroit Country Day School
22305 W. 13 Mile Road

Birmingham, MI 48101
(313) 646-7717

East Lansing

Sleep-over and day camp
for boys 9–17
Contact:
Michigan State University
Summer Sports School
222 Jenison Fieldhouse
East Lansing, MI 48824-1025
(517) 355-5264

Grand Rapids

Day camp for boys 9–12,
12–15, and 10–16
Contact:
Calvin College
Department of Physical
Education
Grand Rapids, MI 49546
(616) 957-6000

MINNESOTA

Mankato

Sleep-over and day camp
for boys 10–20
Contact:
Dean Bowyer Baseball
Camp
Box 28
Mankato State University
Mankato, MN 56001
(507) 389-2689

MISSISSIPPI

Cleveland

Sleep-over and day camp
for boys from age 10

THE BULL PEN
   Q: **On what day is a baseball game never rained out?**
   A: **On Sunday.**

through senior year in high school
Contact:
Bill Marchant
Delta State Baseball Camp
P.O. Box 3141
Delta State University
Cleveland, MS 38733
(601) 846-4291

Jackson

Day camp for boys 8–15
Contact:
St. Andrew's Baseball Camp
4120 Old Canton Road
Jackson, MS 39216
(601) 982-5065

Hattiesburg

Sleep-over and day camp for boys and girls in grades 3–6 and grades 7–12
Contact:
University of Southern Mississippi
Division of Lifelong Learning
Southern Station Box 5056
Hattiesburg, MS 39406-5056
(601) 266-4204

Mississippi State

Sleep-over and day camp for boys 9–17
Contact:
Bulldog Baseball Camp
P.O. Drawer 5327
Mississippi State University
Mississippi State, MS 39762
(601) 325-3597

Oxford

Sleep-over and day camp for boys 9–18
Contact:
University of Mississippi
Ole Miss Baseball Camp
Center for Public Service and Continuing Studies
P.O. Box 879
University, MS 38677
(601) 232-7282

MISSOURI

Columbia

Sleep-over and day camp for boys 12–17
Contact:
Mizzou Baseball Camp
348 Hearnes Building
University of Missouri
Columbia, MO 65211
(314) 882-4087

Maryville

Sleep-over and day camp
Contact:
Jim Johnson
Bearcat Baseball School
Lamkin Gymnasium
Northwest Missouri State University
Maryville, MO 64468
(816) 562-1304

Miller

Sleep-over camp for boys 8–19
Contact:
Mickey Owen Baseball School
P.O. Box 88
Miller, MO 65707
(417) 882-2799 or (during the summer) (417) 452-3211

Table Rock Lake

Sleep-over camp for boys 8–18
Contact:
Sho-Me Baseball Camps
c/o Phil Wilson
Star Route 4, Box 198
Reeds Springs, MO 65737
(417) 338-2603

NEBRASKA

Omaha

Day camp for boys 11–17
Contact:
Athletic Department
University of Nebraska at Omaha
Omaha, NE 68182
(402) 554-2305

NEVADA

Las Vegas

Baseball camp for boys 8–17
Contact:
Coach Rod Soesbe
University of Nevada–Las Vegas
4505 Maryland Parkway
Las Vegas, NV 89154
(702) 876-6761

NEW JERSEY

Hightstown

Sleep-over and day camp
for boys 8–14
Contact:
Baseball U.S.A. Camps
P.O. Box 1134
Mountainside, NJ 07092
(201) 277-3715

Lincroft

Day camp for boys 8–17
Contact:
Ferris Antoon, Director
Sports Camps/Community
Services
Brookdale Community
College
Newman Springs Road
Lincroft, NJ 07738
(201) 842-1900, ext. 315

Piscataway

Day camp for boys 10–17
Contact:
Fred Hill, Director
Rutgers Baseball Camp
Rutgers Athletic Center
P.O. Box 1149
Piscataway, NJ 08855
(201) 932-3553

Princeton

Sleep-over and day camp
for boys 10–17; sponsored
by the Babe Ruth League
Contact:
Conference Services
71 University Place
Princeton University
Princeton, NJ 08544
(609) 258-3369

South Orange

Day camp for boys and
girls 7–17
Contact:
Mike Sheppard
Baseball Coach
94 Tuxedo Parkway
Newark, NJ 07106
(201) 761-9557

Toms River

Day camp for boys and
girls 8–18
Contact:
Office of Community
Education
Ocean County College
CN 2001
Toms River, NJ 08753
(201) 255-0404

Upper Montclair

Sleep-over and day camp
for boys and young men
8–21
Contact:
Big League Baseball Camp
Department M
c/o Vincent Carlesi
2546 Cropsey Avenue
Brooklyn, NY 11214
(718) 946-9827

NEW YORK

Albany

Day camp for boys and
girls 8–17
Contact:
State University of New
York at Albany
c/o Dennis Elkin, Summer
Sport Camp Director
Physical Education Center,
Room 135
1400 Washington Avenue
Albany, NY 12222
(518) 442-3030

Bronx

Sleep-over and day camp
for boys 13–17
Contact:
Dan Gallagher
Championship Baseball
Camp
c/o Baseball Office
Fordham University
Bronx, NY 10458
(212) 579-2439

Brookville

Day camp for boys going
into grades 4–9
Contact:
Brian Carey, Director
Lutheran High School
Summer Program
131 Brookville Road
Brookville, NY 11545
(516) 626-1100

Cooperstown

Sleep-over camp for boys
9–14
Contact:
Baseball U.S.A. Camps
P.O. Box 1134
Mountainside, NJ 07092
(201) 277-3715

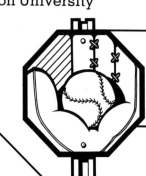

SHORTSTOPS
Until 1884, pitchers were required to pitch underhand.

Cortland

Sleep-over and day camps for boys and girls 10–18. They teach both hardball and softball.
Contact:
Division of Professional Studies
Attn: Cortland Summer Sports School
SUNY/Cortland
P.O. Box 2000
Cortland, NY 13045
(607) 753-2701

Jamaica, Queens

Day camp for boys 8–13
Contact:
St. John's University
School of Continuing Education
Grand Central and Utopia Parkways
Jamaica, NY 11439
(718) 990-6101

Long Island

Sleep-over and day camp for boys 8–18. This camp is held on Long Island, NY, but for information, you need to write to Milford, MA.
Contact:
Bob Horan, Director
Lee Mazzilli and Bud Harrelson All-American Baseball Camp
6 Ridge Road
Milford, MA 01757
(508) 478-0514

Old Westbury

Day camp for boys 7–17, with door-to-door transportation provided throughout Nassau, Suffolk, and Queens counties. (Local programs—no transportation provided—are also offered in Rockville Centre and Bethpage, and at Westbury Junior High School.)
Contact:
New York Baseball Academy
c/o Horizon Program
New York Institute of Technology
Old Westbury, NY 11568
(516) 922-7133

Syosset

Once-a-week training sessions held throughout the year for 3- to 5-year-olds, 6- to 8-year-olds, and 9- to 12-year-olds. Private lessons also available.
Contact:
Eastern Baseball Academy
267 Jericho Turnpike
Syosset, NY 11791
(516) 496-7788

Syracuse

Sleep-over and day camp for boys in grades 8–12
Contact:
Richard Rockwell, Director
LeMoyne Baseball Camp
LeMoyne College
Syracuse, NY 13214
(315) 445-4410

West Point

Sleep-over camp for boys going into grades 6–12
Contact:
Dan Roberts, Director
West Point Baseball Camp
Athletic Department
Building 639 ODIA
West Point, NY 10996
(914) 938-3100

NORTH CAROLINA

Boone

Sleep-over and day camp for boys 13–17
Contact:
Mountaineer Baseball Camp
Office of Conferences and Institutes
Appalachian State University
Boone, NC 28608
(704) 262-3045

Buies Creek

Sleep-over and day camp for boys 10–17
Contact:
Campbell University Baseball Camp
P.O. Box 10
Buies Creek, NC 27506
(919) 893-4111, ext. 2485

Charlotte

Day camp for boys 9–12
Contact:
The Charlotte Country Day Schools

Division of Coordinate and
Summer Programs
1440 Carmel Road
Charlotte, NC 28226
(704) 366-1241, ext. 281

Cullowhee

Day camp for 8- to
15-year-olds
Contact:
WCU Baseball School
Western Carolina
University
Reid Gym, Room 17
Cullowhee, NC 28723
(704) 227-7339

Greenville

Sleep-over camp for boys
6–12 and day camp for
boys 13–17
Contact:
Gary Overton, Director
ECU Baseball Camps
Scales Fieldhouse
East Carolina University
Greenville, NC 27858-4353
(919) 757-4604

Elon College

Sleep-over and day camp
for boys 8–17
Contact:
Mike Harden
Head Baseball Coach
Elon College
Elon College, NC 27244
(919) 584-2420

Fayetteville

Day camps for boys and

**Pro Scout George Biron teaches the
bent leg slide at Mount Wachusett
Baseball Camp.**

girls 8–13 and 13–18
Contact:
Summer Sports Camps
Methodist College
5400 Ramsey Street
Fayetteville, NC 28311
(919) 488-7110

Louisburg

Sleep-over and day camp
for boys from age 10
through senior year of high
school
Contact:
Coach Russ Frazier
Louisburg College
Louisburg, NC 27549
(919) 496-2521

Misenheimer

Sleep-over and day camp
for boys 9 and up
Contact:
Coordinator of Summer
Athletic Camps
Pfeiffer College

Misenheimer, NC 28109
(704) 463-5809

Mount Olive

Sleep-over and day camp
for boys 9–17
Contact:
Coach Roger Jackson
Mount Olive College
Mount Olive, NC 28365

Wilmington

Sleep-over camp for boys
12–17 and day camp for
boys 10–17
Contact:
UNCW Athletic Department
University of North
Carolina at Wilmington
601 South College Road
Wilmington, NC 28403-3297
(919) 395-3233

NORTH DAKOTA

Mayville

Sleep-over and day camp
for boys 12–18
Contact:
MSC Comet Baseball
Camp
Mayville State College
Mayville, ND 58257
(701) 786-2866

OHIO

Akron
Day camp for boys in
grades 6–11
Contact:
Dawn Moore

Coordinator of Zip Sports
Camps
The University of Akron
JAR 183
Akron, OH 44325
(216) 375-7080

Athens

Sleep-over and day camp
for boys 8–18
Contact:
Jerry France, Baseball
Coach
Ohio University
Athens, OH 45701-2979
(614) 593-1180

Bowling Green

Sleep-over and day camp
for boys through grade 12
Contact:
Mel Mahler, Director
Summer Sports School
BGSU Athletic Department
Bowling Green State
University
Bowling Green, OH 43403
(419) 372-2401

Cincinnati

Sleep-over and day camp
for boys in grades 4–11
Contact:
Xavier Summer Camps
O'Connor Sports Center
Xavier University
Cincinnati, OH 45207
(513) 745-3417

Columbus

Sleep-over and day camp
for boys 8–17
Contact:
Dick Finn or Joe Carbone
Baseball Office
Ohio State University
St. John Arena, Room 212
410 Woody Hayes Drive
Columbus, OH 43210
(614) 292-6446

Dayton

Sleep-over and day camp
for boys 8–17
Contact:
Ron Nischwitz or Tom
Brunswick
Wright State Baseball
School
Dayton, OH 45435

Kent

Day camp for boys 7–17
Contact:
Bob Todd Baseball Camp
170 North Prospect Street
Kent, OH 44240
(216) 672-5976

Ridgeville Corners

Day camps for boys and
girls in grades 1–4 and 5–8
Contact:
Community Services
Northwest Technical
College
Route 1, Box 246-A
Archbold, OH 43502
(419) 267-5511, ext. 210

OKLAHOMA

Chandler

Sleep-over camp for boys
8–18
Contact:
Tom Belcher
Baseball Camp
Box 395
Chandler, OK 74834
(405) 258-1720

Norman

Sleep-over and day camp
for boys 8–17
Contact:
Enos Semore Baseball
Camp
University of Oklahoma
401 W. Imhoff
Norman, OK 73069
(405) 325-8354

Stillwater

Sleep-over and day camp
for boys 9–18
Contact:
Baseball Camp Director
201 Gallagher Hall
Oklahoma State University
Stillwater, OK 74078
(405) 744-5000

Tulsa

Sleep-over and day camp
for boys 8–17
Contact:
Oral Roberts University
7777 S. Lewis
Tulsa, OK 74171
(918) 495-7138

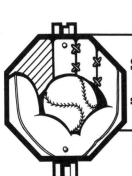

SHORTSTOPS
    Don Mattingly holds the major league record for grand slams in a
single season. In 1987 he cleared the bases six times.

Wilburton

Sleep-over and day camp
for boys 8–14
Contact:
Jerry Smith, Camp Director
Eastern Oklahoma State
College
Wilburton, OK 74578
(918) 465-2361

OREGON

Ontario

Day camp for boys 9–18
Contact:
Rick Baumann's Treasure
Valley Baseball Camp
Treasure Valley Commu-
nity College
650 College Boulevard
Ontario, OR 97914
(503) 889-6493, ext. 276

PENNSYLVANIA

Easton

Day camp for 7- to
18-year-olds
Contact:
Hindelang-Barth Baseball
School
219 Burke Street
Easton, PA 18042
(215) 258-1310

Huntingdon

Day camp for boys and
girls 8–12, sleep-over camp
for boys and girls 13–17
Contact:
Bill Huston
Director of Programming

and Conferences
Juniata College
Huntingdon, PA 16652
(814) 643-4310, ext. 355

Shippensburg

Sleep-over and day camp
for boys 9–18
Contact:
Director of Conferences
Old Main, Box 4
Shippensburg University
Shippensburg, PA 17257
(717) 532-1256

State College

Sleep-over and day camp
for boys going into grades
7–12
Contact:
Kathy Kurchner
Boys Baseball Camp
The Pennsylvania State
University
410 Keller Conference
Center
University Park, PA 16802
(814) 865-7557

SOUTH CAROLINA

Aiken

Day camp for boys 7–17
Contact:
Randy Warrick, Baseball
Coach
University of South
Carolina–Aiken
171 University Parkway
Aiken, SC 29801
(803) 648-6851

Charleston

Sleep-over and day camp
for boys 8–12 and 9–15
Contact:
Chal Port
The Citadel
Charleston, SC 29409
(803) 792-5070

Clemson

Sleep-over camp for boys
from age 12 through senior
year of high school
Contact:
Coach Bill Wilhelm
102 Berry Street
Clemson, SC 29631
(803) 654-5801

Rock Hill

Sleep-over camp for boys
and girls 11–17
Contact:
Horace Turbeville
Winthrop College Baseball
Camp
Winthrop College
Rock Hill, SC 29733
(803) 329-2140

Spartanburg

Day camp for boys 9–12
and 13–17
Contact:
Coach Lon Joyce
Spartanburg Methodist
College
Powell Mill Road
Spartanburg, SC 29301
(803) 587-4000

THE BULL PEN
Q: What went wrong with the Montreal team photo?
A: It was over-EXPOSed!

TENNESSEE

Knoxville

Sleep-over and day camp for boys 12–15 and in high school
Contact:
The Hitting Camp
Baseball Office, Box 47
Knoxville, TN 37901
(615) 974-1261

Sleep-over and day camp for boys 9–16
Contact:
UT Baseball Camp
Box 15016
Knoxville, TN 37901
(615) 974-2056

Nashville

Day camp for boys 7–17
Contact:
Bison Baseball
David Lipscomb University
Nashville, TN 37204-3951
(615) 269-1000

Sleep-over and day camp for boys 8–17
Contact:
Coach Roy Mewbourne
Vanderbilt Athletic
Department
P.O. Box 120158
Nashville, TN 37212
(615) 322-4727

Trevacca

Day camp for boys and girls 7 and older
Contact:

Elliot Johnson
c/o Trevacca College
Nashville, TN 37203
(615) 248-1276

TEXAS

Arlington

Day camp for boys 8–14
Contact:
UTA Baseball Clinic
c/o Butch McBroom
P.O. Box 19079
Arlington, TX 76019
(817) 273-2261

College Station

Sleep-over and day camp for boys 13–17
Contact:
Texas A&M Baseball Camp
Texas A&M University
College Station, TX 77843
(409) 845-1991

Fort Worth

Sleep-over and day camp for boys

Learning to slide on a wet surface is safer—and more fun!

Contact:
Lance Brown
Texas Christian University
Box 32924
Fort Worth, TX 76129
(817) 921-7985

Huntsville

Sleep-over and day camp for boys 9–12 and 13–14
Contact:
San Houston State
University Baseball Camp
SHSU Box 2273
Huntsville, TX 77341
(409) 294-1726

Longview

Day camp for boys 6–10
Contact:
Bob Marsh
LeTourneau College
P.O. Box 7001
Longview, TX 75607
(214) 753-0231, ext. 208

Lubbock

Day camp for boys and girls 10–18
Contact:
Red Raider Baseball Camp
c/o Division of Continuing
Education
Box 4110
Texas Tech University
Lubbock, TX 79409-4110
(806) 742-2777

San Antonio

Full-day and half-day camp for boys and girls

8–15, softball for girls
10–15, and an advanced
skills camp for high school
kids 15–17
Contact:
Jerry Grote's Baseball
World
8206 Rough Rider, Suite 104
San Antonio, TX 78239
(512) 646-9977

UTAH

Cedar City

Baseball camp for boys
Contact:
Maureen Robb
Sports Camp Secretary
Centrum
Southern Utah State
College
Cedar City, UT 84720
(801) 586-7872

Provo

Sleep-over and day camp
for boys and girls 10–17
Contact:
Brigham Young University
Summer Sports Camps,
Conferences and Work-
shops
154 HCEB
Provo, UT 84602
(801) 378-4851

Salt Lake City

Day camp for boys 8–12
and 13–16
Contact:
Baseball Office
University of Utah

Salt Lake City, UT 84112
(801) 581-5323

VIRGINIA

Hampden-Sydney

Six sleep-over camps for
boys 7–10, 10–12, 11–14,
8–12, 13–17, and 8–17
Contact:
Coach Frank Fulton
Hampden-Sydney College
P.O. Box 83
Hampden-Sydney, VA 23943
(804) 223-8975

Harrisonburg

Day camp for boys and
girls 7–9, 10–12, and 13–17
Contact:
Office of Special Events
James Madison University
Harrisonburg, VA 22807
(703) 568-6626

Norfolk

Sleep-over and day camp
for boys 10–14
Contact:
Youth All-Star Camp
Health and Physical
Education Building, Room
232
Old Dominion University

Norfolk, VA 23529-0199
(804) 683-4358

Richmond

Sleep-over and day camps
for boys 8–18
Contact:
Ronnie Atkins
Robins Center
Richmond, VA 23173
(804) 289-8391

WASHINGTON

Auburn

Day camp for boys and
girls 8–14
Contact:
Summer Schools and
Camps
Student Programs Office
Green River Community
College
12401 S.E. 320th Street
Auburn, WA 98002
(206) 833-9111, ext. 337

Yakima

Sleep-over camp for boys
8–17
Contact:
Stottlemyre Baseball Camp
P.O. Box 398
Yakima, WA 98907

**Baseball is by no means a
boys' sport. There are loads
of co-ed camps as well as
camps for just girls.**

(509) 457-1670
(800) 258-5878

Pullman

Day camp for boys and
girls 9–15
Contact:
Cougar Baseball Camp
113 Bohler Gym
Washington State
University
Pullman, WA 99164-1610
(509) 335-4593

WEST VIRGINIA

Wheeling

Sleep-over and day camp
for boys 11–17
Contact:
Steve Blass Baseball Camp
Linsly, Knox Lane
Wheeling, WV 26003
(304) 233-3260

TOURS

CRUISING WITH THE STAR PLAYERS

Some major league
teams hold special
off-season events, such as
cruises, that let fans travel
with the players. Cruises
aren't cheap. They can cost
as much as $1,800 for a
single week. But you'll get
to meet the players, and
even play softball with
them.

For information about
off-season events such as
these, contact the team
office.

There are also cruises
where you can meet
famous baseball veterans.
Custom Cruises is one of
the companies that
organize these trips. You'll
go for a seven-day
Caribbean cruise with the
likes of Willie Stargell and
Ted Williams. The trip
includes card shows,
autograph sessions,
softball games on shore,
and more. It costs $1,349
per person plus airfare.
Kids under 16 must be
accompanied by a parent.

For more information,
contact:

Custom Cruises, Inc., with
the Holland America Line
152 South Saw Mill River
Road
Elmsford, NY 10523
Outside New York: (800)
621-6010
In New York State: (914)
592-6010

STADIUM TOURS

What baseball fan
doesn't long to stand in the
green grass of a major
league outfield? What fan
hasn't daydreamed about
jogging around those
bases, or even just sitting
in the dugout?

One way to do it, of
course, is to make it onto a
major league team. But
don't worry, there's a much
easier method, and it's
open to all.

Many major league
stadiums offer stadium
tours. The tours vary from
team to team, but in most
cases you'll see everything
from the dugouts to the
press box. Not only that,
these tours are almost
always very inexpensive.

Listed below is
information about a
number of these tours.
Details vary from year to
year, though, so when in
doubt, contact the team
office (see Chapter 1). If you
don't see your local team
listed here, don't give up.
Write or call the team
office. For one thing, they
may have recently added a
tour. Or they may be
willing to arrange an
informal tour, especially if
you're part of a large
group.

Minor league stadiums
also offer tours. See
listings for the team offices
in Chapter 1.

Atlanta Braves. They offer
a free stadium tour during
the baseball season. It's
mainly for school groups.

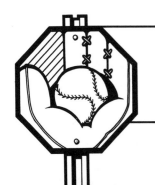

SHORTSTOPS
In 1974, a women's softball game lasted 620 innings!

Contact the team's public relations department. The tour includes a walk around the outfield fence and a visit to the press box.

Baltimore Orioles. They will take schools on group tours of the stadium. Contact the Orioles community relations department. The tour takes you through the stadium, top to bottom, leaving out only the clubhouse. You'll see a video and the exhibit of Hall-of-Fame lockers, and visit the press box.

Boston Red Sox. Out-of-town groups may be able to arrange tours of Fenway through the Sox public relations department. There's no officially established tour.

Chicago Cubs. No tour is offered, except to some contest winners. To keep up to date on these contests, contact the team office.

Chicago White Sox. They offer a tour, mainly for groups. Contact Ms. Susan Summers in the marketing department for information. The tour is free, and it's offered throughout the season except on game days.

Cincinnati Reds. The city of Cincinnati conducts stadium tours for schools and other large groups when the team is playing out of town. For information, call (513) 352-6333.

Cleveland Indians. They offer tours of the stadium for large groups. Contact their community relations department for more information.

Houston Astros. The Astrodome tour is offered three times a day year-round, except when team play or other events get in the way. This one-hour tour will take you from the upper level of the stadium all the way down onto the field. There's also a slide show. Prices: adults, $2.75; kids, $1.50. For more information, contact Mr. Bill Stone of the Astros office at (713) 799-9595.

Kansas City Royals. The Royals tour includes the press box, the Hall of Fame display, the stadium store, the field, and—a rarity on stadium tours—the visiting team's clubhouse.

The tour is offered from June 4 to August 31, Monday through Friday, five times a day: at 9:30,

10:30, and 11:30 A.M., and at 1:30 and 2:30 P.M. There's no 2:30 tour on game days. On Saturdays the tour runs twice, at 10:30 and 11:30 A.M. The cost is $1 for kids and students, $2 for adults. Contact the Royals tour department at (816) 921-2200, ext. 201.

Minnesota Twins. The tour is conducted by the Metropolitan Sports Facilities Commission, which runs the stadium.

You can contact them at (612) 332-0386.

Montreal Expos. For information on their tour, call (514) 252-4737.

Pittsburgh Pirates. You can tour the stadium anytime from spring through fall. You'll see everything from the broadcast booth to the visiting players' dressing room. There's also a two-hour tour that includes the stadium museum and theater, where you'll see a film.

The one-hour stadium tour costs $2.25 for adults, $1.75 for kids 18 and under. The double tour is $3.25 for adults, $2.25 for kids. Tours leave every day of the week from 9:00 A.M. to 4:00 P.M., from Gate C (where free parking is available).

THE BULL PEN
   Q: What baseball player is always ready for Christmas?
   A: The *Santa*-fielder.

You'll need a reservation.

For reservations or more info, write or call:

Spectator Management
Three Rivers Stadium
400 Stadium Circle
Pittsburgh, PA 15212
(412) 321-0650

For a special tour that includes all of the above plus a boat ride, call Gateway Clipper at (412) 355-7980

St. Louis Cardinals. Their stadium tour takes you just about everywhere in the stadium except the locker rooms. You do get to walk through the umpires' corridor, through which the umpires walk to get to the field.

Once out on the field, you get to visit the dugout. (The tour skips the field itself during batting practice.)

The price of the tour is $2.50 for grown-ups and $2.00 for kids. It's offered year-round. During the off season, the tour starts at 11:00 A.M. and 2:00 P.M., five days a week, weather permitting.

During the season, there are tours at 10:00 and 11:00 A.M.; and at 1:00, 2:00, and 3:00 P.M., five days a week, as long as the tour doesn't conflict with a game.

An aerial view of Boston's Fenway Park.

San Francisco Giants. They offer stadium tours for groups only (especially school groups). There's no set schedule, so contact the stadium operations department (you can reach them at the phone number listed for the team in Chapter 1).

Seattle Mariners. The Kingdome Sports Museum (201 South King Street, Seattle, WA 98104; (206) 296-3663) offers tours of the Kingdome.

This tour is offered from mid-April to mid-September at 11:00 A.M. and at 1:00 and 3:00 P.M. It's a one-hour, behind-the-scenes guided tour of the stadium. You'll see everything from the locker rooms (not included in many stadium tours) to the press box, to the highest seat in the house. The tour is accessible to wheelchairs.

The price is $2.50 for adults and teens, $1.25 for seniors 65 and over and children 12 and under. Group tours (for 25 or more) can be arranged year-round with special rates. The tours begin at Gate D.

Texas Rangers. For information on the tour, contact Ms. Della Britain at the team office: (817) 273-5063.

TRIPS TO AWAY GAMES

Let's say the Milwaukee Brewers are playing an

STADIUM QUIZ

Each major league stadium is different from every other. In fact, whole books have been written about the different sizes and features of the various parks.

Some of the most famous features of these stadiums are listed below. Can you match the feature with the stadium and with the stadium's home team?

Answers are listed upside down below.

FEATURES

The Green Monster. The green left-field wall of this old American League stadium is so tall that it earned this nickname. Left-handed pitchers dread playing here, as rightie batters can pull pitches and knock the ball to the wall. Balls that hit the wall are a fielder's nightmare and a hitter's dream. Name the ballpark from the list of parks below.

Ivy-covered Walls. This old stadium was the last to install lights for night games. The fans are separated from the field by a quaint ivy-covered wall.

Astroturf. That's the name of the fake grass used in the first indoor baseball stadium. Name the stadium.

74,208. That's the seating capacity of this, the largest stadium in the major leagues.

The Water Spectacular. This stadium sports six 10-foot-high waterfalls just beyond the outfield wall. Water shows are performed after games.

PARKS

The Astrodome
Wrigley Field
Fenway Park
Cleveland Stadium
Royals Stadium

TEAMS

The Red Sox
The Cubs
The Astros
The Indians
The Royals

CITIES

Chicago
Cleveland
Kansas City
Boston
Houston

The Boston Red Sox play at Fenway, home of the Green Monster. The Chicago Cubs are surrounded by ivy-covered walls at Wrigley Field. If the house is full, the Cleveland Indians play for 74,208 at Cleveland Stadium. The Houston Astros play on astroturf at the Astrodome. The Kansas City Royals play at Royals Stadium, complete with waterfalls.

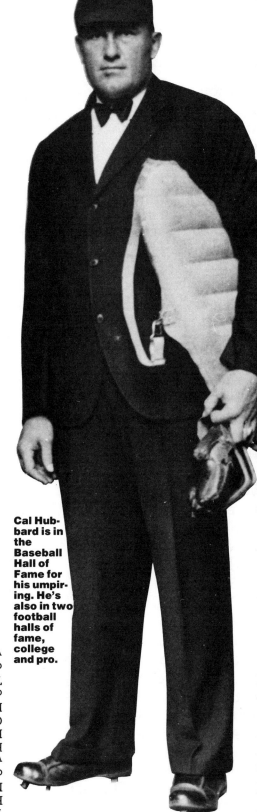

Cal Hubbard is in the Baseball Hall of Fame for his umpiring. He's also in two football halls of fame, college and pro.

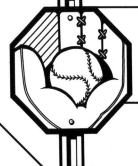

SHORTSTOPS

In the 1930s, the St. Louis Cardinals groundskeeper had a simple method for keeping the grass nice and short. He simply let his goat graze in the outfield!

92

UMPIRE:
NOT ALWAYS A "SAFE!" JOB

What man on the baseball diamond gets yelled at the most? The answer is obvious: the ump.

The players yell at him. The fans yell at him. The coaches yell at him. And sometimes they even kick some infield dirt in his direction (though that usually leads to being ejected from the game).

Every time the ump makes a call, from "Ball One!" to "Safe!" to "Out!" he runs the risk of infuriating one of the two sides. Trying to keep a cool head and a sharp eye under such conditions isn't easy. Some might say the umpire has the hardest job on the field.

When baseball first began, the umpires kept a safe distance—about 20 feet from home plate. Far away from the action, these early umps rested in rocking chairs!

That didn't last long. Umps quickly got caught up in the action, and they took their lives in their hands. In 1907, umpire Billy Evans almost died after a fan beaned him with a pop bottle from high up in the stands.

Attacks on umps haven't stopped. In 1981, a fan got so mad at an ump's call that he ran

The famous pine tar incident. When the ump took his bat away, George Brett got just a wee bit angry.

Umps have to keep the field safe for players. But who keeps the field safe for umps?

onto the field and tackled him. And an ump puts up with all this for what isn't even a high-paying job!

In recognition of their hard and often thankless job, and of the great contribution these talented umps have made to baseball, six umpires have been inducted into the Baseball Hall of Fame. Billy Evans, who survived his terrible attack and continued his famous umping career, was elected to the Hall in 1973.

away game, in Cleveland. Robin Yount pops the ball into the stands for a home run. And what's this? There are cheers from the stands?

Some of these shouting fans are Brewers fans who happen to live in Cleveland. Others have traveled from Milwaukee to see the game.

Booster clubs—large, organized team fan clubs—often plan and arrange for their members to travel to away games and root for the club. Many booster clubs are aimed mainly at grown-ups, however. (For more information on booster clubs, see Chapter 2.)

In addition, some travel agencies specialize in trips to away games for certain major league teams. Contact the team office for more information.

If you're interested in seeing the away games of a lot of major league teams in a short time, you might try George Auerbach's Teen Caravan. These 21-day August outings for kids 13–16 combine outdoor camping and long bus trips with major and minor league games. The cost for the three weeks is $1,375. Contact:

George Auerbach's Teen Caravan
41 German Mills Road
Thornhill, Ontario
Canada L3T 4H4
(416) 731-1862

A BATTY TOUR

Hillerich & Bradsby, the famous bat-makers, offer free tours of their 6½-acre factory (Slugger Park) in Jeffersonville, Indiana. Tours begin at 10:00 A.M. and 2:00 P.M. every weekday.

On this 45-minute tour you'll see new bats being made. You'll also watch a movie about the history of the company and see special exhibits of old and famous bats.

Large groups need to make special reservations. For more info, call toll free: (800) 282-BATS.

WHAT'S YOUR NAME, SHORTY?

If you go to a baseball camp, you're bound to return with improved baseball skills. But that's not all you may come back with—maybe you'll also pick up a nickname.

The word nickname literally means an extra name. Giving players nicknames is an old and usually affectionate baseball tradition. Sometimes nicknames stick for years, long after most can remember how the player got the nickname in the first place.

From A-Train to Yogi is a book (by Chuck Wielgus, Alexander Wolff, and Steve Rushin) written to help fans with just this problem. It lists famous nicknames for players in a number of sports and explains the nicknames' origins. Here are some samples:

Pee Wee Reese. Reese's nickname was so famous that probably few baseball fans can give Reese's real name (it's Harold). According to Reese, he got his nickname from playing marbles as a kid. He always used a special "pee wee" marble.

Mookie Wilson. As a baby, Wilson had trouble with the word "milk." Wilson pronounced it "mookie," and baseball fans have called him that ever since. In fact, fans like to "moo" in his honor. The uninformed think the star is being booed.

Once again, who knows Wilson's real first name? (It's Willie.)

Dave "The Cobra" Parker. A cobra is a deadly snake that lunges at its prey. Opposing pitchers seem to feel that Parker is

Willie "Mookie" Wilson, now with Toronto.

HALL-OF-FAMER GRAVESITES

Baseball fan mania hasn't reached the level of the Elvis Presley craze. Elvis's countless fans make almost a ritual journey to visit Elvis's grave at Graceland, in Memphis, Tennessee.

On the other hand, what baseball fan wouldn't want to visit Babe Ruth's grave (if he or she were near Hawthorne, New York)?

Here's a list of the gravesites of all the Hall-of-Famers. The list comes from the *Baseball Research Journal 1982.* The list was compiled by baseball researcher Bill Ivory. It has been updated with assistance from the Hall of Fame Library staff.

According to Ivory, about one out of every 10 Hall-of-Famer gravesites has a baseball motif. ("Home Run" Baker's grave, for instance, has a bat, ball, and glove.)

If you do visit a famous player's grave, you might want to make a rubbing. You put tracing paper over the grave and rub the paper with special charcoal drawing sticks to get a copy of the words and image. Perhaps such a rubbing will be a valuable collectible some day! (See Chapter 10.)

pretty poisonous when he lunges at their pitches and hits them out for homers. Hence the nickname.

Mike "The Human Rain Delay" Hargrove. Many baseball players go through certain ritual motions as they get ready to bat. Maybe they'll knock the mud from their cleats, wipe their hands, or straighten their cap. Hargrove's prebatting ritual is particularly lengthy. That's how he got his nickname.

Vince "Vincent Van Go" Coleman. This Cardinal's nickname is a humorous version of the name of the famous painter Vincent Van Gogh. Coleman doesn't paint, but he runs like crazy, fast enough to steal base after base.

Tim "Old Second Inning" McCarver. Now a well-known announcer, McCarver used to play catcher. He got his nickname because teammates said that McCarver always needed to go to the bathroom between the first and second inning!

Name	Burial Site
Grover Alexander	Elmwood, St. Paul, NE
Adrian "Pop" Anson	Oakwood, Chicago, IL
Earl Averill	G.A.R., Snohomish, WA
Frank Baker	Spring Hill, Easton, MD
Dave Bancroft	Greenwood, Superior, WI
Ed Barrow	Kensico, Valhalla, NY
Jake Beckley	Riverside, Hannibal, MO
Chief Bender	Ardsley Park, Ardsley, PA
Jim Bottomley	I.O.O.F., Sullivan, MO
Roger Bresnahan	Calvary, Toledo, OH
Dan Brouthers	Wappingers Falls, NY
Mordecai Brown	Roselawn Memorial, Terre Haute, IN
Morgan Bulkeley	Cedar Hill, Hartford, CT
Jesse Burkett	St. John's, Worcester, MA
Max Carey	Woodland, Miami, FL
Alexander Cartwright	Nuvanu, Honolulu, HI
Henry Chadwick	Greenwood, Brooklyn, NY
Frank Chance	Rosedale, Los Angeles, CA
Oscar Charleston	Floral Park, Indianapolis, IN
Jack Chesbro	Howland, Conway, MA
Fred Clarke	St. Mary's, Winfield, KS
John Clarkson	City, Cambridge, MA
Roberto Clemente	Lost at sea; body never recovered
Ty Cobb	Village, Royston, GA
Mickey Cochrane	Cremated; ashes scattered over Lake Michigan
Eddie Collins	Linwood, Weston, MA
Jimmy Collins	Holy Cross, Buffalo, NY
Earle Combs	City, Richmond, KY
Charles Comiskey	Calvary, Evanston, IL
Tommy Connolly	St. Patrick's, Natick, MA
Roger Connor	Old St. Joseph's, Waterbury, CT
Stanley Coveleski	St. Joseph, South Bend, IN
Sam Crawford	Inglewood Park, Inglewood, CA
Joseph Cronin	St. Francis Xavier, Centerville, MA
Candy Cummings	Aspen Grove, Ware, MA
Ki Ki Cuyler	St. Ann's, Harrisville, MI
Dizzy Dean	Bond, Bond, MS
Ed Delahanty	Calvary, Cleveland, OH

Martin Dihigo	Cienfuegos, Cuba
Hugh Duffy	Old Calvary, Mattapan, MA
Billy Evans	Noilwood Mausoleum, Cleveland, OH
John Evers	St. Mary's, Troy, NY
Buck Ewing	Mt. Washington, Cincinnati, OH
Red Faber	Acacia Park, Chicago, IL
Elmer Flick	Crown Hill, Twinsburg, OH
Rube Foster	Lincoln, Chicago, IL
Jimmie Foxx	Flagler Memorial Park, Miami, FL
Ford Frick	Christ Church Columbarium, Bronxville, NY
Frank Frisch	Woodland, Bronx, NY
James ("Pud") Galvin	Calvary, Allegheny, PA
Lou Gehrig	Kensico, Valhalla, NY
Josh Gibson	Allegheny, Pittsburgh, PA
Warren Giles	Riverside, Moline, IL
Vernon Gomez	Novator, CA
Leon "Goose" Goslin	Baptist, Salem, NJ
Henry ("Hank") Greenberg	Hillside, Los Angeles, CA
Clark Griffith	Fort Lincoln, Suitland, MD
Burleigh Grimes	Clear Lake, Clear Lake, WI
Robert ("Lefty") Grove	Memorial, Frostburg, MD
Chick Hafey	St. Helena, St. Helena, CA
Jesse Haines	Bethel, Phillipsburg, OH
Billy Hamilton	Eastwood, South Lancaster, MA
William Harridge	Memorial Park, Skokie, IL
Bucky Harris	Pittston, PA
Gabby Hartnett	All Saints, Des Plaines, IL
Harry Heilmann	Holy Sepulchre, Southfield, MI
Harry Hooper	Mount Calvary, Santa Cruz, CA
Rogers Hornsby	Hornsby Bend, TX
Waite Hoyt	Spring Grove, Cincinnati, OH
Cal Hubbard	Milan, MO
Carl Hubbell	Meeker, OK
Miller Huggins	Spring Grove, Cincinnati, OH
Travis Jackson	Waldo, Waldo, AR
Hugh Jennings	St. Catherine's, Scranton, PA
Byron "Ban" Johnson	Spencer, IN
Walter Johnson	Union, Rockville, MD
Adrian "Addie" Joss	Woodlawn, Toledo, OH
Tim Keefe	City, Cambridge, MA
Willie Keeler	Calvary, Queens, NY
Joe Kelley	New Cathedral, Baltimore, MD
Mike "King" Kelly	Mt. Hope, Boston, MA
George Kelly	Holy Cross, Colma, CA
Chuck Klein	Holy Cross, Indianapolis, IN
Bill Klem	Graceland Memorial Park, Miami, FL
Nap Lajoie	Cedar Hill, Daytona Beach, FL
Kenesaw Mountain Landis	Cremated; Oak Woods, Chicago, IL
Fred Lindstrom	All Saints, Chicago, IL
John Lloyd	City, Atlantic City, NJ
Ernie Lombardi	Mountain View, Oakland, CA
Ted Lyons	Big Woods, Edgerly, LA
Connie Mack	Holy Sepulchre, Philadelphia, PA
Larry MacPhail	Elkland Township, Cass City, MI
Heinie Manush	Memorial, Sarasota, FL
Rabbit Maranville	St. Michael's, Springfield, MA
Rube Marquard	Hebrew, Baltimore, MD
Christy Mathewson	City, Lewisburg, PA

Above: Little Leaguers pay their respects at Ty Cobb's gravesite.

Pirates shortstop Honus Wagner was the first major leaguer to reach the 3,000 hit mark.

Joe McCarthy	Mount Olivet, Tonawanda, NY
Tommie McCarthy	Old Calvary, Mattapan, MA
Joe McGinnity	Oak Hill, McAllister, OK
John McGraw	New Cathedral, Baltimore, MD
Bill McKechnie	Manasota, Sarasota, FL
Joe Medwick	St. Lucas, St. Louis, MO
Kid Nichols	Mt. Moriah, Kansas City, MO
Jim O'Rourke	St. Michael's, Bridgeport, CT
Mel Ott	Metairie, New Orleans, LA
Satchel Paige	Forest Hills, Kansas City, MO
Herb Pennock	Union Hill, New York, NY
Eddie Plank	Greenlawn, Gettysburg, PA
Charles "Hoss" Radbourn	Evergreen, Bloomington, IL
Sam Rice	Cremated
Branch Rickey	Rush Township, Stockdale, OH
Eppa Rixey	Greenlawn, Milford, OH
Jackie Robinson	Cypress Hills, Brooklyn, NY
Wilbert Robinson	New Cathedral, Baltimore, MD
Edd Roush	Montgomery, Oakland City, IN
Red Ruffing	Hillcrest, Bedford Heights, OH
Amos Rusie	Washelli, Seattle, WA
George Herman "Babe" Ruth	Gate of Heaven, Hawthorne, NY
Ray Schalk	Evergreen, Chicago, IL
Al Simmons	St. Adalbert's, Milwaukee, WI
George Sisler	Cremated, Oak Grove, St. Louis, MO
Albert Spalding	Cremated, Byron, IL
Tris Speaker	Fairview, Hubbard, TX
Casey Stengel	Forest Lawn, Glendale, CA
Sam Thompson	Elmwood, Detroit, MI
Joe Tinker	Greenwood, Orlando, FL
Pie Traynor	Homewood, Pittsburgh, PA
Dazzy Vance	Stage Stand, Homosassa Springs, FL
Arky Vaughn	Community, Eagleville, CA
Rube Waddell	Mission Burial Park, San Antonio, TX
Honus Wagner	Jefferson Memorial Park, Pittsburgh, PA
Bobby Wallace	Inglewood Park, Inglewood, CA
Ed Walsh	Forest Lawn, Pompano Beach, FL
Lloyd Waner	Rose Hill, Oklahoma City, OK
Paul Waner	Manasota, Sarasota, FL
John Ward	Rural, Babylon, NY
George Weiss	Evergreen, New Haven, CT
Mickey Welch	Calvary, Queens, NY
Zack Wheat	Forest Hill, Kansas City, MO
Hack Wilson	Rosehill, Martinsburg, WV
George Wright	Holyrood, Brookline, MA
Harry Wright	West Laurel Hill, Bala Cynwyd, PA
Thomas Yawkey	Cremated, Cambridge, MA
Cy Young	Methodist Church, Peoli, OH
Ross Youngs	Mission Burial Park, San Antonio, TX

This bronze tablet honors pitching superstar Christy Mathewson. Among his many feats, Christy holds the record for World Series shut-outs with four.

IN MEMORY OF
CHRISTY MATHEWSON
PITCHER, N.Y. GIANTS, 1900-1916.   COACH, N.Y. GIANTS, 1919-1923.
CAPTAIN, U.S. ARMY, AMERICAN EXPEDITIONARY FORCE, 1918.
BORN, FACTORYVILLE, PA.   DIED, SARANAC, N.Y.
AUGUST 12, 1880   OCTOBER 7, 1925

READ ALL ABOUT IT!

BASEBALL BOOKS, MAGAZINES, AND NEWSLETTERS

Baseball fans love to read about their sport. They read books about baseball history, use baseball reference books to memorize player stats, and relive the sport in baseball novels.

To satisfy this growing market, there are now baseball books on almost every subject—from player biographies to instructional books that teach you how to play. And there are baseball magazines and newsletters for everything from baseball poetry to the youth leagues tournament results.

A lot of these books and magazines are not aimed directly at kids. But that doesn't mean you have to stick to the "kid stuff." Avid young baseball fans are well known for reading whatever baseball information they can get their hands on.

Baseball magazines don't keep track of how many of their readers are kids. But editorial offices of baseball publications field numerous telephone questions from readers with very young-sounding voices.

So remember: There are no age limits on baseball reading material. If you enjoy a publication, don't worry if it's aimed at kids or not!

More has been written about the sport of baseball than many people will read in a lifetime. If you want to read more about baseball, you should have no problem laying your hands on all the reading material you want.

BOOKS
Starting Your Own Baseball Library

Buying books can be an expensive habit. But if you've got the baseball bug, you're going to want to start your own baseball library. For one thing, you'll want to refer to certain reference books, such as books of stats, from time to time. You don't want to have to run to the library every time you and a friend make a baseball trivia bet.

For another thing, it's just fun to have a whole bunch of baseball books lined up in a row on your shelf. Somehow a big collection of baseball books makes a fan feel official!

Anyway, you've already got your library started—with the book you're holding right now. What follows is a look at some of the basics and classics you may want to add to your collection.

There are a number of large (huge!) baseball reference books that list the stats for every baseball player who ever played in a major league game. Like a dictionary, a book such as this makes a good starting point for a home library collection.

The Baseball Encyclopedia, published by Macmillan, is one of the popular one-volume baseball bibles. But books such as these have a problem. As each year's stats are added to new editions, the books keep gaining weight! Macmillan's encyclopedia already weighs 5 pounds 11 ounces. They add about 300 pages to each edition. So far, the book is up to 2,875 pages and contains records for 13,123 ball players! (It costs $45.)

Weighing in at a mere 2,294 pages is *Total Baseball*, with records for every ball player and feature articles on numerous aspects of the game. It's published by Warner Books and edited by John Thorn and Pete Palmer, and it costs $49.95.

If your bookshelf is still standing, you'll want to add some more books with an overview of the sport. *The Baseball Catalog*, by Dan Schlossberg, isn't a catalogue at all, but a reference book that looks at just about every aspect of baseball, from the beginnings of play through the modern day. The book is published by Jonathan David Publishers, Inc., 68-22 Eliot Avenue, Middle Village, NY 11379, and it costs $14.95.

Baseball statistics is an ever-growing field—so much so that some fans complain that stats are taking over. If you get one of the baseball bibles mentioned above, you'll already have hundreds of pages of stats. But you may also want and need at least one book that's got nothing but player stats. There are plenty of such books to choose from.

Great Baseball Feats, Facts and Firsts, by David Nemec, is a handy paperback published by Signet Books for $4.95. The stats are arranged in chronological order from early baseball days to the present. What's nice about this book is that the stats are preselected, arranged by the author into topic headings such as "Famous Firsts" and "Base-Stealing Feats." A book like this isn't that good for looking

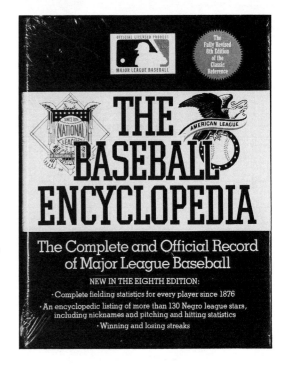

up stats, however; for one thing, there isn't an index.

If you want lots of raw data, and an index, there are books such as *The Complete Baseball Record Book*, by Craig Carter, published by The Sporting News for $12.95.

So far, none of the books mentioned have been written *for* kids. That may be another reason you want to buy them! But if they seem over your head, try *The Kids' World Almanac of Baseball*, by Thomas G. Aylesworth. It's got a little of everything—history, biography, famous quotes, science, salaries, advice from players, and, of course, trivia. The paperback is $6.95 and published by World Almanac/Pharos Books.

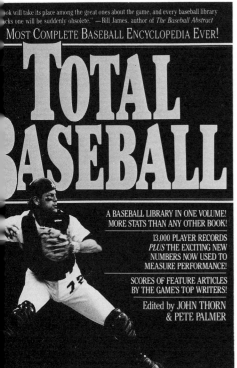

"...k will take its place among the great ones about the game, and every baseball library ...cks one will be suddenly obsolete." —Bill James, author of *The Baseball Abstract*

MOST COMPLETE BASEBALL ENCYCLOPEDIA EVER!

TOTAL BASEBALL

A BASEBALL LIBRARY IN ONE VOLUME!
MORE STATS THAN ANY OTHER BOOK!

13,000 PLAYER RECORDS
PLUS THE EXCITING NEW NUMBERS NOW USED TO MEASURE PERFORMANCE!

SCORES OF FEATURE ARTICLES BY THE GAME'S TOP WRITERS!

Edited by JOHN THORN & PETE PALMER

GROWING UP AT BAT

50 YEARS OF LITTLE LEAGUE BASEBALL

HARVEY FROMMER

Introduction by
A. Bartlett Giamatti,
Commissioner of
Major League
Baseball

For $13.95, Pharos Books also publishes *Growing Up at Bat: The Little League Baseball Official 50th Anniversary Book.* It's a history of the league, with lots of information on famous Little League graduates.

For a book filled entirely with the stories of how today's major league stars fared in Little League, see *Little Big Leaguers*, by Bruce Nash and Allan Zullo. This $7.95 paperback, published by Simon & Schuster, tells how players like Eric Davis and Jose Canseco did on the diamond when they were your age.

Nash and Zullo are also the authors of the *Baseball Hall of Shame* series,

published by Pocket Books for $8.95 each. These books humorously "honor" some of the worst plays ever in baseball history.

Baseball Anecdotes, by Daniel Okrent and Steve Wulf, is an encyclopedia of the great stories of baseball. This bestseller was written for grownups, but it's so good that it's worth the extra time you may have to spend looking up the big words. The paperback is published by Harper & Row for $9.95.

If you're a particular fan of one star player, you can probably get a whole book just about your favorite athlete. Lerner Publications, for example, has a kids' player-profile series with titles such as *Dwight Gooden: Strikeout King* ($8.95). If you're a fan of a specific team, Creative Education publishes a series of kids' books on the individual major league teams.

The Baseball Hall of Fame and Little Simon publishers put out a number of large paperback books for kids. In addition to fun information, these books contain puzzles, games, stickers, quizzes, and other neat stuff.

Titles include *The Official Baseball Hall of Fame Fun and Fact Sticker*

Book, by Bob Carroll and Mark Rucker (Little Simon, 1989, $7.95); *The Official Hall of Fame Answer Book,* by Mark Alvarez (Little Simon, 1989, $6.95); and *The Official Baseball Hall of Fame Book of Superstars,* by Jim Kaplan and Dick Perez (Little Simon, 1989, $4.95). You should be able to find these books at your local bookstore, or you can order directly from the Hall of Fame. For a catalog, write to:

Baseball Gifts
National Baseball Hall of Fame and Museum
Box 590A
Cooperstown, NY 13326

World of Baseball publishes a good series of hardbacks with titles such as *The Sluggers, The Explosive Sixties,* and *October's Game.* The books are aimed at adults but are packed with great photos. They're $14.95 each. For more information, contact:

World of Baseball
P.O. Box 25336
Alexandria, VA 22313
(800) 347-7381

You can also read up on how to hit the ball a mile and catch everything (except the ball you just hit a mile). You have your pick

THE BULL PEN
Q: Why is the start of a baseball game always exciting?
A: It's a big-inning.

of scores of instructional books written just for kids. For instance, there's *Warm Up for Little League Baseball,* by Morris A. Shirts. This low-cost ($2.50) paperback, published by Archway Paperbacks, covers all the bases.

BASEBALL FICTION

So far, all of the titles mentioned have been nonfiction books. These are the books that will help you learn the sport. If you're on a tight budget, as most kids are, you should spend your hard-saved nickels on nonfiction reference books. After all, you can borrow baseball novels from the library and return them after you've read them once.

But that doesn't mean that baseball fiction is less fun than baseball fact. For a baseball fan, a good baseball novel can be pure pleasure. For starters, you can always count on some tense baseball action. And you can almost always count on your team to come from behind and win!

Here are some of the many titles currently in print:

The Atami Dragons, by David Klass, Charles Scribner's Sons (1984).
Baseball Fever, by Johanna Hurwitz, William Morrow (1981).
Baseball Pals, by Matt Christopher, Little, Brown (1972).
The Basement Baseball Club, by Jeffrey Kelly, Houghton-Mifflin (1987).
Benny, Benny, Baseball Nut, by David A. Adler, Scholastic (1987).
Big League Break, by Mark Freeman, Ballantine Books (1989).
Cam Jansen and the Mystery of the Babe Ruth Baseball, by David A. Adler, Viking (1982).
Can You Win the Pennant? by Mitch Gelman, Archway (1983).
Catcher with a Glass Arm, by Matt Christopher, Little, Brown (1985).
The Dog That Pitched a No-Hitter, by Matt Christopher, Little, Brown (1988).
Double Play, by Lance Franklin, Bantam (1987).
First Base Jinx, by John R. Cooper, Wanderer (1982).
The Goof That Won the Pennant, by Jonah Kalb, Houghton-Mifflin (1976).

The Great McGonniggle Switches Pitches, by Scott Corbett, Little, Brown (1980).
Hang Tough, Paul Mather, by Alfred Slote, Harper & Row (1973).
Herbie Jones and the Monster Ball, by Suzy Kline, Putnam (1988).
Here Comes the Strikeout, by Leonard Kessler, Harper & Row (1965).
The Hit-Away Kid, by Matt Christopher, Little, Brown (1988).
Hooray for Snail! by John Stadler, Harper & Row (1985).
How Spider Saved the Baseball Game, by Robert Kraus, Scholastic (1989).
In the Year of the Boar and Jackie Robinson, by Bette Bao Lord, Harper & Row (1984).

Jason and the Baseball Bear, by Dan Elish, Orchard Books (1990).

Jeffrey's Ghost and the Leftover Baseball Team, by David A. Adler, Holt, Rinehart & Winston (1984).

Johnny No Hit, by Matt Christopher, Little, Brown (1977).

The Kid Comes Back, by John R. Tunis, Morrow (1990).

Hooray for Snail!, by John Stadler, Harper & Row (1985).

The Kid Who Only Hit Homers, by Matt Christopher, Little, Brown (1986).

Left-Handed Shortstop, by Patricia R. Giff, Dell (1980).

Look Who's Playing First Base, by Matt Christopher, Little, Brown (1972).

Max, by Rachel Isadora, Macmillan (1987).

No Arm in Left Field, by Matt Christopher, Little, Brown (1974).

Noonan: A Novel about Baseball, ESP and Time Warps, by Leonard E. Fisher (1981).

Old Turtle's Baseball Stories, by Leonard Kessler, Greenwillow (1982).

On Home Ground, by Alan Lelchuk, Gulliver Books/Harcourt Brace Jovanovich (1988).

The Pizza Pie Slugger, by Jean Marzollo, Random House (1989).

Play Ball, Amelia Bedelia, by Peggy Parish, Harper & Row (1972).

Play Ball, Kate! by Sharon Gordon, Troll (1981).

Rabbit Ears, by Alfred Slote, J. B. Lippincott (1982).

Ronald Morgan Goes to Bat, by Patricia R. Giff, Penguin (1988).

The Rookie Arrives, by J. Thomas Dygard, Morrow (1988).

Ruth Marini: Dodger Ace, by Mel Cebulash, Lerner Publications (1983).

Ruth Marini of the Dodgers, by Mel Cebulash, Lerner Publications (1983).

Ruth Marini: World Series Star, by Mel Cebulash, Lerner Publications (1985).

Skinnybones, by Barbara Park, Knopf (1989).

The Spy on Third Base, by Matt Christopher, Little, Brown (1988).

Strike Four! by Harriet Ziefert, Penguin (1988).

Thank You, Jackie Robinson, by Barbara Cohen, Lothrop, Lee and Shepard (1988).

Viola, Furgy, Bobbi and Me, by Kenneth E. Ethridge, Holiday Books (1989).

Winning Season for the Braves, by Nathan Asseng, Chariot Books (1988).

World Series, by John R. Tunis, Harcourt Brace Jovanovich (1987).

Wrongway Applebaum, by Marjorie Lewis, Putnam (1984).

The Year Mom Won the Pennant, by Matt Christopher, Little, Brown (1973).

BOOKS IN PRINT

Your local library and your local bookstore both carry a useful reference work called *Books in Print.* Look under "Baseball" in the *Subject Guide* volume of *Books in Print* and you'll see hundreds and hundreds of titles in categories such as "Baseball History" and "Baseball Biography." This book also lists more than 100 baseball books written just for kids.

You can find some of these books at the library. You can find others on the shelves of a bookstore. And the rest you can order.

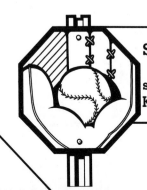

SHORTSTOPS
Many famous baseball players started out in youth leagues. And some youth league graduates have gone on to star in other sports. Kareem Abdul-Jabbar, for instance, once played Little League.

Where? Your bookstore—especially if it's a small one—will order for you from their distributor by using the information in *Books in Print.*

OUT-OF-PRINT BOOKS

The long list of books in *Books in Print* is only the beginning of the list of baseball books available today. There's an even longer list to choose from, but these books are harder to find. They're "out of print," which means that the publisher has stopped printing them.

These are books you'll find in used-book stores, flea markets, and garage sales. They'll expand your library cheaply (unless they're so rare that people have decided they're collectors' items).

If you subscribe to any of the magazines listed later in this chapter, you'll see lots of book ads and offers, for books both new and old. *Sporting News* magazine, for instance, advertises out-of-print baseball books from time to time.

If there's a specific out-of-print baseball book that you've got your heart set on owning, you can go through a book-finding service or out-of-print dealer such as the ones

listed below. But buying a book this way will cost you a lot more than buying a baseball book at your neighbor's garage sale!

THE AUSTIN BOOK SHOP
104-29 Jamaica Avenue
Richmond Hill, NY 11418
(718) 441-1199 or 441-7014
Mailing address:
Box 36
Kew Gardens, NY 11415
Bernard Titowsky, owner

Mr. Titowsky's store specializes in out-of-print baseball books. They have more than one thousand of them in stock. You can order by mail (a catalogue costs $1) or drop into the store on weekends if you live in the area. If they don't have the book you want, they will put out a search for it.

As a former librarian, Mr. Titowsky says he is ready, willing, and able to advise kids about their baseball book needs. Remember, though, rare out-of-print books aren't cheap.

BOOK LOOK
51 Maple Avenue
Warwick, NY 10990
(914) 986-1981

Send a letter or call with the title and author (and publisher and year of publication, if you know it)

of any out-of-print book, and Book Look will search for it for you. The search fee is $2 per month per book. Once they find a copy, they will tell you the book's price and condition and give you the option to buy it or not.

BOOK HUNTERS
P.O. Box 7519
North Bergen, NJ 07047

They'll find out-of-print books for you in four to six weeks. The search fee is added to the cost of the book. Once they find the book, they'll quote you a price and give you an option to buy, with no obligation to do so. The minimum price for a found book is $35.

BOOK CATALOGUES

Let's say that someone were to collect every baseball book ever listed in *Books in Print.* That fan would have a huge collection but still wouldn't have all the baseball books ever published.

There are loads of books distributed by small publishing companies, books that are sold directly to customers through mail order.

Here are some of these publishers, and dealers who distribute these as well as other baseball books. In most cases, you can write to them to receive free catalogues.

ATC SPORT BOOKS
123 West Superior Street
Duluth, MN 55802

They charge $1 for their catalogue. They sell baseball books as well as books on other sports. They also sell old and used books.

BASEBALL AMERICA
P.O. Box 2089
Durham, NC 27702
(919) 682-9635
(800) 845-2726

You can write or call for a free catalogue of their books and publications.

DIAMOND COMMUNICA-TIONS
P.O. Box 88
South Bend, IN 46624
(219) 287-5006

As the name suggests, this small publisher specializes in baseball books.

R. FLAPINGER BASEBALL BOOKS
P.O. Box 1062
Ashland, OR 97520

They charge $2 for their catalogue.

HORTON PUBLISHING CATALOG
P.O. Box 29234
St. Louis, MO 63126

Their catalogue is free if you send a SASE (that's a self-addressed stamped envelope. See page 4 for instructions on SASEs.)

HUMAN KINETICS PUBLISHERS
P.O. Box 5076
Champaign, IL 61820
(800) 342-5457, except in Illinois
In Illinois, call: (800) 334-3665

They publish a few baseball instructional books, such as *High Percentage Base Running*, a book of 28 special base-running plays. Write for a free catalogue.

PHENOM SPORTS CATALOG
P.O. Box 1651
Grand Central Station
New York, NY 10163
(800) 966-7787

Their catalogue costs $1 and comes free if you make a purchase. They carry hundreds of books on baseball history, trivia, superstar biographies, cards and other collectibles, and team histories, as well as a large collection of baseball

audiotapes. (See the article on audio in this chapter.)

The catalogue also offers photos of players, baseball videos, baseball calendars, and other baseball-related items.

THE SPORTING NEWS
121 North Lindberg
St. Louis, MO 63132
(314) 997-7111

They publish a large number of baseball books each year, including a new *Baseball Guide for Kids*, which, for $5.95, comes complete with fold-out poster, layouts of all the major league parks, team schedules, and other information. *The Sporting News* also publishes a complete line of instruc-tional books for youth leagues. Send for a catalogue.

DON WADE BASEBALL BOOKS
31702 Campbell
Madison Heights, MI 48071

The catalogue is free if you send a SASE.

MAGAZINES AND NEWSPAPERS
One great thing about a magazine subscription—it keeps on coming. Whenever it comes—once a month, once every two

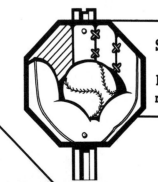

SHORTSTOPS
The very first sports magazine in the United States was started in 1829. It was called the *American Turf Register*. It dealt mainly with race horses.

Pony Baseball's international play brings together young players from all over the world.

If you enjoy some of it, why not subscribe?

Here's an overview of some of the baseball magazines and newspapers out there today (magazines on cards and collecting are listed in Chapter 10). Where subscription prices are listed, remember that prices change often, but they almost never go down!

AMATEUR BASEBALL NEWS
215 East Green
Marshall, MI 49068
(616) 781-2002

This half-size paper is put out seven times a year

by the American Amateur Baseball Congress, a group that promotes youth league play. There's news here of youth league tournament results, plus general advice and information about the game. A year's subscription is $5.

ATHLON'S BASEBALL
220 25th Avenue North
Nashville, TN 37203

This is an annual—it's published each year. For $6.95 you get a look at the current major leaguers, with player profiles, statistics, etc.

months, or even once a year—a magazine is usually a nice surprise each time it arrives.

There are a lot of general sports magazines published in the United States, as well as magazines just about baseball. With the exception of a few, such as *Sports Illustrated for Kids*, these magazines aren't aimed at kids and aren't written for young reading levels.

But don't let that stop you! After all, no one reads every word of a magazine.

A close play at home in the American Amateur Baseball Congress.

BASEBALL BOOKS GONE BONKERS!

You won't find any of these 25 baseball books in stores. They're all made up. They're jokes, and the author names are the punch line. The names spell out words. How many can you translate?

How to Judge a Hitter, by Kenny Sweeng
A Fan's Guide to Major League Umpires, by Hugh R. Aybum
Batting Secrets, by Eileen Forewurd
Base-Stealing Tips, by Bea Crooke
Secrets of a Spitball Pitcher, by Sal I. Vah
The Baseball Stadium Cookbook, by Frank Furter
Step Up to the Plate, by I. M. Ungry
Collecting Baseball Cards, by Sharon Trayd
Where to Find Major League Stars, by Rhonda Field
Measuring Home Runs, by Mark D. Spott
How to Get from First to Second, by Stella Base

Hit by the Pitch, by Phyllis Hurt
How to Get Out of Your Baseball Contract, by SueAnne Kort
Getting in Shape Without Moving, by Ron N. Place
Catching Made Easier, by Annette Helps
Where the Players Spend Their Time, by Doug Owt
Coaching Third, by Gwen Holm
How to Get Involved with Little League, by John D. Teem
The Umps Are Never Wrong, by O. Fischel
How to Stop Baseball Cheaters, by Lynn D. Rools
Don't Slide Headfirst, by Freddy Katz
Practice Makes Perfect, by Betty Winns
Drawing a Game Plan, by Chuck Bord
What Players Will Be Earning in the Year 2000, by Evan Moore
How Umps Can Avoid Injury, by Vera Masque and Stan B. Hinedum

BASEBALL AMERICA
P.O. Box 2089
Durham, NC 27702
(919) 682-9635
(800) 845-2726

For $32.95 a year, you get 24 issues of baseball news, mainly focusing on minor league play and hot major league prospects.

That makes this publication very popular with people playing fantasy league baseball (see the article in Chapter 1). They want to know whom to draft for their team. Card collectors also want to keep up to date on minor leaguers as they judge the value of rookie cards (see Chapter 10).

This is a popular publication, but, as the editors warn, it's only for very serious baseball fans.

BASEBALL DIGEST
990 Grove Street, 3rd Floor
Evanston, IL 60201
(708) 491-6440

This pocket-sized magazine is popular enough to be sold on newsstands. It's been in business since the 1940s and is still going strong. It's also popular with young readers.

Why? It's got fun information about the major league teams and stars, and the articles are short and easy to read. Plus there are puzzles and polls.

A subscription costs $22 for 12 issues. (The same publishers put out a general sports magazine, *Inside Sports*.)

BASEBALL RESEARCH JOURNAL
Society for American Baseball Research (SABR)
P.O. Box 323
Cooperstown, NY 13326

The members of this society are professional baseball historians and other devoted baseball fans. They do research into various aspects of baseball history, and they publish some of their findings in this annual journal.

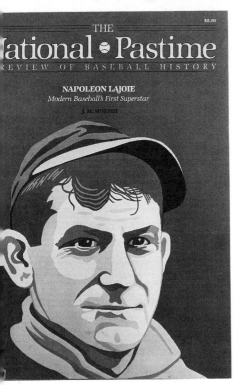

You can buy the annual for $7, or join the society itself for $30 and get it for free. That way you'll also get other SABR publications, such as *The National Pastime*, a softcover glossy magazine about baseball history. And you'll be able to attend SABR conventions and hobnob with other history buffs.

GAME PLAN BASEBALL PREVIEW
P.O. Box 3169
Syracuse, NY 13220
(315) 458-1287

A preview of the upcoming season, put out each year around mid-March or April. You can get it on some newsstands, or directly from the publishers for $4.95 (you can charge it on MasterCard or Visa). It contains complete minor league stats, major league rosters, schedules, etc.

HIGH SCHOOL SPORTS
1230 Avenue of the Americas, Suite 2000
New York, NY 10020
(212) 765-3300

A magazine all about high school sports, including baseball, of course. Most kids get the magazine through their school. You can also subscribe directly, for $10 for five issues.

MAJOR LEAGUE BASEBALL YEARBOOK
1115 Broadway
New York, NY 10010
(212) 807-7100

Another season preview. This one's available only on the newsstands. Watch for it in February. They also publish an annual, *Who's Who in Baseball*, which profiles the stars. This annual hits the stands sometime in March.

BILL MAZEROWSKI'S BASEBALL
Preview Publishing
333 First Avenue West
Seattle, WA 98119
(206) 282-2322

This annual update of baseball stats costs $4.95 on newsstands and comes out toward the end of February each year. For $6.95 (or $7.95, if you live in Canada), you can get a sneak preview copy, direct from the printing press.

Preview Publishing launched *The Show*, a new baseball magazine, in 1990. Sponsored by the Major League Players' Alumni Association, the magazine has fewer stats, and more features and fun facts. In its first year (1990) there were four issues for $9.95 ($12.95 in Canada). They hope to publish more issues per year in the following years.

THE NATIONAL SPORTS DAILY
15 West 52nd Street
New York, NY 10019

An all-sports newspaper that comes out every day except Saturday. It costs 50 cents on the newsstand. To subscribe to the paper and receive it in the mail every day for a year costs $187.20.

OLDTYME BASEBALL NEWS
P.O. Box 833
Petoskey, MI 49770

Every year, with each new major league game, new baseball history is

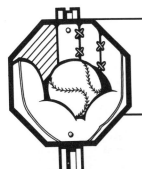

SHORTSTOPS
Softball was started by George Hancock in November 1888.

made. But there's also news from the past, as baseball researchers dig up new facts and stories from seasons gone by. This magazine is devoted entirely to covering what's "new" in baseball history. Six issues a year cost $19.95.

SPORTS ILLUSTRATED
1271 Avenue of the Americas
New York, NY 10020
(212) 586-1212

This famous magazine covers all the sports, weekly. Kids usually start reading it at about age 13.

SPORTS ILLUSTRATED FOR KIDS
P.O. Box 830609
Birmingham, AL 38283-0609

This is the junior version of *Sports Illustrated*. It's about sports in general, with lots of articles about kids in sports. Baseball is covered only occasionally, but each issue comes with nine star athlete cards. A subscription is $15.95 for 12 issues. Subscription orders should be sent to the Alabama address. To contact the magazine itself, write to the address, listed here, for *Sports Illustrated* in New York.

SPITBALL: THE LITERARY BASEBALL MAGAZINE
6224 Collegeview Plaza
Cincinnati, OH 45224
(513) 541-4296

If you're a baseball poet, here's a place to try to publish your poems. This magazine publishes new short baseball fiction and poetry, and reviews new baseball books. They also sponsor the Casey Award. Named for the famous poem about the Mudville slugger ("Casey at the Bat"), the award is given each year to the author of the best new baseball book.

There are four new issues of *Spitball* each year. A subscription costs $12.

SPORT MAGAZINE
Petersen Publishing Company
8940 Sunset Boulevard
Los Angeles, CA 90069
(213) 854-6870

This general-interest sports magazine is popular with kids. It's a monthly, so it doesn't cover current events the way a weekly like *Sports Illustrated* does. Instead it offers more in-depth articles and whole-season previews. The subscription cost is $9.97 for 12 issues.

THE SPORTING NEWS
(See address listing under Book Catalogues.)
For subscriptions: (800) 669-5700

A weekly sports newspaper famous for its baseball coverage. Subscription prices vary, depending on what subscription plan you choose. For instance, you can subscribe just for the baseball season. For a first-time subscriber, the whole year costs $38.92.

MAJOR LEAGUE TEAMS' MAGAZINES
You can get a magazine that has *some* baseball information. You can get a magazine that has *only* baseball information. And

The Cubs' Ryne Sandberg gets set for the pitch.

then you can get a magazine that has *nothing but* baseball information about your favorite team!

Yes, some of the major league teams have their very own magazines and newsletters. A few are listed below. If you don't see your team on this list, check with the team's community relations department. If the team itself doesn't publish a magazine, this department may know of magazines being published by fans. (See Chapter 1 for team listing.)

CHICAGO CUBS VINE LINE
P.O. Box 1159
Skokie, IL 60076

For $17.95 a year you get 12 issues of articles about the Cubs, past and present, plus trivia and Cubs crossword puzzles. The magazine was started by a Cubs fan club.

The A's Rickey Henderson celebrates yet another stolen base. Rickey's already stolen many records, such as most thefts in a season: 130.

NEW YORK METS INSIDE PITCH
Dept. BH
P.O. Box 2331
Durham, NC 27702
(919) 286-1766

This publication offers game summaries, articles about the players and others in the Mets organization, and information on the Mets' minor league teams. They publish 12 issues a year.

THE OAKLAND ATHLETICS MAGAZINE
Oakland Athletics
Baseball Company
Oakland-Alameda County Coliseum
Oakland, CA 94621
(415) 638-4900

At $2.50 for each issue, this magazine offers articles about A's players and general team information.

PHILLYSPORT
Lewis Tower Building
15th & Locust Streets
Suite 820
Philadelphia, PA 19102
(215) 893-4466

This magazine comes
out twice a month with
articles not just about the
Phillies but about the
Eagles, Flyers, and Sixers
as well.

REDS REPORT
Dept. BA
P.O. Box 2331
Durham, NC 27702
(800) 966-7787

The official monthly
newspaper of the
Cincinnati Reds. Included
are features about the
current players, upcoming
prospects, and Reds trivia
quizzes. A year's subscription (12 issues) costs $19.95.

YANKEES MAGAZINE
Yankee Stadium
Bronx, NY 10451
(212) 579-4495

All about the team's
major and minor league
players. The magazine
costs $18 for 12 issues a
year.

NEWSLETTERS
Anyone can send out a
newsletter. Some people
with large families
photocopy their family's

news for all their relatives:
A newsletter is born. (For
advice on starting your
own newsletter, see
Chapter 2.)

Baseball fans tend to be
opinionated, and they like
to share their opinions. As
a result, there are lots of
baseball newsletters!

Many of these newslet-
ters are free. But when a
newsletter catches on and
gets a big readership, it
costs more to produce and
mail out. The newsletter
may then have a subscrip-
tion fee. In fact, some
newsletters charge more
than magazines, even
though all you're getting
are a few pages each
issue. Unless you're sure
you like a particular
newsletter, you're
probably better off sticking
to the free ones.

If you subscribe to any of
the magazines in this
chapter, you'll probably
come across newsletter
ads from time to time. And
in baseball newsletters
themselves there are often
ads for other baseball
newsletters. There's no
end to the mail you can get!

BASEBALL BRIEFS
4424 Chesapeake Street,
N.W.
Washington, DC 20016
(202) 362-6889

This four-pager comes
out once a year, at the end
of each season. It's written
and published by a
baseball historian who
looks at the season's
current events in the light
of baseball's past.

The newsletter is free
(though they may run out
of copies). Send a SASE.

BASEBALL OUR WAY
Our Way Publications
3211 Milwaukee Street, #1
Madison, WI 53714
(608) 241-0549

Eight pages an issue of
commentary on current
ball players. You get 10
issues for $9 a year.

BASEWOMAN
P.O. Box 2292
Glenview, IL 60025
(312) 729-4594

All about women
currently in baseball—
women who are playing
the game and women who
are helping to run teams.
You get this four-page
newsletter each month for
$20 a year.

HERE'S THE PITCH
Mr. W. Lloyd Johnson
205 W. 66th Terrace
Kansas City, MO 64113
(816) 822-1740

Published four times a
year, this newsletter is

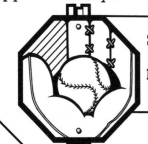

SHORTSTOPS
In 1927, the Yankees started out the season in first place and never
left. They were the first team ever to dominate the league so totally.

paid for by its advertisers and is free to subscribers. Its goal is to serve as a forum for fan opinion about the sport.

PHILADELPHIA BASEBALL FILE
1510 Harrison Street
Philadelphia, PA 19124
(215) 533-5776

Baseball analysis, fine points, humor, poetry. A lot of attention is paid to the Phillies, of course. A subscription for five issues costs $15.

PONY BASEBALL EXPRESS
300 Clare Drive
P.O. Box 225
Washington, PA 15301
(412) 225-1060

A free newsletter about Pony baseball and softball youth leagues. It's really aimed at youth league coaches, but it might be of some interest for older kids involved in Pony baseball.

SPORTS ALERT
Phenom Publishing, Inc.
P.O. Box 1651
Grand Central Station
New York, NY 10163-1354

A free four-page newsletter. Mostly it tries to sell the publisher's books. But, as long as you don't buy any, the newsletter's free!

MAJOR LEAGUE NEWSLETTERS

Just as there are magazines for some of the major league teams, some teams also have newsletters published by the team or by fans. Each team's public relations or community relations department should be able to help you subscribe (see Chapter 1 for team addresses).

Many of these newsletters, such as *Tribe Talk*, a four-page newsletter put out by the Cleveland Indians, are free. All you need to do is write or call and add your name to the mailing list.

Cleveland tries a rundown. For more rundown on the Indians, try the team's newsletter (info on this page).

NOW HEAR THIS— BASEBALL ON AUDIOTAPE

You can read about baseball, you can watch baseball, and you can also *hear* baseball. That's because some companies sell audiotapes of famous radio broadcasts.

These are tapes of actual play-by-play broadcasts of key games, from long ago all the way to the present. For instance, you can hear game five of the 1988 World Series, with Orel Hershiser and the Dodgers scoring an upset win for the championship.

Not all radio broadcasts are rereleased on tape for public sale. But here are two sources with large collections:

Phenom Sports, mentioned in this chapter for their baseball book collection, also offers a large audio selection. You can get their catalogue for $1 from:

Phenom Sports Catalog
P.O. Box 1651
Grand Central Station
New York, NY 10163
(800) 966-7787

If they don't carry the specific game you're looking for, also try:

Danrick Enterprises
Dept. PB1
P.O. Box 1347
Clifton, NJ 07015

YOU'RE ON THE AIR!

BASEBALL ON RADIO AND TV

You're a die-hard Oakland A's fanatic. And you've just gotten some good news and some bad news.

The good news is, your darling A's will clinch the pennant if they sweep the Yankees in this weekend's three-game series.

The bad news is, your family is going to visit Aunt Myrtle this weekend—in Sarasota, Florida. You won't be able to watch the A's play!

Wait! You can still see the games! That's because Channel 24 in Sarasota shows A's baseball. You found out by checking our directory, below. It lists all TV stations, including cable, that broadcast the games of each team.

If you're not traveling all that far from home, this guide will help you tune in your favorite games on the car radio. If you're traveling very far away—away from any of the TV stations listed below—look for a TV that's hooked up to a satellite dish!

The listings also give the address for the main station for each team. If you want to send a letter to one of your team's announcers, this is where to write.

If you're interested in watching college baseball and other nonpro games, many cable networks air the games of local teams. Check with the cable distributors in your area to see what games they carry.

MAJOR LEAGUE BASEBALL

Office of the Commissioner
350 Park Avenue, 17th Floor
New York, NY 10022
(212) 355-0007

CBS Television
51 W. 52nd Street
New York, NY 10019
(212) 975-4531

ESPN
ESPN Plaza
Bristol, CT 06010
(203) 585-2000

605 Third Avenue
New York, NY 10016
(212) 916-9260

CBS Radio
51 W. 52nd Street
New York, NY 10019
(212) 975-4321

AMERICAN LEAGUE

BALTIMORE ORIOLES

Television

Flagship Station: WMAR Channel 2
Games: 45.
6400 York Road
Baltimore, MD 21212
(301) 377-2222

Network Affiliates:
Washington, DC: WDCA
Charlotte, NC: WJZY
Ft. Myers, FL: WBR
Greensboro, NC: WGGT
Orlando-Daytona-Melbourne, FL: WAYK

THE BULL PEN
Q: Who always sits next to the announcer at a ball game?
A: Mike.

Sarasota, FL: W24AT
York, PA: WPNT
Lynchburg, VA: WJPR
Raleigh/Durham, NC: WLFL
Richmond, VA: WRLH
Rocky Mount, NC: WFBE
Salisbury, MD: WMDT

Radio

Flagship Station: WBAL-AM, 1090
Games: 162.
3800 Hooper Avenue
Baltimore, MD 21211
(301) 467-3000

Cable

Network: Home Team Sports
Games: 90.
1111 18th St., NW, Suite 200
Washington, DC 20036
(202) 728-5300
Scrambled Signal: Yes.

Minor League Affiliates

Rochester: WPXY-AM 1280, 146 games.
Hagerstown: WJEJ-AM 1240, 140 games.
Frederick: WQSI-AM 820, 140 games.

BOSTON RED SOX

Director of Broadcasting: Jim
Healey, Boston Red Sox, Fenway
Park, Boston, MA 02215

Television

Flagship Station: WSBK Channel 38
Games: 75.
83 Leo Birmingham Parkway
Boston, MA 02135
(617) 783-3838

Network Affiliates:
Springfield, MA: WGGB
Providence, RI/New Bedford, MA:
WLNE
Hartford, CT: WVIT
Portland, ME: WCSN
Bangor, ME: WLBZ
Burlington, VT: WVNY

White River Jct., VT/Hanover, NH:
WNNE
Palm Bay, FL: WAYK

Radio

Flagship Station: WRKO-AM, 680
Games: 162.
3 Fenway Plaza
Boston, MA 02215
(617) 236-6800

Cable

Network: New England Sports
Network
Games: 82.
70 Brookline Avenue
Boston, MA 02215
(617) 536-9233
Scrambled Signal: No

Minor League Affiliates

Pawtucket: WARA-AM 1320, 146
games.
New Britain: WCNX-AM 1150, 60
games.
Lynchburg: WLLL-AM 930, 140
games.

Winter Haven: WYXY-AM 1360, 70
games.
Elmira: Unavailable, 20 games.

CALIFORNIA ANGELS

Director of Broadcasting: Tom
Seeberg, California Angels,
Anaheim Stadium, 2000 State
College Boulevard, Anaheim, CA
92806

Television

Flagship Station: KTLA Channel 5
Games: 57.
5800 Sunset Boulevard
Hollywood, CA 90078
(213) 460-5500

English Radio

Flagship Station: KMPC-AM, 710
Games: 162.
P.O. Box 710
Los Angeles, CA 90078
(213) 460-5672

From the 1930s to the 1950s, the major league teams' radio announcers didn't cover away games. Instead, they broadcast at home. That meant they had to get the play-by-play over a teletype machine.

To try to make the broadcast sound live and exciting, the announcer knocked on a hollow block of wood with a pencil to make the sound of each hit. Then he played the canned sounds of roaring fans.

Ronald Reagan began his career as a baseball announcer.

Spanish Radio

Flagship Station: XPRS-AM, 1090
Games: 162.
6834 Hollywood Boulevard, 3rd Floor
Los Angeles, CA 90028
(213) 856-5151

Cable

Network: SportsChannel
Games: 35.
1545 26th Street
Santa Monica, CA 90404
(213) 453-1985
Scrambled Signal: Yes

Minor League Affiliates

Midland: KCRS-AM, 550 AM, 136 games.
Quad City: KSTT-AM, 1170, 140 games.
Bend: KRGL-AM, 940, 76 games.

CHICAGO WHITE SOX

Director of Broadcasting: Dan Fabian, Chicago White Sox, 324 West 35th Street, Chicago, IL 60616

Television

Flagship Station: WGN Channel 9
Games: 42.
2501 W. Bradley Place
Chicago, IL 60618
(312) 883-3200

Network Affiliates:
Rockford, IL: WQRF
Noblesville, IN: WMCC
Sarasota, FL: W24AT
Pensacola, FL: WJTC

English Radio

Flagship Station: WMAQ-AM, 670
Games: 162.
19th Floor Merchandise Mart
Chicago, IL 60654
(312) 245-6000

Spanish Radio

Flagship Station: WTAQ-AM, 1300
Games: 40.
9355 W. Joliet Road
La Grange, IL 60525
(708) 352-1300

Cable

Network: SportsChannel Chicago
Games: 114.
820 West Madison Avenue
Oak Park, IL 60302
(708) 524-9444
Scrambled Signal: Yes

Minor League Affiliates

Vancouver: CKWX-AM, 1130, 63 games.
Birmingham: WVOK-AM, 690, 144 games.

Sarasota: WCTQ-FM, 92.1, 24 games.
South Bend: WHME-FM, 103.1, 140 games.
Utica: WIBX-AM, 950, 30 games.

CLEVELAND INDIANS

Director of Broadcasting: Bob DiBiasio, Cleveland Indians, Boudreau Boulevard, Cleveland, OH 44114.

Television

Flagship Station: WUAB Channel 43
Games: 60.
8443 Day Drive
Cleveland, OH 44129
(216) 843-6043

Famous announcer Red Barber mans the mike.

Radio

Flagship Station: WWWE-AM, 1100
Games: 162.
The Park
1250 Superior Avenue
Cleveland, OH 44114
(216) 781-1100

Cable

Network: SportsChannel/Ohio
Games: 45.
6500 Rockside Road
Independence, OH 44131
(216) 328-0333
Scrambled Signal: Yes

Minor League Affiliates

Colorado Springs: KSSS-AM, 740, 144 games.
Canton: WNPQ-FM, 95.9, 140 games.
Kinston: WRNS-AM, 960, 140 games.
Burlington: WBBB-AM, 920, 72 games.

DETROIT TIGERS

Director of Broadcasting: Neal K. Fenkell, Detroit Tigers, Tiger Stadium, Detroit, MI 48216.

Television

Flagship Station: WDIV Channel 4
Games: 45.
550 West Lafayette
Detroit, MI 48231
(313) 222-0444

Network Affiliates:
Kalamazoo, MI: WWMT
Lansing/Jackson, MI: WLNS
Flint/Saginaw, MI: WJRT
Cadillac, MI: WWTV/WWUP
Toledo, OH: WUPW

Radio

Flagship Station: WJR-AM, 760
Games: 162.
2100 Fisher Building
Detroit, MI 48202
(313) 875-4440

Cable

Network: Pro Am Sports System
Games: 71.
24 Frank Lloyd Wright Drive
P.O. Box 3812
Ann Arbor, MI 48106
(313) 930-7277
Scrambled Signal: Yes

Minor League Affiliates

Toledo: WMTR-FM, 95.9, 146 games.
London: CFPL-TV, Channel 10, 12 games.
Fayetteville: WFAI-AM, 1230, 68 games.
Niagara Falls: WJJL-AM, 1440, 30 games.
Bristol: WFGH-AM, 980, 10 games.

KANSAS CITY ROYALS

Director of Broadcasting: C. Dennis Cryder, Kansas City Royals, P.O. Box 419969, Kansas City, MO 64141.

Television

Flagship Station: WDAF Channel 4
Games: 50.
3030 Summit
Kansas City, MO 64108
(816) 753-4567

Network Affiliates:
Columbia, MO: KMIZ
Denver, CO: KWGN
Joplin, MO/Pittsburg, KS: KSNF
Omaha, NE: KPTM
Ottumwa, IA: KOIA

Springfield, MO: KDEB
Topeka, KS: WIBW
Tulsa, OK: KGCT
Wichita, KS: KAKE

Radio

Flagship Station: WIBW-AM, 580
Games: 162.
P.O. Box 119
Topeka, KS 66601
(913) 272-3456

Minor League Affiliates

Omaha: KKAR-AM, 1180, 146 games.
Memphis: WREC-AM, 600, 144 games.
Eugene: KUGN-AM, 590, 76 games.

MILWAUKEE BREWERS

Director of Broadcasting: William Haig, Milwaukee Brewers, Milwaukee County Stadium, Milwaukee, WI 53214.

Television

Flagship Station: WCGV Channel 24
Games: 60.
5445 North 27th Street
Milwaukee, WI 53209
(414) 527-2424

Network Affiliates:
Eau Claire, WI: WQOW
Green Bay, WI: WGBA
La Crosse, WI: WLAX
Madison, WI: WMSN
Rockford, IL: WQRF
Wausau, WI: WAOW

Radio

Flagship Station: WTMJ-AM, 620
Games: 162.
720 East Capitol Drive
Milwaukee, WI 53201
(414) 332-9611

TRIVIA QUIZ
What two baseball announcers are known for using the expression Holy Cow"?

Answer: **The Chicago Cubs' Harry Caray and the New York Yankees' Phil Rizzuto.**

TRIVIA QUIZ
How wide is home plate?

Answer: **17 inches.**

Minor League Affiliates

Denver: KXKL-AM, 1280, 146 games.
El Paso: KHEY-AM, 690, 136 games.
Beloit: WBEL-AM, 1380, 50 games.
Helena: KBLL-AM, 1240, 52 games.

MINNESOTA TWINS

Director of Broadcasting: Laurel Prieb, Minnesota Twins, 501 Chicago Avenue South, Minneapolis, MN 55415.

Television

Flagship Stations: WCCO Channel 4
Games: 33.
90 So. 11th Street
Minneapolis, MN 55403
(612) 339-4444

KITN Channel 29
Games: 27.
7325 Aspen Lane No., Suite 122
Minneapolis, MN 55428
(612) 424-2929

Network Affiliates:
Alexandria, MN: KCCO
Bismarck, ND: KBMY
Fargo, ND: KTHI
Mason City, IA: KIMT
Sioux City, IA: KTIV
Sioux Falls, SD: KSFY
Walker, MN: KCCW

Radio

Flagship Station: WCCO-AM, 830
Games: 162.
625 Second Avenue South
Minneapolis, MN 55402
(612) 370-0611

Cable

Network: Midwest Sports Channel
Games: 31 in Twin Cities metro area; 92 in remainder of Minnesota, parts of Iowa, South Dakota, and North Dakota.
90 So. 11th Street

Minneapolis, MN 55403
(612) 339-4444
Scrambled Signal: Yes

Minor League Affiliates

Portland: KBNP-AM, 1410, 144 games.
Orlando: WWNZ-AM, 740, 144 games.

NEW YORK YANKEES

Director of Broadcasting: John Fugazy, New York Yankees, Yankee Stadium, Bronx, NY 10451.

Television

Flagship Station: WPIX Channel 11
Games: 75.
220 East 42nd Street

Famous for Talking

Night after night, on radio and TV, announcers are the ones telling fans what's going on in baseball. They've got to know the players in the game backwards and forwards. After all, they don't want to run out of things to say!

With all this talking, some announcers are better known to fans than most of the players. Announcers can't make it into baseball's Hall of Fame as official members. But each year an announcer is honored at the induction ceremony with the Ford C. Frick Award.

The winners so far: Mel Allen, Red Barber, Bob Elson, Russ Hodges, Ernie Harwell, Vin Scully, Jack Brickhouse, Curt Gowdy, Buck Canel, Bob Prince, Jack Buck, Lindsey Nelson, and Chicago's much-adored Harry Caray.

How do you get to be a baseball announcer?

Fifty-five of the current big league announcers started out as big league ball players themselves. And six current announcers are in the Hall of Fame as players (Johnny Bench, Don Drysdale, Al Kaline, George Kell, Ralph Kiner, and Brooks Robinson).

For some, baseball announcing doesn't come at the end of a star career—it comes at the beginning. Ronald Reagan began by broadcasting baseball on the radio. (He used to recreate the games from teletyped play-by-play.) Reagan's show biz career led him to politics and all the way to the White House.

11 WPIX Plaza
New York, NY 10017
(212) 949-1100

Network Affiliates:
Binghamton, NY: WICZ
Rochester, NY: WUHF
Hollywood, FL: WDZL
Tampa, FL: WFTS
West Palm Beach, FL: WFLX
New London, CT: WTWS

Radio

Flagship Station: WABC-AM, 770
Games: 162.
2 Pennsylvania Plaza
New York, NY 10121
(212) 613-3800

Cable

Network: Madison Square Garden
Network
Games: 75.
2 Pennsylvania Plaza
New York, NY 10121
(212) 563-8000
Scrambled Signal: Yes.

Minor League Affiliates

Columbus: WBNS-AM, 1460, 146
games.
Albany: WGNA-AM, 1460, 140
games.
Prince William: WPWC-AM 1480,
140 games.

OAKLAND ATHLETICS

Director of Broadcasting: David
Rubenstein, Oakland Athletics,
Oakland-Alameda County
Coliseum, Oakland, CA 94621.

Television

Flagship Station: KPIX, Channel 5
(32 games); KICU, Channel 36 (30
games).
KPIX
855 Battery Street

San Francisco, CA 94111
(415) 362-5550
KICU
P.O. Box 36
San Jose, CA 95109
(408) 298-3636

Network Affiliates:
Arcata, CA: KREQ
Chico, CA: KCPM
Fresno, CA: KAIL
Sacramento, CA: KCRA
Salinas, CA: KCBA
San Jose, CA: KICU
Kingman, AZ: KMOH
Prescott, AZ: KUSK
Las Vegas, NV: KRLR
Reno, NV: KAME
Honolulu, HI: KFVE
Sarasota, FL: WAT24

English Radio

Flagship Station: KSFO-AM, 560
Games: 162.
300 Broadway
San Francisco, CA 94133
(415) 398-5600

Spanish Radio

Flagship Station: KNTA-AM, 1430
Address unavailable.
Games: 162.

Cable

Network: SportsChannel
Games: 50.
901 Battery
San Francisco, CA 94111
(415) 296-8900

Minor League Affiliates

Tacoma: KTAC-AM, 850, 144 games.
Huntsville: WFIX-AM, 1450, 144
games.
Southern Oregon: KMFR-AM, 880, 76
games.

SEATTLE MARINERS

Director of Broadcasting: Randy
Adamack, Seattle Mariners, 411 1st
Avenue S., P.O. Box 4100, Seattle,
WA 98104.

Television

Flagship Station: KSTW Channel 11
Games: 65.
P.O. Box 11411
Tacoma, WA 98411
(206) 572-5789

Network Affiliates:
Anchorage, AK: KTBY
Boise, ID: KTRV
Eugene, OR: KLSR
Honolulu, HI: KFVE
Portland, OR: KPDX
Salt Lake City, UT: KXIV
Spokane, WA: KXLY
Yakima, WA: KAPP

Radio

Flagship Station: KIRO-AM, 710
Games: 162.
P.O. Box C21326
Seattle, WA 98119
(206) 728-7777

Minor League Affiliates

Calgary: Unavailable.
San Bernardino: KCKC-AM, 1350, 21
games.
Wausau: WRIG-AM, 25 games.

TEXAS RANGERS

Director of Broadcasting: Chuck
Morgan, Texas Rangers, P.O. Box
1111, Arlington, TX 76010.

Television

Flagship Station: KTVT Channel 11
Games: 74.
P.O. Box 2495
Ft. Worth, TX 76113
(817) 451-1111

**Ralph Kiner presents Mel Allen with
the first Ford C. Frick Award for his
years of great announcing.**

Network Affiliates:
Amarillo, TX: KCIT
Austin, TX: KBVO
Lubbock, TX: KJTV
Lufkin, TX: KTRE
San Antonio, TX: KABB
San Antonio, TX: The Sports
Channel
Tyler, TX: KLTV
Waco, TX: KWKT
Wichita Falls, TX: K35BO
Salt Lake City, UT: KOOG
Ft. Myers, FL: WBR
Orlando, FL: WAYK
Pensacola, FL: WJTC
Melbourne, FL: WAYK
New Orleans, LA: WCCL
Shreveport, LA: KMSS
Jackson, MS: WAC
Lawton, OK: K53DS
Oklahoma City, OK: KAUT
Tulsa, OK: KOKI

Radio

Flagship Station: WBAP-AM, 820
Games: 162.
1 Broadcast Hill
Ft. Worth, TX 76103
(817) 531-3656

Cable

Network: Home Sports Entertainment
Games: 50.
2080 Highway 360, Suite 260
Lock Box #3
Grand Prairie, TX 75050
(817) 988-9292
Scrambled Signal: Yes

Minor League Affiliates

Oklahoma City: KXY-AM, 1340, 146 games.
Tulsa: KAKC-AM, 1300, 136 games.
Gastonia: WGNC-AM, 1450, 144 games.
Butte: KBOW-AM, 550, 35 games.

TORONTO BLUE JAYS

Director of Broadcasting: Howard Starkman, Toronto Blue Jays, SkyDome, 300 The Esplanade West, Box 3200, Toronto, Ontario, Canada M5V 3B3.

Television

Flagship Station: CFTO Channel 9
Games: 50.
P.O. Box 9
Toronto, Ontario
Canada M4A 2M9
(416) 299-2057

Network Affiliates:
Keewatin, Ont.: CJBN
Kitchener, Ont.: CKCO
North Bay, Ont.: CKNY
Ottawa, Ont.: CJOH
Sault Ste. Marie, Ont.: CHBX
Sudbury, Ont.: CICI
Thunder Bay, Ont.: CHFD
Timmins, Ont.: CITO
Lloydminster, Alb.: CITL
Calgary, Alb.: CFCN
Edmonton, Alb.: CFRN
Vancouver, B.C.: BCTV
Victoria, B.C.: CHEK
Winnipeg, Man.: CKY
St. John's, Nfld.: CHON
Halifax, N.S.: CJCH
Sydney, N.S.: CJCB
Moncton, N.B.: CKCW
Montreal, Queb.: CFCF
Prince Albert, Sask.: CIPA
Regina, Sask.: CKCK
Saskatoon, Sask.: CFQC
Yorkton, Sask.: CICC

Radio

Flagship Station: CJCL-AM, 1430
Games: 162.
40 Holly Street
Toronto, Ontario
Canada M4S 3C3
(416) 488-6397

Cable

Network: The Sports Channel

Games: 50.
1155 Leslie Street
Don Mills, Ontario
Canada M3C 2J6
(416) 449-2244
Scrambled Signal: Yes

Minor League Affiliates

Syracuse: WNOR-AM, 1260, 146 games.
St. Catharines: CKTB-AM, 610, 30 games.
Medicine Hat: CHAT-AM, 1270, number of games unavailable.

NATIONAL LEAGUE

ATLANTA BRAVES

Director of Broadcasting: Wayne Long, Atlanta Braves, P.O. Box 4064, Atlanta, GA 30302.

Television

Flagship Station: WTBS Channel 17
Games: 125.
One CNN Center
Atlanta, GA 30348
(404) 827-1717

Radio

Flagship Station: WSB-AM, 750
Games: 162.
1601 West Peachtree Street, NE
Atlanta, GA 30309
(404) 897-7500

Minor League Affiliates

Richmond: WRNL-AM, 910, 146 games.
Greenville: WFBC-AM, 1330, 144 games.
Durham: WDNC-AM, 620, 140 games.
Idaho Falls: KUPI-AM, 980, 35 games.

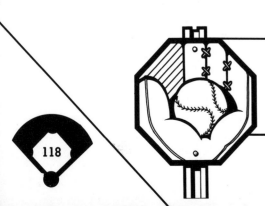

SHORTSTOPS
   In the U.S., the most popular frequency for baseball on radio is 1340 AM. For some reason, 75 different stations broadcast baseball games at this spot on the AM dial.

CHICAGO CUBS

Director of Broadcasting: John McDonough, Chicago Cubs, Wrigley Field, 1060 West Addison Street, Chicago, IL 60613.

The Cubs' beloved announcer, Harry Caray.

Television

Flagship Station: WGN Channel 9
Games: 145.
2501 Bradley Place
Chicago, IL 60618
(312) 528-2311

Network Affiliates:
Des Moines, IA: WHO-TV
Burlington, IA: KJMH
Cedar Rapids, IA: KCRG
Sioux City, IA: KTIV
Ottumwa, IA: KOIA
Champaign, IL: WAND
Davenport, IL: KWQC
Mt. Vernon, IL: WCEE

Peoria, IL: WEEK
Quincy, IL: WGEM
Rockford, IL: WIFR
Fort Wayne, IN: WFFT
Indianapolis, IN: WTTV
South Bend, IN: WNDU
Ft. Pierce, FL: WTVX
Miami, FL: WSVN
Tampa, FL: WTOG

English Radio

Flagship Station: WGN-AM, 720
Games: 162.
435 North Michigan Avenue
Chicago, IL 60611
(312) 222-4700

Spanish Radio

Flagship Station: WOPA-AM, 1200
Games: 30.
509 West Roosevelt Road
Chicago, IL 60607
(312) 738-1200

CINCINNATI REDS

Director of Broadcasting: Stephen H. Schott, Cincinnati Reds, Riverfront Stadium, Cincinnati, OH 45202.

Television

Flagship Station: WLWT Channel 5
Games: 47.
140 West Ninth Street
Cincinnati, OH 45202
(513) 352-5000

Network Affiliates:
Columbus, OH: WTTE

Dayton, OH: WDTN
Lima, OH: WLIO
Zanesville, OH: WHIZ
Indianapolis, IN: WXIN
Bowling Green, KY: WGRB
Hazard, KY: WYMT
Lexington, KY: WDKY
Louisville, KY: WDRB
Charleston/Huntington, WV: WVAH
Lakeland, FL: WTMV
Orlando, FL: WAYK
Charlotte, NC: WHKY
Bristol/Kingsport/Johnson City, TN: WEMT
Nashville, TN: WZTV

Radio

Flagship Station: WLW-AM, 700
Games: 162.
1111 St. Gregory Street
Cincinnati, OH 45202
(513) 241-9597

Cable

Network: SportsChannel/Ohio
Games: 25.
820 W. Madison
Oak Park, IL 60302
(708) 524-9444
Scrambled Signal: No.

Minor League Affiliates

Nashville: WSIX-AM, 980, 146 games.
Chattanooga: WDEF-AM, 1370, 144 games.
Charleston, W. Va.: WCHS-AM, 580, 144 games.
Billings: KCTR-AM, 970, 70 games.

HOUSTON ASTROS

Director of Broadcasting: Jamie Hildreth, Houston Astros, P.O. Box 288, Houston, TX 77001.

Television

Flagship Station: KTXH Channel 20
Games: 85.

8950 Kirby Drive
Houston, TX 77054
(713) 661-2020

Network Affiliates:
Amarillo, TX: KCIT
Austin, TX: K13-VC
Baton Rouge, LA: WKG
Lake Charles, LA: KVNP
Livingston, TX: KETX
Odessa, TX: KPEJ
Palm Bay, FL: WAYK
San Angelo, TX: KIDY
San Antonio, TX: KRRT
Shreveport, LA: KMSS
Waco, TX: KWKT
Wichita Falls, TX: KJTL

English Radio

Flagship Station: KTRH-AM, 740
Games: 162.
510 Lovett Boulevard
Houston, TX 77006
(713) 526-5874

Spanish Radio

Flagship Station: KXYZ-AM, 1320
Games: 162.
2700 E. Pasadena Freeway
Pasadena, TX 77506
(713) 472-2500

Cable

Network: Home Sports Entertainment
Games: 50.
5251 Gulfton
Houston, TX 77006
(713) 661-0078
Scrambled Signal: Yes.

Minor League Affiliates

Tucson: KTKT-AM, 990, 144 games.
Osceola: WMJK-AM, 1220, 70 games.
Asheville: WWNC-AM, 570, number of games unavailable.
Auburn: WMBO-AM, 1340, 20 games.

LOS ANGELES DODGERS

Director of Broadcasting: Dave Van de Walker (KABC), Brent Shyer (Dodgers), Los Angeles Dodgers, Dodger Stadium, 1000 Elysian Park Avenue, Los Angeles, CA 90012.

Television

Flagship Station: KTTV Channel 11
Games: 50.
5746 Sunset Boulevard
Los Angeles, CA 90028
(213) 466-5441

English Radio

Flagship Station: KABC-AM, 790
Games: 162.
3321 South La Cienega Boulevard
Los Angeles, CA 90016
(213) 840-4900.

Spanish Radio

Flagship Station: KWKW-AM, 1300
Games: 162.
6677 Hollywood Boulevard
Los Angeles, CA 90028
(213) 466-8111

Cable

Network: SportsChannel/Los Angeles
Games: 35.
1545 26th Street
Santa Monica, CA 90404
(213) 453-1985
Scrambled Signal: Yes.

Minor League Affiliates

Albuquerque: KOB-AM, 770, 144 games.
San Antonio: KFHM-AM, 1160, 136 games.

GOING, GOING, GONE!

Home runs are always exciting, no matter what the score. And baseball announcers love to describe them. "Going, going, gone!" is probably the most popular home run description among baseball announcers.

Who started it? A Cincinnati announcer named Harry Hartman was the first to use the phrase, in 1929. But it was Yankee announcer Mel Allen who made it famous.

Here are some other well-known home run descriptions:

Vin Scully: "Forget it."

Ralph Kiner: "Kiss it goodbye."

Russ Hodges: "Bye, bye, baby."

Rosey Rowswell: "Open the window, Aunt Minnie, here it comes!" (As a joke, Rowswell made up the idea of an Aunt Minnie with an apartment right near the Pirates' Forbes Field. Every time a player hit a home run, he would smash a light bulb near the mike, as if the ball had just crashed through Aunt Minnie's window.)

Others: "It's outta here!"

"He hit the ball downtown."

"He dialed eight" (the phone number of the bull pen).

Going... going... Pirate Roberto Clemente leaps high trying to grab the ball (see arrow). Gone! Home

ero Beach: WAXE-AM, 1370, 140
ames.
reat Falls: KQDI-AM, 1450, 70
ames.

MONTREAL EXPOS

Director of Broadcasting: Michel
agace, Montreal Expos, P.O. Box
00, Station M, Montreal, Quebec,
anada H1V 3P2.

English Television

Flagship Station: CFCF-TV Channel
2
Games: 28.
05 Ogilvy Street
Montreal, Quebec
anada H3N 1M4
514) 273-6311

Network Affiliates:
St. Johns, Nfld.: CJON
Halifax, N.S.: CJCH
Sydney, N.S.: CJCB
Ottawa, Ont.: CJOH
Sudbury, Ont.: CICI
Kitchener, Ont.: CKCO
Toronto, Ont.: CFTO
Winnipeg, Man.: CKY
Regina, Sask.: CKTV
Saskatoon, Sask.: CFQC
Edmonton, Alb.: CFRN
Calgary, Alb.: CFCN
Vancouver, B.C.: CHAN
Victoria, B.C.: CHEK
Montreal, Que.: CFCF
Sault Ste. Marie, Ont.: CHBX
Thunder Bay, Ont.: CHFD
Yorkton, Sask.: CICC
Lloydminster, Alb.: CITL
Kenora, Ont.: CJBN

French Television

Flagship Station: CBFT Channel 2
Games: 37.
1400 Rene Levesque Boulevard East
Montreal, Quebec
Canada H3C 3A8
(514) 597-5469

English Radio

Flagship Station: CJAD-AM, 800
Games: 162.
1411 Fort Street
Montreal, Quebec
Canada H3H 2R1
(514) 989-2523

French Radio

Flagship Station: CKAC-AM, 730
Games: 162.
1400 Metcalfe Street
Montreal, Quebec
Canada H3A 1X4
(514) 845-5151

Cable

Network: The Sports Network
Games: 25.
1155 Leslie Street

Don Mills, Ontario
Canada M3C 2J6
(416) 449-2244
Scrambled Signal: Yes.

Minor League Affiliates

Indianapolis: WBCI-FM, 100.9, 146
games.
Jacksonville: WJXR-FM, 92.1, 144
games.
Rockford: WROK-AM, 1440, 24
games.

NEW YORK METS

Director of Broadcasting: Michael
Ryan, New York Mets, Shea
Stadium, 126th Street and Roosevelt
Avenue, Flushing, NY 11368.

Television

Flagship Station: WWOR Channel 9
Games: 75.
9 Broadcast Plaza
Secaucus, NJ 07094
(201) 348-0009

English Radio

Flagship Station: WFAN-AM, 660
Games: 162.
34-12 36th Street
Astoria, NY 11106
(718) 706-7690

Spanish Radio

Flagship Station: WJIT-AM, 1480
Games: 100.
655 Madison Avenue
New York, NY 10021
(212) 935-5170

Cable

Network: SportsChannel/New York
Games: 75.
Crossways Park West
Woodbury, NY 11797
(516) 364-3650
Scrambled Signal: Yes.

Minor League Affiliates

Tidewater: WTAR-AM, 790, 146 games.
Jackson: WJDX-AM, 620, 136 games.
St. Lucie: WBL-AM, 1590, 70 games.
Columbia: WOMG-AM, 1320, 144 games.
Pittsfield: WBEC-AM, 1420, 44 games.

PHILADELPHIA PHILLIES

Director of Broadcasting: Jo-Anne Levy, Philadelphia Phillies, P.O. Box 7575, Philadelphia, PA 19101.

Television

Flagship Station: WTXF Channel 29
Games: 85.
4th and Market Streets
Philadelphia, PA 19106
(215) 925-2929

Network Affiliates:
Lancaster/Lebanon, PA: WLYH
Wilkes-Barre/Scranton, PA: WBRE

Radio

Flagship Station: WCAU-AM, 1210
Games: 162.
City Line and Monument Road
Philadelphia, PA 19131
(215) 668-5800

Cable

Network: Prism Cable Company (premium pay) and SportsChannel (basic cable).
Games: Prism 40, SportsChannel 25.
PRISM and SportsChannel
225 City Line Avenue
Bala Cynwyd, PA 19004
(215) 668-2210

Minor League Affiliates

Scranton: WICK-AM, 1400, 146 games.
Reading: WAGO-AM, 1240, 140 games.

Batavia: WBTA-AM, 1490, 20 games.

PITTSBURGH PIRATES

Director of Broadcasting: Dean Jordan, Pittsburgh Pirates, 600 Stadium Circle, P.O. Box 7000, Pittsburgh, PA 15212.

Television

Flagship Station: KDKA Channel 2
Games: 50.
One Gateway Center
Pittsburgh, PA 15222
(412) 392-2200

Network Affiliates:
Altoona, PA: WWPC
Erie, PA: WETG
Charleston/Huntington, WV: WVAH
Johnstown, PA: WWCP
Steubenville, OH: WTOV
York, PA: WPMT
Youngstown, OH: WKBN

Radio

Flagship Station: KDKA-AM, 1020
Games: 162.
One Gateway Center
Pittsburgh, PA 15222
(412) 323-5096

Cable

Network: KBL Entertainment Network
Games: 60.
294 West Stuben Street
Pittsburgh, PA 15205
(412) 922-9610
Scrambled Signal: No.

Minor League Affiliates

Buffalo: WGR-AM, 550, 146 games.
Harrisburg: WCMB-AM, 1460, 140 games.
Salem: WROV-AM, 1240, 140 games.
Welland: CHOW-AM, 1470, number of games unavailable.

ST. LOUIS CARDINALS

Director of Broadcasting: Dan Farrell, St. Louis Cardinals, 250 Stadium Plaza, St. Louis, MO 63102.

Television

Flagship Station: KPLR Channel 11
Games: 78.
4935 Lindell Boulevard
St. Louis, MO 63108
(314) 367-7211

Network Affiliates:
Fayetteville, AR: KHOG
Ft. Smith, AR: KHBS
Little Rock, AR: KASN
Ft. Myers, FL: W07BR
Jacksonville, FL: WAWS
Miami, FL: WDZL
Orlando, FL: WAYK
Pensacola, FL: WJTC
Panama City, FL: WPGX
Sarasota, FL: W24AT
Tallahassee, FL: W17AB
Tampa, FL: WTMV
Burlington, IA: KJMH
Cedar Rapids, IA: KOCR
Davenport, IA: KLJB
Marshalltown, IA: K39AS
Ottumwa, IA: KOIA
Sioux City, IA: KTTV
Champaign, IL: WCCU
Peoria, IL: WYZZ
Quincy, IL: WGEM
Rockford, IL: WQRF
Springfield, IL: WRSP
Evansville, IN: WEVV
Paducah, KY: KBSI
Columbia, MO: KOMU
Joplin, MO: K57DR
Springfield, MO: KDEB
St. Joseph, MO: KQTV
Oklahoma City, OK: KAUT
Jackson, TN: WMTV
Memphis, TN: WLMT

Radio

Flagship Station: KMOX-AM, 1120
Games: 162.
One Memorial Drive
St. Louis, MO 63102

(314) 621-2345

Cable

Network: Cencom Cable Network
Games: 50.
14522 S. Outer Forty Road
St. Louis, MO 63017
(314) 576-4446
Scrambled Signal: Yes.

Minor League Affiliates

Louisville: WAVG-AM, 970, 146 games.
Arkansas: KARN-AM, 920, 68 games.
Springfield: KRVI-FM, 96.7, 84 games.

SAN DIEGO PADRES

Director of Broadcasting: James A. Winters, San Diego Padres, 9449 Friars Road, P.O. Box 2000, San Diego, CA 92120.

Television

Flagship Station: KUSI Channel 51
Games: 51.
7377 Convoy Court
San Diego, CA 92111
(619) 571-5151

Network Affiliates:
El Centro, CA: Imperial Valley Cable
Kingman, AZ: KMOH-TN
Prescott, AZ: KUSK
Tucson, AZ: KTTU
Yuma, AZ: Sun Cable
Pensacola, FL: WJTC
Honolulu, HI: KMGT
Albuquerque, NM: KKTO
Las Vegas, NV: KRLR
Ogden, UT: KOOG

English Radio

Flagship Station: KFMB-AM, 760
Games: 162.
7677 Engineer Road
San Diego, CA 92111
(619) 292-7600

Spanish Radio

Flagship Station: XEXX-AM, 1420
Games: 162.
353 3rd Ave., Suite 201
Chula Vista, CA 92010
(619) 427-1420

Cable

Network: San Diego Sports Network
Games: 50.
5159 Federal Boulevard
San Diego, CA 92105
(619) 263-9251
Scrambled Signal: No.

Minor League Affiliates

Las Vegas: KVEG-AM, 840, 144 games.
Wichita: KQAM-AM, 1410, 136 games.
Waterloo: KCFI-AM, 1250, 140 games.
Charleston, S.C.: WSCE-AM, 1390, 72 games.
Spokane: KJRB-AM, 790, 76 games.

SAN FRANCISCO GIANTS

Director of Broadcasting: Bob Hartzell, San Francisco Giants, Candlestick Park, San Francisco, CA 94124.

Television

Flagship Station: KTVU Channel 2
Games: 50.
P.O. Box 2222
Oakland, CA 94623
(415) 834-1212

Network Affiliates:
Reno, NV: KAME
Sacramento, CA: KRBK
Fresno/Visalia, CA: KMPH
Monterey, CA: KMST
Honolulu, HI: KFVE

English Radio

Flagship Station: KNBR-AM, 680
Games: 162.
1700 Montgomery Street, #400
San Francisco, CA 94111
(415) 951-7000

Spanish Radio

Flagship Station: KLOK-AM, 1170
Games: 162.
2905 So. King Road
San Jose, CA 95122
(408) 274-1170

Cable

Network: SportsChannel
Games: 55.
901 Battery Street
San Francisco, CA 94111
(415) 296-8900
Scrambled Signal: No.

Minor League Affiliates

Phoenix: KMPX-AM, 1230, 40 games.
Shreveport: KEEL-AM, 710, 136 games.
San Jose: KSJS-FM, 90.7, 62 games.
Clinton: KROS-AM, 1340, 70 games.
Everett: KWYZ-AM, 1230, 76 games.

WHAT'S IN A NAME?

Some radio stations don't just carry baseball—they've named themselves after the game! Check out these station names:
KURV 719 AM—Edinburg, Texas (they broadcast Houston Astros games)
WRUN 1150 AM—Utica, New York (Yankees)
WBAT 1400—Marion, Indiana (Cubs)
WIFF 1570 AM—Auburn, Indiana (Cubs and White Sox)
WRBI 103.9 FM—Batesville, Indiana (Reds)

DIAL-A-GAME
SPORTS PHONES

Former President Gerald Ford once goofed by saying he liked to "watch" sports on the radio. You can't watch baseball on the radio, but you *can* listen to the score on the phone.

All over the country, there are phone numbers you can call for special tape-recorded announcements with updated sports scores. If you're desperate to find out if your beloved Padres won, say, and you're away from the TV and radio (hopefully you sometimes are!), then sports phone numbers come in handy.

There's a catch, though. In most cases you'll be charged for the call. Numbers that begin with the area code 800 are free. 900 numbers are not. Within your area code, local numbers that begin with a 976 or 540 also charge.

The prices vary, but 50 cents a call is pretty much the minimum. So be sure you know the price before you start checking in regularly!

For sports phones in your area, check your telephone directory or call Information. Below are a few 900 numbers to get you started. Remember: A 900 number isn't the same as an 800 number. A 900 call isn't free!

Scores... Plus
(900) 226-8000

You pay 95 cents per minute for score updates for all the major national sports.

Sports Illustrated Hotline
(900) 988-7777

Scores and updates on teams around the nation, at 77 cents per minute.

Baseball Card Phone Shoppers
(900) 860-9242

You pay $2 for the first minute, $1 for each additional minute. You get hobby news and price updates, and hear about collectibles for sale. This service can also put you in touch with other collectors who want to buy and sell memorabilia.

WATCHING BASEBALL:
THE HIDDEN GAME

If you've watched or played much baseball, you're probably pretty familiar with the basic rules of the game. But few fans know the whole story.

Baseball looks a lot simpler than it is. In fact, whole books have been written on the game "behind the scenes."

What follows is just a brief overview. For more information, read a book such as *How to Watch Baseball*, by Steve Fiffer (it's published by Facts on File Publications). This book is written for adults, but it's pretty easy to follow.

Catchers don't want anyone stealing their signs. Just how many fingers is Johnny Bench holding up?

The Pitch

In the major leagues, it's not enough for a pitcher to have a sizzling fastball. If he throws the same pitch every time, the batters will catch up with it eventually. They'll be waiting for it, adjusting to it, and, after a while, walloping it out of the park.

The most successful pitchers are the ones who vary their pitches. Let's say the pitcher starts the batter off with two fastballs and blows them right by him. Now the batter is thinking, "I've got to swing sooner, faster!"

So on the next pitch the pitcher may come up with a change-up. He throws it just like a fastball (so there's no way to tell it's coming), but he holds the ball differently. The ball comes in much more slowly, and the eager batter swings before the ball even gets to the plate!

If you can learn to follow the pitcher's strategy, you'll find yourself thinking along with him: What should I throw next? What is the batter expecting?

If you're at the stadium, you'll probably have a hard time picking up the pitches, unless you're sitting down low. But on TV you can, if they show you the right angle. The announcers will often call the pitches, but they make mistakes. Here are some of the basic types of pitches that pitchers throw:

Fastball. The pitcher's fastest ball. A "rising" fastball rises as it approaches home plate. That means it's not where the batter hoped it would be, and he swings under it. If he hits the bottom of the ball, he may pop up. Or he may miss it altogether.

A "straight" fastball comes in straight, without rising. It'd better be fast!

Change-up. Thrown like a fastball but with a different grip, this slower pitch is designed to throw off the batter's timing.

Curveball. The most common of what are known as the "breaking" pitches. These are pitches that change, or break, direction, just as they reach the plate. As you can imagine, that makes them very hard to hit.

The curveball breaks down. The batter swings over it, grounding out or missing completely.

Slider. Like the curveball, except that it breaks down and across the plate. A right-hander's slider breaks into the left-handed hitters, jamming them, and breaks down and away from the righties.

Screwball. It breaks in the opposite direction from a slider. So a right-hander's slider jams the righties and breaks away from the lefties.

Pitchers use different pitches in different situations. For one thing, the pitcher has to keep track of the count of balls and strikes.

As you know, the batter gets four balls or three strikes. But, quick! How many different counts are there in baseball?

The answer is nine. 1 & 0, 2 & 0, 3 & 0, 1 & 1, 2 & 1, 3 & 1, 1 & 2, 2 & 2, 3 & 2. The count can never be "4 and anything" or "anything and 3." In those cases, the batter will have jogged down to first with a walk or walked sadly back to the dugout, having been struck out.

When the pitcher has more strikes on the batter than balls, he is said to be "ahead in the count." He's closer to striking the batter out than he is to walking him.

When the pitcher is ahead, he's more likely to throw a "waste pitch." That's a pitch out of the strike zone. It may be up and in—right under the batter's chin, say. That's to move the batter back in the batter's box. Then on the next pitch the pitcher can throw low and outside. The backed-up batter swings and misses.

There are only nine different possible counts, but each one can come up in an infinite number of different situations. In an early inning, say, or a late inning. With runners on base. With nobody on. When the pitcher's team is behind. When it's ahead. Every different situation affects the pitcher's choice of pitch.

The catcher helps the pitcher "call the game" by giving him suggestions for each pitch, using special signs.

If the pitcher and catcher are working well together, they'll agree on each pitch right away. If they disagree often, you'll see the pitcher shaking his head to veto the catcher's suggestions.

THE CATCHER'S SIGNS

To give the signs, the catcher holds a certain number of fingers between his legs. If you're watching on TV you'll be able to pick up the signs. The standard sign system is: one finger for a fastball, two fingers for a curve, three for a slider, four for a change-up.

Watch the sign and then watch the pitch to see what system the catcher is using.

You won't be the only one who's trying to decipher the catcher's signals. The batter himself may try to sneak a peek. And if a player from the batter's team has made it to second base, he can see the signs and signal to the batter. If the batter knows what pitch is coming and where, the pitcher's in trouble.

So with a runner on second, the catcher may switch to a harder sign system, to keep the signals safe. For instance, he may use an "indicator."

Let's say the pitcher and catcher agree that with a runner on second the indicator is four. The catcher flashes the signs: three, four, two, one. He ended with one, to fool the runner on second. But the sign after the indicator (four) was a two. The pitch will be a curve.

Another code system the catcher may use is the pump system. In this system, the number of signs given is what counts, not the signs themselves. If the catcher flashes a three, then a two, then a one, the sent signal is three—the total number of signs. The pitch will be a slider.

The catcher also indicates to the pitcher whether the pitch should be thrown inside or outside, high or low. He can do this with the location of his fingers in giving the sign. He also sets up his mitt as a target to show where he wants the ball thrown.

Of course, as with all baseball signs, the location of the mitt may be a decoy to throw the batter off. And once the ball is caught, watch the catcher closely. He will move the mitt as he catches the ball—toward the strike zone. When the ump looks to see where the ball was caught, he'll see a strike.

STEALING SIGNS

If you're watching baseball on TV and have access to a VCR, you can tape the game and replay it to help you decipher the signs.

There are lots of signs to watch for. In fact, signals are being sent all over the field throughout the game.

Each team's manager calls the game from the dugout. He sends in the signals to his third-base coach in code. The third-base coach then uses a different code to relay the plays to his batter and base runners.

A third-base coach giving signals is often an amusing sight. He scratches his head, pats his stomach, puts his finger on his nose, all in rapid succession.

It's not a funny sight to the opposing team, though.

The players in the opposing dugout study the third-base coach trying to "steal" his signs—and crack his code.

Most third-base coaches use three basic systems. The simplest is to agree on set parts of the body or uniform to indicate certain plays. If the coach touches his knee, the runner on first knows to try to steal second base on the next pitch.

This easy method is a little too easy for the opposing team to pick up. (On the other hand, the code can't be *too* complicated. The coach doesn't want to fool his own players!)

The coach can also use the indicator system, as discussed above. The only sign that counts is the one that comes right after he pulls his left ear, say. Or he

can use the pump system—when the total number of signs is all that matters. These numbers stand for the plays.

When the opposing team figures out the signs, they can put on a play of their own, to counter it. If they see that a steal is on, the pitcher can whirl and pick the runner off. Or throw a pitchout.

That means that the catcher steps out of the batter's box for the throw. He's then in good position to whip the ball down to second and catch the runner.

To make their codes harder to crack, teams may use different codes for different players. If a team suspects that its signs are being stolen, they'll change the signs. To safely check if their signs are being stolen, teams use a

"take-off" sign. Here's how it works. The coach gives the sign for a bunt. Let's say he's using his arms crossed as an indicator. So he touches his knee, coughs, rubs his tummy, crosses his arms, then wipes his right sleeve, then touches his foot.

The crossed arms indicate that the next sign is the one. Wiping his right sleeve is the signal to steal. But touching his foot is the take-off sign. It means to disregard the play.

If the opposing team has figured out the signals but hasn't yet cracked the take-off sign, the opposing manager may signal his pitcher to pitchout. Time to change the signs!

BASIC PLAYS

The third-base coach has lots of plays to signal in. Here's a sample:

Bunt. Instead of swinging, the batter holds the bat steady and just taps the ball. Ideally, the ball plops down between the catcher and pitcher. It takes them too long to reach it. The runner beats the throw to first.

Sacrifice bunt. Same play, but the goal is different. There's a runner on base and the manager wants to get him into "scoring position." Scoring position means the runner is on second or third. He can score even if the batter hits only a single.

On a sacrifice bunt, the surprise factor is usually lost. So the batter probably won't make it safely to first. If the runner advances, though, the batter's done his job.

Steal. The base runner takes off with the pitch. That gives him a "jump" on the catcher. By the time the catcher has the ball and is ready to throw it, the runner is well on his way to stealing the next base.

Hit and run. The steal is on, and the batter is instructed to swing at anything. He's protecting the runner by trying to hit the ball. If he gets a hit, the runner has gotten a big jump and may pick up an extra base, or score.

Double steal. Two base runners are told to steal at the same time. Let's say there are runners "at the corners" (on first and third). The runner on first breaks for second. As the catcher throws down to second, the runner on third is breaking for home. The first runner acts as a decoy to help the second runner score.

Squeeze. The runner on third breaks for home with the pitch. The batter bunts. If the play succeeds, the runner scores. If the batter

Warren Spahn shows off his sweeping overhand form. At this point in his career, he already had won 20 or more games in 13 different years!

misses the bunt, though, the catcher is holding the ball and just waiting for the runner from third. Whoops.

DEFENSE

While the third-base coach, batter, and base runners are signaling each other, the fielders are busy signaling as well.

If you watch the second baseman and shortstop, you'll see them signal on almost every play. If there's a runner on first, for instance, they have to decide who's going to cover second. (They may use hand signals, open or close their mouths, signal with their gloves, or even whistle.)

They also watch their teammate, the catcher. Then they relay the pitch to the rest of the defense. When the players on the field know what pitch is coming, they know which way to move when the pitch is thrown.

For instance, if the pitcher is throwing an inside pitch to a lefty, the first baseman may move toward first base with the pitch. Since the batter is likely to pull the ball (hit it down the baseline), the fielder wants to guard the line (keep the ball from getting between him and the bag and into the outfield for extra bases).

In fact, players and very experienced fans claim they can tell what pitch is coming by watching the fielders as the pitch is thrown. Of course, this could help the opposing team, as well.

That's why the fielders don't move until the pitch is thrown. With a 90 m.p.h. hardball whizzing toward

home, the batter doesn't have much time for looking at the fielders!

Fielders have many plays to signal to each other. They may put on a "wheel," for instance, a complicated play in which several players rotate positions.

There are also some simple, classic decoys that you can watch for. The simplest is one you've probably used yourself. The pitcher throws the ball to first, trying to pick off the runner. "Safe," signals the ump. But the first baseman only *pretends* to throw the ball back to the pitcher. The runner takes his lead again, stepping off the base, and the fielder tags him out.

Believe it or not, this play is still used in the major leagues, and some players are still fooled by it!

Here are a couple of subtler decoys that happen frequently down at second. The batter hits the ball into the outfield. He rounds first fast, planning on stretching his hit into a triple. But the shortstop is crouched at second, about to receive the throw from the outfielder.

"How did they get to the ball that fast?" wonders the runner. And perhaps he slows down. But there is no throw about to come into second. The fielder was putting on an act—a decoy.

The next batter hits the ball into the outfield as well. He rounds first hoping for a double. The fielder now stands on second ever so nonchalantly. There is no throw coming into second, it seems. Maybe the outfielder bobbled the ball?

The runner comes into second standing up, not sliding. The ball gets there before him. He's been decoyed, and he's tagged out.

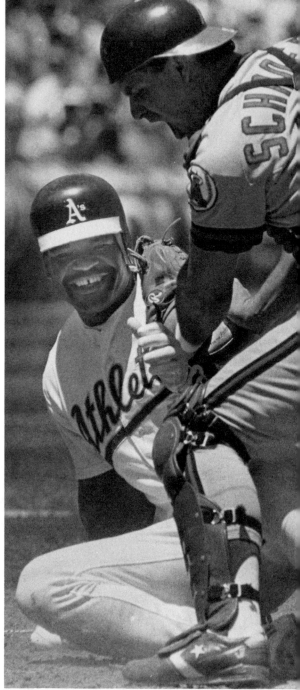

With this smile, Dave Henderson must be safe!

HITTING THE CUT-OFF

When there's a long throw from the outfield to home plate, an infielder serves as the "cut-off" man. He stands in the path of the ball and either catches it—cuts it off—or lets it go to the catcher.

If he thinks the runner who's racing home is going

catcher tags the runner out and the runner holds at first.

BACKING UP

Here's an aspect of the game that's best seen at the stadium, not on TV—and, of course, you can't see it on radio! Most fans follow the ball. They watch the pitcher throw the ball, the hitter swing at the ball, the fielder field the ball, etc.

So do the TV cameras. But many of the other fielders are in on each play in ways that are interesting to watch. For instance, on any given play fielders may have to back up their teammates. If there's a throw home, it's the pitcher's job to run and back up the catcher. If the throw gets by the catcher, the pitcher will get it, and keep other runners from scoring.

The catcher can't stand still either—he often has to back up first. The left-fielder backs up third base, and so on. And while they're racing around off camera, so are the umpires! They keep running to be closer to the play, so they can make accurate calls.

OTHER ASPECTS

All this is just the tip of the iceberg. For instance, there are players rarely seen on the field who play important roles. The most important of these off-field players is the manager.

Fans love to think along with the manager as he makes his moves throughout the game. They also love to second-guess the manager and argue about the mistakes they think he made.

Should Tommy LaSorda take Fernando Valenzuela out of the game? No, you say. But he does. Then the relief pitcher lets in three runs... It looks like you made the right call. Of course, we'll never know what would have happened if Fernando had stayed in the game.

The more you know about baseball strategy, the more you can second-guess, and play along with the players on and off the field. It's all part of the game within the game.

Managers have to know when to replace their pitchers—even aces like Fernando Valenzuela.

to beat the throw anyway, he cuts it off. Now he can at least keep the runner who hit the ball from advancing any further.

Then again, he may decoy. He pretends he's going to cut off the throw, trying to slow the base runner down. Then he lets the ball go through to catch the runner at home. If all works perfectly, the

WHO'S ON FIRST?

BASEBALL ON VIDEO

How long do you think it would take you to watch every Hollywood baseball movie ever made? You better not try to watch them all in one sitting. It would take you around 114 hours!

According to *The Guinness Book of Movie Facts and Feats*, between 1910 and 1987 Hollywood made 53 baseball movies. And new films about the sport, such as *Major League* and *Eight Men Out*, are coming out all the time.

Not only that, there are home videos with baseball highlights, bloopers, and tips on how to play better ball. There's even a film that teaches the art of baseball card collecting. This chapter will tell you what's out there and how to get hold of it. You can start a home video library and be all set for a rainy day. While the pros have to wait out a rain delay, you can pop in a video and "catch" the baseball action!

Rating system:
Strikeout—Not worth your time!
Single—Not bad
Double—Good
Triple—Very good
Home Run—Excellent
Grand Slam—Out of the park! Fabulous!
Walk—No rating. The film company didn't provide a tape for review.

FEATURE FILMS

Here's a selection of some of the best-known baseball features

available on home video. If your local video store doesn't carry one of the films listed below, they can order it for you.

Once you've viewed all of these, check out the drama checklist later in this chapter for 33 more titles. Unfortunately, only a few of these baseball movies are available on videotape. But many films, such as *The Babe Ruth Story* and *Kill the Umpire*, show up often on TV. So keep an eye on your local listings.

The Bad News Bears, 1976—Home Run. Walter Matthau is the down-and-out coach, Morris Buttermaker, whose foul-mouthed Little League team is in last place. Then he recruits an 11-year-old girl (Tatum O'Neal) with a wicked fastball. Funny and moving.
VHS, Beta, $19.95; Laser, $29.95
Paramount Home Video

There are two sequels: *The Bad News Bears in Japan* and *The Bad News Bears in Breaking Training.* But *don't* watch for them! They both rate a Strikeout.

Bang the Drum Slowly,
1973—Home Run.
Robert De Niro stars as a rookie catcher dying of Hodgkin's disease. It's a very sad movie, but a great one.
VHS, Beta, $66.95
Paramount Home Video

Casey at the Bat,
1986—Single.
Elliott Gould, Carol Kane, and Howard Cosell star in a short film based on the famous poem. Will there be any joy in Mudville if Casey strikes out?
VHS, Beta, $19.95
Playhouse Video
c/o CBS/Fox Video
1211 Avenue of the Americas
New York, NY 10036
(800) 2-CBS-FOX

Damn Yankees,
1958—Home Run.
Did you ever daydream about being a great pro ball player and helping your team win the pennant? In this classic 1958 musical, a fan makes that daydream come true. But he has to sell his soul to do it.
VHS, Beta, $59.95
Warner Home Video, $59.95

Eight Men Out,
1988—Triple.
Charlie Sheen and John Cusack star in the story of the Chicago White Sox scandal of 1920. Eight players were accused of losing the World Series on purpose.
VHS, Beta, $89.98
Orion Home Video

The Kid from Left Field,
1979—Double.
Gary Coleman plays a batboy whose expert advice helps a sad-sack Padres team to victory. A likable TV movie remake

of a 1953 film.
VHS, Beta, $69.95
Vestron Video

Major League,
1989—Double.
The owner of the Cleveland Indians tries to ruin her own team in this silly but fun comedy.
VHS, Beta, $29.95
Paramount Home Video

The Natural, 1984—Double.
Robert Redford stars as an aging rookie with one last chance for glory. A little on the spooky side, but this film has some good baseball action.
VHS, Beta, $19.95
RCA/ Columbia Pictures Home Entertainment

The Naughty Nineties,
1945—Single.
This is the film in which Abbott and Costello do their famous "Who's On First?" routine. It's a classic, but the rest of the movie isn't. This time the two clowns get mixed up with riverboat gamblers on the Mississippi.
VHS, Beta, $19.95
MCA Home Video Inc.

The Pride of the Yankees,
1942—Grand Slam.
Many call this the greatest baseball flick ever. Gary Cooper stars as the "Iron Man," Lou Gehrig. Gehrig

Tatum O'Neal is bad news for hitters in *The Bad News Bears*.

As his illness worsens, Lou Gehrig (Gary Cooper) slips and falls in the locker room *(The Pride of the Yankees)*.

played in 2,130 straight games—a record—before he came down with a rare illness.
VHS, Beta, $19.98
CBS/Fox Video

HIGHLIGHTS AND BLOOPERS

The bases are loaded. Two outs, bottom of the ninth. The home team is down by three runs. The batter swings.... It's a long fly ball, deep to center. The outfielder races to the wall. He leaps. It's out of here! Grand slam!

Every baseball fan longs for such moments. But large parts of most games are slow-paced. In fact,

that's part of the beauty of the sport.

On the other hand, sometimes it's fun to see non-stop thrilling baseball highlights, on videotape. Or you can watch blooper tapes and guffaw over back-to-back bonehead plays. Here's what's out there:

The Batty World of Baseball—Double. Famous Chicago announcer Harry Caray hosts this humorous look at the characters of the game.
VHS, BETA, $39.95 plus $3.00 shipping and handling. Order through your video store. The tape

is sold by RCA/Columbia Pictures Home Video.

Major League Baseball Productions
1212 Avenue of the Americas
New York, NY 10036
(212) 921-8100
(800) 421-7020

Major League Baseball Productions sells a total of 355 different baseball videos! They have scads of highlight films, bloopers, how-tos, baseball history, and more. Write or call for the complete catalogue.

The Greatest Comeback Ever—Double. Highlights of the 1978 Yankees as they rose from 14 games back to beat the Red Sox in their famous playoff game. A lot of fun, unless you're a Sox fan, of course.
VHS, $14.98

VidAmerica, Inc.
235 East 55th Street
New York, NY 10022
(212) 355-1600

They also carry a number of other baseball highlights and blooper tapes. Write them for a complete listing.

The Official 1989 World Series Video—Triple. With this well-made video

THE BULL PEN
Q: Why did the movie producer want to make a horror movie about baseball?
A: He saw a doubleheader.

WHY WAS "WHO" ON FIRST?

"Who's on first?" asks Costello.

"Yes," replies Abbott. For on this crazy team "Who" is the name of the first baseman!

In the 1940s, Abbott and Costello's "Who's On First?" routine was such a success that it turned the two comedians into major stars.

How did they get the idea? (Or should we say, "*Who* had the idea?")

No one knows for sure. But Chris Costello's biography of his father offers a possible answer.

As a kid, Lou Costello used to play a lot of baseball with his friends. He was short and not a good hitter, and he rarely got more than a single. But he was fast and often stole second.

So when he was on first base, the pitcher used to warn his teammates, "Lou's on first!"

You can see Abbott and Costello perform the routine in their flick *The Naughty Nineties* (see page 131). Here's how it goes:

COSTELLO: Hey, Abbott!
ABBOTT: What do you want, Costello?
COSTELLO: Look, Abbott, I understand you're going to be the manager of the Lou Costello Junior Youth Foundation Baseball team....
ABBOTT: Yes, we just organized the thing.
COSTELLO: You did?
ABBOTT: Sure!
COSTELLO: Well, I'd like to play on the team myself. You know, I know something about baseball.

ABBOTT: That could be accomplished.
COSTELLO: I'd like to know some of the guys' names on the team, so when I meet them on the street or in the ballpark I can say hello to them.
ABBOTT: Why, surely I'll introduce you to the boys. You know, strange as it may seem they give these ball players nowadays very peculiar names.
COSTELLO: You mean funny names?
ABBOTT: Nicknames... pet names... like Dizzy Dean...
COSTELLO: And his brother Daffy?
ABBOTT: Daffy Dean.
COSTELLO: I'm their French cousin.
ABBOTT: French cousin?
COSTELLO: Goo Fay!
ABBOTT: Goo Fay? *(Laugh)* Well, now, let's see, we have on the bags—We have Who's on first, What's on second, I Don't Know's on third...
COSTELLO: That's what I want to find out.
ABBOTT: What silly names... I say Who's on first, What's on second, I Don't Know's on third...
COSTELLO: Are you the manager?
ABBOTT: Yes.
COSTELLO: Do you know the fellas' names?
ABBOTT: Well, I should.
COSTELLO: Well, then, who's on first?
ABBOTT: Yes.
COSTELLO: I mean, the fella's name.
ABBOTT: That's it.
COSTELLO: That's who?
ABBOTT: Yes.
COSTELLO: Well, go ahead and tell me.
ABBOTT: Who.
COSTELLO: The guy on first.
ABBOTT: Who.
COSTELLO: The first baseman.
ABBOTT: Who!

COSTELLO: Have you got a first baseman?
ABBOTT: *Who* is on first!
COSTELLO: I'm asking *you* who's on first!
ABBOTT: That's the man's name!
COSTELLO: That's who's name?
ABBOTT: Yes.
COSTELLO: Now, tell me who's on first.
ABBOTT: That's right.
COSTELLO: I wanna know what's the guy's name on first base...
ABBOTT: Naw... No... What's on *second* base.

COSTELLO: I'm not asking who's on second.
ABBOTT: *Who* is on *first!*
COSTELLO: I don't know...
ABBOTT: He's on third... Let's get together here.
COSTELLO: How did I get on third base?
ABBOTT: You happened to mention the man's name.
COSTELLO: If I mentioned the third baseman's name, who did I say is playing third base?
ABBOTT: No, *Who's* playing *first!*
COSTELLO: I'm not asking who's playing first!
ABBOTT: Who *is* on first!
COSTELLO: I'm asking

you what's the guy's name on third?

ABBOTT: What's on *second.*

COSTELLO: Who's on second?

ABBOTT: Who's on *first!*

COSTELLO: I don't know!

ABBOTT: He's on *third!*

COSTELLO: There I go... Back on third again!

ABBOTT: I can't change their names.

COSTELLO: You got a first baseman?

ABBOTT: Absolutely!

COSTELLO: When you pay him off every month, who gets the money?

ABBOTT: Every dollar of it. Why not? The man's entitled to it!

COSTELLO: Who is?

ABBOTT: Yes.

COSTELLO: So, who gets it?

ABBOTT: Sure he does!

COSTELLO: Look, the left fielder's name?

ABBOTT: Why.

COSTELLO: Because!

ABBOTT: Oh, he's *center* field!

COSTELLO: Eeeeeeee!

ABBOTT: Now you know these players as well as I do!

COSTELLO: You got a catcher?

ABBOTT: Surely!

COSTELLO: The catcher's name?

ABBOTT: Today.

COSTELLO: Today. And Tomorrow's pitching?

ABBOTT: Now you've got it!

COSTELLO: Now I've got it? Well, I'm a pretty good catcher myself.

ABBOTT: So they tell me...

COSTELLO: Now, I'll catch today... myself. And Tomorrow's pitching on the team. Now Tomorrow throws the ball and the guy up bunts. Now, me being a

good catcher, I wanna throw the guy out at first base, so I pick up the ball and throw it to who?

ABBOTT: That's the first thing you've said right!

COSTELLO: I don't even know what I'm talking about!

ABBOTT: Well, that's all you have to do!

COSTELLO: Is to throw the ball to first base?

ABBOTT: Yes.

COSTELLO: Now, who's got it?

ABBOTT: Naturally.

COSTELLO: If I throw the ball to first base, somebody's got to get it. Now, who's got it?

ABBOTT: Naturally.

COSTELLO: Naturally?

ABBOTT: Naturally!

COSTELLO: Oh, so I throw the ball to Naturally!

ABBOTT: You do nothing of the kind. You throw the ball to Who.

COSTELLO: Naturally.

ABBOTT: That's it!

COSTELLO: That's what I said!

ABBOTT: No, you didn't... No, you didn't!

COSTELLO: I throw the ball to Naturally...

ABBOTT: But you don't.

COSTELLO: I throw it to who?

ABBOTT: Naturally!

COSTELLO: That's what I'm saying.

ABBOTT: But that's *not* what you said!

COSTELLO: I throw the ball to who?

ABBOTT: Naturally.

COSTELLO: You ask me.

ABBOTT: You throw the ball to Who?

COSTELLO: Naturally! Same as you! I throw the ball to who.

ABBOTT: Naturally.

COSTELLO: Naturally. Now, whoever it is drops the ball, so the guy runs to I Don't Know, I Don't Know throws it back to Tomorrow—triple play!

Another guy gets up and hits a long fly ball to be caught. Why? I Don't Know! He's on third and I don't give a darn!

ABBOTT: What'd you say?

COSTELLO: I said I don't give a darn!

ABBOTT: Oh, he's our shortstop.

COSTELLO: Abbott!!!!!!

you can relive the highlights of the Series. Billed as "The Showdown by the Bay," the games were almost stopped by a powerful earthquake.

CBS/Fox Sports Video
1211 Avenue of the Americas
New York, NY 10036
(212) 819-3200
(800) 635-GIFT

They also carry a number of other baseball videos. Ask for a catalogue.

TEAM VIDEOS

Many of the major league teams sell their own home videos. The Philadelphia Phillies, for example, offer six videos, with everything from a look at 100 years of Phillies history to a 30-minute tape of the Phillies Phanatic, the team mascot, in action. (That tape is called "The Phillie Phanatic Phollies." Sounds like it's phull of laphs for Phillies phans!)

To find out what each team offers, prices, and how to order, contact each team directly, using the listings in Chapter 1.

HOW-TO VIDEOS

You're watching a videotape that teaches you how to play baseball.

"Okay," says the coach on the videotape, "now swing!"

CRASH! Your bat whacks into your dad's VCR, smashing it beyond repair.

Clearly, learning to play ball by watching TV has its problems!

A few how-to tapes remind you not to swing a bat in the house. Most explain that watching tapes won't help you unless you also spend hours playing ball for real—outside. But videos can give you lots of useful tips on strategy and form.

You might be able to find a few of these tapes at your video store. But for most you'll need to write or call the company.

All Sports Book & Video Distributors
P.O. Box 5793
Denver, CO 80217
(303) 778-8383
(800) 525-9030

They sell 34 baseball how-to films, including a film that teaches you how to umpire. Call for a catalogue.

The Art of Hitting—Walk. Vada Pinson, the former Cincinnati Reds star, tries to get you "in the swing" of hitting well.
60 min., VHS, $39.95

RMI Media Productions, Inc.
2807 West 47th Street
Shawnee Mission, KS 66205
(913) 262-3974

Babe Ruth: The Fence Buster—Walk.
Prize-winning newsreel documentary of the Sultan of Swat. For $49.95, you also get Lou Gehrig and Connie Mack.
45 min., VHS, Beta.

Two Star Films
P.O. Box 495
Saint James, NY 11780
(516) 584-7283

The Baseball Bunch—Walk.
An Emmy Award-winning kids' TV series, hosted by Johnny Bench. A video store can order the episodes through Warner Bros. Home Video.
60 min., VHS, Beta, $14.98

Jim Rice helps Johnny Bench explain the game's fine points in Bench's instructional series, *The Baseball Bunch*.

THE BULL PEN
Q: What do you call it when someone watches a baseball video three times?
A: A triple play.

Baseball Card Collector—
Strikeout.
A video to get you started in the hobby of collecting baseball cards. Unfortunately, it's slow-moving and doesn't have a lot of information. Seems like you're better off with a book on this subject, rather than a videotape (see page 202).
65 min., VHS, $29.99

Best Film & Video Corp.
98 Cutter Mill Road
Great Neck, NY 11021
(516) 487-4515
(800) 527-2189

The Baseball Masters—
Single.
A series of four tapes on pitching, hitting, fielding, and baserunning. Hall of Famer Al Kaline instructs.
40 min., VHS, $14.95

Congress Video Group
1776 Broadway, Suite 1010
New York, NY 10019
(212) 581-4880
800-VHS-TAPE

They also carry *The Mark Cresse School of Baseball.* It's a 120-minute tape of tips for young players from the coach of the Los Angeles Dodgers.
VHS, $49.95

Baseball Sports Clinic—
Double.
Garry Templeton, Jerry

Reuss, and other pros coach you on all aspects of the game. It's not exciting to watch, but it's easy to follow and should be helpful.
80 min., VHS, $19.99
Best Film & Video Corp.
(See listing opposite for *Baseball Card Collector.*)

Baseball the Yankee Way—Single.
Filmed in 1965 at the Yankee training camp.

There's footage of Roger Maris, Mickey Mantle, Whitey Ford, Elston Howard, and Al Downing as they hone their skills. The players narrate, giving tips and chatting about the game. Has nostalgia appeal.
45 min., VHS, $19.95

Rhino Video
2225 Colorado Avenue
Santa Monica, CA 90404
(213) 828-1980
(800) 432-0020

KNOW YOUR BASEBALL MOVIES?

Take This Trivia Quiz!

1. Which sport has been played in the most Hollywood movies?
A) Baseball
B) Boxing
C) Horse racing
D) Football
E) Car racing

2. How many movies have been made based on Ernest Thayer's 1888 ballad "Casey at the Bat"?
A) More than three
B) Two
C) None

3. In what film did the great Babe Ruth play the role of—Babe Ruth?
A) *The Pride of the Yankees*
B) *The Bad News Bears*
C) *The Babe Ruth Story*
D) *Babes in Toyland*

4. Old-time film star Joe E. Brown loved baseball so much he:
A) Left Hollywood to play ball

B) Refused to make movies that weren't about baseball
C) Made his film company start a baseball team just for him

5. What position does Tatum O'Neal play in *The Bad News Bears*?
A) Catcher
B) Left field
C) Shortstop
D) Pitcher

6. Which of these movie stars *never* made a baseball movie?
A) Ronald Reagan
B) Jimmy Stewart
C) Robert De Niro
D) Tom Hanks

ANSWERS

6. D) Tom Hanks
5. D) Pitcher
the Joe E. Brown All-Stars!
a baseball team for him called
4. C) Warner Brothers started
film *The Babe Ruth Story*.)
played Babe Ruth in the 1948
Gehrig. (William Bendix

George Brett's Secrets of Baseball—Triple.
A flashier video than most how-tos. And who knows more about hitting than eleven-time All-Star George Brett? There are lots of highlight clips as George shows the opposing pitcher his fine batting form.
25 min., VHS, Beta, $14.95

New World Video
1440 South Sepulveda Boulevard
Los Angeles, CA 90025
(213) 444-8100

Little League Baseball: Instruction for 8- to 14-Year-Olds—Double.
Two tapes—one on hitting and running, the other on pitching and fielding. The tapes offer all kinds of tricks for helping you master—and remember—good baseball form.
30 min., VHS, $9.99

Goodtimes/Kids Klassics Distribution Corp.
401 Fifth Avenue
New York, NY 10016
(212) 889-0044

Little League's Official How to Play Baseball Video—Double.
Almost all of the plays are shown and narrated by kids. The Little Leaguers help make this a lively tape.
70 min., VHS, Beta, $19.95

Mastervision
969 Park Avenue
New York, NY 10028
(212) 879-0448

Mickey Mantle's Baseball Tips for Kids of All Ages—Double.
Along with two Little Leaguers, Mickey Mantle leads you through baseball basics. A little

George Brett's powerhouse swing. To improve your swing, check out *George Brett's Secrets of Baseball*.

slow-moving, but they cover all the bases.
CBS Fox Sports Video (see page 135 for address).

This photo is a hint for question 3.

1. A) Boxing is first with 179 movies. Then come horse racing, football, and car racing, in that order. Baseball is fifth.

2. B) Counting cartoon versions, Casey's been done 11 times! The first film, in 1899, was a silent movie made by Thomas Alva Edison. The most recent movie about Casey is available at video stores. See page 131.

3. A) The Babe played himself in *The Pride of the Yankees*, the classic movie about Lou

TIPS FROM THE TAPES

It's a Hit. Most experts say that hitting is the hardest part of the sport. Here's a tip from *George Brett's Secrets of Baseball.* As you swing, keep your front foot pointing toward the plate. Don't let it "open up" and point toward the mound.

Heading "Down" to First. It's not enough just to hit the ball; you've got to beat the throw to first. In *Little League Baseball: How to Hit & Run,* Dr. Bragg Stockton offers this advice for sprinting to first base:

Keep your head down, your body leaning forward, and your toes pointing straight ahead. Your elbows should be parallel to the ground. Your fists should pump up and down, not across your body.

Rounding the Bag. Whenever you hit the ball out of the infield, you should *round* first base. That means, you're starting toward second—and, you hope, a double.

According to *Mickey Mantle's Baseball Tips for Kids of All Ages,* when rounding first you should touch the inside corner of the bag with your left foot. This saves time and helps you push off toward second.

Unfeeling Fielding. Here's a pain-saving tip from the *Little League's Official How-to-Play Baseball by Video.* Cup your hand inside your glove. The air space between the glove and your hand will help cushion the blow when you catch the ball.

Throw Straight. In *Baseball the Yankee Way,* old-timer Whitey Ford offers this important pitching reminder. Don't throw curveballs or other trick pitches until you're 16. You could hurt your arm and damage a future pitching career. Besides, a well-controlled fastball is enough to win lots of ball games.

Veteran stars Monte Irvin (left) and Jackie Robinson give pointers to Little Leaguers in 1962.

BASEBALL DRAMA CHECKLIST

Baseball has starred in more than just movies. It's been the subject of thousands of American artworks, from sculptures to comic strips. If you're interested in a complete guide to these works, check your library or bookstore for *Everything Baseball,* by James Mote (published by Prentice-Hall, Inc.). The book claims to list "every baseball song, poem, novel, play, movie, TV and radio show, painting, sculpture, comic strip, cartoon, and more"!

Printed opposite are two film checklists to get you started, one for baseball feature films, the other for baseball cartoons. With one exception, only films released since 1939 are listed. According to *Everything Baseball,* films made before that year are almost impossible to find. Also, feature films already listed in this chapter aren't listed again here.

Where indicated, some of these films are available on home video (ask your local video store to order). And just because it's not marked here as a home video release doesn't mean it hasn't been released on home video since this catalogue was written. Again, your local video store will have the most up-to-date listings.

For those films not yet on home video, watch your TV listings. And if you're lucky enough to live near a film and TV library collection such as New York's Museum of Broadcasting, you'll be able to check off many more films on these lists!

CHECKLIST FOR BASEBALL FEATURE FILMS

☐ *Angels in the Outfield*
MGM, 1951
☐ *The Babe Ruth Story*
Allied Artists
Productions, Inc., 1948
(Available on home video)
☐ *The Big Leaguer*
MGM, 1953
☐ *The Bingo Long Traveling All-Stars and Motor Kings*
Universal, 1976
(Available on home video)
☐ *Blue Skies Again*
Warner Bros., 1983
(Available on home video)
☐ *Brewster's Millions*
Universal Pictures, 1985
(Available on home video)
☐ *Fear Strikes Out*
Paramount Pictures, 1957
☐ *Goodbye, Franklin High*
Cal-Am Artists, 1978
☐ *The Great American Pastime*
MGM, 1956
☐ *The Heckler*
Columbia Pictures, 1940
☐ *Here Come the Tigers*
Filmways Pictures, 1978
American International Pictures
☐ *It Happened in Flatbush*
Twentieth Century-Fox, 1942
☐ *It Happens Every Spring*
Twentieth Century-Fox, 1949
☐ *It's My Turn*
Columbia Pictures, 1980

Rastar
(Available on home video)
☐ *The Jackie Robinson Story*
Eagle-Lion, 1950
(Available on home video)
☐ *Jim Thorpe—All American*
Warner Bros., 1951
(Available on home video)
☐ *The Kid from Cleveland*
Republic Pictures Corp., 1949
☐ *The Kid from Left Field*
Twentieth Century-Fox, 1953
☐ *Kill the Umpire*
Columbia Pictures, 1950
☐ *Ladies' Day*
RKO Radio Pictures, 1943
☐ *Lovable Trouble*
Columbia Pictures, 1941
☐ *Mr. Noisy*
Columbia Pictures, 1946
(Remake of *The Heckler*)
☐ *The Pride of St. Louis*
Twentieth Century-Fox, 1952
☐ *Rhubarb*
Paramount Pictures, 1951
☐ *Roogie's Bump*
Republic Pictures Corp., John Bash Productions, 1954
☐ *Safe at Home!*
Columbia Pictures Corp., Naud-Hamilburg Productions, 1962
☐ *The Slugger's Wife*
Columbia Pictures Corp., Rastar, 1985
☐ *Stealing Home*
Warner Bros., 1988
☐ *The Stratton Story*
MGM, 1949
☐ *Take Me Out to the Ball Game*
MGM, 1948
(Available on home video)
☐ *Two Mugs from Brooklyn*
Favorite Films, 1942
☐ *Whistling in Brooklyn*
MGM, 1944
☐ *The Winning Team*
Warner Bros., 1952

Say it ain't so, Charlie Sheen! In *Eight Men Out*, he and other players lose the World Series on purpose.

CHECKLIST FOR BASEBALL CARTOONS

☐ *Abner the Baseball*
Paramount Pictures
Corp., 1961

☐ *The Ball Game*
(Aesop's Fables)
Van Beuren Corp., 1932
(Available on home
video)

☐ *Base on Bawls*
(Starring Mr. Magoo)
UPA Pictures, Inc., 1960

☐ *Baseball*
(Starring Roger Ramjet)
Ken Snyder Productions,
1965

☐ *Baseball Bugs*
(Bugs Bunny)
Warner Bros., 1946

☐ *Base Brawl*
Paramount Pictures, Inc.

☐ *Bats in the Ballpark*
(Starring King and Odie)
Total Television
Productions, Inc., and
Leonardo Productions,
1962

☐ *Battery Up*
(Starring Popeye)
King Features
Productions, 1962

☐ *Batty Baseball*
MGM, 1944

☐ *The Berenstain Bears
Play Ball*
(Starring the Berenstain
Bears)
NBC, 1983
(Available on home
video)

☐ *Big League Freddie*
(The Flintstones)
Hanna-Barbera
Productions, 1964

☐ *The Case of the Big Ball
Game*
(Starring Courageous
Cat and Minute Mouse)
Trans-Artists
Productions, Inc., 1961

☐ *Casey at the Bat*
Walt Disney Produc-
tions, 1946
(Available on home
video)

☐ *Casey at the Bat*
McGraw-Hill Book Co.,
1966

☐ *Casey at the Bat*
Concord, 1968

☐ *Casey at the Bat*
AIMS Instructional
Media, Inc., 1976

☐ *Casey Bats Again*
Walt Disney Produc-
tions, 1954

☐ *Charlie Brown's
All-Stars*
(Starring the Peanuts
gang)
CBS, 1966
(Available on home
video)

☐ *Clyde Crashcup Invents
Baseball*
(Starring Clyde
Crashcup)
Format Films and
Bagadasarian Film
Corp., 1962

☐ *Dinky at the Bat*
(Starring Dinky Dog)
Hanna-Barbera
Productions, 1979

☐ *The Foul Ball Player*
Paramount Pictures,
1940

☐ *Gone Batty*
(A Looney Tune Cartoon)
Warner Bros.

☐ *The Horse That Played
Center Field*
ABC, 1979

☐ *How to Be a Good
Umpire*
(Starring Mr. Know It All)
Hooper Productions in
association with Jay
Ward Productions, 1964

☐ *How to Play Baseball*
Walt Disney Produc-
tions, 1942
(Available on home
video)

☐ *Kiddie League*
(starring Woody
Woodpecker), 1959

☐ *King of Swat*
(Starring Tooter Turtle)
Total Television
Productions, Inc., and
Leonardo Productions,
1962

☐ *Ladies' Day*
(Starring the Flintstones)
Hanna-Barbera
Productions, 1963

☐ *The Late T.C.*
(Starring Top Cat)
Hanna-Barbera
Productions, 1962

☐ *The Little Big League*
(Winsome Witch)
Hanna-Barbera
Productions, 1967

☐ *Mexican Baseball*
(starring Gandy Goose)
Twentieth Century-Fox,
1947

☐ *Nine Strikes, You're Out*
(Starring Atom Ant)
Hanna-Barbera
Productions, 1966

☐ *Operation Barney*
(Starring the Flintstones)
Hanna-Barbera
Productions, 1962

☐ *Porky's Baseball
Broadcast*
(Starring Porky Pig)
Warner Bros., 1940

☐ *Slide, Donald, Slide*
(starring Donald Duck)
Walt Disney Produc-
tions, 1949

☐ *Take Me Out to the Ball
Game*
(Starring the Flintstones)
Hanna-Barbera
Productions, 1962

☐ *Take Me Out to the
Brawl Game*
(Starring Popeye)
Hanna-Barbera
Productions, 1979

☐ *Take Me Up to the Ball
Game*
Nelvana Ltd., 1982
(Available on home
video)

THE BEST AND THE WORST

MOST MEMORABLE: Many thought it would never be broken. Babe Ruth's record of 714 career home runs seemed untouchable. But on April 8, 1974, Hank Aaron knocked his 715th out of the park.

Aaron went on to rack up 755 four-baggers. But it was his 715th that people would remember.

Tug McGraw had a good lifetime ERA of 3.13. But he made it into the Hall of Shame (see story on this page).

In 1976, sports writers voted that homer the most memorable moment in all of baseball history.

FOR SHAME: Few players make the Hall of Fame. What's worst, they may enter Bruce Nash and Allan Zullo's *Baseball Hall of Shame!* To be listed in this series of books, you have to make one of the worst—and zaniest—plays ever.

For instance, there's the time the 1965 Mets let the Pirates turn a routine ground ball into a grand slam.

To do it, the Mets made three errors in one play. And when it was over, no one was "out" except the Mets pitcher, Tug McGraw. Tug swore at his teammates so loudly that he was thrown out of the game.

FLIPP TIPPS

You can't exactly lug a VCR out onto the baseball diamond to check up on proper form. But there is a kind of video that you can carry in your pocket and view whenever you like.

Known as "Flipp Tipps," these are small flip books of famous players in action. When you flip the pages fast, the image appears to move as in a movie or video. By using "Flipp Tipps," you can check out Mickey Mantle's swing just before you make your own.

Visionation, Inc., makes these little flip books and sells them for $6.95 each. The company is in Los Angeles. You can get more information or order the books over the phone by calling toll free: (800) 388-8832.

PINSTRIPE POWER
WHERE TO GET AUTHENTIC UNIFORMS AND OTHER EQUIPMENT

HOME

ROAD

You can play some forms of baseball with almost no equipment at all. For a pickup game of stickball, for instance, all you need is a broom handle and a rubber ball.

But if you play hardball on any kind of serious team, there's a lot of equipment you'll need—from a mitt to a batting helmet to a uniform.

These listings will give you a broad selection of equipment to choose from. You can buy or order most of this equipment through your local sporting goods store. But some of the specialty items listed here are available only through the companies that make them. You'll find every-

thing here from decals for your team's batting helmets to a special device for breaking in your glove.

Some of the companies listed here take mail and phone orders. They'll probably have a catalogue they can send you.

Some company catalogues are free, while other companies charge a fee. If the company has an 800 number, that's toll free. So there's no cost for calling and finding out if they'll send you a catalogue, how much the catalogue costs, and whether or not you can buy equipment directly from them.

Many of the companies listed in this chapter are too big to sell to individuals. *They'll sell only in large quantities, to a whole team, say.* Or, in some cases, to a whole

league. If they do sell to an individual, they'll have to add a large service charge. That makes it cheaper to buy some of these products from a sporting goods store, since stores buy at the bulk rate.

On the other hand, a few of these large companies also sell mail-order items. Hillerich and Bradsby, the bat makers, for instance, sell most of their products only to sporting goods stores or to major and minor league players. But they do offer some mail-order items that you can buy directly from them, such as a personalized bat (your name goes on it), bat key chains, and bat racks and hangers.

And, even if the company sells only in bulk, they will probably be able to direct you to a store that carries their product.

HOW TO USE THESE LISTINGS

Under each item of equipment there is a list of some of the companies that carry it. First find the item you're interested in. *Now turn to the second half of the chapter (starting on page 158) to find the address and phone number of the*

THE BULL PEN
Q: What was the baseball mitt arrested for?
A: Breaking in.

company. The companies are listed in alphabetical order.

Few know it, but women have been playing organized baseball since 1875!

PLAYING EQUIPMENT

ATHLETIC JACKETS AND PARKAS

Many large sporting goods stores can add numbers and letters to jackets and parkas. In fact, the first company in this list (ADC) makes and sells the equipment for lettering the jackets. They sell this to sports stores.

If you're only looking for a jacket for yourself, or for a small group, use the local store. Most of the following companies handle very large bulk orders only.

ADC (Athletic Die Co.)
Aladen Athletic Wear
Alpha Sportswear
Antler
Artex Mfg. Company
Bacharach Rasin Sporting Goods
Bike Athletic Company
Bristol Products Corp.
Buccaneer Mfg. Co.
Butwin Sportswear Co.
Centralia Knitting Mills
Chalk Line
Challenger/General
CMG/Cannon Sports
Cran Barry
Dunbrooke Sportswear Co.
Empire Sporting Goods Mfg. Co.
Fab-Knit Manufacturing Co.
Famous Sportswear Specialty Co.
Felco Athletic Wear Co.
Four Seasons Garment Co.
Gameday/Raceday Sportswear
Gem Sportswear
Hanco-M. Handelsman Co.
Hartwell Garment Co.
Hascall Sportswear
Hatchers Manufacturing
Hi Style Lettered Sportswear Co.
Hilton Athletic Apparel
Horizon Sportswear
Joslin's
King Louie International
Leslie, Richard A. Co.
Maple Mfg. Co.
Mark V Sales
Meca Sportswear
Needlecraft of Woonsocket
Nike
Rainbow Sports Enterprises
Rennoc
Roman Art-Roman Pro Lara
Russell Athletic
Sipes, Howe K. Co.
Southland Athletic Mfg. Co.
Spalding Sports Worldwide
Speedline Athletic Wear
Starter Sportswear
Swingster Athletic Apparel
T.M. Athletics
Transorient
Wilson Sporting Goods Co.

ATHLETIC SUPPORTERS

Athletic supports—or "jock straps," as they are more commonly called—are a necessary part of any male ball player's equipment. According to Mark Atwater, starting at about age six or seven boys should wear them whenever they play.

Mark Atwater is the president of Royal Textile Mills in Yanceyville, North Carolina. His company makes over a million "Duke" athletic supporters a year.

"As soon as you get past the T-ball stage, you should be wearing an athletic supporter with a protective cup," says Mr. Atwater.

In addition to athletic supporters, his company also makes shin pads, wrist bands, and knee and ankle supports. But, for all of their products, they deal only with sporting goods stores and a few pro teams.

So, unless you're buying for a large team or league of players, go through a sporting goods store.

Alchester Mills Co.
All Star Sporting Goods
Bacharach Rasin Sporting Goods
Becton Dickinson & Company
Bike Athletic Co.
Champion Products
CMG/Cannon Sports
Empire Sporting Goods Mfg. Co.
Franklin Sports Industries
Hanco-M. Handelsman Co.
Pennsylvania Sporting Goods Co.
Richardson Sports
Royal Textile Mills
Standard Merchandising Co.
Swingster Athletic Apparel
Venus Knitting Mills
Wilson Sporting Goods Co.

BALLS

Major league teams go through whole bags of balls in a day. (In a major league game, once the ball is scuffed, it's set aside.)

But, again, you can probably get all the baseballs you need at a local store. The companies listed below want orders in the hundreds.

The Automated Batting Cages Corporation (ABC) will sell balls in quantities as low as a dozen. But these aren't regular leather hardballs we're talking about. These are polyurethane, seamless, dimpled practice balls meant for use in pitching machines. You can't use them in official games. But for practice they're waterproof, cheap, and long-lasting.

ABC's main business is the making and selling of coin-operated batting cage systems where you put in a quarter, say, for every 10 pitches. A pitching machine hurls the balls over the plate and you practice your hitting. To find a coin-operated batting cage in your area, check your Yellow Pages telephone book under "Batting Cages."

Of course, if you've got a whole *lot* of money on hand, you can set up your own batting cage system. ABC sells the cages for about $100,000 apiece.

Andia Progress Co.
Automated Batting Cages Corp.
Bacharach Rasin Sporting Goods
Baden Sports
Bravo International
BSN Corporation
Champion Sports Products Co.
CMG/Cannon Sports
Collette Mfg. Co.
Cooper International

Diamond Sports Company
Franklin Sports Industries
General Sportcraft Co.
Hutch Sporting Goods Company
Jelinek Sports
Kenko Sports International
Kent Sporting Goods Company
MacGregor Sporting Goods
Markwort Sporting Goods Co.
Master Pitching Machine
North American Recreation
Pick Point Enterprises
Pinckard Baseballs & Softballs
Rawlings Sporting Goods Co.
Regent Sports Corp.
Renosol Corporation
Richardson Sports
Spalding Sports Worldwide
Sportime
Steele's Sports Co.
T.G. Sports Co.
U. S. Games
Wa-Mac
Wilson Sporting Goods Co.
Winston Sports Corp.
Worth Sports Co.

BAT GRIPS AND TAPES

You step up to the plate. It's up to you to bang in the winning run. Just then, your hands start to sweat. And the bat slips in your hand.

To avoid this, many bats have special grips or tape on the handle. If you have an untaped bat, you can buy a grip for it at the local sports store.

The companies below make some of the different kinds of bat grips and tapes. Grabbit Grip Products, for instance, makes a plastic-rubber grip that you can wrap on yourself without any glue or tape.

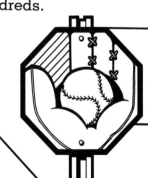

SHORTSTOPS
An official major league hardball must weigh between 5 and 5¼ ounces.

Grabbit deals mainly in large orders. For an order of 144 grips, their price is $1.75 per grip. They're willing to handle a smaller order, but they'll have to add a service charge. In the stores, their retail price is $3.95 to $4.95.

Bat Grips
Easton Sports
Grabbit Grip Products
Ideal Tape, Inc./Athletic Division
Johar of California
Physicians & Nurses Mfg. Corp.
SSK America Incorporated
Totes

Bat Tape
ATEC
Bacharach Rasin Sporting Goods
CMG/Cannon Sports
Easton Aluminum
Gexco Enterprises
Grabbit Grip Products
Hillerich and Bradsby Co., Inc.
Ideal Tape, Inc./Athletic Division
Totes, Inc.
Vukas Products
Worth Sports Company

BAT WEIGHTS

Bat weights are used by the pros when they warm up in the on-deck circle. The weights make the bat heavier and then make the unweighted bat seem light and easy to swing hard. But these weights have been outlawed in some places. They can come flying off the bat and hurt people.

Not only that, some experts feel that kids shouldn't use weights of any kind, since their bodies are still forming.

Bacharach Rasin Sporting Goods
Champion Sports Products Co.
CMG/Cannon Sports
Markworth Sporting Goods Co.
Pennsylvania Sporting Goods Co.
Regent Sports Corp.
Worth Sports Company

BATS

On average, a major league ball player uses up to 25 bats a season! Many use more—players such as Bo Jackson, for instance. He's known for snapping bats like twigs over his thigh in moments of frustration.

Not only do the major leaguers use a lot of bats, but they have very special bat requirements. Hillerich and Bradsby, the famous bat makers, keep more than 300 special bat specifications on file for major league players.

For most of us mere mortals, however, one or two bats can last a lifetime. Especially if the bat is made of aluminum.

Among kids, the popularity of aluminum bats continues to grow. It's easy to see why. Aluminum bats last longer and hit farther.

On the other hand, wooden bats have tradition and history—and the major leagues—on their side. It's unlikely that the majors will allow aluminum anytime soon.

Most sporting goods stores carry bats, both aluminum and wood, in all sizes, and store personnel can advise you about a good size for you. You can also get catalogues from some of the large bat makers listed below. You can use these catalogues in ordering from the store. And some of the companies, such as H&B, offer certain bats through mail order.

Aluminum Athletic Equipment Co.
Bacharach Rasin Sporting Goods
Cooper International
Easton Aluminum
Easton Sports
General Sportcraft Co.
Hillerich and Bradsby Co.
Hutch Sporting Goods Co.
Jayfro Corp.
MacGregor Sporting Goods
Markwort Sporting Goods Co.
Marshall-Clark Mfg. Co.
North American Recreation
Pick Point Enterprises, Inc.
Rawlings Sporting Goods Co.
Regent Sports Corp.
Richardson Sports
Show-Tags
Spalding Sports Worldwide
Sportsotron, Inc. and Hy Sport
Steele's Sports Co.
T.G. Sports Co.
U.S. Games Inc.
Venus Knitting Mills
Wilson Sporting Goods Co.
Winston Sports Corp.
Wittek Golf Supply Co.
Worth Sports Company

BATTING HELMETS/ FACEGUARDS

Batting helmets are a must when playing hardball. Getting hit with a hardball pitch is no joke. If your team doesn't supply them, you can get them yourself at a sporting goods store. If the store doesn't have what you want, they should be able to order it from one of the major suppliers listed below.

Faceguards provide added protection for the batter. These are see-through plastic guards that fit onto the helmet and protect your face from the nose up.

All Star Sporting Goods
American Baseball Cap, Inc.
Apsco Sports Enterprises
Bacharach Rasin Sporting Goods
Champion Sports Products Co.
CMG/Cannon Sports
Face Guards
Hutch Sporting Goods Co.
Joslin's
MacGregor Sporting Goods
Markwort Sporting Goods Co.
Nocona Athletic Goods Co.
Pro-tec
Rawlings Sporting Goods Co.
Riddell
Schutt Mfg. Co.
Unique Sports Products
U.S. Games
Wilson Sporting Goods Co.
Wittek Golf Supply Co.

CAPS

Baseball caps come in different materials, from polyester to wool (which is warmer) to twill to corduroy. The majors mainly use a polyester and wool mix. Some caps come with a mesh back, to keep you cool. Others have a solid back, to keep you warm.

If you're looking for a souvenir cap as a fan, you'll need to go to the stadium of your team or sporting goods store.

Stores can order caps for your own team from the distributors listed below. Or, if you've got a large order, your team may be able to order directly from the cap maker. California Headwear, for example, has a minimum order of 50 hats. If you give them artwork for your team's logo, their machines can embroider it onto each cap.

AJD Cap Company
Apsco Enterprises
California Headwear
Derby Cap Mfg. Co.
Eddy Bros. Co.
EDS West
Fairfield Line
Famous Sportswear Specialty Co.
Farnham Hall Sportswear
Foremost Athletic Apparel
Funk Bros. Hat & Cap Co.
Goorin Bros.
Huffer Corporation
Julie Hat Co.
Kratish Hat & Cap Co.
Leader Mfg. Co.
London Cap Co.
Louisville Mfg. Co.
New Era Cap Co.

Northern Cap Mfg. Co.
Pearson, Drew Enterprises
Pioneer Industries
Pro Line Cap Co.
Roman Art-Roman Pro-Lara
Segal International
Sportcap
Sports Specialties
Stevens Hat Co.
Town Talk Cap Mfg. Co.

CLEATS

Cleats are the little metal spikes on baseball shoes that help you grip the ground as you run. You'll need to go through a sporting goods store for this item. Cleat makers send the cleats—just the cleats, not the shoes—to stores. The cleats screw into the shoes.

Blazer Manufacturing Co.
General Sportcraft Co.
Gold Medal Recreational Products
MacNeill Engineering Co.
Richardson Sports

COACHING JACKETS

This is a style of windbreaker popular among coaches, especially coaches of youth teams. Sporting goods stores carry them. They can order them from the large distributors listed below.

Centralia Knitting Mills
Challenger/General
Champion Products
JPM Company
Leslie, Richard A. Co.
Louisville Mfg. Co.
Powers Mfg. Co.

Rainbow Sports Enterprises
Swingster Athletic Apparel

CUP SUPPORTERS

Cups are hard-plastic protectors worn by male players to protect the groin. (See Athletic Supporters.) Purchase them at the sporting goods store unless you're ordering a large quantity.

Alchester Mills Co.
Becton Dickinson & Co.
Bike Athletic Co.
Cooper International
Flaherty, John B. Co.
Franklin Sports Industries
Standard Merchandising Co.

DECALS

The decal companies listed here can help you decorate your team's batting helmets. Award Decals, for instance, makes decals of team logos for $1.50 each (on a minimum order of 15).

All they would need from you (in addition to the money!) is a copy of your team's logo. How do you get that? You can xerox it off your baseball cap. Send them the xerox and they'll make up the decals. For more information, call their toll-free 800 number.

Award Decals
Chase-Taylor Company
Collegiate Pacific
Muehleisen Mfg. Co.
SportDecals

MAKING BATS AND BASEBALLS

BALLS

Small changes in a baseball can have a big effect on how it acts in a game (see the "Balata Ball" article on page 148). When Rawlings makes an official major league ball, they have to follow countless rules. For example, the cork center with its rubber coat must weigh $7/8$ ounce.

The rubber-lined cork center is wound tightly with layers of yarn and wool. (The tighter the winding, the livelier the ball.)

First they wind a layer of blue-gray yarn, then a layer of white wool, then another layer of blue-gray yarn. Now comes a layer of white cotton yarn. In all, that's about a quarter of a mile's worth of yarn wrapped inside every baseball!

Next this yarnball is coated with rubber cement. The cover goes on in two pieces that are stitched together by hand.

When the ball is dry, it's ready for testing in a driving range, to see if it comes off the bat at the exact speed required by the majors.

BATS

It takes a long time to make a wooden bat. For one thing, bats have to age, like cheese! Here's an overview of the process.

Step One: Lumber companies chop down ash trees. Ash wood is considered to be the most powerful. The ash tree is cut into 40-inch-long pieces that are stacked up to dry for one or two years. If this process is botched, the bat will be weak.

Step Two: The bats are "turned" on a lathe, a machine that spins and cuts the wood to a certain shape. The wood is sanded and put into a flame to harden its outside.

Step Three: The trademark is inscribed onto the bat—sometimes with a player's signature. The bat is coated with a lacquer to seal the wood and protect it.

Since major leaguers are finicky about the exact size and shape of their favorite bats, some bat makers store the bat models in a fireproof vault. When the player wants more bats, they bring out the model and copy it.

Bats are a crucial part of a player's game. Many star players visit the bat makers in person to oversee the process. You yourself can visit a batmaker. Hillerich and Bradsby, one of the oldest and most famous, offers daily free tours of its $6\frac{1}{2}$-acre factory, Slugger Park, in Jeffersonville, Indiana (see page 94 for details).

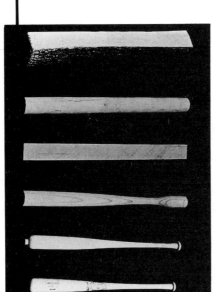

DIE-CUT LETTERS AND NUMERALS

Companies such as Bomark Sportswear in Houston provide a relatively cheap way to number and letter team T-shirts. Bomark offers an iron-on kit for lettering a whole team's shirts for $47.85 (that's with the fuzzy flocked material) or for $57.35 (with film).

Bomark Group
Centralia Knitting Mills
Crown Prince
Dyer Specialty Co.
Insta Graphic Systems
Midwest Lettering Co.
Quik-Set Lettering
Rainbow Sports Enterprises
Roman Art-Roman Pro Lara Ltd.
SportDecals
Troy Corp.

FOOD SUPPLEMENTS

Drinking a lot of water during a game can make you feel heavy and tired. So companies have come up with special sport drinks, such as Gatorade, Quick Kick, and Mueller Sport Drink. These drinks vary in terms of calories, salt, and other factors.

You can get more specific information from the companies listed below. They'll be able to direct you to the dealer closest to you.

Drackett Company
Mueller Sports Medicine
Quaker Oats Company (Gatorade)
Ross Laboratories (Exceed)
Twin Laboratories

GLOVE OIL

One of the pleasures of owning a fine mitt is the fun of oiling it. It needs it, too, to keep it from hardening and, eventually, cracking. But mitts don't need to be oiled that often. In fact, once a year is probably plenty.

On the other hand, over-oiling doesn't do much harm, though it can make the glove a little heavier.

Neat's-foot oil is the oil most often used. Some players use mink oil or saddle soap. You can get neat's-foot at most hardware or sporting goods stores. If you have any trouble finding these products, large distributors are listed below. Cramer, for example, will direct you to the store nearest you, or sell to you directly if there's no outlet in your area.

Bacharach Rasin Sporting Goods
CMG/Cannon Sports
Cooper International
Cramer Products
Easton Sports
Franklin Sports Industries
General Sportcraft Co.
Hillerich and Bradsby Co.
Hutch Sporting Goods Co.
MacGregor Sporting Goods
Pennsylvania Sporting Goods Co.
Rawlings Sporting Goods Co.
Regent Sports Corp.
Saranac Glove Co.
Spalding Sports Worldwide
Wa-Mac

GLOVE REPAIR

The owner, founder, and sole employee of the American Baseball Glove Company is Ray Piagentini. For as little as $3 (or

BALATA BALL

When home-run hitters around the league aren't hitting lots of homers, the opposing pitchers rarely get much credit. People start to wonder, is there something wrong with the baseballs?

Slight changes in the way hardballs are made *can* make a difference in players' home-run production. There are lively balls that seem to jump off the bat and carry for miles. And there are less lively balls that don't seem to want to leave the ballpark, ever.

For instance, in 1943 the United States needed rubber for its war effort. So the major leagues started the season by using special "balata balls."

The balls used rubbery balata from balata trees instead of rubber. Balata is used in a lot of golf balls, but it didn't work

out in baseballs. The balata balls were used for 72 games. During those games, American League hitters managed only nine home runs.

Then new balls were brought in. That same day, in the American League six of these new balls went out of the park for home runs.

as much as $20, depending on how much repair is involved), Mr. Piagentini will repair your mitt's webbing, recondition the glove, and give you instructions on better mitt care.

Players all over the country send Mr. Piagentini their broken mitts. Catcher's mitts are the ones he most often has to repair. (No wonder, with the pitcher steaming the ball into it, pitch after pitch!)

American Baseball Glove Co.

GLOVE SHAPER

Staco Enterprises in Overland Park, Kansas, offers a new baseball and softball glove shaper device. According to Staco, many pros are now using these shapers to break in their new mitts.

The device fits in the pocket of a ball glove. Its three bendable fingers hold the pocket in the shape you want, breaking in the pocket in two to three days. Storing the device in the glove when not in use will help the pocket keep the shape.

Staco handles single orders. The shaper is $7.95 plus $2.00 for postage and handling.

Staco Enterprises

GLOVES—BATTING AND FIELDING

Rusty Staub is said to be the man who made batting gloves popular in the majors. He got so many hits with them, it's no wonder they caught on.

Batting gloves help in two ways. They help you grip the bat—or grip the grip, if you've added a batting grip or tape. The gloves can also cut down on the stinging pain caused by the bat vibrating in your hand when you hit the ball.

You can also wear a special glove-within-a-glove while fielding. These so-called palm-guard gloves give your hand extra protection from pain when catching those wicked line drives.

Get both through the local sports store. They can order from the large distributors below.

All Star Sporting Goods
Andia Progress Co.
Bacharach Rasin Sporting Goods
Champion Glove Mfg. Co.
CMG/Cannon Sports
Crown Global Corp.
Dorson Sports
Easton Sports
Flaherty, John B. Co.
Franklin Sports Industries
Game Master Athletic Co.
General Sportcraft Co.
Hutch Sporting Goods Company
Jelinek Sports
MacGregor Sporting Goods

Markwort Sporting Goods Co.
Midwest Glove Co.
North American Recreation
Regent Sports Corp.
Richardson Sports
Rodel
Saranac Glove Co.
Show-Tags
Spalding Sports Worldwide
Sportsotron, Inc. and Hy Sport
SSK American Incorporated
Steele's Sports Co.
Trophy Glove Co.
U.S. Games
Venus Knitting Mills
Wilson Sporting Goods Co.
Worth Sports Company

GLOVES—CATCHER, FIELDER, AND FIRST BASE

When people think about buying baseball equipment, the first thing they think about getting is the mitt.

A baseball mitt is a special item. Mitt owners often take pride in (and feel quite attached to) a well-broken-in, well-oiled glove.

Outfielders tend to use longer gloves for snagging flies. Infielders may want a shorter glove so they can get the ball out of the glove in a hurry.

Rawlings, one of the largest and oldest glove makers in the country, makes gloves in all sizes and styles. Rawlings gloves sell for a range of prices. The top of the line is their Gold Glove (named after the fielding awards that Rawlings gives every year—see Chapter 12).

What Rawlings recommends is starting with one of their cheaper gloves, learning to care for it properly, and then gradually moving up the line.

Rawlings, like most glove makers, sells only through their dealers, the sporting goods stores. The dealer will have their catalogue. (Rawlings doesn't send out copies to individual consumers.)

What should you look for in a glove? You'll need to go to a sporting goods store and try on mitts till you find one that feels comfortable for you. Then, you'll have to see if it plays well at your position.

Amko
Andia Progress Co.
Bacharach Rasin Sporting Goods
Champion Sports Products Co.
CMG/Cannon Sports
Collette Mfg. Co.
Cooper International
Easton Sports
Franklin Sports Industries
Hillerich and Bradsby Co.
Hutch Sporting Goods Co.
Jelinek Sports
MacGregor Sporting Goods
Markwort Sporting Goods Co.
Nelson/Weather-Rite Products
Nocona Athletic Goods Co.
North American Recreation
Rawlings Sporting Goods Co.
Regent Sports Corp.
Show-Tags
Spalding Sports Worldwide
Sportsotron, Inc. and Hy Sport

SSK America Incorporated
U.S. Games, Inc.
Wilson Sporting Goods Co.
Winston Sports Corp.

GRIPPING AIDS

More tapes and other sticky products for helping batters grip the bat (see Bat Grips, above).

Alchester Mills Co.
Gexco Enterprises
Pennsylvania Sporting Goods Co.
Physicians & Nurses Mfg. Corp.
Pitt Barbell & Healthfood Corp.
Standard Merchandising Co.
Surgrip U.S.A.
Unique Sports Products
Vukas Products Inc.

HEAT TRANSFERS

A common method for adding team names, logos, and numbers to uniforms, T-shirts, etc. Your local sporting goods store can order through the following companies.

Centralia Knitting Mills
Crown Prince
Holoubek Studios Iron-On
Insta Graphic Systems
Lone Star Athletic Designs
Midwest Lettering Company
Quik-Set Lettering Inc.

JACKETS

Sporting goods stores can handle team orders for team jackets with team names and logos either sewn on or put on with heat transfers. (Sewn-on patches last longer and

cost more.)

Stores can order the jackets for you through the following companies.

Alpha Sportswear
Butwin Sportswear Co.
Centralia Knitting Mills
Champion Products
Collegiate Pacific
Farnham Hall Sportswear
Holloway Sportswear
Leslie, Richard A. Co.
Majestic Athletic Wear
Meca Sportswear
Needlecraft of Woonsocket
Powers Mfg. Co.
Pyramid Outerwear
Rainbow Sports Enterprises
Roman Art-Roman Pro Lara
Venus Knitting Mills
Wilson Sporting Goods Co.
Wolf, H., & Sons

JERSEYS

In sportswear, the term jersey usually refers to a replica of a major league uniform. Many youth teams use these. If the uniform is letterless and numberless, that's called a uniform. The idea is that you'll have the sporting goods store add the team name and the player's name and number.

Your sporting goods store can order from the following companies:

Alpha Sportswear
Bomark Mills
Champion Products
Collegiate Pacific
Farnham Hall Sportswear
Majestic Athletic Wear
New Era Knitting Mills
Powers Mfg. Co.

BATTER UP!
HOW TO PICK THE RIGHT BAT

According to Hillerich and Bradsby (makers of the Louisville Slugger), a bat that's too long and heavy won't help you. To hit the ball longer and harder, they say, you need to swing the bat faster. That means, you need a bat that's just the right size for you.

Here are the charts H&B uses to help boys and girls pick the right-sized bat. Find your weight on the left. Then move your finger straight across to the column that lists your height. Your finger should now be resting on the length of the perfect bat for you!

BATS FOR BOYS

Player Weight	Batter's Height								
	3'-3'4"	3'5"-3'8"	3'9"-4'	4'1"-4'4"	4'5"-4'8"	4'9"-5'	5'1"-5'4"	5'5"-5'8"	5'9"-6'
Under 60 lbs.	26"	27"	28"	29"	29"	—	—	—	—
61-70	27"	27"	28"	29"	29"	30"	—	—	—
71-80	—	28"	28"	29"	30"	30"	31"	—	—
81-90	—	28"	29"	29"	30"	30"	31"	32"	—
91-100	—	28"	29"	30"	30"	31"	31"	32"	—
101-110	—	29"	29"	30"	30"	31"	31"	32"	—
111-120	—	29"	29"	30"	30"	31"	31"	32"	—
121-130	—	29"	30"	30"	30"	31"	32"	33"	33"
131-140	—	29"	30"	30"	31"	31"	32"	33"	34"
141-150	—	—	30"	30"	31"	31"	32"	33"	34"
151-160	—	—	30"	31"	31"	32"	32"	33"	34"
Over 160	—	—	—	31"	31"	32"	32"	33"	34"

BATS FOR GIRLS

Player Weight	Batter's Height						
	3'5"-3'9"	3'10"-4'	4'1"-4'4"	4'5"-4'8"	4'9"-5'	5'1"-5'4"	5'5"-5'9"
Under 40 lbs.	26"	26"	27"	28"	—	—	—
40-45 lbs.	26"	27"	28"	29"	30"	—	—
46-50 lbs.	26"	27"	28"	29"	30"	—	—
51-60 lbs.	27"	27"	28"	29"	30"	31"	—
61-70 lbs.	27"	28"	29"	30"	31"	32"	—
71-80 lbs.	27"	28"	29"	30"	31"	32"	33"
81-90 lbs.	—	29"	30"	31"	32"	33"	33"
91-100 lbs.	—	29"	30"	31"	32"	33"	34"
101-110 lbs.	—	—	30"	31"	32"	33"	34"
111-120 lbs.	—	—	31"	32"	33"	34"	34"
121-130 lbs.	—	—	31"	32"	33"	34"	34"
Over 130 lbs.	—	—	—	32"	33"	34"	34"

Girls competing for #1 honors in the Little League World Series.

Rawlings Sporting Goods Co.
Soffe, M.J., Co.
Sports Belle
Venus Knitting Mills

LETTERING

These stick-on letters and numbers are applied with a heat-transfer machine. Your local sporting goods store can order through the following companies.

Centralia Knitting Mills
Dalco Athletic Lettering
Holoubek Studios Iron-On Express
Lone Star Athletic Designs
Meistergram
Miracle-Grip Lettering
Quik-Set Lettering
Rainbow Sports Enterprises
Roman Art-Roman Pro Lara
Stahls'
Troy Corp.

MASKS

Catchers and umpires should wear masks, even in a casual pickup game of softball. Any player—even a major leaguer—can accidentally throw a bat. It might simply slip out of his hands.

Your local sporting goods store can order masks from some of the following large distributors.

All Star Sporting Goods
Bacharach Rasin Sporting Goods
Champion Sports Products Co.
CMG/Cannon Sports
Cooper International
Hutch Sporting Goods Co.

Jelinek Sports
MacGregor Sporting Goods
Markwort Sporting Goods Co.
North American Recreation
Rawlings Sporting Goods Co.
U.S. Games
Venus Knitting Mills
Wilson Sporting Goods Co.

PINE-TAR CLOTHS

Pine tar is a black, sticky substance. Players use pine-tar cloths to put the goo on their hands and bat to improve the grip. (See page 163)—"The Infamous Pine Tar Incident.")

Check your local sporting goods store. Large distributors are listed below.

All Star Sporting Goods
Bacharach Rasin Sporting Goods
Cooper International
MacGregor Sporting Goods
Markwort Sporting Goods Co.
North American Recreation
Pennsylvania Sporting Goods Co.
Rawlings Sporting Goods Co.
Vukas Products
Worth Sports Company

PITCHER'S TOE PLATES

A pitcher's motion is a complicated thing. When a winning pitcher starts to lose lots of games, coaches and announcers start to analyze his motion. Maybe something has gone wrong with the pitcher's "mechanics," they say. They mean his body

motion as he delivers the pitch.

If you watch the delivery of a major league pitcher in slow motion, you'll see that he scrapes either the left or right foot along the ground with each pitch. It's all part of trying to heave that ball at the plate even faster. But it can be kind of hard on the toes.

So pitchers wear plastic toe plates to protect themselves. If you're a pitcher and have this problem, you can get a toe plate at your sporting goods store, or they can order one for you from the companies listed below. The plates come in lefty and righty shapes and in different foot sizes.

Bolco Athletic Co.
MacGregor Sporting Goods
North American Recreation
Poly Enterprises
Tuff Toe

PROTECTIVE GEAR— CATCHER, UMPIRE

If you're catching or umping a hardball game, you'll need padding. Listed below are some of the large distributors. Your sporting goods store can order from the following companies.

All Star Sporting Goods
Apex Athletic Equipment
Bacharach Rasin Sporting Goods
Bike Athletic Co.

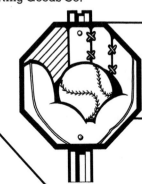

SHORTSTOPS
First baseman Hank Greenberg used such a long glove that a rule was passed limiting first basemen to mitts 12 inches long and 8 inches wide.

Champion Sports Products Co.
CMG/Cannon Sports
Cooper International
Easton Sports
Flaherty, John B. Co.
Hutch Sporting Goods Co.
Jelinek Sports
MacGregor Sporting Goods
Markwort Sporting Goods Co.
Nocona Athletic Goods Co.
North American Recreation
Rawlings Sporting Goods Co.
Royal Textile Mills
Safe-Play Tuf Wear Mfg. Co.
U.S. Games
Venus Knitting Mills
Wilson Sporting Goods Co.

ROSIN

That's the sticky stuff that helps sweaty palms grip the ball. Pitchers keep little rosin bags "handy" and touch the rosin every so often. You should be able to find this product just about anywhere—including in the coin-dispensed machines in bowling alleys. Some of the large distributors of the product are listed below.

Bacharach Rasin Sporting Goods
Cramer Products
Franklin Sports Industries
North American Recreation
Pennsylvania Sporting Goods Co.
Unique Sports Products
Vukas Products
Wa-Mac

SCREEN PRINTING

This is another method, like heat transfers, for putting team names on T-shirts and uniforms.

Order through a sporting goods store.

Central Park
Centralia Knitting Mills
Dyer Specialty Co.
Holoubek Studios Iron-On Express
JPM Company
Lone Star Athletic Designs
McArthur Towels
McCarthy, Bob, Athletic Wear
Quik-Set Lettering
Rainbow Sports Enterprises
SportDecals
Uniforms Unlimited

SHOES

For cleated shoes specially designed for baseball, check your sporting goods store. They can order from the following large distributors.

Adidas U.S.A.
American Athletic Shoe Co.
Asics Tiger Corporation
Avia
Bacharach Rasin Sporting Goods
Bike Footwear
Brookfield Athletic Shoe Co.
Brooks Shoe
Champion Products
Converse
Cosby, Gerry Co.
Easton Sports
Everlast Sporting Goods Mfg. Co.
Franklin Sports Industries
Hyde Athletic Industries
Jelinek Sports
Joslin's Inc.
KangaROOS U.S.A.
Kazmaier International
Mitre Sports
Nike
Pony Sports & Leisure
Puma USA
Rawlings Sporting Goods Co.
Wilson Sporting Goods Co.

SLIDING PADS

"Slide! Slide!"
Sliding along the ground to avoid the tag is good baseball, but it also leads to bruises, scrapes, and more serious injuries.

Pro Sports Products makes a special pair of pants with an enclosed girdle of padding that protects you when sliding into the base.

The product is relatively new but has begun to catch on in the majors. The Yankees and Mets ordered the pants for their entire rosters. Pittsburgh's Andy Van Slyke personally phones in his order each year.

Sliding pants for kids come in the following waist sizes: Youth 20–22, Junior 24–26, and Small 28–30. You can purchase the product directly from the company listed below. If you're getting fewer than 10 pairs of sliding pants, the price is $35 per pair plus shipping.

(By the way, sliding pants used to be worn in the early 1900s but went out of style).

Pro Sports Products

SOCKS

A sporting goods store

can order entire uniforms for your team, from top to bottom. Speaking of the bottom, here are some of the large distributors of socks.

ABC Sports Socks
Adidas U.S.A.
Alchester Mills Co.
AMBI Athletic Shoes
Bacharach Rasin Sporting Goods
Ballston Knitting Co.
Bristol Products Corp.
Broner
Buccaneer Mfg. Co.
Champion Products
Chipman Union
CMG/Cannon Sports
Collegiate Pacific
Comfort Cushion Mills
Converse
Cooper International
Cosby, Gerry Co.
Cran Barry
Dorson Sports, Inc.
East-Tenn Mills
Empire Sporting Goods Mfg. Co.
Felco Athletic Wear Co.
Fox River Mills/Rockford Textile
Franklin Sports Industries
General Sportcraft Co.
Hanco-H. Handelsman Co.
Harriss & Covington
Hole in None
Hot Sox
Jefferies Socks
Jobst Institute
Kayser-Roth
Kiwi Consumer Products
MacGregor Sporting Goods
Maple Mfg. Co.
Markwort Sporting Goods Co.
Medalist Apparel
Mizuno Sports
Moretz Sports
Nelson Knitting Co.
Nike
Pennsylvania Sporting Goods Co.
Pine Hosiery Mills
Pony Sports & Leisure
Pro Feet
Rainbow Sports Enterprises
Rawlings Sporting Goods Co.

Ridgeview Mills
Russell National Sport Socks
SAI by Kemfast
Softouch Co.
Spalding Socks
Sportsotron, Inc. and Hy Sport
Striker Uniforms
Thor-Lo
Top-Comfo Athletic Sox
Trenway Textiles
Twin City Knitting Co., Inc.
Uniforms Unlimited
Union Jacks
U.S. Games
Venus Knitting Mills
Wa-Mac
Wigwam Mills
Wilson Sports Socks

STIRRUPS

A fancy baseball uniform also includes stirrups—cloth hose that hold the socks up. Your team will get them if they order complete uniforms.

Bacharach Rasin Sporting Goods
Bristol Products Corp.
Champion Products
CMG/Cannon Sports
East-Tenn Mills
Empire Sporting Goods Mfg. Co.
Hole in None
Majestic Athletic Wear
Markwort Sporting Goods Co.
Powers Mfg. Co.
Rawlings Sporting Goods Co.
Ridgeview Mills
Top-Comfo Athletic Sox
Trenway Textiles
Uniforms Unlimited
U.S. Games
Venus Knitting Mills
Wilson Sporting Goods Co.

TOE GUARDS

Toe guards for pitchers (see Pitcher's Toe Plates). If you send your pitching shoe (the foot that drags) to

Tuff Toe, they'll mold a polyurethane guard right onto it for $16 plus tax. That includes the cost of shipping it back.

Eclectic Products, Inc.
Tuff Toe

TOWELS

If you're involved with a youth team that uses a locker room and needs a towel supply, here's a list of towel suppliers.

And for the team that has everything, you can always get personalized towels. A company such as Crown Prince, Inc., will print the name of the team on the towel, or the names of the players, or whatever you want. (They also do T-shirts.) Order directly from the company.

Sweat Buddy, Inc., is the designer of a special towel that hooks onto the waist so it's always available for wiping sweaty hands during the game. It was made with football quarterbacks in mind, but a number of baseball players have taken to using it as well.

Crown Prince
McArthur Towels
Sweat Buddy

UMPIRE INDICATORS

If you're umping a game,

154

these hand-held clicker devices help you keep track of balls, strikes, outs, and runs. That way, when angry players yell at you about the score, you can just show them the clicker.

Your sporting goods store can order umpire indicators from the following companies.

Cramer Products
Everlast Sporting Goods Mfg. Co
MacGregor Sporting Goods
Markwort Sporting Goods Co.
Pennsylvania Sporting Goods Co.
Richardson Sports
Roman Art-Roman Pro Lara Ltd.
Tide-Rider
Venus Knitting Mills

UNIFORMS AND JERSEYS

Unless you're buying for a large league, your team should order through a sporting goods store. (See also the listing for jerseys earlier in this chapter.) Here are some of the large distributors.

ADC (Athletic Die Co.)
Adidas U.S.A.
Aladen Athletic Wear
Alpha Sportswear
Bacharach Rasin Sporting Goods
Betlin Mfg. Co.
Bike Athletic Co.
Bristol Products Corp.
Capital Industries
Champion Products
CMG/Cannon Sports
Cooper International
Cosby, Gerry Co.
Cran Barry Inc.
Dodger Mfg. Co.
East-Tenn Mills

Empire Sporting Goods Mfg. Co.
Fab-Knit Mfg. Co.
Felco Athletic Wear Co., Inc.
Flaherty, John B. Co.
Foremost Athletic Apparel
Game Master Athletic Co.
Gold Medal Recreational Products
Hanco-M. Handelsman Co.
Harv-Al Athletic Mfg.
Hi Style Lettered Sportswear Co.
Hutch Sporting Goods Co.
Jesco Athletic Co.
Johnstown Knitting Mill Co.
Joslin's

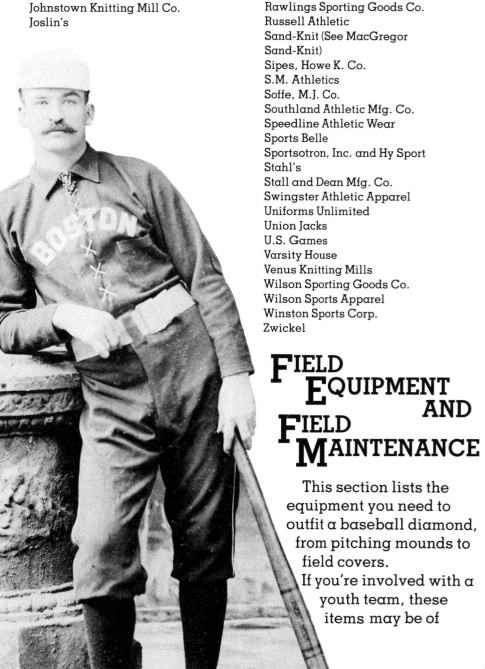

Katzenberg Bros.
Letrell Sports
Majestic Athletic Wear
MacGregor Sand-Knit
Maple Mfg. Co.
Mark V Sales
Markwort Sporting Goods Co.
MBF Sports
New Era Knitting Mills
Newsouth Athletic Co.
Powers Mfg. Co.
Ranger Athletic Mfg.
Rawlings Sporting Goods Co.
Russell Athletic
Sand-Knit (See MacGregor Sand-Knit)
Sipes, Howe K. Co.
S.M. Athletics
Soffe, M.J. Co.
Southland Athletic Mfg. Co.
Speedline Athletic Wear
Sports Belle
Sportsotron, Inc. and Hy Sport
Stahl's
Stall and Dean Mfg. Co.
Swingster Athletic Apparel
Uniforms Unlimited
Union Jacks
U.S. Games
Varsity House
Venus Knitting Mills
Wilson Sporting Goods Co.
Wilson Sports Apparel
Winston Sports Corp.
Zwickel

FIELD EQUIPMENT AND FIELD MAINTENANCE

This section lists the equipment you need to outfit a baseball diamond, from pitching mounds to field covers.

If you're involved with a youth team, these items may be of

interest to your team.

BASE SPIKES

For securing the bases in the ground.

Everlast Sporting Goods Mfg. Co.
Ju-Do Mfg. Co.
MacGregor Sporting Goods
North American Recreation
Pennsylvania Sporting Goods Co.
Spalding Sports Worldwide

BAT RACKS AND HANGERS

For storing large numbers of bats. Hillerich and Bradsby sells these through its mail-order catalogue.

Bacharach Rasin Sporting Goods
Beacon Products Company
CMG/Cannon Sports
GSC Athletic Equipment
Hillerich and Bradsby Co.
Rawlings Sporting Goods Co.
Spalding Sports Worldwide
Stackhouse Athletic Equipment
U.S. Games
Worth Sports Company

BATTING TEES

Used in the youth game known as T-ball and also used in batting practice, these tees hold the ball in place and let you whack it.

Blazer Manufacturing
CAPS (Creative Athletic Products & Services, Inc.)
Diamond Sports Products
Game Master Athletic Co.
General Sportcraft Co.
Jayfro Corp.
MacGregor Sporting Goods

North American Recreation
Pennsylvania Sporting Goods Co.
Poly Enterprises

COVERS—FIELD

To protect the field from rain, for instance.

Anchor Industries
BSN Corporation
Carron Net Company
Cover Sports USA
Covermaster
Douglas Industries
Griffolyn Division, Reef Industries
Ju-Do Mfg. Co.
North American Recreation
OTA, Inc.
Putterman, M. & Co.
Revere Plastics
Stuart, D. Co.
Victory Sports Nets
West Coast Netting

FIRST-BASE SAFETY PROTECTOR

A large net that protects the first baseman during batting practice. If you go to the ballpark early and watch the majors during batting practice, you'll see that the first baseman is warming up the infielders while the batters hit. This net keeps the first baseman from getting clobbered.

Gold Medal Recreational Products
Jayfro Corp.
Ju-Do Mfg. Co.
North American Recreation
Patterson-Williams Mfg. Co.

INFIELD DRAG MATS

For smoothing out the infield—and getting a truer hop on grounders.

Austin Athletic Equipment Corp.
Beacon Products Company

NETS

To be used in protectors such as the first base protector, or to protect fans from sharply hit foul balls.

ATEC
Beacon Products Company
Douglas Industries
Gold Medal Recreational Products
Jayfro Corp.
Jugs Pitching Machines
K-Lin Specialties
North American Recreation
Patterson-Williams Mfg. Co.
Putterman, M. & Co.
R.B.I. Industries
Victory Sports Nets
Wittek Golf Supply Co.

PITCHBACKS

A net that helps you practice pitching, since it bounces the ball back your way. North American Recreation sells it directly to individuals.

Franklin Sports Industries
Gold Medal Recreational Products
Jayfro Corp.
North American Recreation
T&R Sale

PITCHER SAFETY PROTECTORS

To protect the person

throwing batting practice from getting whammed by a shot right back to the mound. Protects the lower half of the body while allowing him or her to pitch.

Austin Athletic Equipment Corp.
Jayfro Corp.
Ju-Do Mfg. Co.
K-Lin Specialties
North American Recreation

PITCHING MACHINES

For $449 to $779, Granada Pitching Machines will sell you a pitching machine that will hurl a special kind of plastic ball at you at 70 m.p.h. Why would you buy a machine that whips the ball at you? These machines are terrific ways to practice your hitting. The machines can even throw curveballs!

Most batting practice is done with pitches in the 70-m.p.h. range. But Granada's pitching machines can throw the ball faster, up to 100 m.p.h.

However, the makers of pitching machines don't set the machines that fast because it's just not safe for the hitters. (Of course, major league batters regularly have to face 90-m.p.h. pitches in games.)
ATEC

Austin Athletic Equipment Corp.
Bacharach Rasin Sporting Goods
CMG/SBC Sports
Granada Pitching Machines
Hillerich and Bradsby Co.
Joslin's
Jugs Pitching Machines
K-Lin Specialties
Master Pitching Machine
North American Recreation
Pick Point Enterprises
Sports Equipment
Trius Products
Tru-Pitch

PITCHING MOUNDS

CAPS will ship you by truck an entire fiberglass pitching mound and rubber. It's covered in artificial turf, and it's portable. In some leagues, it can be used in games. CAPS sells different varieties for hardball and softball.

CAPS (Creative Athletic Products & Services, Inc.)

PROFESSIONAL SERVICES

For designing and building a baseball diamond from scratch.

Arena Group
Eggers Group, P.C.
Ellerbe Becket
Gaudreau, Inc. Architects/
  Engineers/Planners
Geiger, Gossen, Hamilton & Liao
  P.C.
Gordon, Jack L. Associates
Hansen/Murakami/Eshima, Inc.,
  Architects/Planners
Hastings & Chivetta
Heery/Sports International
HOK Architects

Howard Needles Tammen &
  Bergendoff (HNTB)
Odell Associates
Paoletti/Lewitz/Associates
Powell, Milton & Partners
Rossman, Schneider, Gadbury,
  Architects
Sink Combs Dethlefs
Stanmar
Sverdrup Corp.
Tomblinson Harburn York
  and Associates
Tully, Daniel F. Associates,
  Architects/Engineers
Wight and Company

SHORT-TOSS MACHINE

Less expensive pitching machine that throws the ball at you from closer up.

R.B.I. Industries

TRAINING AIDS

These are devices to help you learn good baseball form. For instance, CAPS sells (direct, not through stores) a special bunt bat with a pocket at the end. You try to catch the ball in the pocket, thus learning a good gentle bunt form.

They also carry a flat glove that helps teach good fielding habits. To snag a grounder with this flat glove, the fielder must watch the ball all the way and "give with the ball," gently moving the glove back as the ball hits it. These are key habits to get into and should improve your fielding—once you switch back to a normal glove!

R.B.I. sells a number of training devices, including a motorized batting instructor. A ball on a string rotates around you at up to 60 m.p.h. Each time it comes through the batter's box, you try to hit it. If you do hit it, it will get back on track within a few rotations.

CAPS (Creative Athletic Products & Services, Inc.)
R.B.I. Industries, Inc.

TUNNELS

These are 70-foot-long tunnels of netting for batting practice. (That way you don't have to keep chasing the balls.)

R.B.I. Industries, Inc.

WALL MATS

To protect outfielders when they run into the wall as they chase down long fly balls.

OTA
Putterman, M. & Co.

COMPANY LISTINGS

ABC Sports Socks
255 North Elm Street
High Point, NC 27261
(919) 889-7071
(800) 334-2741

Acuvision Systems, Inc.
355 Lexington Avenue,
Suite 200
New York, NY 10017
(212) 687-3080

ADC (Athletic Die Co. Inc.)
P.O. Box 1128
78 Sadler Road
Amelia Island, FL 32034
(904) 261-5588
(800) 874-8674

Adidas U.S.A., Inc.
15 Independence Boulevard
Warren, NJ 07060
(201) 580-0700
FAX: (201) 580-0480

Aerobics Inc.
30 Colfax Avenue
Clifton, NJ 07013
(201) 773-4143

Aircast, Inc.
P.O. Box T
Summit, NJ 07901
(201) 273-6349 (NJ)
(800) 526-8785 (except in NJ)
FAX: (201) 273-1060

AJD Company
3301 Castlewood Road
Richmond, VA 23234

(804) 233-9683

AKZO Industrial Systems Co.
P.O. Box 7249
One North Pack Square
Asheville, NC 28802
(704) 258-5050
FAX: (704) 258-5059

Aladen Athletic Wear
51 Cannonball Road
Pompton Lakes, NJ 07442
(201) 839-4744

Alchester Mills Co., Inc.
314 South 11th Street
Camden, NJ 08103
(609) 964-9700
FAX: (609) 964-9135

All American/Maxpro
1320 Taylor Street
Elyria, OH 44035
(216) 327-0750
FAX: (216) 366-0041

All Star Knitwear, Inc.
331 North 6th Street
P.O. Box 571
Griffin, GA 30224
(404) 227-5016
(800) 241-0246

All Star Sporting Goods
1 Main Street
P.O. Box 1356
Shirley, MA 01464
(508) 425-6266
(800) 777-3810
FAX: (617) 425-4610

Alleson, Don, Athletic
2921 Brighton-Henritta

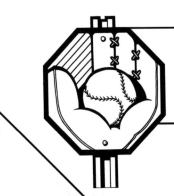

SHORTSTOPS
The first baseball glove was used by Charles G. Waite, a Boston first baseman in 1875. It wasn't padded. Ouch.

Town Line Road
Rochester, NY 14623
(716) 272-0630

Alpha Sportswear, Inc.
2525 16th Street
San Francisco, CA 94103
(415) 552-3570
(800) 227-4266 (except in CA)
(800) 222-6630 (CA only)
FAX: (415) 552-3573

Altus Athletic Mfg. Co.
OK-1
5 Miles North, Highway 283
Altus, OK 73522
(405) 482-0891
(800) 654-3955
FAX: (405) 482-2760
Mailing Address:
P.O. Box 7361
Altus, OK 73522

Aluminum Athletic
Equipment Company
4 Portland Road
West Conshohocken, PA
19428
(215) 825-6565
(800) 532-5471 (except in PA)
FAX: (215) 825-2378

AMBI Athletic Shoes

P.O. Box 249
Jonesboro, AR 72401
(501) 935-2611

American Athletic, Inc.
200 American Avenue
Jefferson, IA 50129
(515) 386-3125
(800) 247-3978
FAX: (515) 386-4566

American Athletic Shoe Co.
P.O. Box 777
15 South Street
Ware, MA 01082
(413) 967-3511

American Baseball Cap,
Inc.
310 Station Road
Media, PA 19063
(215) 565-0945

American Baseball
Coaches Association
P.O. Box 3545
Omaha, NE 68103-0545
(402) 733-0374
FAX: (402) 734-7166

American Baseball Glove
Company
5834 W. Gunnison

Chicago, IL 60630
(312) 202-8434

American Eagle Sports
450 Market Street
Perth Amboy, NJ 08861
(201) 324-2300

American Electric
1555 C Lynnfield
Memphis, TN 38119
(901) 682-7766
FAX: (800) 843-6561

American Medical Sales,
Inc.
8476 Warner Drive
Culver City, CA 90232
(213) 558-0600
(800) 423-3535

Amko, Inc.
P.O. Box 5809
Huntsville, AL 35814-5809
(205) 837-3603
(800) 289-2656
FAX: (205) 837-3606

Anchor Industries, Inc.
1100 Burch Drive
Evansville, IN 47733
(812) 867-2421
Mailing Address:

PITTSBURGH

PHILADELPHIA

CHICAGO

Uniforms for three of the eight National League teams in 1903.

P.O. Box 3477
Evansville, IN 47733

Andia Progress Co., Inc.
47 Soundview Avenue
White Plains, NY 10606
(914) 948-2685
(800) 431-2775
FAX: (914) 948-7325

Anjon Corporation
915 Broadway
Kansas City, MO 64105
(816) 474-1507
FAX: (816) 842-0952

Antler
10 West 33rd Street
New York, NY 10001
(718) 361-2800

Apex Athletic Equipment,
Inc.
141 Lanza Avenue
Garfield, NJ 07026
(201) 772-7400

Apsco Enterprises
50th Street & First Avenue
Building No. 57
Brooklyn, NY 11232
(718) 965-9500
FAX: (718) 965-3088

The Arena Group
999 Peachtree Street, N.E.
Atlanta, GA 30367
(404) 892-0841

Aris Isotoner, Inc.
417 Fifth Avenue
New York, NY 10016
(212) 532-8627

(800) 223-2218
FAX: (212) 576-9530

Arkla Industries
810 Franklin
P.O. Box 534
Evansville, IN 47704
(812) 424-3331

Arnold Health Equipment
Co.
P.O. Box 205
La Porte, IN 46350
(219) 325-0582

Artcraft Concepts
P.O. Box 20404
1450 South Burlington
Avenue
Los Angeles, CA 90006
(213) 385-1646

Artex Mfg. Co.
7600 Wedd
Overland Park, KS 66204
(913) 631-4040

Asics Tiger Corporation
10540 Talbert Avenue
West Building
(714) 754-0451
(800) 854-6133
FAX: (714) 754-0507

ATEC
9011 Southeast Jannsen
Road
P.O. Box 451
Clackamas, OR 97015
(503) 657-3275
(800) 331-4337
FAX: (503) 675-5718

Atlantic Fitness Products
6701 Moravia Park Drive
Baltimore, MD 21237
(301) 488-2020
(800) 445-1855
FAX: (301) 488-3059

Athletic Helmet, Inc.
(See Schutt Mfg. Co.
listing)

Athletic Institute
200 Castlewood Drive
North Palm Beach, FL 33408
(407) 842-3600

Augusta Sportswear
P.O. Box 14939
Augusta, GA 30919
(404) 860-4633
(800) 237-6695
FAX: (404) 868-5672

Austin Athletic Equipment
Corp.
705 Bedford Avenue, Box
423
Bellmore, NY 11710
(516) 785-0100

Automated Batting Cages
Corp.
8811 Huff, N.E.
Salem, OR 97303
(503) 390-5714

Autry Industries, Inc.
11420 Reeder Road
Dallas, TX 75229
(214) 241-7793
(800) TXA-UTRY (TX only)
(800) USA-UTRY (except in
TX)

FAX: (214) 241-9774

Avia
16160 S.W. Upper Boones
Ferry Rd.
Portland, OR 97224
(503) 684-0490
(800) 547-3213
FAX: (503) 684-3963

Avita Health & Fitness
Products
P.O. Box 3547
Redmond, WA 98073-3547
(206) 885-1010
(800) 222-9995
FAX: (206) 881-3099

Award Decals
P.O. Box 3449
Boca Raton, FL 33427
(407) 479-4384
(800) 525-9395

Bacharach Rasin Sporting
Goods, Inc.
802 Gleneagles Court
Towson, MD 21204
(301) 825-6747

Baden Sports, Inc.
1120 Southwest 16th
Renton, WA 98055
(206) 235-1830
FAX: (206) 235-1892

Ballston Knitting Co., Inc.
P.O. Box 30
Ballston Spa, NY 12020
(518) 885-6701

Bally Fitness Products
Corporation
(See Life Fitness, Inc.)

Bassett-Walker Inc.
P.O. Box 5423
Martinsville, VA 24115
(703) 632-5601

Battle Creek Equipment
Co.
307 West Jackson Street
Battle Creek, MI 49017-2385
(616) 962-6181
(800) 253-0854 (except in
Michigan)
(800) 632-5620 (in Michigan)

Beacon Products Company
P.O. Box 4115
Madison, WI 53711
(608) 274-5985
(800) 747-5985

Becton Dickinson & Co.
One Becton Drive
Franklin Lakes, NJ
07417-1883
(201) 848-7100

Betlin Mfg. Co.
1445 Marion Road
Columbus, OH 43207
(614) 443-0248
FAX: (614) 443-4658

BFCO Fitness Products
5310 Southern Avenue
South Gate, CA 90280
(213) 564-5701
FAX: (213) 564-9717
Mailing Address:
P.O. Box 1070
South Gate, CA 90280

Bike Athletic Company
P.O. Box 666

Knoxville, TN 37801
(615) 546-4703
(800) 251-9230 (except in TN)
(800) 362-9256 (TN only)
FAX: (615) 525-2471

Billmeyer, Robert E. Co.,
Inc.
277 Rowayton Avenue
Rowayton, CT 06853
(203) 852-0638
FAX: (203) 854-5766

Binghamton Block Co.
P.O. Box 1256
Binghamton, NY 13902
(607) 772-0420

Biodex Corporation
P.O. Drawer S
Shirley, NY 11967
(516) 924-9300
FAX: (516) 924-9241

Bio-Dyne Corp.
400 Wharton Circle, S.W.
Atlanta, GA 30336
(404) 691-0983

Blazer Mfg., Inc.
P.O. Box 266
Columbus, NB 68601
(402) 721-2525
FAX: (402) 721-4647

Body Sculpture
1299 Grand Avenue
Baldwin, NY 11510
(516) 379-6920

Body-Builder Industries
Inc.
1253 New Market Avenue
South Plainfield, NJ 07080

(201) 757-2200

Bolco Athletic Co., Inc.
2638 Lee Avenue
South El Monte, CA 91733
(818) 579-6612
(800) 423-4321

Bolen Leather Products Inc.
P.O. Box N
Springfield, TN 37172
(615) 384-9541

Bollinger Fitness
(a Bollinger Industries Co.)
222 West Airport Freeway
Irving, TX 75062
(214) 445-0386
(800) 527-1166
FAX: (214) 438-8471

Bomark Mills, Inc.
5040 Layton Lane
Collegedale, TN 37315
(615) 236-4238

Bomark Sportswear
5804 South Rice
Houston, TX 77081
(713) 664-7272
(800) 231-3351 (except in TX)
(800) 392-0616 (TX only)

Boyle, John & Co., Inc.
P.O. Box 791, Salisbury Road
Statesville, NC 28677
(704) 872-8151

Bravo International
P.O. Box 2515
Boston, MA 02208
(617) 767-1007

Bristol Products Corp.
700 Shelby Street
P.O. Box 158
Bristol, TN 37620
(615) 968-4140
(800) 336-8775

Bristol Sports Corp.
481 Johnson Avenue
Bohemia, NY 11716
(516) 567-8300

British Knights
138 Duane Street
New York, NY 10013
(212) 227-6236
FAX: (212) 513-1438

Broner, Inc.
359 Robbins Drive
Troy, MI 48083
(313) 589-1919
(800) 521-1318
FAX: (313) 583-7724

Brookfield Athletic Shoe
Company, Inc.
Centennial Industrial Park
Peabody, MA 01961
(617) 532-9000

Brooklyn Officiating
Supply Services (B.O.S.S.)
Inc.
1842 Brown Street
Brooklyn, NY 11229
(718) 769-6163
Mailing Address:
3178 Avenue W
Brooklyn, NY 11229

Brooks Shoe, Inc.
9341 Courtland Drive, N.E.

Rockford, MI 49351
(616) 866-5500
FAX: (616) 866-1041

BSN Corporation
1901 Diplomat
Farmers Branch, TX 75234
(214) 484-9484
(800) 527-7510
FAX: (214) 484-0457
Mailing Address:
P.O. Box 7726
Dallas, TX 75209

Buccaneer Mfg. Co.
35 York Street
Brooklyn, NY 11201
(718) 855-7171
(800) 221-0560 (except in NY)
(800) 522-8894 (NY only)
FAX: (718) 802-9307

Burlington Socks
(See Kayser-Roth)

Butwin Sportswear Co.
3401 Spring Street N.E.
Minneapolis, MN 55413
(612) 331-3300
(800) 328-1445 (except in MN)
(800) 238-0303 (MN only)
FAX: (612) 331-5420

California Gym Equipment
Company
3140 East Pico Boulevard
Los Angeles, CA 90023
(213) 264-2715
FAX: (213) 261-2693

California Headwear, Inc.
661 Rio
Los Angeles, CA 90023

(213) 268-7112
(800) 421-6404
FAX: (213) 268-5975

Cambridge Career
Products, Inc.
One Players Club Drive
Charleston, WV 25311
(304) 344-8550
(800) 468-4227
FAX: (304) 344-5583

Cap Barbell, Inc.
1830 S. 54th Avenue
Cicero, IL 60650
(312) 780-0200

Capital Industries Inc.
P.O. Box 689
De Soto, TX 75115
(214) 223-8440
(800) 527-3114

CAPS (Creative Athletic
Products & Services Inc.)
P.O. Box 7731
Des Moines, IA 50322
(515) 270-6352
(800) 227-4574
FAX: (515) 270-2249

Carron Net Co., Inc.
P.O. Box 177
Two Rivers, WI 54241
(414) 793-2217
(800) 558-7768

Casco/USA
3677 N.W. 19th Street
Lauderdale Lakes, FL 33311
(305) 486-0300
(800) 327-9285

Central Park
3287 Northwest 65 Street
Miami, FL 33147
(305) 693-7000

Centralia Knitting Mills,
Inc.
P.O. Box 269
1002 West Main
Centralia, WA 98531
(206) 736-3994

Chalk Line, Inc.
West 11th Street
P.O. Box 38
Anniston, AL 36202
(205) 238-1540
(800) 633-2304
FAX: (205) 237-9025

Challenger/General
555 Mount Tabor Road
New Albany, IN 47150

(812) 945-0462
(800) 543-1505
FAX: (812) 948-6927

Champion Barbell
2007 Royal Lane
Dallas, TX 75229
(214) 484-9484

Champion Glove Mfg. Co.
2200 East Ovid
Des Moines, IA 50313
(515) 265-2551
(800) 247-4537
FAX: (515) 265-7210

Champion Products, Inc.
P.O. Box 850
3141 Monroe Avenue
Rochester, NY 14603
(716) 385-3200
FAX: (716) 385-6987

THE INFAMOUS PINE TAR INCIDENT

In the major leagues, there's a rule that says players can't put pine tar more than 18 inches up the bat. That rule led to what has come to be known as the Pine Tar Incident. Here's what happened:

July 24, 1983—With two outs in the ninth inning and his team trailing by a single run (baseball's most dramatic situation), the Royals' hitting master George Brett steps up to the plate. He's facing the Yankees' imposing speedballer Goose Gossage.

Going... going... GONE! Brett wins the showdown with a two-run homer that puts the Royals ahead 5–4.

But wait. Yankee manager Billy Martin protests to the umpire that Brett's bat has more than 18 inches of pine tar. The umpire checks the bat, agrees with Martin, and takes back the home run. Brett has a tantrum. He screams at the umpire until he is thrown out of the game.

But wait, it's not over yet. Days later the scene shifts to the offices of the American League president, Lee MacPhail. MacPhail examines the bat in question.

There are indeed more than 18 inches of sticky black goo. But MacPhail says that the purpose of the pine tar rule is to keep the balls from getting gooey and dirty. Brett wasn't cheating, he says. The umpire should

simply have asked Brett to use a cleaner bat from then on.

MacPhail rules that the game be finished. The Yankees take their last licks and lose 5–4. They take the case all the way to court. They lose again.

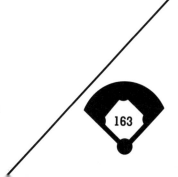

163

Champion Sports Products
Company
10 Embroidery Street
P.O. Box 138
Sayreville, NJ 08872
(201) 238-0330

Chase-Taylor Company
Box 1739
Tahoe City, CA 95730
(916) 583-7205
(800) 582-7205 (CA only)

Chipman Union Inc.
500 Sibley Avenue
Union Point, GA 30669
(404) 486-2112
FAX: (404) 486-4963

Chronomix Corporation
650F Vaqueros Avenue
Sunnyvale, CA 94086
(408) 737-1920
(800) 538-1548

CMG/Cannon Sports
P.O. Box 11179
Burbank, CA 91510-1179
(800) 223-0064 (except in CA)
(800) 247-3102 (CA only)
FAX: (818) 503-9169

Collegiate Pacific
81 Adams Drive
Totowa, NJ 07512
(201) 256-8600

Collette Mfg. Co./Crown
Recreation Inc.
Building No. 9 De Graff
Street
Amsterdam, NY 12010
(518) 842-0510

Comfort Cushion Mills, Inc.
1101 - 18 St. Rogers Circle
Boca Raton, FL 33487
(305) 994-3001
(800) 327-5012

Continental Sports
1403 East Alfred Street
Tavares, FL 32778
(904) 343-2096

Converse, Inc.
1 Fordham Road
North Reading, MA 01864
(508) 664-1100
(800) 225-5079 (except in
Maine)
(800) 556-1190 (MA only)
FAX: (508) 664-7259

Cooper International, Inc.
1707 Ridge Road, Route 104
Lewiston, NY 14092
(716) 754-4391
FAX: (716) 754-2704
(800) 232-2667 (except in NY)
(416) 763-3801 in Canada
FAX: (416) 763-0994

Cosby, Gerry Co., Inc.
3 Pennsylvania Plaza
New York, NY 10001
(212) 563-6464
(800) 548-4003
FAX: (212) 967-0876
Telex: 928297

Cover Sports USA Inc.
P.O. Box 1060
Exton, PA 19341
(800) 445-6680 (except in PA)
(800) 262-8668 (PA only)

Covermaster, Inc.
100 Westmore Drive, Unit
11-D
Rexdale, Ontario
Canada M9V 5C3
(416) 745-1811
(800) 387-5808 (U.S. WATS)
(800) 387-1942 (Canada
WATS)
FAX: (416) 749-4449

Cramer Products, Inc.
153 West Warren Street
Gardner, KS 66030
(913) 884-7511
(800) 225-6621
FAX: (913) 884-5626
Mailing Address:
P.O. Box 1001
Gardner, KS 66030

Cran Barry Inc.
2 Lincoln Avenue
Marblehead, MA 01945
(617) 631-8510

Creative Awards by Lane
1575 Elmhurst Road
Elk Grove, IL 60007
(312) 593-7700
FAX: (312) 593-1155
Mailing Address:
P.O. Box 1467
Elk Grove Village, IL 60009

Crown Global Corp.
7291 Garden Boulevard
Garden Grove, CA 92641
(714) 895-4307

Crown Health Equipment
Co., Inc.
P.O. Box 751

Mt. Vernon, OH 43050
(614) 397-1060

Crown Prince, Inc.
7439 Harwood Avenue
Milwaukee, WI 53213
(414) 476-1500 (WI only)
(800) 558-0858 (except in WI)
FAX: (414) 476-5121

Cybex Division, Lumex Inc.
2100 Smithtown Avenue
Ronkonkoma, NY 11779
(516) 585-9000

Cyrk, Inc.
P.O. Box 1499
3 Pond Road
Gloucester, MA 01930
(617) 283-5800

Dalco Athletic Lettering,
Inc.
P.O. Box 28312
Dallas, TX 75228
(214) 494-1455
(800) 527-4016 (except in TX)
(800) 492-9125 (TX only)

Derby Cap Mfg. Co., Inc.
P.O. Box 34220
Louisville, KY 40232
(502) 587-8495
(800) 443-3729
FAX: (502) 587-7771

Diamond Sports Company
10671 Humbolt Street
Los Alamitos, CA 90720
(213) 598-5717
FAX: (213) 598-0906

Diversified Products
309 Williamson Avenue
Opelika, AL 36803
(205) 749-9001

D.L.C. Fabricating Co.,
Inc.
4809 Miami Street
St. Louis, MO 63116
(314) 351-9778

Dodger Mfg. Co.
1702 21st Street
Eldora, IA 50627
(515) 858-5464
(800) 247-7879 (except in IA)
(800) 542-7972 (IA only)
FAX: (515) 858-2485

Donjoy
5966 La Place Court
Carlsbad, CA 92008
(619) 438-9091
FAX: (619) 438-3210

Dorfman-Pacific Co., Inc.
2615 Boeing Way
Stockton, CA 95206
(209) 982-1400
(800) 621-3241 (except in CA)
(800) 221-5176 (CA only)
FAX: (209) 982-1596

Dorson Sports, Inc.
195 Lauman Lane
Hicksville, NY 11801
(516) 822-2424
(800) 645-7215
FAX: (516) 935-1464

Douglas Industries, Inc.
3441 S. 11th Avenue
Eldridge, IA 52748

(319) 285-4162
(800) 553-8907
Mailing Address:
P.O. Box 393
Eldridge, IA 52748

The Drackett Company
201 East Fourth Street
Cincinnati, OH 45202
(513) 632-1844

Dunbrooke Sportswear Co.
P.O. Box 430
Lexington, MO 64067
(816) 259-2241
(800) 821-3020
FAX: (816) 258-2011

Duraflex
401 East Thomas Street
Wilkes-Barre, PA 18773
(717) 825-4501

Dyer Specialty Co., Inc.
1550 Corona
Lake Havasu City, AZ 86403
(602) 453-8600
FAX: (602) 453-8641

Eagle Performance
Systems
151-24th Avenue, N.W.
Owatonna, MN 55060
(507) 455-0217

Easton Aluminum/Van
Nuys Division
7800 Haskell Avenue
Van Nuys, CA 91406
(818) 782-6445

Easton Sports, Inc.
577 Airport Boulevard,

THE BULL PEN
Q: What state makes the most baseball uniforms?
A: New Jersey.

8th Floor
Burlingame, CA 94010
(415) 347-3900
(800) 227-0484 (CA only)
(800) 227-5990 (except in CA)
FAX: (415) 347-1035

East-Tenn Mills, Inc.
P.O. Drawer 420
3112 Industrial Drive
Johnson City, TN 37601
(615) 928-7186
(800) 251-0269
FAX: (615) 928-8901

East-West Trading Co.
P.O. Box 19188
Irvine, CA 92713
(714) 660-0888
FAX: (714) 660-0611

Eaton Corp., Golf Grip
Division
Highway 401 North Bypass
P.O. Box 1848
Laurinburg, NC 28352
(919) 276-6901
FAX: (919) 277-3700

Eclectic Products, Inc.
1111-B Watson Center Road
Carson, CA 90745-4205
(213) 830-5190
(800) 421-5779
FAX: (213) 830-4318

Eddy Bros. Co., Inc.
11252 Sunco Drive
Rancho Cordova, CA 95670
(916) 635-0116

EDS West Inc.
1201 S. Jellick Avenue

City of Industry, CA 91748
(818) 810-3322
(800) 854-6200 (except in CA)
(800) 633-4177 (CA only)
FAX: (818) 913-6074

The Eggers Group P.C.
440 Ninth Avenue
New York, NY 10001
(212) 629-4100

Elaston Company
574 Castle Boulevard
Akron, OH 44313
(216) 836-4742
FAX: (216) 836-4742

Elexis Corporation
7000 Northwest 46th Street
Miami, FL 33166
(305) 592-6069
(800) 327-1033
FAX: (305) 599-0936

Ellerbe, Becket
1 Appletree Square
Bloomington, MN 55420
(612) 853-2000
FAX: (612) 853-2271
Kansas City Office:
4739 Belleview Avenue
Kansas City, MO 64112
(816) 561-0657
FAX: (816) 561-2863

Elmer's Weights, Inc.
P.O. Box 16326
Lubbock, TX 79490
(806) 745-6724
(800) 858-4568
FAX: (806) 745-6726

Empire Sporting Goods

Mfg. Co., Inc.
443-5-7 Broadway
New York, NY 10013
(212) 966-0880
(800) 221-3455
FAX: (212) 941-7113

Engineering Dynamics
Corp., Exercise Equipment
Division
120 Stedman Street
Lowell, MA 01851
(508) 458-1456
(800) 225-9020
FAX: (508) 458-9064

Everlast Sporting Goods
Mfg. Co.
750 East 132nd Street
Bronx, NY 10454
(212) 993-0100
FAX: (212) 665-4116

Exceed
(See Ross Laboratories)

Excel, The Exercise Co.
9935 Beverly Boulevard
Pico Rivera, CA 90660
(213) 699-0311
(800) 392-2258 (except in CA)
(800) 826-9353 (CA only)
FAX: (213) 699-6626

Exercise Equipment of
Tennessee
5814 E. Sunset Road
Knoxville, TN
(615) 938-1358
Mailing Address:
P.O. Box 5405
Knoxville, TN 37918

TRIVIA QUIZ
 What was the name of Roy Hobbs's magical bat in the Robert
Redford movie *The Natural?*

Answer: Wonderboy.

Exercycle Corporation
667 Providence Street
Woonsocket, RI 02895
(401) 331-0113
(800) 367-6712
Mailing Address:
P.O. Box 1349
Woonsocket, RI 02895

Exerflex
6786 Hawthorn Park Drive
Indianapolis, IN 46220
(317) 849-6181
(800) 428-5306
FAX: (317) 842-5384

Exer-Genie, Inc.
1628 South Clementine
Anaheim, CA 92802
(714) 772-3912

Exim Sales Corporation
1128 Sunrise Highway
Copiague, NY 11726
(516) 842-1200
(800) 221-2022
FAX: (516) 671-8264

Fab-Knit Mfg. Co.
1415 North 4th Street
Waco, TX 76707
(817) 752-2511
(800) 433-3380

Fabrication Enterprises
Trent Building
South Buckbout St.
Irvington, NY 10533
(914) 591-9300
(800) 431-2830
FAX: (914) 591-4093

Face Guards, Inc.
P.O. Box 8425
Roanoke, VA 24014
(703) 774-1696
(800) 336-9683

Fairfield Line Inc.
2-10 Exchange Place
P.O. Box 520
Hanover, PA 17331
(717) 637-6235
(800) 247-3383
FAX: (717) 637-8135

Famous Sportswear
Specialty Company
P.O. Box 23368
2060 Hardy Parkway
Columbus, OH 43223
(614) 875-8180

Farnham Hall Sportswear
P.O. Box 149
39 Sunset Road
West Haven, CT 06516
(203) 932-1900

Felco Athletic Wear Co.,
Inc.
900 Passaic Avenue
Harrison, NJ 07029
(201) 484-4200
(800) 221-8240
FAX: (201) 484-8868

Fitness Equipment Co.,
Inc.
P.O. Box 167
Clanton, AL 35045
(205) 755-4953

Fitness Master
1260 Park Road
Chanhassen, MN 55317
(612) 474-0992
FAX: (612) 474-0416

Fitness Systems, Inc.
P.O. Box 266
Independence, MO 64051
(816) 765-3303
(800) 821-3126
FAX: (816) 765-8709

Flaherty, John B. Co., Inc.
120 Bruckner Boulevard
Bronx, NY 10454
(212) 292-4030
(800) 221-8742

Foremost Athletic Apparel
1307 East Maple Road
P.O. Box 427
Troy, MI 48099
(313) 689-3850
(800) 882-4333 (MI only)
(800) 433-9486 (except in MI)

Four Seasons Garment
Company
1111 Western Row Road
Mason, OH 45040
(513) 398-3695
(800) 543-3028 (OH only)
(800) 543-4611 (except in OH)

Fox River Mills/Rockford
Textile
227 Poplar Street
P.O. Box 298
Osage, IA 50461
(515) 732-3798
(800) 247-1815 (sales only)
FAX: (515) 732-5128

Franklin Sports Industries, Inc.
P.O. Box 508
17 Campanelli Parkway
Stoughton, MA 02072
(617) 344-1111
(800) 225-8647
FAX: (617) 584-4003

Funk Bros. Hat & Cap Co.
2528 Texas Avenue
St. Louis, MO 63104
(314) 771-8800
(800) 325-7156
FAX: (314) 771-0696

Game Master Athletic Co.
P.O. Box 236
582 Goddard Avenue
Chesterfield, MO 63017
(314) 532-4646
(800) 325-4141
FAX: (314) 536-2721

Gameday/Raceday
Sportswear
7801 Mesquite Bend, Suite 105
Irving, TX 75063
(214) 556-0807
(800) 458-0711
FAX: (214) 556-0870
Mailing Address:
Drawer 160486
Irving, TX 75016

Gatorade
See Quaker Oats Company

Gaudreau, Inc., Architects/
Planners/Engineers
810 Light Street
Baltimore, MD 21230

(301) 837-5040

Geiger, Gossen, Hamilton
& Liao P.C.
322 Eighth Avenue, 19th
Floor

New York, NY 10001
(212) 989-9400
FAX: (212) 989-9401

Gem Sportswear Mfg. Co.
Star Route 708
P.O. Box 56
Russells Point, OH 43348
(513) 843-2020
FAX: (513) 843-5122

General Seating Co.
585 Tennis Court Lane
P.O. Box 5699
San Bernardino, CA 92412
(714) 884-9447
(800) 843-9512 (CA only)
FAX: (714) 888-3644

General Sportcraft Co.,
Ltd.
140 Woodbine Street
Bergenfield, NJ 07621
(201) 384-4242
FAX: (201) 387-8128

Gerstung, Inc.
6310 Blair Hill Road
Baltimore, MD 21209
(301) 337-7781
FAX: (301) 337-0471

Gexco Enterprises
P.O. Box 1216
Huntington Beach, CA 92647
(714) 848-9393

Gold Medal Recreational
Products
Blue Mountain Industries
Blue Mountain, AL 36201
(205) 237-9461

An Orioles bat boy lugs some lumber.

(800) 633-2354
FAX: (205) 237-8816

Gold Star Fitness
10910 W. Bellfort, Suite 405
Houston, TX 77009
(713) 774-6288

Goorin Bros., Inc.
115 Park Lane
Brisbane, CA 94005
(415) 467-9195

Gordon, Jack L. Architects
43 West 23rd Street, 5th
Floor
New York, NY 10010
(212) 633-0909
FAX: (212) 633-2085

Grabbit Grip Products
250 Blair Avenue
Reading, PA 19601
(215) 372-2143

Granada Pitching
Machines
P.O. Box 3926
5055 Dobrot Way
Central Point, OR 97502
(503) 664-2176

Griffolyn Division, Reef
Industries Inc.
P.O. Box 750250
Houston, TX 77275
(713) 943-0070
FAX: (713) 947-2053

GSC Athletic Equipment,
Inc.
15672 Producer Lane
Huntington Beach, CA

92649
(213) 831-0131

Gymjazz Inc.
8016 Via Verona
Burbank, CA 91504
(818) 767-7439
(818) 954-0077

Hadar Athletic Mfg. Co.
405 Main Street
Dakota City, IA 50529
(515) 332-5312

Haden Industries, Inc.
2707 Satsuma
Dallas, TX 75229
(214) 241-3552
(800) 527-7305

Hanco-M. Handelsman Co.
1323 South Michigan
Avenue
Chicago, IL 60605
(312) 427-0784
(800) 621-4454
FAX: (312) 427-0787

Hansen/Murakami/Eshima,
Inc., Architects, Planners,
Interior Designers
424 Second Street
Oakland, CA 94607
(415) 444-7959

Harrison-Hoge Industries,
Inc.
P.O. Box 944
Smithtown, NY 11787
(516) 724-8900

Harriss & Covington Inc.
124 East 38th Street

New York, NY 10016
(212) 532-0404

Hartwell Garment Co.
Bowman Road
P.O. Box 160
Hartwell, GA 30643
(404) 376-5421
(800) 241-7136
FAX: (404) 376-2951

Harv-Al Athletic Mfg., Inc.
P.O. Box 91
409 West Main Street
Ranger, TX 76470
(817) 647-3776
FAX: (817) 647-3777

Hascall Sportswear, Inc.
161 Border Street
East Boston, MA 02128
(617) 567-4160

Hastings & Chivetta
Architects, Inc.
101 South Hanley, Suite
1700
St. Louis, MO 63105
(314) 863-5717
FAX: (314) 863-2823
Michigan Office:
26200 Town Center Drive
Suite 125
Novi, MI 48050
(313) 347-2920
FAX: (313) 347-2926
Illinois Office:
Hamilton Lakes, One
Pierce Place
Itasca, IL 60143
(312) 773-0074

Hatchers Mfg. Inc.
31 Green Street
Marblehead, MA 01945
(617) 631-9373
(800) 225-6842

Hauser Enterprises
P.O. Box 1090
Morgan Hill, CA 95037
(408) 779-9140

Heery/Sports International,
Architects, Engineers, and
Planners
999 Peachtree Street, N.E.
Atlanta, GA 30367
(404) 881-9880
FAX: (404) 881-9880, ext.
2305

Hi Style Lettered
Sportswear Co., Inc.
Highway 65 North
Carrollton, MO 64633
(816) 542-3410
(800) 821-3610
FAX: (816) 542-3467

Hillerich and Bradsby Co.,
Inc.
P.O. Box 35700
Louisville, KY 40232
(502) 585-5226
(800) 282-2287
FAX: (502) 585-1179

Hilton Athletic Apparel
3700 Morse Avenue
Lincolnwood, IL 60645
(312) 675-1010

Hoggan Health Industries
111 East 12300 South

Draper, UT 84020
(801) 572-6500
FAX: (801) 572-6514

HOK Architects/Sports
Facilities Group
323 West 8th Street, Suite
700
Kansas City, MO 64105
(816) 221-1576
FAX: (816) 221-1578, ext. 200

Hole in None, Inc.
1247 West Webb Avenue
Burlington, NC 27215
(919) 228-1758
(800) 334-3728
Mailing Address:
PO Drawer 2198
Burlington, NC 27215

Holloway Sportswear, Inc.
607 East Pike Street
Jackson Center, OH 45334
(513) 596-6193
(800) 543-6181
FAX: (513) 596-6283

Hollywood Bases, Inc.
10032 S. Pioneer Boulevard
Santa Fe Springs, CA 90670
(213) 949-8155
(800) 421-2243 (except in CA)
FAX: (213) 948-3593

Holoubek Studios Iron-On
Express
W238N 1800 Rockwood
Drive
Waukesha, WI 53186
(414) 547-0500
(800) 558-0566

Horizon Sportswear, Inc.
190 Ajax Drive
Madison Heights, MI 48071
(313) 589-2000
(800) 521-9792
FAX: (313) 589-2006

Hot Sox, Inc.
1441 Broadway
New York, NY 10018
(212) 354-5310

Howard Needles Tammen
& Bergendoff (HNTB)
9200 Ward Parkway
Kansas City, MO 64114
(816) 333-4800
FAX: (816) 333-9327

Huffer Corporation
14455 North 79th Street
Scottsdale, AZ 85260
(602) 998-9621
(800) 528-7355
FAX: (602) 998-0968

Hutch Sporting Goods
Company
1835 Airport Exchange
Boulevard
Erlanger, KY 41018
(606) 282-9000
FAX: (606) 282-9012
(800) 727-4511

Hyde Athletic Industries,
Inc.
Centennial Drive
Peabody, MA 01960
(508) 532-9000
(800) 223-4933
FAX: (508) 532-6105

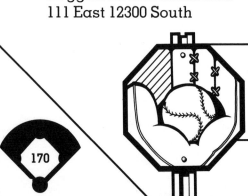

SHORTSTOPS
    A Boston Braves player named Bill Voiselle had one of the highest
numbers ever—96. He requested it in honor of his hometown:
Ninety-Six, South Carolina.

Hydra-Gym Athletics, Inc.
2121 Industrial Boulevard
P.O. Box 599
Belton, TX 76513
(817) 939-1831
(800) 433-3111 (except in TX)
(800) 792-3013 (TX only)
FAX: (817) 939-8312

Ideal Tape, Inc./Athletic
Division
1400 Middlesex Street
Lowell, MA 01851
(508) 458-6833
(800) 343-0300
FAX: (508) 458-0302

Imex Corporation
9716 Old Katy Road
Houston, TX 77055
(713) 827-0556

Incrediball, Inc.
185-B Mason Circle
Concord, CA 94520
(415) 798-0203
FAX: (415) 798-0207

Insta Graphic Systems
13925 East 166th Street
Cerritos, CA 90702
(213) 404-3000
(800) 421-6971
FAX: (213) 926-3023

Institute of Athletic
Motivation (ISAM)
One Lagoon Drive, Suite
141
Redwood City, CA
94065-1563
(415) 598-0700

International Seaway
Trading Corporation
6680 Beta Drive
Mayfield Village, OH 44143
(216) 446-1000
FAX: (216) 446-1018

International Seeds, Inc.
P.O. Box 168
Halsey, OR 97348
(503) 369-2251

Ivanko Barbell Company
P.O. Box 1470
San Pedro, CA 90733-1470
(213) 514-1155
(800) 247-9044 (except in CA)
FAX: (213) 514-1363

J&L Knitwear
Valley Forge Bus Center
2430 Boulevard of the
Generals
Norristown, PA 19403
(215) 630-4500
(800) 523-0204
FAX: (215) 275-3959

Jansport, Inc.
P.O. Box 1817
2425 West Packard Street
Appleton, WI 54913
(414) 734-5700
(800) 346-8239
FAX: (414) 734-2741

Jayfro Corp.
976 Hartford Turnpike
P.O. Box 400
Waterford, CT 06385
(203) 447-3001
(800) 243-0533

Jefferies Socks
P.O. Box 1680
1176 N. Church St.
Burlington, NC 27215
(919) 226-7315
(800) 334-6831
FAX: (919) 229-9920

Jelinek Sports
781 Westgate Road
Oakville, Ontario
Canada L6L 5L7
(416) 825-4100

Jesco Athletic Co.
P.O. Box 1716
316 Rose Street
Williamsport, PA 17701
(717) 326-2083
(800) 233-8750

Jim Viola Company
5600 W. Maple Road, Suite
B215
West Bloomfield, MI 48322
(313) 737-8777
FAX: (313) 737-1962

Jobst Institute, Inc.
653 Miami Street
Toledo, OH 43694
(419) 698-1611
(800) 537-1063
FAX: (419) 693-2162

Johar of California
15934 South Figueroa
Gardena, CA 90248
(501) 633-8161
(800) 248-1232 (except in CA)
FAX: (501) 633-1507

Johnson & Johnson
501 George Street
New Brunswick, NJ 08903
(201) 524-2193
FAX: (201) 524-2299

The Johnstown Knitting
Mill Company
309 West Montgomery
Street
Johnstown, NY 12095
(518) 762-3156

Joslin's Inc.
5955 Eden Drive
Fort Worth, TX 76117
(817) 834-7169
(800) 433-1500

JPM Company
350 Fifth Avenue, Suite 1808
New York, NY 10118
(212) 564-4328

Ju-Do Mfg. Co., Inc.
P.O. Box 311
San Gabriel, CA 91778
(818) 285-3378

Jugs Pitching Machines
P.O. Drawer 365
Tualatin, OR 97062
(503) 692-1635
(800) 547-6843
FAX: (503) 692-6774

Julie Hat Company, Inc.
Industrial Park Drive
P.O. Drawer 518
Patterson, GA 31557
(912) 647-2031
(800) 841-2592 (except in GA)

(800) 342-3387 (GA only)
FAX: (912) 647-2605

KangaROOS U.S.A., Inc.
1809 Clarkson Road
Chesterfield, MO 63017
(314) 532-3357
(800) 822-2803 (except in
MO)
(800) 544-3414 (MO only)
FAX: (314) 532-4967

Katzenberg Bros., Inc./
Merrygarden Athletic Wear
3500 Parkdale Avenue
Baltimore, MD 21211
(301) 669-4400

Kayser-Roth, Inc.
2303 W. Meadowview Road
Greensboro, NC 27407
(919) 852-2030
FAX: (919) 854-4352

Kazmaier International
Corporation
1455 Concord Street
Framingham, MA
01701-9130
(508) 788-0904
FAX: (508) 877-8031
Telex: 408010

Keen, Cliff, Athletic Inc.
P.O. Box 1224
1235 Rosewood
Ann Arbor, MI 48106
(313) 769-9555
(800) 992-0799
FAX: (313) 769-0412

Keiser Sports Health
Equipment
411 South West Avenue
Fresno, CA 93706-9952
(209) 266-2715
(800) 888-7009 (except in CA)
FAX: (209) 266-6203

Kenko Sports International
242 East Route 109
Farmingdale, NY
11735-1503
(516) 293-2277
(800) 258-1414

Kent Sporting Goods
Company, Inc.
433 Park Avenue
Route 60 South
New London, OH 44851
(419) 929-7021
(800) 537-2970
FAX: (419) 929-1769

King Louie Intl., Inc.
13500 15th Street
Glenview, MO 64030
(816) 765-5212
(800) 521-5212

Kiwi Products International
P.O. Box 5009
Woodland Hills, CA 91365
(818) 888-7494

K-Lin Specialties, Inc.
15701 Container Lane
Huntington Beach, CA
92649
(714) 897-8878
(800) 654-5553 (except in CA)

TRIVIA QUIZ:
When Hank Aaron hit his 715th home run (and broke the record), he was wearing number 44. But what number was the opposing pitcher wearing?

Answer: **Number 44.** The pitcher was Al Downing of the Los Angeles Dodgers.

172

Koch Asphalt Company
P.O. Box 2338
Wichita, KS 67201
(316) 832-5608

Korney Board Aids
312 Harrison Avenue
Roxton, TX 75477
(214) 346-3269

Kratish Hat & Cap Co.
305 North Laurel Avenue
Los Angeles, CA 90048
(213) 651-3797
FAX: (213) 380-3987

Kuranda USA, Inc.
1001 Paca Lane
Annapolis, MD 21403
(301) 269-5504

Lafayette Instrument Co.
P.O. Box 5729
Lafayette, IN 47903
(317) 423-1505

Landice Products Corp.
269 East Blackwell Street
Dover, NJ 07801
(201) 328-6560

Lannom Mfg. Co.
(See Worth Sports Co.)

Lasco, Inc.
West 35 Main
Spokane, WA 99201
(509) 456-8180
(800) 833-1845

Leader Mfg. Co., Inc.
3693 Forest Park Parkway
St. Louis, MO 63108

(314) 652-2500
(800) 325-2666
FAX: (314) 652-6928

Lee, Dean Co., Inc.
718 West Algonquin Road
Arlington Heights, IL 60005
(312) 640-0888

Lenox Hill Brace, Inc.
11-20 43rd Road
Long Island City, NY 11101
(781) 392-3320
FAX: (718) 786-5814

Leslie, Richard A. Co.
7 Corporate Drive
Orangeburg, NY 10962
(914) 359-5200
FAX: (914) 356-1456

Letrell Sports
3004 Industrial Parkway
West
Knoxville, TN 37921
(615) 546-8070
(800) 325-3975
FAX: (615) 523-5996

Letterworks
151-51 7th Avenue
Whitestone, NY 11357
(718) 767-2700
(800) 365-3883

Liebe Company
582 Goddard Avenue
Chesterfield, MO 63017
(314) 532-1614
(800) 325-4141
FAX: (314) 536-2721

Life Fitness, Inc.

9601 Jeronimo Road
Irvine, CA 92718
(714) 359-1011
(800) 543-2925 (Consulting
Division)
(800) 634-8637 (Communica-
tions Division)
FAX: (714) 458-5711

Lifeline International, Inc.
15318 N.E. 95th
Redmond, WA 98052-2517
(206) 881-7477
(800) 553-6633

London Cap Co., Inc.
150 Bay Street
Jersey City, NJ 07302
(201) 333-2554

Lone Star Athletic Designs,
Inc.
P.O. Box 214
104 Frankston Highway
Palestine, TX 75801
(214) 729-1643

Lotto USA, Inc.
2301 McDaniel Drive
Carrollton, TX 75006
(214) 351-2537
(800) 527-5126
FAX: (214) 247-3347

Louisville Mfg. Co.
P.O. Box 1436
301 South 30th Street
Louisville, KY 40201
(502) 774-8711

Lurie, Dan, Barbell Co., Inc.
219-10 South Conduit
Avenue

173

Springfield Gardens, NY
11422
(718) 978-4200
FAX: (718) 52-LURIE

MacGregor Sand-Knit
330 Trowbridge Drive
Fond du Lac, WI 54935
(414) 921-8200

MacGregor Sporting Goods
25 East Union Avenue
East Rutherford, NJ 07073
(201) 935-6300
FAX: (201) 935-5166

MacNeill Engineer Co., Inc.
289 Elm Street
Marlborough, MA 01752
(508) 481-8830
(800) 652-4267 (orders only)
FAX: (508) 460-9778
Mailing Address:
P.O. Box 735
Marlborough, MA 01752

Magnetic Sportboards
1550 Orchid Court
Longview, WA 98632-3421
(206) 425-0228

Majestic Athletic Wear Ltd.
636 Pen Argyl Street
Pen Argyl, PA 18072
(215) 863-6161
(800) 345-3134 (except in PA)
(800) 322-9050 (PA only)
FAX: (215) 863-7006

Maple Mfg. Co.
1309 Noble Street
Philadelphia, PA 19123
(215) 925-2313

Marcy Gymnasium
Equipment Company
1901 S. Burgundy Place
Ontario, CA 91761
(714) 986-2729
(800) 423-3920

Mark V Sales, Inc.
50 West 34th Street
New York, NY 10001
(212) 695-4546

Markwort Sporting Goods
Company
4300 Forest Park Avenue
St. Louis, MO 63108
(314) 652-3757
(800) 669-6626 (except in
MO)
(800) 392-0207 (MO only)
FAX: (314) 652-6241

Marquette Electronics
8200 West Tower Avenue
Milwaukee, WI 53233
(414) 355-5000
(800) 558-5120
FAX: (414) 357-0415

Marshall-Clark Mfg. Corp.
20-40 Marshall Street
Kearny, NJ 07032
(201) 991-2821
FAX: (201) 991-6981

Marty Gilman, Inc.
Gilman Road
Gilman, CT 06336
(203) 889-7334
(800) 243-0398

Master Pitching Machine,
Inc.
4200 Birmingham Road

Kansas City, MO 64117
(816) 452-0228
FAX: (816) 452-7581

Maximus Fitness Products
208 East 2nd Avenue
La Habra, CA 90633
(213) 694-0800
FAX: (213) 694-6283
Mailing Address:
P.O. Box 277
La Habra, CA 90633-0277

MBF Sports
3940 Higuera Street
Culver City, CA 90230
(213) 204-1551
(800) 247-9786

MCA Sports
6600 Artesia Boulevard
P.O. Box 5041
Buena Park, CA 90620
(714) 670-9400
FAX: (714) 670-9457
NYC Sales Office:
689 Fifth Avenue
New York, NY 10022
(212) 688-3400

McArthur Towels, Inc.
Box 448
Baraboo, WI 53913
(608) 356-8922
(800) 356-9168
FAX: (608) 356-7587

McCarthy, Bob, Athletic
Wear, Inc.
1535 6th Street
Detroit, MI 48226
(313) 964-5536
(800) 921-3153

McDavid Knee Guard, Inc.
P.O. Box 9
Clarendon Hills, IL 60514
(312) 969-1280
(800) 237-8254

Meca Sportswear, Inc.
2363 University Avenue
Saint Paul, MN 55114
(612) 646-4886
FAX: (612) 646-7327

Medalist Apparel, Inc.
803 North Downing Street
Piqua, OH 45356
(513) 773-3152
(800) 543-8952
FAX: (513) 773-5367
Mailing Address:
P.O. Box 914
Piqua, OH 45356

Megg-Nets USA
P.O. Box 13111
Roseville, MN 55113
(612) 483-5588
(800) 346-3775

Meistergram, Inc.
3517 West Wendover
Avenue
Greensboro, NC 27402
(919) 854-6200
(800) 321-0486
FAX: (919) 855-0106

Mid-American's All Star
Enterprises, Inc.
P.O. Box 639
Stillwater, OK 74076
(405) 744-3259

Midwest Glove Co., Inc.
2425 North Sheffield
Avenue
Chicago, IL 60614
(312) 871-8700

Midwest Lettering
Company
645 Bellefontaine Avenue
Marion, OH 43302
(614) 382-1905
(800) 848-8289

Miracle-Grip Lettering
440 Speedwell Avenue
Morris Plains, NJ 07950
(201) 540-1589

Mitre Sports
Genesco Park 538-A
Nashville, TN 37202
(800) 826-7650 (except in TN)
(800) 342-5795 (TN only)
FAX: (615) 367-7320

Mizuno Sports, Inc.
577 Airport Boulevard, 8th
Floor
Burlingame, CA 94010
(415) 347-3900
(800) 227-0484 (CA only)
(800) 227-5990 (except in CA)
FAX: (415) 347-1035

Moretz Sports
514 West 21st Street
Newton, NC 28658
(704) 464-0751
(800) 438-9127
FAX: (704) 465-4203

Muehleisen Mfg. Co.
823 Gateway Center Way,

Suite A
San Diego, CA 92102
(619) 266-1616
(800) 654-8567 (except in CA)
(800) 321-0756 (CA only)
FAX: (619) 527-0307
Mailing Address:
P.O. Box 8130
San Diego, CA 92102-0130

Mueller Sports Medicine,
Inc.
One Quench Drive
Prairie du Sac, WI 53578
(608) 643-8530
(800) 356-9522
FAX: (608) 643-2568

MVP Productions
P.O. Box 1057
Fern Park, FL 32730
(407) 339-2690

Nasco Inc.
27 North Main Street
Springfield, TN 37172
(615) 384-0100
(800) 621-0883
FAX: (615) 384-0100, ext. 335

Nathan Equipment Mfg.
Corp.
139 Banker Street
Brooklyn, NY 11222
(718) 388-2527
(800) BARBELL
FAX: (718) 384-5990

National Fabricators
937 Saw Mill River Road
Yonkers, NY 10710
(914) 963-4080

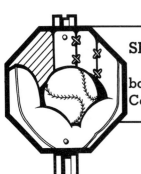

SHORTSTOPS
    In his entire 14-year career, Hall-of-Famer Joe Sewell used only one bat. (He kept it in shape by rubbing it with chewing tobacco and a Coke bottle.)

RETIRING NUMBERS

When a rookie player is assigned a famous number, it sometimes brings with it a lot of pressure. Do you think you can play as well as so-and-so? the rookie is asked. Can you fill old number 11's shoes?

But for some of the most famous numbers ever, players don't have this problem. One of the ways baseball honors its greatest players is to retire their number. That team decides it will never assign the number again.

As of 1989, 80 players' numbers had been retired. Here's a list. (Remember, the numbers are retired only for the one team.)

AMERICAN LEAGUE

Baltimore Orioles
Earl Weaver	4
Brooks Robinson	5
Frank Robinson	20
Jim Palmer	22

Boston Red Sox
Bobby Doerr	1
Joe Cronin	4
Ted Williams	9

California Angels
Gene Autry	26
Rod Carew	29

Chicago White Sox
Nellie Fox	2
Luke Appling	4
Minnie Minoso	9
Luis Aparicio	11
Ted Lyons	16
Billy Pierce	19

Cleveland Indians
Earl Averill	3
Lou Boudreau	5
Bob Feller	19

Detroit Tigers
Charlie Gehringer	2
Hank Greenberg	5
Al Kaline	6

Kansas City Royals
Dick Howser	10

Milwaukee Brewers
Hank Aaron	44

Minnesota Twins
Harmon Killebrew	3
Rod Carew	29

New York Yankees
Billy Martin	1
Babe Ruth	3
Lou Gehrig	4
Joe DiMaggio	5
Mickey Mantle	7
Yogi Berra	8
Bill Dickey	8
Roger Maris	9
Phil Rizzuto	10
Thurman Munson	15
Elston Howard	32
Casey Stengel	37

NATIONAL LEAGUE

Atlanta Braves
Warren Spahn	21
Phil Niekro	35
Eddie Mathews	41
Hank Aaron	44

Chicago Cubs
Ernie Banks	14
Billy Williams	26

Cincinnati Reds
Fred Hutchinson	1
Johnny Bench	5

Houston Astros
Jim Umbright	32
Don Wilson	40

Brooklyn/Los Angeles Dodgers
Pee Wee Reese	1
Duke Snider	4
Jim Gilliam	19
Walter Alston	24
Sandy Koufax	32
Roy Campanella	39
Jackie Robinson	42
Don Drysdale	53

New York Mets
Gil Hodges	14
Casey Stengel	37
Tom Seaver	41

Philadelphia Phillies
Richie Ashburn	1
Robin Roberts	36

Pittsburgh Pirates
Bill Meyer	1
Ralph Kiner	4
Willie Stargell	8
Bill Mazeroski	9
Pie Traynor	20
Roberto Clemente	21
Honus Wagner	33
Danny Murtaugh	40

St. Louis Cardinals

Stan Musial	6
Ken Boyer	14
Dizzy Dean	17
Lou Brock	20
Bob Gibson	45

New York/San Francisco Giants

Bill Terry	3
Mel Ott	4
Carl Hubbell	11
Willie Mays	24
Juan Marichal	27
Willie McCovey	44

This isn't Roger Maris's real jersey. The 61 stands for his record-breaking home run total.

National Merchandise Co.
P.O. Box 600
Mechanicsville, VA 23111
(804) 788-4377

National Sporting Goods
Corp.
25 Brighton Avenue
Passaic, NJ 07055
(201) 779-2323
FAX: (201) 779-0084

Nautilus Sports/Medical
Industries
P.O. Box 809014
Dallas, TX 75380-9014
(214) 490-9155
(800) 874-8941
FAX: (214) 490-3736

N.D.L. Products, Inc.
P.O. Box 1867
Pompano Beach, FL 33061
(305) 942-4560
(800) 843-3021 (except in FL)
(800) 843-3022 (FL only)
FAX: (305) 578-9496

Needlecraft of Woonsocket,
Inc.
565 North Main Street
Woonsocket, RI 02895
(401) 766-1000
(800) 222-1312
FAX: (401) 766-7680

Neff Company
P.O. Box 218
Greenville, OH 45331
(513) 548-3194

Nelson Knitting Co.
909 South Main Street

P.O. Box 1211
Rockford, IL 61101
(815) 962-8829
(800) 435-0701
FAX: (815) 962-8110

Nelson/Weather-Rite
Products, Inc.
P.O. Box 14488
14760 Santa Fe Trail Drive
Lenexa, KS 66215
(913) 492-3200
(800) 255-6061
FAX: (913) 492-8749
New Jersey Address:
125 Enterprise Avenue
Secaucus, NJ 07094
(201) 348-0400
(800) 631-3721
FAX: (201) 348-2252
California Address:
6000 Peachtree Street
Commerce, CA 90040
(213) 747-7351
(800) 533-5355
FAX: (213) 747-1525

New Era Cap Co. Inc.
8061 Erie Road
Derby, NY 14047
(716) 549-0445

New Era Knitting Mills, Inc.
4101 West Parker Avenue
Chicago, IL 60639
(312) 486-0871

Newsouth Athletic Co. Inc.
P.O. Box 398
1010 North Main Street
Lowell, NC 28098
(704) 824-4678
(800) 438-9934

Nike
3900 Southwest Murray
Boulevard
Beaverton, OR 97005
(503) 641-6453
FAX: (503) 641-0731

Nissen Corporation
4121-16th Avenue S.W.
Cedar Rapids, IA 52406
(319) 396-9626
(800) 553-7901

Nocona Athletic Goods Co.
209 Baylor Street
Nocona, TX 76255
(817) 825-3326
(800) 433-0957

NordicTrack
141 Jonathan Boulevard
North

Chaska, MN 55318
(612) 448-6987
(800) 328-5888 (except in MN)
FAX: (612) 448-6120

North American Recreation
P.O. Box 430, FH Station
New Haven, CT 06513
(203) 789-1811
(800) 243-5133
FAX: (203) 776-1461

Northern Cap Mfg. Co., Inc.
510 First Avenue North
Minneapolis, MN 55403
(612) 332-8979
(800) 328-4589
FAX: (612) 332-1748

Odell Associates, Inc.
Commerce Center
129 West Trade Street

Charlotte, NC 28202
(704) 377-5941
FAX: (704) 377-5941, ext. 225

Oklahoma Leather
Products, Inc.
402 Newman Road
North Miami, OK 74354
(918) 542-6651
FAX: (918) 542-6653

Omni Scientific, Inc.
827 Arnold Drive, No. 100
Martinez, CA 94553
(415) 228-5330
(800) 448-OMNI (except in
CA)

Omnisport/Deerfoot
128 Singleton Street
Woonsocket, RI 02895
(401) 769-7000

OTA, Inc.
135 High Avenue
Oshkosh, WI 54901
(414) 235-3200

Pacer Industries
1121 Crowley
Carrollton, TX 75006
(214) 446-3535
(800) 873-9090
FAX: (214) 242-3415

Paoletti/Lewitz/Associates
Inc.
40 Gold Street
San Francisco, CA 94133
(415) 391-7610
FAX: (415) 391-0171
Utah Office:
5263 South 300 West

Players model the official uniforms for the first Little League World Series for girls in 1974.

Salt Lake City, UT 84107
(801) 266-3605

Paramount Fitness
Corporation
6450 East Bandini
Boulevard
City of Commerce, CA
90040
(213) 721-2121
(800) 421-6242

Patch, A.T. Co.
P.O. Box 682, Dept. 136
Littleton, NH 03561
(603) 444-3423

Patterson-Williams Mfg.
Co., Inc.
P.O. Box 4040
Santa Clara, CA 95054
(408) 988-3066

Pearson, Drew Enterprises
17103 Preston Road, Suite
288
Lock Box 102
Dallas, TX 75248
(214) 733-0880
FAX: (214) 733-0657

Pennsylvania Sporting
Goods Company
1360 Industrial Highway
Southampton, PA 18966
(215) 322-9100
(800) 535-1122
Mailing Address:
P.O. Box 451
Southampton, PA 18966

Performance-USA Fitness
Ltd.
106 Regal Row

Dallas, TX 75247
(214) 637-2500
(800) 292-5866
FAX: (214) 637-5506

Physicians & Nurses Mfg.
Co.
P.O. Box 68
Larchmont, NY 10538-0068
(914) 576-0216
(800) 535-1110
FAX: (914) 633-5876
California Address:
P.O. Box 1723
Huntington Beach, CA
92647-1723

Pick Point Enterprises, Inc.
Windleblo Road
Mirror Lake, NH 03853
(603) 569-1338

Pinckard Baseballs &
Softballs
P.O. Box 6670
Woodland Hills, CA 91365
(818) 709-8805

Pine Hosiery Mills, Inc.
P.O. Box 98
South Main Street
Star, NC 27356
(919) 428-2185
(800) 342-2948
FAX: (919) 428-9367

Pioneer Industries, Inc.
11702 W. 85th Street
Lenexa, KS 66214
(913) 888-6760
(800) 255-0406
FAX: (913) 541-0592

Pitt Barbell & Healthfood
Corp.
126 Penn Hills Mall
Pittsburgh, PA 15235
(412) 371-4366

Plank's Printing Service,
Inc.
505 South Ninth Street
Goshen, IN 46526
(219) 533-1739, 533-1031

Playfield Industries, Inc.
P.O. Box 8, Murray
Industrial Park
Chatsworth, GA 30705
(404) 695-4581
(800) 221-7449
FAX: (404) 226-6243

Plus Fours
12970 Maurer Industrial
Drive
St. Louis, MO 63187
(314) 525-0614
(800) 325-9516

Polar Electro, Inc., USA
300 Cottonwood Avenue,
Suite 1
Hartland, WI 53029
(414) 367-4944
(800) 262-7776 (customers
only)
FAX: (414) 367-5147
Mailing Address:
P.O. Box 920
Hartland, WI 53029

Polaris by Iron Company
P.O. Box 1458
Spring Valley, CA 92077
(619) 670-7976

(800) 858-0300
FAX: (619) 258-2605

Poly Enterprises
230 East Pomona
Monrovia, CA 91016
(818) 358-5115
FAX: (818) 358-7862

Pony Sports & Leisure, Inc.
201 Route 17, North
Rutherford, NJ 07070
(201) 896-0101
(800) 654-7669
FAX: (201) 935-3312

Powell, Milton & Partners
5207 McKinney Avenue
Dallas, TX 75205
(214) 526-2151

Powercise International
3201 Orange Grove Avenue
North Highland, CA 95660
(916) 971-8500
FAX: (916) 481-0489

Powers Mfg. Co.
Box 2157
Waterloo, IA 50704
(319) 233-6118
FAX: (319) 234-8048

Precor USA
20001 North Creek Parkway
North
Bothell, WA 98011
(206) 486-9292
(800) 662-0606
Mailing Address:
P.O. Box 3004
Bothell, WA 98041-3004

Pro Feet, Inc.
1208 Belmont Street
Burlington, NC 27216
(919) 226-0237
(800) 334-1101
FAX: (919) 229-9920
Mailing Address:
P.O. Box 2720
Burlington, NC 27216

Pro Line Cap Company
P.O. Box 5098
8224 White Settlement
Road
Fort Worth, TX 76108
(817) 246-4931

Pro Orthopedic Devices,
Inc.
4101 S. Longfellow Avenue
Tucson, AZ 85714
(602) 790-9330
(800) 523-5611
FAX: (602) 750-0355
Mailing Address:
P.O. Box 31401
Tucson, AZ 85751

Pro Sports Products
2438 West Anderson Lane
Austin, TX 78757
(512) 451-7141
(800) 444-1158

Pro Star Sports, Inc.
1120 S.W. 28th Street
Blue Springs, MO 64015
(816) 229-1554
(800) 821-8482
FAX: (816) 229-1566

Professional Gym, Inc.
P.O. Box 188

805 Cherokee Lane
Marshall, MO 65340
(816) 886-9628
(800) 821-7665
FAX: (816) 886-3041

Pro-Grip Division
22 Skokie Highway
Lake Bluff, IL 60044
(312) 234-8100
(800) 323-3133
FAX: (312) 234-8160
FAX (WATS): (800) 447-7722

Pro-Mate USA
3135 Diablo Avenue
Hayward, CA 94545
(415) 782-8471
(800) 521-6327

Pro-Tec Sports International, Inc.
5181 Argosy Drive
Huntington Beach, CA
92649
(714) 893-3330
(800) 453-5332 (except in CA)
(800) 423-6382 (CA only)
FAX: (714) 895-4324

Puma USA, Inc.
492 Old Connecticut Path
Framingham, MA 01701
(617) 875-0660
FAX: (617) 872-9895
Mailing Address:
P.O. Box 1369
Framingham, MA
01701-1369

Putterman, M. & Co., Inc.
4834 South Oakley Place
Chicago, IL 60609

THE BULL PEN
Q: Why is Dracula afraid of baseball?
A: Players sometimes throw the bat.

(312) 927-4121
(800) 621-0146
FAX: (312) 650-6028

Pyramid Fitness Industries,
Inc.
854 S. Irvine Avenue
Masury, OH 44438
(216) 448-1872
(800) 448-1888
FAX: (412) 962-0866

Pyramid Outerwear
33-34th Street
Building No. 7
Bush Terminal
Brooklyn, NY 11232
(718) 965-9100

Quaker Oats Company
321 North Clark
Chicago, IL 60610
(312) 222-7709
FAX: (312) 222-8191

Quik-Set Lettering Inc.
26 Israel Street
P.O. Box 232
Westerville, OH 43081
(614) 891-1370
(800) 848-8893 (except in OH)
(800) 292-8813 (OH only)
FAX: (614) 891-4461

Rainbow Sports Enter-
prises, Ltd.
6621 Richmond Highway
Alexandria, VA 22306
(703) 768-6050

Ranger Athletic Mfg., Inc.
407 West Main Street
Ranger, TX 76470

(817) 647-3771
(800) 433-5518
FAX: (817) 647-3777 (Ranger)
FAX: (214) 276-9608 (Dallas)

Rawlings Sporting Goods
Co.
1859 Intertech
Fenton, MO 63026
(314) 349-3500
(800) RAWLING
FAX: (314) 349-3588
Mailing Address:
P.O. Box 22000
St. Louis, MO 63126

R.B.I. Industries, Inc.
9737 Larston Drive
Houston, TX 77055
(713) 468-5748

Red Lion Products
176 Patton Lane
Wayne, PA 19087
(609) 365-0220
(800) 526-2363
FAX: (609) 964-9135

Regent Sports Corp.
45 Ranick Road
Hauppauge, NY 11787
(516) 234-2800

Rennoc
S.E. Boulevard & Sheridan
Avenue
Vineland, NJ 08630
(609) 825-7720

Renosol Corporation
5500 South State Street
Ann Arbor, MI 48106
(313) 429-5418

FAX: (313) 429-5351

Revere Plastics Inc.
16 Industrial Avenue
Little Ferry, NJ 07643
(201) 641-0777

Richardson Sports, Inc.
3490 West First Avenue
Eugene, OR 97402
(503) 687-1818
(800) 545-8686
FAX: (503) 687-1130

Riddell, Inc.
3670 North Milwaukee
Avenue
Chicago, IL 60641
(312) 794-1994
FAX: (312) 794-6155

Ridgeview Mills, Inc.
2101 North Main Avenue
P.O. Box 8
Newton, NC 28658
(704) 464-2972
(800) 438-9517

Roadmaster Corporation
East Street & Radio Tower
Road
Olney, IL 62450
(618) 393-2991
FAX: (618) 395-1057
Mailing Address:
P.O. Box 344
Olney, IL 62450

Rocky Mountain Gym
Equipment Co., Inc.
5745 Monaco Street
Commerce City, CO 80022
(303) 287-8095

DETROIT

CHICAGO

WASHINGTON

Rodel Inc.
451 Bellevue Road
Newark, DE 19713
(302) 366-0500

Roman Art-Roman
Pro-Lara Ltd.
443 Summer Street
Brockton, MA 02402
(617) 583-5515

Ross Laboratories, Inc.
625 Cleveland Avenue
Columbus, OH 43215
(614) 227-3333
FAX: (614) 229-7088

Rossman, Schneider,
Gadbery Shay Architects
4601 East McDowell Road
Phoenix, AZ 85008
(602) 273-7188
FAX: (602) 840-3024

Royal Textile Mills
P.O. Box 250
Yanceyville, NC 27379
(919) 694-4121
(800) 334-9361
FAX: (919) 694-9084

RS Productions, Inc.
3819 Wooded Creek
Farmers Branch, TX 75244
(214) 243-5440

Russell Athletic
Alexander City, AL 35010
(205) 329-4000
FAX: (205) 329-4474

Russell National Sport
Socks
P.O. Drawer 9
Star, NC 27356
(919) 428-2131
(800) 334-9661
FAX: (919) 428-2131, ext. 324

S & C Sales Company
3826 Zane Trace
Columbus, OH 43228
(614) 876-1156
(800) 848-7978 (national)

Safe-Play Tuf Wear Mfg.
Co., Inc.
P.O. Box 239, 16th & Hickory
Sidney, NB 69162
(308) 254-4011
(800) 445-5210

SAI by Kemfast
10 North Summit Street

Granite Falls, NC 28630
(704) 396-2154
(800) 438-2371

Saiz Group
1485 Bayshore Boulevard
San Francisco, CA 94124
(415) 821-7775
FAX: (415) 467-0991

Saranac Glove Co.
P.O. Box 786
1201 Main Street
Green Bay, WI 54305
(414) 435-3737
(800) 558-7302 (except in WI)
(800) 242-6656 (WI only)

School Health Supply Co.
300 Lombard Road
Addison, IL 60101
(312) 543-9216
(800) 323-1305 (except in IL)
FAX: (312) 543-9231

Schutt Mfg. Co.
Box 345
610 South Industrial Drive
Litchfield, IL 62056
(217) 324-3978
FAX: (217) 324-2855

Schwinn Bicycle Company
217 N. Jefferson Street
Chicago, IL 60606
(312) 454-7400

SciPro
2333 San Ramon Valley
Boulevard
Center Plaza, Suite 200
San Ramon, CA 94583
(415) 837-8081
FAX: (415) 837-6157

Segal International
1220 Spring Garden Street
Philadelphia, PA 19123
(215) 922-2100

Sentinel Fitness Products
130 North Street
Box S
Hyannis, MA 02601
(617) 775-5220
(800) 323-5005 (except in MA)
(800) 323-5001 (MA only)
FAX: (617) 771-1554

SGI
480 Jefferson Boulevard
Warwick, RI 02886
(401) 732-5520
(800) 423-2247
FAX: (401) 822-1710

Show-Tags, Inc.
P.O. Box 7468
2110 Veasley Street
Greensboro, NC 27407
(919) 292-7564
(800) 248-3687 (except in NC)
(800) 854-5168 (NC only)

Sink Combs Dethlefs
1900 Grant Street, Suite
1250
Denver, CO 80203
(303) 830-1200

Sipes, Howe K. Co., Inc.
P.O. Box 9099
249 E. Mallory Avenue
Memphis, TN 38109
(901) 948-0378
(800) 238-2682

S.L.M. Action Sports
P.O. Box 2000
Morrisville, NC 27560
(919) 469-4111
FAX: (919) 467-1888

S.M. Athletics, Inc.
10334 Cogdill Drive
Knoxville, TN 37922
(615) 966-3434

Snitz Mfg. Co.
2096 South Church Street
East Troy, WI 53120
(414) 642-3991
(800) 558-2224
FAX: (414) 642-9591

Soffe, M.J., Co., Inc.
One Soffe Drive
Fayetteville, NC 28301
(919) 483-2500
(800) 444-0337 (except in NC)
(800) 682-2547 (NC only)

Softouch Co., Inc.
1167 N.W. 159 Drive
Miami, FL 33169
(305) 624-5581
(800) 327-1539 (except in FL)

(800) 432-3633 (FL only)
Mailing Address:
P.O. Box 4144
Miami, FL 33269

Sonata USA, Inc.
9948 Bryn Mawr Avenue
Rosemont, IL 60018
(312) 671-0040
FAX: (312) 671-0216

Southland Athletic Mfg.
Co.
P.O. Box 280
Terrell, TX 75160
(214) 563-3321
FAX: (214) 563-0943

Spalding Apparel
(See Warnaco listing)

Spalding International
Athletic Footwear
470 Park Avenue South
New York, NY 10016
(212) 683-8503

Spalding Socks
200 Madison Avenue
New York, NY 10016
(212) 532-2510

Spalding Sports Worldwide
425 Meadow Street
Chicopee, MA 01013
(413) 536-1200
FAX: (413) 536-1404
Mailing Address:
P.O. Box 901
Chicopee, MA 01021-0901

Spectrum Corporation
10048 Easthaven

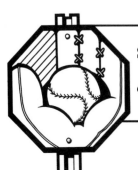

SHORTSTOPS
The major league infield bags at first, second, and third base are all 15 inches wide. Home plate is 17 inches.

Houston, TX 77075
(713) 944-6200
(800) 392-5050
FAX: (713) 944-1290

Spectrum Sports
2069 Midway Drive
Twinsburg, OH 44087
(216) 425-3481
(800) 321-4145

Speedline Athletic Wear
1804 North Habana
Tampa, FL 33607
(813) 876-1375

Spenco Medical Corporation
Box 2501
Waco, TX 76701-2501
(817) 772-6000
(800) 433-3334
FAX: (817) 772-3093

Sport Tech
85 Madison Circle Drive
East Rutherford, NJ 07073
(201) 460-1888
FAX: (201) 460-0125

Sportcap, Inc.
3515 West Artesia
Boulevard
Torrance, CA 90504
(213) 538-3312
(800) 421-5511 (except in CA)
(800) 821-2786 (CA only)
FAX: (213) 324-3898
Mailing Address:
P.O. Box 6460
Torrance, CA 90504

SportDecals
P.O. Box 358
Crystal Lake, IL 60014
(815) 455-0431
(800) 435-6110
FAX: (815) 455-9044

Sportech, Inc.
P.O. Box 99101
Cleveland, OH 44199
(216) 566-7873 (OH)
(800) 221-1258 (except in OH)

Sportime
2905-E Amwiler Road
Atlanta, GA 30360-2897
(404) 449-5700
(800) 444-5700
FAX: (404) 263-0897

Sports Belle Inc.
6723 Pleasant Ridge Road
Knoxville, TN 37901
(615) 938-2063
(800) 251-9836
FAX: (615) 947-4466
Mailing Address:
P.O. Box 50243
Knoxville, TN 37950

Sports Equipment Inc.
P.O. Box 280777
Dallas, TX 75228
(214) 412-4031
(800) 727-2444

Sports Specialties
25 Hughes
Irvine, CA 92718
(714) 768-4000
(800) 535-2222

Sports Systems Inc.
437 Bulkley Building
Cleveland, OH 44115
(216) 696-1126
FAX: (216) 861-3624

Sportsotron, Inc. and Hy
Sport
115 Orville Drive
Bohemia, NY 11716
(516) 567-9300
(800) 645-1140

Sport-Star Company
7360 S.W. 84th
Portland, OR 97223
(503) 245-2393

Sportyme, Inc.
126 South York Road
Hatboro, PA 19040
(215) 675-0270
(800) 634-8311

SSK America Incorporated
17101 S. Central Avenue,
Unit 1C
Carson, CA 90746
(213) 638-9338
(800) 421-2674
FAX: (213) 637-1355

Stackhouse Athletic
Equipment, Inc.
P.O. Box 12276
Salem, OR 97309
(503) 363-1840
FAX: (503) 363-0511

Staco Enterprises, Inc.
P.O. Box 12511
Overland Park, KS 66212
(913) 894-6044

THE BULL PEN
    Q: What baseball player is always ready for Halloween?
    A: The catcher—he wears a mask.

(800) 282-0042
FAX: (913) 321-7853

Stadiums Unlimited, Inc.
P.O. Box 627
Grinnell, IA 50112
(515) 236-6535
(800) 782-3486

Stahls
20600 Stephens
St. Clair Shores, MI 48080
(313) 772-6161
(800) 521-3100
(800) 521-9702 (For Orders)
FAX: (800) 346-2216
FAX: (313) 772-6237 (Intl/MI)
Mailing Address:
P.O. Box 628
St. Clair Shores, MI 48080

Stall & Dean Mfg. Co., Inc.
P.O. Box 698
95 Church Street
Brockton, MA 02401
(508) 586-2414

Standard Merchandising
Co.
1125 Wright Avenue
Camden, NJ 08103
(609) 964-9700
FAX: (609) 964-9135

Stanmar Inc.
Boston Post Road
Sudbury, MA 01776
(508) 443-9922

Star City Productions
C/O Rob Ellis
P.O. Box 6134
East Lansing, MI 48826

(517) 355-3419

Star Quality Sports
2210 Wilshire Boulevard,
Suite 328
Santa Monica, CA 90403

Starter Sportswear
360 James Street
New Haven, CT 06513
(203) 787-4291
(800) 243-6170
FAX: (203) 773-1383
Mailing Address:
P.O. Box 1547
New Haven, CT 06506

Stedman Corporation
450 Hanes Mill Road
Winston-Salem, NC 27102
(919) 744-2400

Steele's Sports Co.
1044 Vivian Drive
Grafton, OH 44044
(216) 926-2831
(800) 321-3885

Stevens Hat Co.
3601 Leonard Road
St. Joseph, MO 64502
(816) 233-8031

Stone Enterprises, Inc.
P.O. Box 2024
14 Hanover Street
Hanover, MA 02339
(617) 826-4668
(617) 826-9511

Stone, Rock & Associates
612 Pleasure Street
Route 4, Box 184

Chetek, WI 54728
(715) 924-4374

Strength, Inc.
432 Highland Avenue
Twin Falls, ID 83301
(208) 734-6883

Striker Uniforms
161 West State Street
Doylestown, PA 18901
(215) 348-9400

Stromgren Supports, Inc.
2801 Hall Street
Hays, KS 67601
(913) 625-4674
FAX: (913) 625-9036
Mailing Address:
P.O. Box 1230
Hays, KS 67601

The Stuart, D. Co., Inc.
691 Gana Court
Mississauga, Ontario
Canada L5S 1P2
(416) 670-1177
FAX: (416) 670-4981

Surgrip U.S.A.
1014 16th Street
Modesto, CA 95353
(209) 521-6260
FAX: (209) 521-5971
Mailing Address:
P.O. Box 3212
Modesto, CA 95353

Sverdrup Corporation
801 North Eleventh
St. Louis, MO 63101
(314) 436-7600
(800) 325-7910

FAX: (314) 436-2959

Sweat Buddy, Inc.
P.O. Box 1743
Cleveland, TX 77327
(713) 592-1151

Swingster Athletic Apparel
10450 Holmes Road
Kansas City, MO 64131
(816) 943-5000
(800) 255-0006
FAX: (816) 943-5150

Tacki-Mac Grips, Inc.
8740 Flower Road
Rancho Cucamonga, CA
91730
(818) 944-9681
(800) 423-2549
FAX: (818) 944-0493

T-Brace Co.
522 Colusa
El Cerrito, CA 94530
(415) 527-9809
(800) 234-8272

T.G. Sports Co./Trans
Global Sports Co.
13104 S. Avalon Boulevard
Los Angeles, CA 90061
(213) 321-9714
FAX: (213) 327-6465

Thera-Care, Inc.
1320 Hill Street
El Cajon, CA 92020
(619) 588-7711

Things from Bell, Inc.
4 Lincoln Avenue
P.O. Box 706

Cortland, NY 13045
(607) 753-8291

Thor-Lo
P.O. Box 5440
Statesville, NC 28677
(704) 872-6522
(800) 438-0209
FAX: (704) 878-9861

Tide-Rider, Inc.
85 Corporate Drive
Hauppauge, NY 11788
(516) 434-1030
FAX: (516) 434-1774
Mailing Address:
P.O. Box 12427
Hauppauge, NY 11788

Time Out
2412 St. Mary's Avenue
Omaha, NE 68105
(402) 342-2985

Titan Exercise Equipment,
Inc.
1440 LeMay, Suite 110
Carrollton, TX 75007
(214) 245-3000

T.M. Athletics
163 South Jackson Street
Seattle, WA 98104
(206) 624-3756
FAX: (206) 587-5334

Tom Sports Company
777 Chestnut
Abilene, TX 79604
(915) 677-4844
(800) 351-1374

Tomblinson Harburn
Associates
1800 Crooks Road
Troy, MI 48084
(313) 362-3046
FAX: (313) 235-3999

Top-Comfo Athletic Sox,
Inc.
P.O. Box 10304
Lynchburg, VA 24506
(804) 237-2323

Totes, Inc.
East Kemper Road
Loveland, OH 45140
(513) 583-2300
FAX: (513) 683-4765

Tournament Sports
Marketing
P.O. Box 700
55 Canbar Street
Waterloo, Ontario
Canada N2J 4B8
(519) 886-3600
FAX: (519) 886-5673

Town Talk Cap Mfg. Co.,
Inc.
P.O. Box 4009
Lousville, KY 40204
(502) 584-2163
FAX: (502) 585-2367

Transorient, Inc.
9591 York Alpha Drive
North Royalton, OH 44133
(216) 582-0144

Trenway Textiles, Inc.
P.O. Drawer 2180
Westside Industrial Park

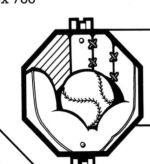

SHORTSTOPS
A major league bat cannot be more than 42 inches long.

ohnson City, TN 37601
615) 928-8196
800) 251-7504
FAX: (615) 928-8138

Trius Products, Inc.
P.O. Box 25
221 South Miami Avenue
Cleves, OH 45002
513) 941-5682
FAX: (513) 941-7970

Trophy Glove Co.
122 Washington Avenue
East
Albia, IA 52531
515) 932-2183
800) 323-2928
FAX: (515) 932-7430

Trotter, Inc.
1073 Main Street
Millis, MA 02054
617) 376-4500

Troy Corp.
2300 West Diversey Avenue
Chicago, IL 60647
312) 227-2400
800) 331-8769 (except in IL)
800) 223-8769 (In IL)

Tru-Fit Inc.
680 Lynnway
Lynn, MA 01905
617) 592-6544
800) 225-6848
FAX: (617) 593-7602

Tru-Pitch Inc.
13150 38th Street North
P.O. Box 1728
Clearwater, FL 34290

(813) 573-9701

Tuff Toe
255 Tivoli Drive
Long Beach, CA 90803
(213) 434-5168

Tully: Architecture,
Planning, Engineering
99 Essex Street
Melrose, MA 02176
(617) 665-0099
FAX: (617) 662-0873

Tunturi, Inc.
P.O. Box 3825
1776 136th Place, N.E.
Bellevue, WA 98009
(206) 643-1000
(800) 426-0858
FAX: (206) 644-1642

Twin City Knitting Co., Inc.
710 1st Street East
Conover, NC 28613
(704) 464-4830
(800) 438-6884
Mailing Address:
P.O. Box 1179
Conover, NC 28613

Twin Laboratories, Inc.
2120 Smithtown Avenue
Ronkonkoma, NY 11779
(516) 467-3140
(800) 645-5626 (except in NY)
FAX: (516) 471-2375

Uniforms Unlimited
P.O. Box 45
175 Tompkins Avenue
Pleasantville, NY 10570
(914) 769-6845

Union Jacks
3525 Roanoke
Kansas City, MO 64111
(816) 561-5550
FAX: (816) 561-1722

Unique Sports Products,
Inc.
840 McFarland Road
Alpharetta, GA 30201
(404) 442-1977
(800) 554-3707 (orders only)
FAX: (404) 475-2065

Uniquity
P.O. Box 6
215 Fourth Street
Galt, CA 95632
(209) 745-2111

Universal Fitness
Products/Universal Gym
Co.
20 Terminal Drive
Plainview, NY 11803
(516) 349-8600
(800) 645-7554

Universal Gym Equipment
Inc.
4121—16th Avenue S.W.
Cedar Rapids, IA 52406
(319) 396-9626
(800) 553-7901
Mailing Address:
P.O. Box 1270
Cedar Rapids, IA 52406

Universal Industries, Inc.
5 Industrial Drive
Mattapoisett, MA 02739
(617) 758-6101
(800) 225-8194

Making Your Own Baseball Souvenir

As you can tell from the article in this chapter, making a major league baseball is a complicated process. What if you want to make your own?

Tom Hubben, a New York toy maker and avid baseball fan, decided to do just that. By studying a real baseball, he made himself a toy baseball souvenir. Then he drew out the pattern below. You can use it to make a toy ball of your own.

It won't be a ball you can bat around (not more than once, anyway!). But if you follow the pattern exactly, it will be major league size. You can use the same number of stitches as a major league ball has (108), and the same stitching pattern.

WHAT YOU'LL NEED

Needle and thread. Major league balls use red thread. You can use red for authenticity, or any color you like just for fun!

Cloth. Use any kind or color you like that's easy to cut and sew.

Stuffing. Again, it's up to you. You can use anything from a bag of beans to pieces of paper crumpled around a rock.

WHAT TO DO

Trace the shapes below and use it as a pattern to cut out the two pieces of cloth. If you're having trouble seeing how the two pieces form a ball, it helps to look at a real baseball.

Basically, you need to form one piece into a C-shape. Start by sewing one of the large ends of the other piece into the C-shaped opening you've just formed with the first piece.

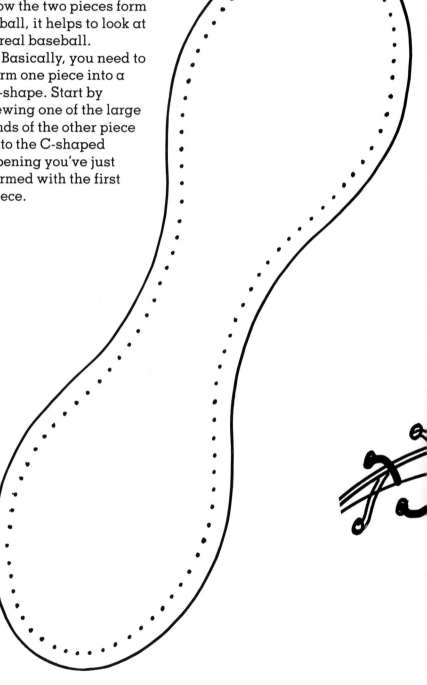

SEWING

If you're not a good sewer, don't worry too much about the major league sewing pattern shown below. You can sew the two pieces together any which way, or even glue them to your stuffing.

If you want to be official and fancy, sew two threads as shown in the diagram. With the first thread go over and under, skipping a hole each time. Now go back with the second thread and do the same thing with all the missed holes.

Before you've sewed the first thread all around, fit the stuffing inside.

FAX: (617) 758-4786
Mailing Address:
P.O. Box 1060
Mattapoisett, MA 02739

U.S. Barbell Products, Inc.
P.O. Box 747
Summit, NJ 07901
(201) 464-7134
FAX: (201) 464-7134 (P.M.)

U.S. Cap & Jacket
214 New Haven Road
Prospect, CT 06712
(203) 758-4437
(800) 243-4150
FAX: (203) 758-3277

U.S. China Trading Corp.
7827 Quincy Avenue
Willowbrook, IL 60521
(312) 654-0606
(800) 284-0319
FAX: (312) 654-0530

U.S. Games, Inc.
1901 Diplomat Drive
Farmers Branch, TX 75234
(214) 484-9484
(800) 327-0484
FAX: (214) 484-0457
Mailing Address:
P.O. Box 117028
Carrollton, TX 75011-7028

Varsity House
1462 62nd Street
Brooklyn, NY 11219
(718) 232-1110

Venus Knitting Mills, Inc.
140 Spring Street
Murray Hill, NJ 07974

(201) 464-2400

Vibra-Whirl & Co.
P.O. Box 966
Panhandle, TX 79068
(806) 537-3526
FAX: (806) 537-3442
Justin, TX Office:
150 Highway 156
Justin, TX 76247
(800) 255-8722
FAX: (817) 648-2700

Victory Sports Nets
927 First Street
Menominee, MI 49858
(906) 863-5531
(800) 338-9860

Vienna Health Products
54 Phillips Way
Sharon, PA 16146
(412) 342-2525

Vitronics, Inc.
350 East Orangethorpe
Avenue
Placentia, CA 92670
(714) 579-0224

Voyager Emblems, Inc.
3707 Lockport Road
Sanborn, NY 14132
(716) 731-4121
(800) 828-1603

Vukas Products, Inc.
1457 Woodland Drive
Ann Arbor, MI 48103
(313) 769-7894

Wa-Mac, Inc.
P.O. Box 128

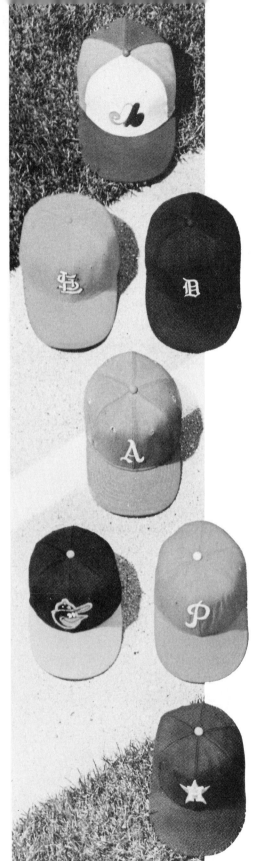

178 Commerce Road
Carlstadt, NJ 07072
(201) 438-7200
(800) HI-SKORE (except in NJ)
FAX: (201) 438-1494

Warnaco
7915 Haskell Avenue
Van Nuys, CA 91409
(818) 782-7568
(800) 547-8770
FAX: (818) 375-1698

Wate-Man Sales, Inc.
29123 8 Mile Road
Livonia, MI 48152
(313) 477-7245

Weider Health & Fitness
Box 864
21100 Erwin Street
Woodland Hills, CA 91367
(818) 884-6800
(800) 423-5590

Weightlifter's Warehouse, Inc.
5542 South Street
Lakewood, CA 90713
(213) 531-3731

Weslo, Inc.
P.O. Box 10
Logan, UT 84321
(801) 750-5000
(800) 824-3109
FAX: (801) 753-0209

The West Bend Company
400 Washington Street
West Bend, WI 53095
(414) 334-2311

(800) 438-5326

West Coast Netting, Inc.
P.O. Box 728
8978 Haven Avenue
Cucamonga, CA 91730
(818) 330-3207
(714) 987-4708
(800) 854-5741
FAX: (714) 944-7396

Whitely Fitness Products
135 South Washington Avenue
Bergenfield, NJ 07621
(201) 384-9711
FAX: (201) 384-3494

Whitland Corporation
P.O. Box 1049
Lawrence, MA 01842
(617) 685-5109

Widen Tool & Stamping Inc.
1206 South Front Street
St. Peter, MN 56082
(507) 931-5778

Wight and Company, Inc.
814 Ogden Avenue
Downers Grove, IL 60515
(312) 969-7000
FAX: (312) 969-7979

Wigwam Mills, Inc.
3402 Crocker Avenue
Sheboygan, WI 53081
(414) 457-5551
(800) 558-7760
FAX: (414) 457-0311
Mailing Address:
P.O. Box 818

Sheboygan, WI 53082-0818

Wilson Sporting Goods Co.
2233 West Street
River Grove, IL 60171
(312) 456-6100
FAX: (312) 452-3132

Wilson Sports Apparel
16002 West 110th Street
Lenexa, KS 66219
(913) 888-0640
(800) 255-1065
FAX: (913) 888-8721

Wilson Sports Socks
124 East 38th Street
New York, NY 10016
(800) 243-4640

Windjammer Inc.
525 North Main
Bangor, PA 18013
(215) 588-0626
(800) 872-7500 (PA only)
(800) 441-6958 (except in PA)

Windless Inc.
800 31st Street
Altoona, PA 16603-0730
(814) 944-6144
(800) 458-3479 (orders only,
except in PA)
(800) 342-2909 (orders only,
PA)
FAX: (814) 944-0369

Winston Sports Corp.
200 Fifth Avenue
New York, NY 10010
(212) 255-6870

Wittek Golf Supply Co.
3650 Avondale
Chicago, IL 60618
(312) 463-2636
(800) 533-3101
FAX: (312) 463-2150

Wladyka, Joe
7 Wilson Avenue
Rutherford, NJ 07070
(201) 935-3917

Wolf, H., & Sons, Inc.
10139 Commerce Park Drive
Cincinnati, OH 45246
(513) 874-8000
(800) 543-7451
FAX: (513) 874-8992

World Famous Trading
Company Ltd.
4850-B Cass Street
San Diego, CA 92109
(619) 274-2710
(800) 621-0852 (CA only)
(800) 347-0151 (except in CA)
FAX: (619) 274-1306

Worth Sports Company
P.O. Box 88104

41A Highway
Tullahoma, TN 37388-8104
(615) 455-0691
FAX: (615) 455-7451

Yarrington Mills Corp.
412 S. Warminster Road
Hatboro, PA 19040
(215) 674-5125
FAX: (215) 674-0586
Mailing Address:
P.O. Box 397
Hatboro, PA 19040

York Barbell Co.
3300 Board Road
York, PA 17402
(717) 767-6481
(800) 358-YORK
FAX: (717) 764-0044
Mailing Address:
Box 1707
York, PA 17405

Zwickel, Inc.
346 East Courtland Street
Philadelphia, PA 19120
(215) 329-9410

Since 1895, 2¾ inches has been the maximum legal bat diameter. 42 inches has been the maximum length since 1893.

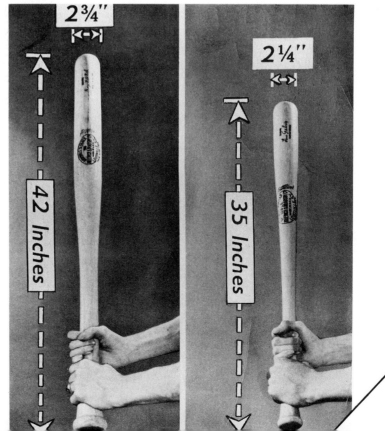

191

WHAT A CARD!

HOW TO COLLECT BASEBALL CARDS AND OTHER MEMORABILIA

All over America, people love to keep collections. People collect bottle caps, marbles, jigsaw puzzles, rubberbands—you name it.

In a country of collectors, one item stands out from all the rest. Right now, the most popular collector's item of all is probably the baseball card.

Just listen to these figures: There are more than 3,500 baseball card stores in the United States today. And according to *Sports Illustrated,* each year people spend a total of more than $200 million on baseball cards and buy about 5 billion cards! (That's counting both new cards and old ones.)

Baseball fans collect more than cards. In fact, they collect almost anything that's in any way related to the game. These other items are referred to as baseball memorabilia or collectibles.

Among many other collectibles, fans collect autographs of players, baseball bats, baseball board games, caps, coffee mugs, coins, cleats from the shoes of famous players, decals, flip books, gloves and other equipment, jerseys, jewelry (such as souvenir charm bracelets with a charm for each player on the team), letters from players, magazines, pennants, photos of players, pins, porcelain plates with pictures of players, postcards, posters, programs, radios, schedules, scorecards, stamps, statues, stickers, team yearbooks, ticket stubs, and toys!

Collecting baseball cards and collectibles used to be something kids and adults did just for fun. "Just for fun" is still the best reason for collecting baseball memorabilia. But nowadays the prices of baseball collectibles have skyrocketed.

In one year, from 1986 to 1987, the price of baseball cards rose 123 percent. To get an idea of how big a jump that is, compare it with the price of rare stamps. That year, the price of rare U.S. stamps barely rose at all, just 1 percent.

More and more adults have gone to their attics searching for their old card collections, hoping against hope that their mothers didn't throw out the cards! Some of these collections have turned out to be worth thousands of dollars. One very rare card, of Honus Wagner, has sold for as much as $110,000!

News of people making that kind of money has brought more and more collectors into the field, and that's driven the prices up even more.

Some say that the boom has hit its peak and that prices won't go up so quickly from now on. In the meantime, though, the

THE BULLPEN
Q: Why were the St. Louis players so crazy about collectibles?
A: Because they were CARDinals.

high prices have changed the card-collecting business. Some say the high prices have ruined things for the fun seekers.

On the other hand, if you follow a few simple rules, you can still collect just for fun. And someday your collection may make you a profit! Here are some basic tips to get you started.

STARTING A CARD AND COLLECTIBLES COLLECTION

The first step in starting a baseball card and collectibles collection is

simple. It'll cost you about 40 cents.

Go to your local candy store, department store, supermarket, or sporting goods store and buy a pack of baseball cards.

You can buy a "wax pack," which comes wrapped in wax paper and often includes a stick of gum. Or you can buy a "cello" pack, which is a pack wrapped in cellophane.

In the good old days of card collecting, you could take these cards home and play with them, shuffle through them, stick them in the spokes of your bike. Maybe you'd flip them against a friend. (If your flip matches your friend's, with both cards landing face up, then you win your friend's card.) You'd store your growing collection of cards by putting a rubberband around them and tossing them into your closet.

You can still do all those things, but not if you want to protect the future value of your cards. If you're interested in cards as an investment, you'll have to take very good care of your merchandise.

Nowadays, some collectors of particularly valuable cards store the collections in vaults and

take out insurance to protect them!

You certainly don't need to go that far! But most card collectors do store all their cards in see-through plastic sheets in loose-leaf binders. That's because tight rubberbands can roughen a card's edges. Lots of handling can crease the card. Any kind of wear and tear can drastically lower the card's value.

You can get plastic card protectors at card shops and card shows. You can also order them from dealers who advertise in card-collecting magazines. (See the listing of price guides starting on page 206. Also see this chapter's guide for judging a card's condition.)

Surprisingly, some collectors *don't even open* some packs of cards. That's not only to protect the cards. Unopened packs can become very valuable over the years. According to Bruce Chadwick and Danny Peary's book *Baseball Cards and Collectibles*, a single unopened pack of 1954 Bowman baseball cards now sells for about $400!

When you first start collecting, it will probably be impossible for you to resist opening all of your packs to see what players you got. You're hoping that you got some players you know and love. Those cards will have sentimental value for you. You may also have gotten some cards that will be worth some money.

STAR CARDS, ROOKIES, AND COMMONS

Basically, the cards in any pack break down into three groups—star cards, rookies, and commons.

Star cards are the cards for star players, players whose names are known in every household. These are players with names such as Jose Canseco and Dave Winfield. Rookie cards are cards for this year's rookies. Commons are all the rest.

The star cards are worth more than most. The rookie cards have a lot of potential. And the commons are worth very little indeed, unless you need them to fill out a set (more on that later).

Let's say you opened a pack in 1986 and found a card for star player Kirby Puckett. You had heard stories about thousands of dollars being made from baseball cards. Are you rich? Can you take all your

friends to Disneyland?

Afraid not. A 1986 Topps card for Kirby in mint condition was worth about $1.75 in 1990, four years later. Still, that's not a bad profit. After all, you paid only 3 cents for the card in 1986 (40 cents per pack divided by 15 cards per pack equals 3 cents each).

Some investors make their money by buying single cards in large quantities, called lots. If they think Kirby Puckett is going to grow into a bigger and bigger star, they buy lots of his cards now and hold onto them. If someone bought hundreds of Topps cards for Puckett for 3 cents each in 1986, they could make thousands of dollars by selling the cards for $1.75 a pop in 1990. (Anybody can buy lots, but they're expensive. And if you're collecting for fun, who wants hundreds of duplicates?)

When you open your pack of cards, you can check each card's value in a card price guide (see the listings on page 206). But don't start counting up your dollars too quickly. The prices listed there are the prices dealers will charge you as a buyer. When you try to *sell* your cards to the dealers, they'll pay you a lot less than

what the price guide says—as little as one tenth!

In a way, managing a good card collection is like managing a major league team. You need good players, and you have to decide which ones are going to play well their whole careers. The value of a player's card is directly related to his performance on the field. (And sometimes his performance off the field as well. The value of Pete Rose's card went way down when news of his gambling scandal reached the papers.)

Rookies who play well at the start of the season send up the value of their cards. So sharp card investors follow the box scores of the minor league games and keep track of up-and-coming stars. Then they buy huge numbers of these players' rookie cards.

There are also minor league baseball cards. Investing in these cards is much like investing in rookie cards. The cards of players who make it big in the majors will be the cards that become the most valuable.

Now that you know that star cards are more

valuable than commons, and that rookie cards may turn out to be valuable, there are two things to watch for when buying your card packs.

For one thing, you're better off buying several packs at a time, from the same box. Why? A card company such as Topps packs 36 wax packs into each box, and those 36 packs contain about half of that year's entire set of cards. So if you buy the packs from the same box, you should be increasing your chances of getting star cards and rookies.

You should be. But you won't be if the packs have been opened (and perhaps resealed). Someone may have already removed the star cards and left you with commons. Beware!

One of the neat things about cello packs is that you can see two of the cards you'll be getting. Look for packs with star and rookie cards showing through.

If you want to buy the whole box, and you've got the money to do it, don't buy it at the candy store. They'll charge you the same price ($14.40) as if you'd bought all 36 packs one at a time for 40 cents each.

You can get whole card boxes at card shows for $11. (You've also got to figure on the admission price of the show. which could be as much as $5.

But probably you'll be getting several items, and, you hope, saving money on each one.)

Remember those unopened packs of cards? Well, an unopened box can also "grow up" to be valuable, over the years. So can unopened sets—the entire collection of the cards of one company for the year. (When you buy a set from a card company, you're guaranteed that it's complete, so you don't have to open it up to check. You can buy a complete new Topps or Score set for about $20.)

COMPLETE SETS

Speaking of sets, cards that are part of a complete set are usually worth more than they would be by themselves. If you don't have the money to buy a complete set of this year's cards, you may be able to build one. As you pick up wax and cello packs, you'll start getting doubles (these are cards you already have) and triples. Start trading your doubles with friends.

Just for the fun of it, you can make up a special set and try to complete it. A set of all the players on a single team, say. Or all of the rookies from a

Jose Canseco has been a star since his rookie year, making his baseball cards more valuable than most.

"THE CASE OF THE FLYING DUTCHMAN"

Read this baseball mystery and see if you can solve the crime!

"Well, Kate," said J.J. happily, "Isn't our card show a success?"

"So far so good," agreed Kate. "But it's not over yet."

The two teenagers were sitting on the stage of their high school gym. Below them, the card show they had organized—their first ever—was in full swing.

At table after table, card dealers were selling, buying, and trading baseball cards and other memorabilia. Countless fans stood in line to get autographs from J.J.'s uncle, former baseball player Chucky Waddell. They were paying $1 a pop! And more and more fans were coming in the front door, paying $2 admission each. (To give Kate and J.J. a break, Kate's dad was taking the tickets for a while.)

"You're such a worrywart," laughed J.J. "What could go wrong now?"

Just then, there was a commotion over at Table #17. A young boy could be heard yelling, "Somebody stole it! Somebody stole it!"

The noisy gym suddenly fell totally silent. Then it became noisier than ever as everyone reacted. J.J. rushed to the mike.

"Don't worry folks," he said. "Keep dealing. We'll have this straightened out in no time."

Then he and Kate hurried over to Table #17.

It was Louis Chadwick's table. Louis Chadwick was one of the biggest dealers at the show. He had his 12-year-old son Nick by the arm, and he was squeezing that arm pretty tightly.

"We need the police, and fast," he told J.J. and Kate. "Somebody stole our Flying Dutchman."

"We don't need the police," Kate assured him. "We can straighten this out ourselves."

"Straighten it out?" cried Chadwick. "Don't you kids know anything about cards? This is a T206 Honus Wagner tobacco card we're talking about, Near Mint! This card is worth thousands of dollars!"

J.J. was starting to sweat. "What happened?" he asked. "I mean, when did you notice it was stolen?"

"Just now," fumed Chadwick. "You see, I left my son Nick here in charge of the table for an hour, while I looked at the rest of the show. All he had to do was *stay* at the table. But this nincompoop left the table unguarded."

"I wanted to get Waddell's signature," said Nick tearfully.

"Sure you did," said Chadwick. "And you got it. You know, someday that signature might be worth $20. If you're lucky. In the meantime, we're out thousands."

Kate turned to the dealer at Table #16. He was a large, gruff-looking man wearing a Phillies cap that was too small for his head.

"Did you see anyone going through their stuff while Nick was gone?" Kate asked.

The man blew a large pink bubble of bubblegum before he answered. "I'm busy dealing my cards, lady," he drawled. "I don't have time to babysit Chadwick's display."

"Yes," said J.J. "But just now, when the table was empty..." He turned to Nick. "How long were you gone?"

"About five minutes."

J.J. turned back to Dealer #16. "Did you see anyone at the table during those five minutes?"

"Not a soul," grinned the dealer.

"That's probably true," said Louis Chadwick. "Because you probably took the card yourself!"

"Tell it to the cops," the dealer answered.

"That's exactly what I will do. I'm calling them right now!"

"Please don't do that," said Kate. "This is our first card show. A scandal could sink us. Just give us one more minute."

As she said this, Kate caught the eye of Dealer #18, who smiled kindly.

"Did you see anyone at Chadwick's table while Nick was gone?" she asked.

"Didn't look," he replied apologetically. "I was too busy selling a card to this gentleman here. Made a good sale, too. Sold him a 1986 Topps Wally Joyner for $ in cash."

The customer at his table showed Kate the card. "Did I make a good buy?" he asked.

Kate smiled. "He overcharged you by about fifty cents!"

J.J. had been busy trying to stall Chadwick. Now he turned to the dealer at Table #15, Mrs. Piersall. "What about you?" J.J. asked. "Did you notice anyone snooping around while Nick was gone?"

"Well, I was pretty busy with my own table of course," said Mrs. Piersall, nervously straightening the cards in front of her. "But I did

e that boy there."
She pointed to a
.nny teenager in a
ie Janet Jackson
:hirt. He was one of a
ge crowd of gawkers
o were watching the
ene.

.J. whirled around to
: who she was
inting at. "You mean
vin McInnis? My
:h-rival?"

Hey, J.J.," said Kevin.
ice show. Too bad
out the theft. This will
n you for sure."

hat was all J.J.
eded to hear. "Is that
at you did it for,
vin? To ruin my show?
is this the only way
i know how to make
ney from baseball
ds ... by stealing!"

Before you go
owing around any
re accusations,"
swered Kevin, "you
ght want to know that
idn't take any Honus
gner card. I looked at
adwick's table while
:k was gone, sure. I
in't see any Flying
tchman. Whoever
k it must have taken
efore I got there.
arch me, if you like."

I would like," replied
angrily. "Empty your
:kets."

neering, Kevin
ned his pockets
ide out. They
tained a pack of
rt-up common Topps
ds, a pink stick of
bblegum with lint on

it, and a wooden pen
shaped like a bat.

"Terrific!" yelled
Chadwick. "You found
me some bubblegum. I
want the police and I
want them now!"

"Okay," stammered
J.J., his voice cracking.
"I'll go call them."

"Remember how you
said 'Don't worry,'" Kate
reminded him in a
whisper. "You said,
'What could go wrong
now?'"

"Don't tease me," J.J.
whispered back. "I think
I'm about to have a
nervous breakdown." He
fumbled in his pants
pocket. "Great," he told
her. "I don't even have a
quarter to make the
phone call."

Kate searched her
pockets for a quarter. No
luck. She looked at
Dealer #18. He
immediately reached
into his own pockets.

"Sorry," he said. "I
don't have a dime on
me." He opened his
wallet to show it was
also empty.

"Here," said
Chadwick, slapping a
quarter into J.J.'s hand.
"I'd make the call
myself, but I'm afraid to
leave my table again.
The way you've run this
card show, there would
probably be nothing left
of my collection when I
got back!"

"Right," said J.J. "I'll
go call the cops."

"Oh," smiled Kate.
"There's no need to do
that."

"No need?!!" screamed
Chadwick.

"That's right," said
Kate. "I've caught the
crooks."

*Can you figure out who
took the card? The
answer is printed upside
down, below.*

For his alibi, Dealer #18
claimed that he was busy
selling a card for $3 in cash.
But when Kate needed a
quarter, he didn't have a cent.
After Kate confronted him
with this lie, Dealer #18
agreed to let Kate, J.J., and
Chadwick search his booth.
There they found the Flying
Dutchman.

particular year. Or all the players with the letter Z in their names!

It's up to you. Sets such as these make collecting more fun and give the common cards some meaning.

ERROR CARDS

Like everyone else, card companies make mistakes. But their errors can make cards worth more than the correct ones. In 1988, Topps printed pitcher Al Leiter's name on the wrong card. They quickly corrected the mistake, making the error card rare. And valuable. Soon the wrong Leiter card was worth $3.

BASEBALL STICKERS

Baseball stickers are much like baseball cards. One main difference: Since you stick them into albums, stickers don't have information on the backs! But the sticker albums themselves print the player's stats under the space where you stick the player's photo.

Panini USA is one of the largest makers of stickers. They put out 388 baseball stickers in 1989. The stickers include players, teams, and highlight shots. That year, kids

bought about 40 million of Panini's stickers alone!

Will the sticker craze ever match the card craze? Will stickers someday soar in value? It's too early to say, according to a spokesperson for Panini. But collectors are buying whole sets of stickers and keeping them unopened so that they'll remain in mint condition. These investors apparently feel that stickers will, um, stick around.

TRADING STICKERS. You can't buy stickers from Panini itself, but only from retail stores such as Woolworth's. But Panini does offer a special trade-in deal, detailed in the back of any Panini album. You can trade your duplicate stickers with Panini for any Panini sticker you're missing.

Check out a Panini album for rules and details before you send any stickers. You'll need to send your stickers to:

Panini USA
P.O. Box 5218
Department B-90
FDR Station
New York, NY 10150

COLLECTING COLLECTIBLES

Just because you've got a small budget doesn't mean you can't start a baseball memorabilia collection. To begin with, collectors recommend going to every major league giveaway day you can.

You'll end up with all kinds of items, from bats to towels. (For more information on giveaway days, see Chapter 2, or contact the team's offices listed in Chapter 1.)

When you go to a major league game, on a giveaway day or a regular day, save the ticket stub. If you've got some extra allowance money, also purchase items such as the program, the yearbook, the scorecard, or a pennant. Save them.

And, of course, if you're lucky enough to catch or retrieve a ball hit into the stands, save that too. Maybe you can even get the player who hit the ball out of the park to autograph it for you after the game.

BASEBALL CARDS CAME IN CRACKER JACKS?

A LOOK AT BASEBALL CARD HISTORY

Quick! How old is the oldest baseball card ever made? 10 years old? 20? 50?

In 1990, the correct answer was 122. In 1868, a sporting goods company called Peck and Snyder gave out the first baseball cards free, as advertising gimmicks. The very first cards were for a team known as the Brooklyn Atlantics.

But baseball cards didn't really catch on until the late 1880s, when tobacco companies got into the act. They stuck their cards into packs of cigarettes, and the craze began.

In 1909, a group of tobacco companies known as the American Tobacco Trust started printing a card of Honus Wagner among its selection of 523 players.

A famous shortstop, Wagner was known for his ferocity at the plate (he won his league's batting championship eight times). Off the field he was known for his kind, gentle character.

When Honus found out that his card was helping sell tobacco, he made them stop printing it. The company obeyed. That made the cards they had already printed quite rare. Today, a mint-condition Wagner card sells for more than $100,000! It's the most famous card in baseball history.

Since cards came with tobacco, they weren't for kids. That changed in 1888, when a company called G&B Chewing Gum entered the card market. They sold cards with gum, and the era of kid card collectors began.

The photos on this gum company's cards were quite primitive. Live-action shots were faked in a studio, as players pretended to hit or catch a ball that was hanging on a string.

Gum makers weren't the only ones who tried their hand at baseball cards. A caramel company started making them in 1909. From 1914 to 1915, cards were used as the prize in boxes of Cracker Jacks. Fleer, one of the modern card giants, started out by selling cards with a cherry-flavored cookie.

The Topps Chewing Gum Co. started printing its cards in 1951. Soon, Topps grew to be all-powerful in the card business.

Years later, the Fleer Company had to go to court to win the right to make cards again. Topps claimed it was the only company with the right to make baseball cards, but a Pennsylvania court said no. Fleer got back into the business in 1981. The Donruss Company started making its cards the same year. The fourth modern card-making biggie, Score, started its card line in 1988.

Today, you can still get a pink stick of hard gum with a pack of baseball cards. But snacks, candy, and tobacco are all long gone from the card business.

The old cards aren't gone, though. Not hardly. With baseball cards growing more and more popular, the old cards are still very much with us. They're being displayed, bought, and sold at auctions, card shops, and weekly card shows. And the old cards are selling for higher and higher prices.

Someday such a ball could be very valuable, especially if it's a home run hit by a star. In December of 1989, a single baseball signed by Babe Ruth was auctioned off for $2,750!

(See the article on page 204 for tips on where to sit to improve your chances of snagging a souvenir ball.)

AUTOGRAPHS

A star player's autograph can turn a photograph, baseball, glove, or bat into a valuable collectible. It won't increase the value of a baseball card, though. Not even if the player signs his very own card.

If you look at the guidelines on page 203 for judging a card's condition, you'll see that writing on a card lowers its condition to "Fair," one of the worst grades a card can get.

In the good old days, before card and collectibles prices went through the roof, all players gave out autographs for free. Today, many players charge for their autographs. They'll make an appearance at a card show and charge fans as much as $20 per signature!

Some fans object. But players point out that

A young Mickey Mantle signs free autographs. But did these kids save the signatures?

many signature seekers are trying to make money off the players.

If you're not willing to shell out the bucks for a star's autograph at a card show, there are still ways to get it for free.

For one thing, many teams hold special autograph sessions (see Chapter 2 for more details). Some teams hold these sessions regularly before weekend home games.

By hanging out near the team's dugout you may be able to hand a cap or glove to a player to sign.

You can also write to your favorite team's publicity department and ask for a free signed photo of your favorite player. If that doesn't work, buy your own photo and send it to the player directly. And if that doesn't work, take the photo to the stadium.

OLD COLLECTIBLES

Buying old collectibles at card shows means spending a lot of money. The uniform of a retired star player, for example, can go for thousands of dollars.

That's out of most people's league—kids and adults alike.

But you can still collect some old memorabilia by hunting at antiques stores, thrift shops, garage sales, and flea markets. (Thrift shops are good places to look for old sports magazines. Remember, they have to be in good condition to be worth much.)

If you find an old major league glove or other equipment, it could be worth more than you pay for it. Once again, price guides will give you a sense of how much you should pay.

Don't forget the famous catch about price guides. It's worth repeating: To make an immediate profit, you'll need to buy for a lot less than the price listed in the price guide. When you go to sell, dealers may offer you as little as one tenth of the prices listed in the guides.

CARD SHOWS

Card shows are held just about every week all over the country. You can find listings for them in card magazines and at your local card shop.

You'll have to pay an admission fee. But once inside you'll find a card collectors' paradise, with thousands of new, old, and rare cards on sale. There'll be people to chat with about cards, people to buy from, sell to, and trade with!

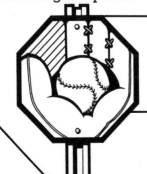

SHORTSTOPS
In addition to cards for the players today, you can also buy cards for all the major league umps!

MAIL-ORDER COLLECTIBLES

In addition to card shows and shops, cards and collectibles are for sale via mail order from hundreds of dealers. You'll find ad after ad in the pages of any card price guide or collectibles magazine.

If you'd like to see their complete line of products and also get some extra mail, you can get free catalogues from many of these dealers. Some others will charge you only the postage it costs them to send you the catalogue ($1, say). Still others will send a free catalogue along with your first purchase.

SPECIAL CARD CLUBS

What cards will prove to be the most valuable? Some card clubs (like book clubs) sell you cards that are preselected by card experts.

You can find these clubs listed in the card magazines. For example, there's the Sporting News Rookie Card Club. This group's panel of experts includes stars such as Yogi Berra. They select cards for you each month, picking from the year's rookies.

Will their choices someday prove valuable? Time will tell. In the meantime, though, the club is expensive. Even with the cheapest plan, you'll have to buy $19.95 worth of cards each month. To join, contact:

The Sporting News Rookie Card Club
One Old Country Road
Carle Place, NY 11514
(800) 876-7117
(516) 294-0040

STARTING YOUR OWN CARD AND COLLECTI-BLES BUSINESS

You don't need a store to trade with friends. And you can always set up a free shop on your front lawn, sort of a baseball-card version of the old lemonade stand.

To set up a table at a card show may cost you $400 or more. That's out of most kids' price range. But some kids make so much money off their card collections, they work their way up to being dealers.

One of the most successful of these young card stars is 21-year-old Harlan J. Werner of southern California. He started collecting baseball cards at age 10. He rapidly expanded his collection by making extra money mowing lawns. He spent all the cash at card shows.

By age 14, he was selling his own cards at shows. At 16, he and a friend started their own mail-order card business. One year later, he started his own card store. And by age 17, he was organizing whole card shows of his own and hiring star athletes such as Muhammad Ali to come and sign autographs.

With a successful card show, Werner now makes about $50,000!

Not everyone can have this kind of incredible success, at least not so quickly. But if you do get to the point of starting your own business, Sports Fantasy Inc. is a company that may be of some assistance. For information, write to:

Mr. Reese Davis
Director of Franchise
Development
Sports Fantasy, Inc.
P.O. Box 910
Phoenix City, AL 36868
(205) 297-5494

SOFTWARE FOR COLLECTORS

Even if you're starting a collection from scratch, you'll probably find that it gets big, fast. Soon it won't be so easy to remember what cards you have and what cards you need.

If you've got a home computer, companies make software specifically for card collectors. Look for ads in the price guides. There are programs that list card price guides on computer disk, help you keep track of all your cards, and more. Here are two of the companies that make such software:

Lineup
Emerald City Sports Cards
8046 S. 114 Street
Seattle, WA 98178
(206) 772-4266
(for IBM PC or IBM compatible)

Compu-Quote
6914 Berquist Avenue,
Dept. SS
Canoga Park, CA 91307
(800) 782-6775
In California, call: (828) 348-3662 (for IBM, Macintosh, and Apple II)

FURTHER READING

Whole books have been written on the art of collecting cards and other collectibles as a way to make money. If you want to get more serious about your collecting, check your local bookstore for titles such as these:

A Beginner's Guide to Baseball Card Collecting: A Step-by-Step Guide for the Young Collector, by

Casey Childress and Linda McKenzie. It was published by C. Mack Publications in 1988.

Collecting Baseball Cards, by Donn Pearlman, published by Bonus Books, Inc. If you can't find this book at a bookstore, write to the publisher at 160 East Illinois Street, Chicago, IL 60611. (The book comes with a free baseball card, so when you buy this book you also start your collection!)

How to Buy, Trade, and Invest in Baseball Cards and Collectibles, by Bruce Chadwick and Danny Peary. It's published by Simon & Schuster, Inc.

How to Invest in Baseball Cards, by Stanley Apfelbaum. It's published by the Baseball Card Society, FCI Press, One Old Country Road, Carle Place, NY 11514. They have a toll-free number: (800) 645-6075. If you're calling from New York State, dial (516) 294-0040.

Start Collecting Baseball Cards, by David Plant, published by Running Press in 1989.

You can find more books—and more information—in baseball card magazines. Where do you get these magazines?

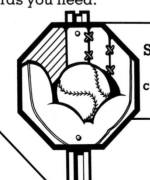

SHORTSTOPS
In 1909, the Colgan Gum Company started making *round* baseball cards, the size of silver dollars.

The best place to look is at your local card shop. And if you don't have a card shop in your area (which is not very likely!) there's a guide to some of these publications on page 206.

HOW TO JUDGE A CARD'S CONDITION

In card collecting, mint isn't a good flavor of ice cream. It stands for the best condition a card can be in.

A "mint" is a place where coins are made. For a card to be in "Mint Condition" it must be in the condition that it was in when it was first made—just like new!

A card in mint condition is always worth more than a beat-up, wrinkled, or stained card. In fact, a card's condition can make it worth hundreds of dollars or just pennies.

So if you're buying and trading cards, you'd better keep track of the condition of the cards or you'll be getting bad deals. How do you judge what condition a card is in?

Going by the guidelines listed in *Sports Collectors Digest,* here are the rankings and descriptions of what they mean:

Mint: Perfection! To be rated as "Mint," the card can't be creased or bent or nicked or stained in any way. It can't be yellowed with age or faded from sitting out in the sun.

The corners of the card have to be sharp and straight, not thumbed, bent, and rounded. And the photo of the player has to be perfectly centered on the card.

Near Mint: When you first look at it, a "Near Mint" card seems to be mint. Only when you study it will you find its single flaw. The photo, for instance, may not be perfectly centered. Or one corner may be slightly worn.

Excellent: An "Excellent" card's photo can be off-center. But the card can't be stained or creased. On the other hand, the glossy surface of the card can have faded a bit. And the corners of the card can be a little worn.

Very Good: A "Very Good" card has been touched quite a bit. It can have little creases, and the corners can be rounded from wear. The card can even have a large stain from gum or wax. But it can't have big creases, and it can't be written on.

Good: A good card is worn badly, but it doesn't look like anyone damaged the card on purpose. It can have major creases and very rounded corners.

Fair: A fair card can have writing on it (an autograph, say). It can be creased badly. It can have holes in it from being tacked on a bulletin board. But it has to be whole. It can't have a piece ripped off of it, for instance. If it's not whole, it's not in "Fair" condition—it's "Poor." Either way, it's not going to be worth much.

How would you rate the condition of these cards?

WHERE TO SIT TO CATCH SOUVENIR BASEBALLS

Not every fan who goes to a major league game hopes to catch a foul ball or homer. In fact, many fans would like to sit somewhere safe from line drives! Right behind the home-plate netting is completely safe and gives fans a great view—that's why these are some of the best, and most expensive, seats in the house.

"But I *want* to catch a foul ball!" you exclaim.

You're not alone. Many kids take their mitts to the games, hoping to catch the fouls and homers. Where should you sit? Cliff Frohlich and Gary R. Scott of the Society for American Baseball Research have done a study of the subject.

First of all, they found that the chances of getting a free souvenir ball are slim. They calculate that a fan can hope to get a free ball only once in every 350 to 3,000 games.

To increase your chances, they say, go to games with low turnouts. The fewer people there, the more chance you'll have of being the first one to get to a ball that lands in empty seats.

The researchers also found that players hit more fouls and homers in some stadiums than they do in others. Of the stadiums they studied, Toronto's Exhibition Stadium had the highest average number of balls hit into the stands—29 per game.

The most important factor, though, is where you sit. If you sit behind the netting at home plate, you're obviously not going to get any souvenirs. (Be glad the netting is there. It keeps you from getting conked in the head by a screaming foul.)

Frohlich and Scott suggest sitting in the following places:

If you're in the upper stands, sit in the lower half of the first three sections, right behind home plate (that's above the netting).

In the lower stands, try to sit along the first-base line, and a little beyond it. That's for teams with lots of right-handed hitters. For teams with lots of lefties, you're better off along the third-base line in the lower stands. (That's because hitters "pull" the ball, with lefties hitting to the left side and righties hitting to the right.)

For homers, you want to stay away from seats out beyond straightaway center. That's the longest distance for the ball to go, and it doesn't go there often. That's another reason hitters try to pull the ball. They're aiming to get it out of the stadium on the shortest route possible, to the left or right.

If you follow these strategies and still don't get any balls hit your way, don't despair. Remember, you can always buy a souvenir ball at the stadium. If you get a player to sign it, it makes a nice addition to your collection. And it could be worth something someday.

In addition, every team sells souvenir balls signed by that year's entire team. The ball of the team that wins the World Series will be worth the most in years to come. That's why the signed balls of the heavily favored teams will cost the most.

But if you buy the souvenir ball of a long-shot team and they win, you've made a good investment.

Arthur Meyer's baseball collection. He didn't catch all these at the ballpark!

204

THE PRICE IS RIGHT!

Prices of baseball collectibles aren't always easy to guess. If you don't believe it, take a crack at this mini-game show quiz.

First, see if you can rank the following items, from least expensive to most expensive. The correct order is listed upside down, below.

Then see if you can guess what each item sold for—or was priced at—in 1989. You can play this game with a friend. Take turns guessing a price for each item. Whoever guesses closest to the sale price—without going over—wins.

How can you know what costs what? Just guess! You'll probably be way off on a lot of them. That's why they publish price guides. (These prices come from price guides and from Bruce Chadwick and Danny Peary's book *Baseball Cards and Collectibles.*)

A) A Mickey Mantle coffee mug from 1955.

B) A new porcelain 9"-high statue of Bob Gibson, the Cardinals Hall of Fame pitcher, in a limited edition. (That means that a small number are being made, not an infinite number, and each statue should therefore be more valuable.)

C) A catcher's mask from the 1930s. The player who wore it is unknown.

D) Don Mattingly's high school yearbook.

E) A Brooklyn Dodger wooden pen-and-pencil set (both shaped like baseball bats) in the original wooden box.

F) The poster for the famous baseball movie *Pride of the Yankees*, starring Gary Cooper.

G) A home-game jersey of Atlanta Braves star Hank Aaron from 1973.

H) Lou Gehrig's 1929 car registration form, signed by Gehrig.

I) The 1973 National League All-Star ring.

J) A color 8 × 10 photo of Yogi Berra, signed by Yogi himself.

K) A bat autographed by Babe Ruth and used by him in a game.

L) A baseball signed by Nolan Ryan.

M) A 1953 Mickey Mantle Topps baseball card in "Near Mint" condition.

N) A 1953 Mickey Mantle Topps baseball card in "Excellent" condition.

O) A 1953 Bowman baseball card of Mickey Mantle in "Near Mint" condition.

P) A 1974 Topps card of Carl Yastrzemski in "Near Mint" condition.

Everybody likes to get players' autographs—even presidents! Here Maris signs for President Kennedy.

Game 2 answers:
In 1989, the asking prices (or selling prices) for these items were:

A) $122 **B)** $200 **C)** $50 **D)** $200 **E)** $550 **F)** $275 **G)** $2,100 **H)** $1,502 **I)** $600 **J)** $11 **K)** $2,000 **L)** $49.95 **M)** $1,900 **N)** $1,000 **O)** $300 **P)** $9

Game 1 answers:
The order of the prices from *least expensive* to *most expensive* is:
P, J, L, C, A, B and D (they're the same price), F, O, E, I, N, H, M, K, G

205

You're at a card show and you see a 1986 Sportflics card for Vince Coleman, your favorite Cardinal speedster. The dealer is asking $10. The card is in mint condition. Is it a fair price?

No! According to the January 5, 1990, *Sports Collectors Digest,* a fair price is only $2.

If you don't keep up to date on the market values, you're going to get ripped off. You can buy price guide books that are updated each year. Or, if you want even more current prices, you can subscribe to some of the monthly or weekly magazines.

Price guides are available at every card shop. Or you can order directly, using the information listed below. (For some of these magazines, you can get a free sample copy if you write and ask for it.)

Baseball Card Digest. A magazine for card collectors. They publish six issues each year. A year's subscription costs $5.75. The address for the magazine is:

Baseball Card Digest
22203 John R Road
Hazel Park, MI 48030

Baseball Card Investment Report. This is a monthly newsletter that deals with expensive cards. It's really meant for the investor who's looking to spend big bucks. It probably won't be of much use to kid collectors. But you can get a free copy to check it out for yourself. (A year's subscription costs $29.) For a free copy, write to:

Baseball Card Investment Report
American Card Exchange
125 East Baker, Suite 150
Costa Mesa, CA 92626

Baseball Hobby News. A monthly 100-page magazine with price guides and articles about collecting. Single copies are $1.95. A year's subscription costs $18. Write to:

Baseball Hobby News
4540 Kearny Villa Road, Suite 215
San Diego, CA 92123

The Sports Collectors Digest. This large weekly collection of collectibles information is edited by Bob Lemke. A year's subscription costs $39.95. It's published by:

Krause Publications
700 E. State Street
Iola, WI 54945

Toll-free phone: (800) 258-0929

Also available from Krause are *Baseball Card News, Sports Collectors Digest Baseball Card Price Guide, Baseball Cards Magazine,* and *Baseball Card Price Guide Monthly.* They also publish special single issues such as *The Baseball Card Boom,* a look back at the soaring card prices of the 1980s, and *A Beginner's Guide to Baseball Card Collecting.*

Current Card Prices. A monthly price guide for $19.95 a year. Write to:

Current Card Prices
433 North Windsor Avenue
Brightwaters, NY 11718

Another big publisher of price guides is:

Beckett Publications
3410 MidCourt, Suite 110
Carrollton, TX 75006

Some of their publications are listed below. If you're ordering a book, you'll need to add $1 for postage.

Beckett's Baseball Card Monthly. A one-year subscription to this monthly magazine is $18.95.

Dr. Beckett's Price

Guide to Baseball Collectibles. This price guide sells for $9.95.

The Sport Americana Alphabetical Baseball Address List. This $9.95 book lists addresses for almost every major leaguer, both currently playing and retired. Autograph collectors use this book to write to players directly, hoping for signatures.

The Sport Americana Baseball Card Price Guide, by Dr. James Beckett and Dennis W. Eckes. A large book that costs $12.95.

The Official Price Guide to Baseball Cards. A price list, also edited by Dr. Beckett, that costs $4.95. This comes out once a year. It's pocket-size, which means it's easy to take to a card show as a ready reference.

The Sport Americana Alphabetical Baseball Card Checklist. An alphabetical list, by player, of all the baseball cards ever made. It costs $8.95.

The Sport Americana Baseball Collectibles Price Guide. Lists the market value prices for just about everything *except* cards. It costs $9.95.

MINOR LEAGUE CARDS

For minor league information, there's the *Guide to Pre-Rookie Prices.* Order from:

Cornelius Collectibles
102 2nd Avenue
Bagley, IA 50026

A year's subscription (4 issues) is $8.50. Also available:

Tuff Stuff. A monthly price guide ($17.95 for 12 issues) that has lots of information on rookie and minor league cards. Write to:

Tuff Stuff
Box 1637
Glen Allen, VA 23060

The Old Judge. This newsletter provides prices for old cards. A subscription is $8, and you get six issues. The address is:

The Old Judge
c/o Lew Lipset
P.O. Box 137
Centereach, NY 11720

THE OLDEN TIMES

Outfielder/third baseman Freddie Lindstrom had a lifetime batting average of .311 over 13 seasons.

In 1932, the U.S. Caramel Company held a special contest to promote its baseball cards. The company printed 32 cards that year. They announced that if any fan could collect all 32 cards, they would win a free baseball.

Not a very big prize, right? But no one could do it. There didn't seem to be a card #16! In fact, many collectors gave up looking for it. They assumed that the company never printed a #16, so that no one would win!

Then, in 1988, a #16 was finally found. Caramel Card #16 is of Freddie Lindstrom, a famous third baseman. And it's worth about $35,000!

PLAY BALL!
GAMES AND SOFTWARE

What's only an inch or so long and is used all over America to hit grand slams? It's a joystick, and it's a key part of the software game craze.

Thanks to joysticks, home computer users now have more control over their pitches than Fernando Valenzuela ever has. They can wiggle the ball all the way to home plate, and they can make the batter swing at any part of the strike zone.

Computer baseball simulations have grown better and better—and more elaborate.

On the other hand, computer games haven't stopped the makers of baseball board games. Many people still prefer to play ball on a cardboard game board rather than on a TV screen. Classic baseball board games such as Strat-O-Matic show no signs of fading.

Either way, simulated baseball games provide a very specific pleasure. With these games, you can imagine that you're playing in the majors, helping your team win the pennant with your heroic play.

Ex-Mets star Lenny Dykstra once whacked a game-winning homer in the play-offs. After the game, he gushed to reporters that nothing that exciting had happened to him since he played Strat-O-Matic!

This chapter will help you shop around for both board games and software games and let you know what's out there.

In some cases, you may be able to get a better price in a local store than by mail order. That's because a store orders in bulk, while you'd be ordering only a single game. But sometimes you'll find mail-order bargains. And some of the games listed here are available only through mail order. Write, or call if there's an 800 toll-free number, for a free brochure or catalogue.

And, as you go through this chapter, keep a pencil handy. There are plenty of baseball puzzles to play right here! (For the answers, turn to the "Scorecard" section at the end of this chapter.)

BOARD GAMES

Most baseball board games use actual batting averages and other statistics of real players to determine how well the player will do in the game. (There are also some pure trivia games; two are listed at the end of this section.)

Chance is involved in stats games, thanks to devices such as spinners and dice. But, over the long haul, players will perform roughly according to their stats, just as in the

Q: Joey played a baseball board game with his brother Tom. He lost the game. Then he demanded a rematch. Why wouldn't Tom play again?
A: The game was lost, and they couldn't find it.

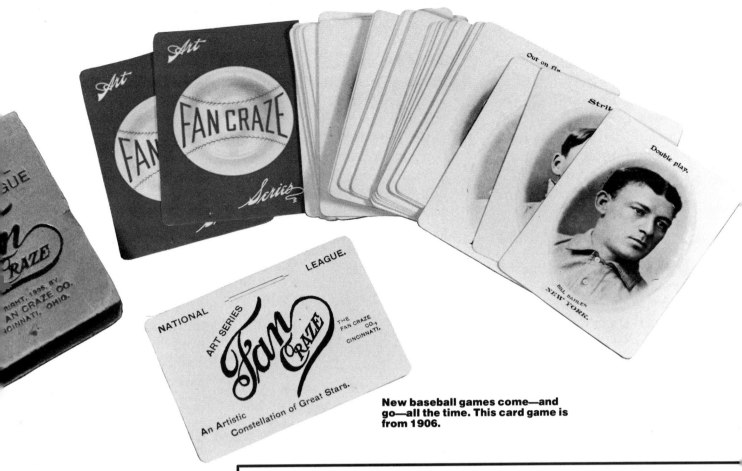

New baseball games come—and go—all the time. This card game is from 1906.

big leagues. And that lets you be the manager of big league players.

New versions of this kind of game crop up all the time. They may be worth trying. But one advantage of the tried and true companies such as Strat-O-Matic is that they're more likely to last from year to year. New board games come and go. And if they don't catch on, you won't be able to get new stats cards for the next season's crop of players.

TRACE AROUND THE BASES!

How fast can you race —um, make that *trace*— around these bases?

Start with the point of your pencil at the START HERE dot on the pitching rubber. You have to trace your way around the rubber, around the pitcher's mound, down to home plate, and around all the bases, including home plate, *without going over any part of the line twice.*

Note: you will be recrossing points (intersections) on the line, but you can't redraw any section of the line.

If you make it around first but get stuck tracing second, credit yourself with a single. If you get past second, and get stuck at third, that's a double. If you trace through third but home isn't traced, that's a triple. Trace everything without retracing your

steps and you've hit it out of the park.

Trace the line very fast on the first try, without getting stuck, and you've got yourself an *inside the park* homer!

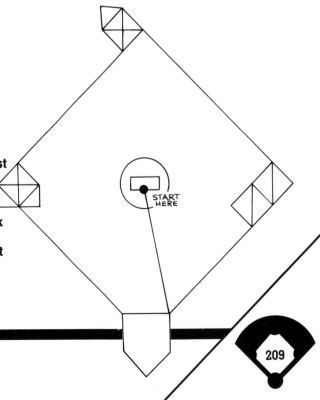

STATS GAMES

All-Star Baseball. One of the 65 board games made by Cadaco. It's produced in cooperation with the Major League Baseball Players' Association, and it comes with 62 player discs to fit onto the spinner. Price: $12.95.

Cadaco recommends you buy their game through stores such as Toys R Us or K-Mart, but if you're having trouble finding it, they will sell to you directly. Contact them at:

Cadaco
4300 West 47 Street
Chicago, IL 60632
(312) 927-1500

APBA Major League Players Baseball. You get 520 player cards, and you can pick from any of the major league teams. You can also get cards for famous teams from baseball history, so you can see how well they'd play against the modern-day stars. Price: $32.95.

Order from:

APBA Game Company, Inc.
P.O. Box 4547
Lancaster, PA 17604
(800) 334-APBA, ext. 11B

Big League Manager. A detailed stats game that uses the current season's players. Price: $39.95.

Order directly from:

Big League Game Company
321 East Superior Street
Duluth, MN 55802
(218) 722-1275

INFO Baseball. A strategy card game that calls for card-playing skills, as opposed to trivia knowledge. Recommended for kids 9 and up. This company also makes football and basketball versions. Available in stores and by mail order. Price: $7.95.

For more information, contact:

Information Games, Inc.
7 Central Street
Montague Center, MA 01351
(413) 367-2412

Statis-Pro. A diceless stats game that comes with current players and old stars. Price: $39.

For a free catalogue, write or call:

The Avalon Hill Game Company
4517 Hartford Road
Baltimore, MD 21214
(301) 254-5300

Pursue the Pennant. This stats game comes with 729 players. And you have a choice of stadiums to play in (different players will do better or worse depending

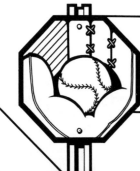

SHORTSTOPS
The first baseball board game was invented way back in the 1860s, not long after baseball itself!

on what stadium you pick).
Price: $44.95.

You can order directly
from:

Pursue the Pennant
P.O. Box 1045
Brookfield, WI 53008
(800) 288-4PTP

Strat-O-Matic. A classic—
they've been in business
since 1961. The game is
played with cards and
dice. There's an advanced
and more complex version
that includes more of the
fine points of baseball
strategy. You can get the
game in the stores. Price:
$15 or $34.50, deluxe.

You can also send for a
free brochure or order the
game itself from:

Strat-O-Matic
46 Railroad Plaza
Glen Head, NY 11545
(516) 671-6566
(800) 645-3455, if you're
calling from outside New
York State

BASEBALL TRIVIA

**Classic: A Major League
Baseball Boardgame.**
Players race each other
around the infield and
score runs by answering
baseball trivia. The game
comes with 100 special
game cards that could
have some collectibles
value.

There's also a travel
version of the game. If you
don't come across the
game in stores, the Score
Board is one company that
sells it, along with a
number of baseball
collectibles. Price: $21.95.

For a catalogue write or
call:

The Score Board
100 Dobbs Lane, Suite 206
Cherry Hill, NJ 08034
(800) 356-2193

**Grand Slam Baseball
Board Game.** In this trivia
game, teams form a lineup
based on trivia-ability. For
each at-bat, a player picks
the degree of difficulty he
or she wants to try for.

The simplest questions
are worth singles. Answer
a "single" correctly and
you can move your marker
down to first. Make a
wrong answer and you're
out. Three outs a side, of
course. Price: $27.95.

Write or call:

Grand Slam Inc.
P.O. Box 2049
Elizabethtown, KY 42701
(502) 765-6692

SOFTWARE

Since it takes a while to master any video game, most players like to stick to one game. Here's a sampling of the many computer baseball games on the market. If you're looking for a new ball game, most of these companies will send free brochures or catalogues, which is a nice way to browse.

APBA Major League Players Baseball. An IBM and Apple computer version of the popular board game. Price: $59.95.

For a brochure or to order, contact:

McGraw-Hill Educational Resources
11 West 19 Street
New York, NY 10011
(800) 843-8855

Bad News Baseball. A Nintendo game, available in both boy and girl modes. It throws 11 different kinds of pitchers. Price: $44.99.

For a brochure, write to:

TECMO Games
18005 S. Adria Maru Lane
Carson, CA 90746
(213) 329-5880

Baseball Simulator 1.000. In addition to regular computer ball, this Nintendo system lets you play out an entire fantasy season. The computer will play out a 165-game pennant race among six teams. If you like, you can use it to simulate the current major league season, or you can make up fantasy teams.

Ultra-play features let you design crazy plays such as fielders who leap hundreds of feet in the air to catch flies. Price: $49.95.

For more information, write to:

Culture Brain U.S.A. Inc.
15315 N.E. 90th
Redmond, WA 98052
(206) 882-2339

Bo Jackson Baseball. This advanced IBM computer game system can be connected via modem to a sports information network. The program will update its player statistics daily! Price: $49.95.

Write to:

Data East USA
1850 Little Orchard Street
San Jose, CA 95125
(408) 286-7074

Earl Weaver Baseball 1.5. An updated version of the popular old software game. Now available for

DOUBLE TALK

There are 21 baseball terms hidden in this word jumble. Use our word list. The words can go up, down, across, back, and diagonally. After you've circled all the words, the leftover letters will spell out the answer to this riddle:

Q: At a ballpark, what seats are always the cleanest?

Word List

BALL
BALKS
BATS
BUNT
CLOUT
DOUBLE
ERRORS
FOUL
FUNGO
GROUNDER
GROUND RULE
HOMER
RBI
SIGNS
SLUGGER
STRIKE
SWAT
SWINGING
THROW
TRIPLES
WALK

S	N	G	I	S	K	L	A	B
W	O	R	H	T	T	T	H	W
I	S	O	E	E	O	R	A	A
N	E	U	F	D	G	T	I	L
G	L	N	B	O	N	L	T	K
I	P	D	I	U	U	U	U	H
N	I	R	B	B	F	L	O	E
G	R	U	A	L	R	M	L	R
C	T	L	T	E	E	H	C	E
R	L	E	S	R	O	R	R	E

212

IBM only. Price: $39.95.

You can't order directly from the company, but you can get information from them:

Electronic Arts
1820 Gateway Drive
San Mateo, CA 94404
(414) 571-7171

Hardball! Put out in 1985, the first version of this game sold more than 500,000 copies. Now they've got Hardball II, which lets you mix and match players and make up your own all-star teams with current and former stars. And there are seven stadiums to choose from.

The game is for IBM, Apple, Atari ST, or Amiga. Price: $14.95 for Hardball!, $39.95 for Hardball II.

If you can't find it at the store, you can order directly from:

Accolade
550 South Winchester Boulevard
San Jose, CA 95128
(800) 245-7744

Full Count. A software strategy game based on actual major league statistics. You can play the game on Commodore 64/128, IBM, Apple, or Atari ST. Price: $39.99.

For a free brochure or to order, contact:

Lance Haffner Games
P.O. Box 100594
Nashville, TN 37210
(615) 242-2617

R.B.I. Baseball. A Nintendo game made by Tengen. How popular is it? It's sold more than 2 million copies! Price: $49.95.

To order directly, get a brochure, or find out the dealer nearest you, call toll free:

(800) 2-TENGEN.

Sporting News Baseball. A game that combines statistics with arcade action, it is available for Commodore, IBM, and Apple. The makers of this game also sell Street Sports Baseball, a computer stickball game set in a city street. Price: $39.95.

For information or to order, contact:

Epyx Computer Products
600 Galveston Drive
Redwood City, CA 94063
(415) 368-3200

Tommy Lasorda Baseball. For this Sega Genesis ball game you'll need a Genesis console, TeleGenesis modem, and game cartridge. Price: $55.80.

For more information, write to:

Sega of America, Inc.
P.O. Box 2167
South San Francisco, CA 94080
(415) 742-9300 or (800) USA-SEGA

TV Sports Baseball. Another computer game that aims to combine arcade fast action with interesting statistics. Price: For IBM and Amiga, $49.95; for C64, $34.95.

For information:

Cinemaware
4165 Thousand Oaks Boulevard
Westlake Village, CA 91362
(805) 495-6515

ELECTRONIC GAMES

Then there are games that you plug in or that run on batteries. These games are sort of a cross between the board game and the computer game. One version, "Belly Ball," an electronic baseball card game, is available from:

The Main Street Toy Company, Inc.
540 Hopmeadow Street
Simsbury, CT 06070
(203) 651-4986

Hand-held electronic games are like mini-com-

THE BULL PEN
    Q: How did the Count feel after he ate three hot dogs and drank two sodas?
    A: The Count was full.

puter games. One outlet that sells them is Tiger Electronics in Vernon Hills, Illinois. They make a Bo Jackson Combo Baseball and Football game (since Bo stars in both sports). They also put out a basic hand-held ball game, and a fancier tabletop version that talks, calling out the balls and strikes and making other comments on the game. (The talking game retails for about $30.)

You can't order directly from Tiger. If you can't find a local store that carries their products, ask a large toy store near you to order for you.

In general, talking baseball games don't seem to be doing that well.

LJN Toys, for instance, quickly discontinued its line of talking baseball cards. (Maybe this will make them collectors'

MAJOR LEAGUE SCRAMBLE

This year's pennant race is certainly a jumble. Can you sort it out?

To solve the puzzle, you'll need to find the names of teams hidden in this block of letters. The words to look for are listed below. They can go up, down, across, back, or diagonally.

The leftover letters will spell out the answer to this riddle:

Why did the policeman try to arrest Rickey Henderson?

Word List

ANGELS
ASTRO
ATHLETICS
ATLANTA
BRAVES
CARDINALS
CHICAGO
CLEVELAND
CUBS
GIANTS
JAY
LOS ANGELES
NEW YORK METS
PHILS
RED SOX
REDS
SAN DIEGO
SEATTLE
TWIN
YANKEES

```
H E C A R D I N A L S L
Y A N K E E S L E C E O
A T D O D S C T I G V S
O L H R S E L T L I A A
G A C T O E E A G A R N
E N H S X L V U E N B G
I T I A H S E A T T L E
D A C T L S L I S S N L
N S A E T N A I O B J E
A L G E I N N B H A U S
S N O W A S D E Y P S C
A S T E M K R O Y W E N
```

items someday?) You put the card in a special machine and hear that player talk about his career and stats for two and a half minutes.

You can still buy the cards (but not the playing machines) directly from LJN at $5.95 for a set of four. (LJN also makes a Nintendo computer game called Major League,

which you can get through stores.)

LJN Toys, Ltd.
1107 Broadway
New York, NY 10010
(212) 243-6565

Parker Brothers put out a line of talking baseball games in 1989, and by 1990 the toys all bit the dust. You'll have to hunt in stores and garage sales to

SHORTSTOPS
Baseball pitchers used to be allowed to throw a lot more balls than they are today, without walking the batter. In 1879, *nine* balls meant a walk.

find them. Parker Brothers has no old games in stock.

It's hard to believe that Parker Brothers won't someday get back into the baseball game business. To keep informed of their games, send for a catalogue. You can order their games direct:

Parker Brothers
50 Dunham Road
Beverly, MA 01927
(508) 927-7600

TRADE-INS

A number of companies will "buy back" your old computer games (especially Nintendo games). In some cases, you won't get the money. You'll get a markdown on your new game purchase. If you're interested, look for ads in computer games magazines, which you can find on most big newsstands (there's one listed in the next section of this chapter).

Here's a trading company for Nintendo games. They recommend calling first to find out the prices they're offering for your old game:

The Fun Company
Funco, Inc.
4948 Highway 169 North
New Hope, MN 55428
(612) 533-8118

The Ultimate Game Club buys and sells used software games of all kinds. There's a $10 annual membership fee. For more information, call:

(800) TOY-CLUB

HIGH SCORES

First you got addicted to your baseball computer game. Then, after long hours of practice, you became a pro. You can beat the computer every time, with astronomical scores.

What's your reward?

Sometimes software companies sponsor game contests. Watch computer magazines and stores for ads.

In the meantime, *Gamepro* magazine publishes high scores each month for Nintendo, Sega, Genesis, and Atari (7800 or XE) games. So you can brag about your high score, and win a *Gamepro* T-shirt.

For subscription information, write to:

Gamepro Magazine
P.O. Box 2096
Knoxville, IA 50198-2096

A subscription costs $19.97 for 12 monthly issues.

FANTASY LEAGUE SOFTWARE

If you get into fantasy or Rotisserie™ league play (see page 68), you'll want to start keeping track of major and minor leaguers' current statistics. Fantasy league play involves made-up teams of players from various teams in the majors. The success of your hodgepodge team depends on the ever-changing stats of the individual players.

How do you keep track of all these stats? There are

plenty of software programs on the market to help you. Look for ads in the back of collectibles magazines (see Chapter 10). Here's one of the many companies that offer them:

Jacobsen Software Designs
Attn: Order—PBX
1590 E. 43 Avenue
Eugene, OR 97405
(503) 343-8030

INVENT YOUR OWN BASEBALL GAME!

If you get tired of shelling out your allowance money on other people's baseball games, why not invent your own?

It's fun to play your own board game with friends. And if you want to get more serious and try to sell your invention, here's a brochure that can help guide you:

Game Plan: The Game Inventor's Handbook
Game Inventors of America, Inc.
P.O. Box 58711
World Trade Center
Dallas, TX 75258
(214) 331-4587

The pamphlet costs $12. You can order it by having your parents send a check for that amount (it costs more outside the U.S.) to the above address.

SLUGGER FEST!

Here's a grand whammy of a hidden word puzzle. (Of the three word scrambles in this chapter, this one's by far the toughest. So be prepared!)

Hidden in this word jumble are 31 of baseball's greatest hitters, past and present.

If you find all 31, the remaining letters will spell out the answer to the riddle below.

The 31 names can go across, backward, up, down, and diagonally. Use the word list below, and look only for the words spelled out with capital letters.

Riddle: Why did the famous slugger eat 42 cherry pies in an hour?

Slugger List

HANK AARON
WADE BOGGS
(george) BRETT
ROBERTO CLEMENTE
TY COBB
JOE DIMAGGIO
(carlton) FISK
(george) FOSTER
(lou) GEHRIG
(rogers) HORNSBY
(kent) HRBEK
(reggie) JACKSON
AL KALINE
(ralph) KINER
(dale) LONG
MICKEY MANTLE
(roger) MARIS
KEVIN (mitchell)
(johnny) MIZE
(stan) MUSIAL
MEL OTT
(dave) PARKER
BOOG (powell)
KIRBY (puckett)
JIM RICE
(frank) ROBINSON
PETE ROSE
BABE RUTH
HONUS WAGNER
(ted) WILLIAMS
CARL YASTRZEMSKI

M	K	T	M	S	H	G	N	O	L	O	M	I	E	T
A	I	Y	H	U	A	O	O	T	H	T	E	K	T	E
R	N	C	B	J	S	P	R	D	F	T	L	S	N	J
I	E	O	K	R	A	I	A	N	I	E	O	M	E	O
S	R	B	T	E	I	C	A	R	S	R	T	E	M	E
U	E	B	A	R	Y	K	K	L	K	B	T	Z	E	D
N	N	I	R	B	P	M	N	S	N	E	Y	R	L	I
S	G	G	O	B	E	D	A	W	O	E	R	T	C	M
M	A	T	B	R	T	R	H	N	O	N	G	S	O	A
A	W	M	I	Z	E	A	U	H	T	I	E	A	T	G
I	S	N	N	B	R	T	A	T	R	L	K	Y	R	G
L	U	I	S	V	O	Y	S	H	H	A	E	L	E	I
L	N	V	O	H	S	O	E	O	I	K	B	R	B	O
I	O	E	N	T	E	G	G	T	F	L	R	A	O	E
W	H	K	E	C	I	R	M	I	J	A	H	C	R	R

216

TRIPLE PLAY!

How many words can you make using only the letters in the two words "triple play"? No proper nouns or contractions are allowed. But the words can be of any length. Since there are two P's in "triple play," you can use words with two P's, such as "pep." But you can't use a word such as "patter" since "triple play" has only one T.

There's a list of 102 possible words in the "Scorecard" section at the end of this chapter. Can you make that many? More?

Mickey Mantle, the superstar slugger from Spavinaw, Oklahoma.

BASEBALL-GRAMS

An anagram is a word made out of another word, using all of the same letters. For instance, an anagram of the word "throw" is "worth." Can you find the baseball words and phrases hidden in these anagrams?

RIB
EAR
TATS
HONE RUM
OLE BUD (becomes one word)
SLOWER RIDES (becomes two words)
NOBLE AS LABS (becomes three words)

Now that you've got the hang of anagrams, try your hand at this anagram story. Your job is to fill in the blanks in the following way. For the first blank, take the word "IS," add one letter, and make a word that makes sense out of the sentence.

For the next blank, you'll have to add a letter to your first answer, and make a word out of that. And so on.

THE WHIFFER

It's the bottom of the ninth, and Marvin Whiffer I S at the plate. "Two outs," thinks Whiffer. "It would be

a ____ ____ ____ to strike out!"

The fans begin to

____ ____ ____ ____ :

"Whiffer's going to whiff, Whiffer's going to whiff!"

Here's the pitch. Fastball. Marvin swings with all his might—and hits it. As he races for first, he thinks, "I hope I didn't

____ L ____ ____ ____ the bat!"

Marvin's ____ ____ ____

____ ____ ____ wins the game!

THE CASE OF SLUGGER MCWHAM'S MISSING BAT

Slugger McWham is due up at bat and the bases are loaded. But the opposing team has filled the bat rack with fake McWham whammers. Can you find McWham's bat in time? Which of the six bats on the right exactly matches the bat on the left?

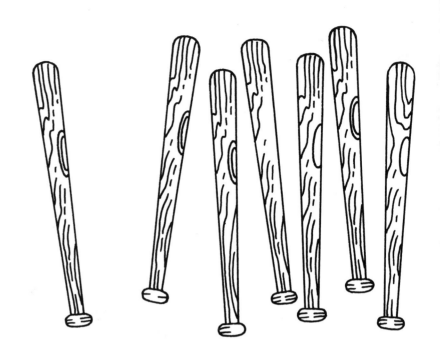

PHONE BALL

729-48-2468-76-563. That's a phone number, but don't try calling it. It's code for a famous baseball quote. To decipher it, look at a phone dial. Each one of these numbers stands for one of three letters. It's up to you to figure out which letter.

1	ABC 2	DEF 3
GHI 4	JKL 5	MNO 6
PRS 7	TUV 8	WXY 9
*	0	#

Look at the background and the scoreboard in this Normal Rockwell painting. Which team wants this game stopped?

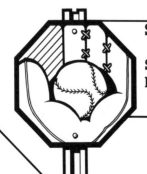

SHORTSTOPS

In his 15 seasons Jim Wohlford played in Kansas City, Milwaukee, San Francisco, and Montreal. Few know his name, but many know his famous quote: "Ninety-percent of this game is half mental." What was wrong with Wohlford's arithmetic?

QUOTE-BALL

Here are some more famous baseball quotes to decipher. The quote goes from left to right, in the blank boxes. The shaded-in boxes mark the spaces between the words.

Under each row of boxes are the letters to fill into them. The problem is that the letters may or may not be out of order.

For instance, in the first puzzle there's a W, I, and Y under the first row of boxes. So the quote starts with one of those three letters.

Hint: Start by looking for rows with only one or two letters. Try filling in the letters and see if they make words. As soon as you make one or two words, you'll be able to eliminate some of the letters in certain rows. And you'll be on your way.

1. Here's one of the most famous baseball quotes of all time. It's from turn-of-the-century writer Grantland Rice:

W	O	U		O	L	A	L	O	T	E	E	I	E	A	M	Y	O	W
I	T	N		P	R	T	T	W	S	H	T	H	G	S		H	O	U
Y	I	S		N	O			H	E			T	R		E			

2. The start of some very famous baseball lyrics:

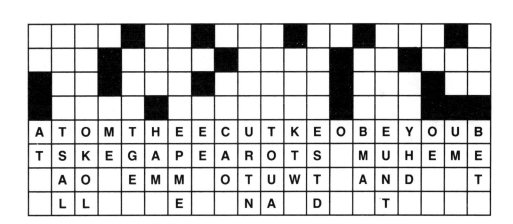

A	T	O	M	T	H	E	E	C	U	T	K	E	O	B	E	Y	O	U	B
T	S	K	E	G	A	P	E	A	R	O	T	S		M	U	H	E	M	E
	A	O		E	M	M		O	T	U	W	T		A	N	D			T
	L	L			E			N	A	D			T						

3. Hidden in this puzzle is a famous quote from Satchel Paige:

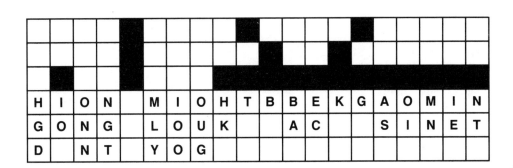

H	I	O	N		M	I	O	H	T	B	B	E	K	G	A	O	M	I	N
G	O	N	G		L	O	U	K			A	C			S	I	N	E	T
D		N	T		Y	O	G												

CAN YOU NAME THIS MYSTERY PLAYER?

If you solve this baseball crossword puzzle, you'll find out the identity of the mystery player in the center photo. Here's a hint: He plays first base.

Across

1. The first name of the mystery player (see photo, and see 22 Down for the mystery player's last name.)
4. _____-pitch softball. One of the two kinds of softball.
7. __ __ L L. Fill in the letters and you have the word for something round, with 108 stitches in it, that major leaguers love to hit.
9. Exists
10. What a fielder tries hard not to make.
12. A long thin fish.
13. What an outfielder catches.
15. A word that means all of us.
16. __ __ D. Fill in the letters and you have the word for a ballplayer from Cincinnati.
17. A kind of plant.
18. With 25 Down. These players play a special game once a year.
19. The fifth letter of the alphabet.
20. __ V __. Fill in the letters and you have a special award given each year to one superstar in each of the major leagues.

23. Along with "and," one of the most commonly used words in English.
26. The _____ Horse. A nickname for Lou Gehrig.
27. Gooey substances.
30. Accuse.
31. What a batter does after getting his fourth ball.
33. Friend.
34. See 9 Across.
35. Things.
37. A pitcher better have a good one of these. In fact, in baseball lingo this word *means* a pitcher.
39. Instant _____ (you see thi on some major league scoreboards).
41. This abbreviation stands for a subject you study in school.
43. The initials for the town th Cardinals play in.
44. A routine grounder or simple pop-up is known as an _____ _____ (two words).

Down

1. Annoy.
2. Not awake.
3. Sharp.
4. Abbreviation that stands for "older." It's used when a father and son share the same first name.
5. One reason an ump calls a pitch a ball is because it's _____.
6. Certain minerals.
7. Rowdy fans drink too much of this at ball games.
8. The initials for one of the major leagues.
11. __ yne __ andberg. Add the initials and you've got a Chicago second baseman who won the MVP in 1984, leading his team to the pennant.
12. This abbreviation stands for the most important statistic kept on a pitcher.

14. Anger.
19. __ __ bacco. Add two letters and you've got something that many ball players used to chew.
20. A part of a play.
22. The second half of the mystery player's name.
23. __ __ __ D E. Add three letters to make a word that means swapping players.
24. A Greek poet whose name is mentioned whenever a batter hits the ball out of the park.
25. See 18 Across.
26. Sick.
28. Effortlessness. As in the sentence, "The shortstop fielded the grounder with _____."
29. Something a good ball player must have.

30. What you round after hitting the ball.
32. __ __ __ T. Add the first three letters and you have a common baseball word. It refers to the mathematical way people keep track of how well someone is playing.
33. The afternoon. Abbreviation.
36. "Good _____ !" Players say this to congratulate their hitter when he doesn't swing at a bag pitch.
37. Long _____ . (In the past.)
38. A member of a certain New York team.
40. Abbreviation. It's used to mark a special note at the end of a letter.
42. Don Mattingly plays here. (Abbreviation.)

220

THE SCORECARD
Answers to Puzzles and Games in This Chapter

TRACE AROUND THE BASES
One possible solution.

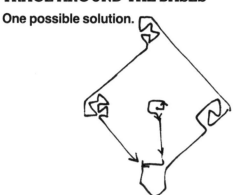

DOUBLE TALK

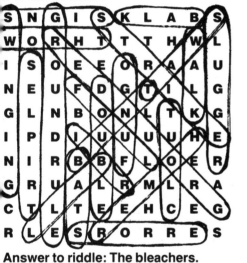

Answer to riddle: The bleachers.

MAJOR LEAGUE SCRAMBLE

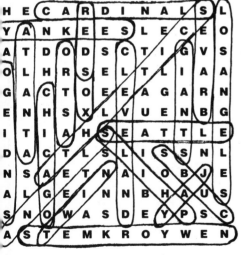

Answer to riddle:
He leads the leagues in stolen bases.

SLUGGER FEST

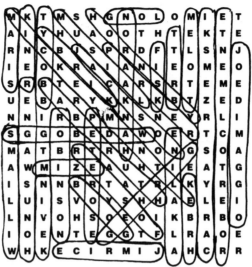

Answer to riddle:
So that he'd turn into a heavy hitter.

THE CASE OF SLUGGER McWHAM'S MISSING BAT

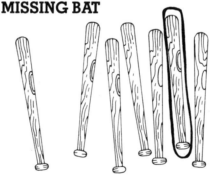

CAN YOU NAME THIS MYSTERY PLAYER?

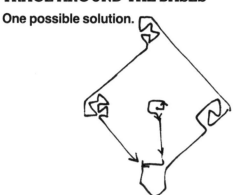

TRIPLE PLAY

AT, IT, PA, AIL, AIR, ALE, ALP, APT, ARE, ART, ATE, AYE, EAR, EAT, ELL, ERA, IRE, LAP, LAY, LEA, LET, LIE, LIP, LIT, LYE, PAL, PAP, PAR, PAT, PAY, PEA, PEP, PER, PET, PIE, PIT, RAP, RAT, RAY, RIP, RYE, TAP, TAR, TEA, TIP, YAP, YEA, YEP, YET, ALIT, APER, ARTY, LAIR, LATE, LEAP, LYRE, PAIL, PAIR, PARE, PART, PEAR, PERT, PILE, PLAY, PLEA, PRAY, RAIL, RAPE, RATE, RILE, RIPE, TAIL, TAPE, TEAR, TILE, TIRE, TRAP, TRAY, TRIP, TYPE, APPLE, APPLY, APTLY, PALER, PAPER, PARTY, PLATE, PLEAT, PRATE, LATER, LAYER, RATER, RELAY, RIPER, TAPER, TRAIL, TRIAL, TRIPE, RIPPLE, TIPPLE, TIPPER, YAPPER.

BASEBALL-GRAMS

RIB = RBI, EAR = ERA, TATS = STAT, HONE RUM = HOME RUN, OLE BUD = DOUBLE, SLOWER RIDES = WORLD SERIES, NOBLE AS LABS = BASE ON BALLS

THE WHIFFER: SIN, SING, SLING, SINGLE

PHONE BALL

Say it ain't so, Joe.

QUOTE-BALL

1. It's not whether you win or lose, it's how you play the game.
2. Take me out to the ball game. Take me out to the crowd. Buy me some peanuts and…
3. Don't look back. Something might be gaining on you.

221

THAT'S THE TICKET!

A SCHEDULE OF KEY EVENTS

Come March, most baseball fans start to get excited. With spring training games in the news, fans know a new season is just around the corner. The long winter baseball drought has ended.

Actually, there's something going on in baseball every month. If your family has enough time and money, plus a desire to travel, you could probably attend baseball events just about all year 'round!

For many of baseball's bigger events, you need to plan way ahead to get tickets. This chapter can help you do just that. Baseball schedules vary from year to year, but here's an overview of a typical season's calendar:

JANUARY

Early this month, the major leagues announce their season schedules for the new year. Fans begin to look ahead, hoping this will be the year for their team to win.

But January is also a time for looking back. Since 1936, the baseball writers have been selecting baseball heroes to be inducted into the Hall of Fame, part of the Baseball Museum at Cooperstown, New York.

To be eligible, a player must have played at least 10 seasons in the big leagues and have been retired for at least five years. The new inductees are named in January, but the induction ceremony isn't held until the latter part of July or August.

FEBRUARY

Most names for the Hall of Fame are announced this month. These people are selected by a special Veterans Committee. The committee honors umpires, baseball executives, and other people who would not otherwise be eligible.

In mid-February (or thereabouts), pitchers and catchers begin reporting to spring training in Arizona and Florida.

MARCH

Spring training games are underway, and the

1989 inductees to the Hall of Fame: (left to right) Schoendienst, Barlick, Yastrzemski, and Bench.

drama of the new season begins to unfold. For spring training ticket information, see special listings in this chapter.

And for people who play fantasy baseball (see page 68), it's time to pick team players in their fantasy league drafts.

Traditionally, the President of the United States or another high public official throws out the first ball at an opening day game.

Who plays whom in April? The official schedule of major league play is announced in

all the picked players will be headed for the minors. But sometimes a player picked in the June draft is so talented you'll see him playing in the majors come April.

In addition to getting drafted into the majors, this month players can try out for the United States national team. This team plays for the U.S. in international tournaments (see July). Most players are specifically invited to the tryouts, but there's also an open tryout day. (Players need to be at least 17 years old.)

President Taft throws out the first baseball of the season (April 14, 1910).

APRIL–MAY

A new season of professional baseball begins. The major leagues usually begin play in the first week of April.

January of each year.

JUNE

In early June, the major league holds its summer free-agent draft. Almost

At age 15 (plus 10 months and 11 days), Joe Nuxhall pitched for the Reds. He was the youngest major leaguer ever.

The tryouts are held in Millington, Tennessee. For information about watching the tryouts, or trying out yourself, contact the United States Baseball Federation (USBA) (see page 24).

Also in early June, the eight top U.S. college teams meet in Omaha, Nebraska, for the College Baseball World Series. For ticket information, contact the Younkers Ticket Office in Omaha at (402) 399-6640.

There are five other college divisional championships, which take place in late May and June.

June 25 is the usual date for the annual national old-timers game. Today,

some of baseball's most famous veterans limber up for one more showdown. For more information about this game, you can write to the Association of Professional Ball Players (see page 24).

JULY

In early July all major league play stops for a three-day All-Star Game break (the exact schedule of the break and game varies from year to year). The players who go to the All-Star Game are chosen

by the fans. You can get ballots by going to your local stadium. The ballots are also printed in the newspaper *USA Today*.

To get tickets to the All-Star Game, you need to contact the office of the team hosting the game that year. That team often uses a lottery system to decide who gets to go. To have a chance, you need to contact the team early, months before the season even begins!

To find out what team is hosting this year's All-Star

The stars from the first All-Star game in 1933. Babe Ruth's 2-run shot won for the AL, 4-2.

Game, contact the American League or National League office (see pages 59-60.)

In the latter part of July, or sometimes in August, players elected to the Hall of Fame in January are officially inducted. The ceremony is held at the Hall of Fame in Cooperstown, New York. The ceremonies are open to the public, free of charge. To find out who's being inducted and when, contact the Hall of Fame (see page 45).

July and August are busy times for international baseball, with the U.S. national team in action every year.

For instance, the Summer Olympics, which are held every four years, are adding baseball as an official sport in Barcelona, Spain, in 1992. For more information, contact the USBA (see page 24).

The Pan American Games are also held every four years, with the 1991 games to be played in Cuba. These games are open to the national teams of countries in North and South America. There is also the Intercontinental Cup, the World Championships (held every two years), and the Goodwill Games. To find out more about any of these four events, contact the International Baseball Federation (IBA) (see page 65).

AUGUST

August is championship play-off time for many youth leagues. For example, the Khoury Leagues play their world series in Missouri over the course of one August weekend. Tickets are free.

The Little League holds its international world series in Williamsport, Pennsylvania. That's for 11- and 12-year-olds. Three other Little League age groups play tournaments in other cities.

On the third Thursday in August, the Pony League plays its championship in Washington, Pennsylvania. On the same day the Bronco League holds its championship in Sacramento, California. The Colt and Palomino leagues also play championships, in different cities.

The Babe Ruth Leagues hold championships in August. So do the Dixie Leagues, which have seven world series tournaments this month. For specific information about any of the youth league championships, contact the league in question (see Chapter 1 listings).

There are two national U.S. youth teams, sponsored by the IBA. The AA team is for 13- to 15-year-olds, the AAA for 16- to 18-year-olds. Chosen by the USBA, these kids represent the U.S. in world championships every year, usually in August and September. For information about these championship games, contact the IBA.

SEPTEMBER

September is usually the final month of major league ball (though sometimes season play continues into early October). It's an exciting

---

TRIVIA QUIZ

What's the highest number of hits a team can get in nine innings and still not score a single run?

Answer: Each inning, a team can get a maximum of six hits without scoring. For instance, they can load the bases with three singles. Then let's say two players are picked off. Two more singles load the bases again, but no runs score. Then the batter hits one of the base runners with what would have been a hit. The runner is out. The batter gets a hit. That's six hits per inning, for a nine-inning total of 54.

The Little League's very first champs pose with the league's founder, Carl Stotz, in 1930.

month in baseball, as teams in the pennant race head for the finish line!

Teams with a chance at a pennant make an announcement in September about how to get tickets for the play-offs. Season-ticket holders usually have the best shot.

In early September it's time for the Triple-A Classic. That's the best-of-seven world series for the AAA American League and International Minor League. The series is held in the cities of the competing teams. As with the major league World Series, tickets are available through the two teams' offices.

The AAA Pacific Coast League plays its own play-off series in early September. The four division winners play in a best-of-five series. The winners of these games play another best-of-five series for the championship.

There's also another youth league championship this month. The American Amateur Baseball Congress holds its annual championship in Battle Creek, Michigan.

OCTOBER

The Major League Championship Series (LCS) begins in early October. The four pennant

winners play a best-of-seven series to see who goes to the World Series.

The World Series itself begins sometime in mid-October. This series starts in the city of either the NL or AL champion—it alternates every year. On even years the series starts in the NL team's city.

NOVEMBER

There are four big awards in major league baseball: Most Valuable Player (MVP), Cy Young, Rookie of the Year, and the Gold Glove. All but the Gold Gloves are announced this month, usually in successive weeks.

Famed baseball commissioner, Judge Kenesaw Mountain Landis.

MVP

It's officially known as the Kenesaw Mountain Landis Award (named after a former baseball commissioner). But most people known it as the MVP, the most valuable player. It goes to the player who has done the most to help his team win.

Every year, the Baseball Writers' Association of America selects two writers in each major league city. Then all these writers cast their ballots and elect an MVP for each league.

MVP awards have been given since 1911. To date, the first choice has been unanimous only twelve times.

Ty Cobb (1911) and Babe Ruth (1923) are among the few who have gotten all the first-place votes for their year. Recently, Jose Canseco was voted a Most Most. He won unanimously for the NL in 1988.

ROOKIE OF THE YEAR

Canseco had entered the big leagues only two years earlier, in 1986. And that year he was named AL Rookie of the Year.

The baseball writers have been giving out this award since 1940. To be previous seasons, has

Cy Young, whose name has come to stand for great pitching.

eligible for Rookie of the Year, a player has to be in his first full season.

The rules protect players who are called up from the minors to fill in briefly for injured players. If a player has had only 130 at-bats in

played under 50 innings, or has spent only 45 days on the roster, he's still considered a rookie.

CY YOUNG

Many people feel that the MVP award should never go to a pitcher. Their reasoning is this: Since the pitcher plays only one out of every four or five games, how can he be as valuable to the team as a player who's in every game?

The rules are clear. Pitchers are eligible for MVP, and a number of pitchers have won. But most of the time, the award goes to a nonpitcher.

To correct this imbalance, in 1956 the baseball writers began naming the best pitcher as well as MVP. The first year they gave the award to pitcher Don Newcombe. He won the MVP award as well!

The best-pitcher awards are named after Cy Young. From 1890 to 1911 Cy Young racked up 511 career wins. That record still stands. In fact, no other pitcher has even come close.

Two Cy Young Award winners are picked every year, one pitcher in each league.

DECEMBER

The major and minor leagues hold their annual winter meetings. The exact times and locations vary. Team owners meet to talk business and often end up talking trades. Watch for big trade announcements before the meetings are through.

At the meetings, the last major awards of the season are often announced—the Gold Gloves. Every year the players and managers select the best fielders at each position. (They can't vote for a player on their own team!)

As a trophy, the winners

"THE SHOT HEARD 'ROUND THE WORLD"

October 3, 1951—It is one of the single most famous hits in all baseball history. And in Brooklyn, it's still a sore subject.

On August 12, the New York Giants were 13½ games behind Brooklyn's star-studded Dodgers. The pennant was in the bag. But it got out.

First, the Giants clawed their way back to a first-place tie as the season ended. Then, the two teams met for a best-of-three-game play-off.

The Giants won the first game 3 to 1. The Dodgers, with stars such as Frankie Robinson, romped in the second game, 10 to 0.

And they were leading the second game 4–2 in the bottom of the ninth. With two men on base, pitcher Ralph Branca came in to try for the save. He faced Bobby Thompson.

Brooklyn fans should not read any further. Because Thompson hit a ball to left field that just managed to make it out of the stadium. Three runs scored and—though the fans couldn't believe it—Brooklyn had lost.

receive special Rawlings mitts that have been coated with gold. The mitts hold two gold baseballs—a nice catch for the player.

Great fielders tend to be

more consistent about their fielding than great hitters are at the bat. Perhaps as a result, a number of star players have won the Gold Glove for their position year after year. Keith Hernandez, for instance, won at first base for 10 straight years, beginning in 1978.

The famous over-the-shoulder grab by Willie Mays is known as "*The* Catch."

WARM TIX!

Come February and March, pro players head south, to Florida and Arizona. It's spring training time—time for the players to warm up for the season, and stay warm while they do it. (See the article on the Grapefruit and Cactus leagues on page 71.)

Spring training games usually start on the first weekend in March and last the month. During the regular season, you'll probably need to contact the team office for info (see listing in Chapter 1). Closer to March, you can get spring training schedule information and tickets directly from the spring training centers:

Atlanta Braves
Municipal Stadium
715 Hank Aaron Drive
West Palm Beach, FL 33401
(305) 683-6100
For TIX: Call, or write to P.O. Box 2619 at the above address.

Baltimore Orioles
Bobby Maduro Miami Stadium
2301 NW 10th Avenue
Miami, FL 33127
(305) 635-5395
TIX: Contact the Spring Training Ticket Manager, at the same address.

Boston Red Sox
Chain O' Lakes Park
Cypress Gardens Boulevard
Winter Haven, FL 33880
(813) 293-3900

California Angels
Gene Autry Complex
4125 East McKellips
Mesa, AZ 85206
(602) 830-4137
also:
Angels Stadium
Sunrise and Barristo Roads
Palm Springs, CA 92263
(619) 323-3329
TIX: Call (619) 325-4487 or write to P.O. Box 609 at the second address above.

Chicago Cubs
HoHoKam Park
1235 North Center Street
Mesa, AZ 85201
(602) 964-4467

Chicago White Sox
Payne Park
2052 Adams Lane (off Washington Street)
Sarasota, FL 34237
(813) 953-3388
TIX: Chicago White Sox
      Payne Park
      P.O. Box 1702
      Sarasota, FL 33578

Cincinnati Reds
Reds Spring Training Complex
1900 South Park Road
Plant City, FL 33566
(813) 752-7337

Cleveland Indians
Hi Corbett Field
Randolph Park
Tucson, AZ 85726
(602) 325-2621
TIX: Call or write to P.O.
Box 27577 at the above
address.

Detroit Tigers
Joker Marchant Stadium
Lakeland Hills Boulevard
Lakeland, FL 33801
(813) 682-1401

Houston Astros
Osceola County Stadium
1000 Osceola Boulevard
Kissimmee, FL 32743
TIX: Houston Astros
      Osceola County
      Stadium
      P.O. Box 2229
      Kissimmee, FL
      32742
      (305) 933-5400

Kansas City Royals
The Stadium at
Boardwalk and Baseball
Boardwalk and
Baseball, Inc.
Intersection Interstate 4
& Highway 27
Orlando, FL 32802
From Florida call:
800-367-2249
From rest of U.S. call
800-826-1939
From Canada call:
813-424-2424

Los Angeles Dodgers
Holman Stadium
Dodgertown
4001 26th Street
Vero Beach, FL 32961
(305) 569-4900
TIX: Call, or write to P.O.
Box 2887 at the above
 address.

Milwaukee Brewers
Compadre Stadium
1425 W. Ocitillo Road
Chandler, AZ 85248
(602) 821-2200
TIX: Milwaukee Brewers
      3800 S. Alma School
      Road
      Suite 300
      Chandler, AZ 85248
      (602) 899-9111

Minnesota Twins
Tinker Field
Tampa Avenue at
Church Street
Orlando, FL 32855
(305) 849-6346
TIX: Call, or write to P.O.
Box 5645 at the above
address.

Montreal Expos
Same address as Atlanta
Braves
TIX: Municipal Stadium
      P.O. Box 2546
      West Palm Beach,
      FL 33401
      (305) 689-9121

New York Mets
St. Lucie County Sports
Complex
West Peacock Street
Port St. Lucie, FL 33452
(305) 335-3695
TIX: Call, or write to P.O.
Box 8808 at the above
address.

New York Yankees
Ft. Lauderdale Stadium
5301 NW 12th Avenue
Ft. Lauderdale, FL 33309
(305) 776-1921

Oakland Athletics
Phoenix Municipal
Stadium
5999 East Van Buren
Phoenix, AZ 85008
(602) 275-0500
TIX: Credit card orders,
call (602) 829-5555.

Philadelphia Phillies
Jack Russell Stadium
800 Phillies Drive
Clearwater, FL 33515
(813) 441-8638
TIX: Write to the above
address or call (813)
442-8496.

Pittsburgh Pirates
McKechnie Field
17th Avenue and 9th
Street West
Bradenton, FL 33505
(813) 748-4610

San Diego Padres
Desert Sun Stadium
1440 Desert Hills Drive
Yuma, AZ 85364
(602) 782-2567
TIX: San Diego Padres
      Caballeros de Yuma
      Chamber of
      Commerce
      P.O. Box 230
      Yuma, AZ 85364
      (602) 782-2567

San Francisco Giants
Scottsdale Stadium
7408 East Osborne Road
Scottsdale, AZ 85251
(602) 994-5123

Seattle Mariners
Diablo Stadium
2200 W. Alameda
Tempe, AZ 85282
(602) 731-8381

St. Louis Cardinals
Al Lang Stadium
180 2nd Avenue S.E.
St. Petersburg, FL 33701
(813) 896-4641
TIX: Write to the above
address or call (813)
894-4773.

Texas Rangers
Charlotte County
Stadium
2300 El Jobean Road
Port Charlotte, FL 33949
(813) 625-9500
TIX: Call (813) 624-2211 or
write to P.O. Box 3609 at
the above address.

Toronto Blue Jays
Grant Field
311 Douglas Avenue
Dunedin, FL 34698
(813) 733-9302
TIX: Call, or write to P.O.
Box 957 at the above
address.

WHAT GOES UP MUST COME DOWN

1939—As a publicity stunt, Lefty O'Doul, the manager of a minor league team, dropped a baseball out of a dirigible, 1,200 feet up. His catcher, Joe Sprinz, claimed to see the ball all the way. He said it looked no bigger than an aspirin.

He didn't make the catch, though. The ball hit him in the jaw and knocked him out.

Other high high pops *have* been caught. On August 25, 1894, a catcher named Pop Schriver caught a ball dropped from the top of the Washington Monument—555 feet up.

IT'S NOT POLITE TO POINT!

October 1, 1932—It's the third game of the World Series between the New York Yankees and the Chicago Cubs. Wrigley Field is packed with screaming fans. The score is tied 4–4 in the fifth. Guess who's up? Babe Ruth.

Ruth had just missed a hard catch in right, and the crowd was razzing him nonstop. So the great Bambino pointed to the bleachers. Was he telling the crowd where he planned to hit his next homer?

Some say the Babe was only signaling the count, not pointing. But that's not how the legend has it. One thing's for sure—what happened next: With the count at 2 and 2, Ruth smacked the ball right into the bleachers. The Yankees won the game and swept the Series.

HAVE A SEAT!

Whether you're buying your tickets through the mail or at the stadium, it's a good idea to get familiar with the stadium layout. For instance, if you're looking to snag a foul ball souvenir at a Detroit Tigers home game, don't buy a lower box seat in section 122, because you'll be behind the home plate screen.

On the other hand, you'll have one of the best views in the house. (For advice on where to sit to improve your chances of grabbing a foul ball, see the article on page 204.)

A complete layout for Tiger Stadium is shown below. You can get a layout for any other major league stadium by writing or calling the team office (Chapter 1). They'll send you a flyer of ticket-buying information that will probably include helpful information such as how to read your baseball ticket. Ushers at the stadium can also direct you.

KALINE DRIVE

UPPER BLEACHERS

GRANDSTAND RESERVED

DETROIT TIGERS

TIGER STADIUM

COCHRANE AVENUE

TRUMBULL AVENUE

LOWER BLEACHERS

LOWER BOXES

LOWER RESERVED

UPPER BOXES

UPPER RESERVED

MICHIGAN AVENUE

SEASON'S GREETINGS!
BASEBALL CALENDARS

On June 26, 1901, the Red Sox arrived in Philadelphia, all set to play baseball. There was just one little problem. Their scheduled game was in Baltimore. Clearly, they needed to pay closer attention to their calendar!

You probably don't have as many appointments to keep in mind as a ball player does. But a calendar can help you stay organized—reminding you of everything from your mom's birthday to the day your school science project is due.

And if you use a *baseball* calendar, your calendar can also remind you of famous dates in baseball history, the birthdays of famous players, and other baseball fun facts.

Included in this chapter is a baseball calendar with a baseball tidbit for every day of the year. You can use this calendar daily to find out what happened on this day in baseball history, or you can read the calendar straight through.

This chapter will also tell you where you can order other baseball calendars, including a baseball card calendar and a wall calendar for baseball parks. You can start a calendar collection.

You can also use one of these baseball calendars to make your own baseball diary. Each day, add an interesting baseball fact from the current season— something you've read in the papers, heard on TV, or seen for yourself at a game. By the end of the year, you'll have a calendar that tells a story of that year in baseball.

For your next trick, see if you can gather a bit of baseball news for all 365 days of the year. During the off season, baseball isn't always in the news. In fact, filling in the off-season days with current baseball events could take you a number of years!

CALENDARS TO BUY

BASEBALL AMERICA'S GREAT MINOR LEAGUE BASEBALL PARKS CALENDAR

Each year since 1984, Baseball America has been publishing a wall calendar that highlights 12 of baseball's great minor league stadiums, with color photos and information about park size and history.

The calendar costs $6.95. Order directly from Baseball America: (800) 845-2726.

THE BASEBALL CARD ENGAGEMENT BOOK, by Michael Gershman

Published by Houghton Mifflin, this notebook-style book has space for you to write in all your upcoming appointments. And while

THE BULL PEN
Q: Why are baseball calendars always so popular?
A: They have a lot of dates.

you're keeping organized, there are pictures of classic and unusual baseball cards to entertain you, plus baseball facts, stats, and player quotes.

The book comes with special baseball cards made just for the calendar. It costs $10.95. You can buy it in bookstores starting in August. And starting in July you can also order directly from Houghton Mifflin's warehouse: (800) 225-3362 (outside Massachusetts); (617) 272-1500 (in Massachusetts).

MAJOR LEAGUE BASEBALL CALENDAR

Published by Macmillan in cooperation with the Major League Players' Association, this wall calendar features 13 color action shots of the great plays of the two previous seasons. In addition, there are 175 fun baseball facts.

The calendar costs $8.95. You can get it in bookstores starting sometime in August, or order directly from Macmillan: (800) 323-7445.

MAJOR LEAGUE INDIVIDUAL TEAM CALENDARS

If you're crazy for one particular team and don't want to be bothered with baseball facts about anybody else, you'll probably want to get that team's calendar. Most major league teams publish a new wall calendar each year, with photos of the players, team history, player quotes, and trivia.

To order, contact your team office (see Chapter 1). These calendars usually cost around $10.

PLAY BALL!

If you're into birthdays, this wall calendar is the one for you. It's got the birthdays for all the current major leaguers, as well as other fun facts. The cost is $9.95 in the U.S. and $14.95 in Canada. The publisher is:

Tidemark
P.O. Box 8311
East Hartford, CT
06108-0311

You can order directly from the publisher, or you may also be able to get the calendar on sale from the Phenom Sports Catalogue for $8; call (800) 966-7787. (Phenom carries other marked-down baseball calendars as well, including some major league team calendars and the *Baseball Card Engagement Book*.)

365 DAYS OF SPORTS FACTS

These are page-a-day calendars—you tear off the sheets as you go along. There's a fun sports fact listed for each day of the year. (They don't publish a baseball-only calendar, so you'll have to put up with facts about other sports as well!)

The calendars are $9.95 apiece including shipping. They're usually available sometime in August.

Your parents can order by credit card by calling (800) 722-7202. Or they can send a check or money order made out to Workman Publishing to:

Workman Publishing
708 Broadway
New York, NY 10003

1/1/1911. Hank Greenberg is born. He'll grow up to be a power-hitting, MVP-winning first baseman for the Tigers.

1/2/1836. Dickey Pearce, the inventor of the bunt, is born.

1/3/1920. The worst baseball deal of all time—at least as far as Red Sox fans are concerned. Harry Frazee of the Boston Red Sox sells Babe Ruth to the Yankees for $125,000.

1/4/1931. Home-run great Roger Connor dies.

1/5/1864. Future American League president Ban Johnson is born.

1/6/1976. Ted Turner buys the Atlanta Braves for $11 million.

1/7/1945. Tony Conigliaro is born. His career will be stopped short by a tragic accident. Hit near the eye by a pitch, Tony C's vision is damaged and his career ruined.

1/8/1927. Ty Cobb switches from the Tigers, his team of 22 years, to the Philadelphia A's.

1/9/1903. New York City gets a baseball team. First called the Highlanders, later the team will change its name to the Yankees.

1/10/1938. Willie McCovey is born. In his great career, the San Francisco Giant will knock in 1,555 runs.

1/11/1973. The American League team owners vote for a designated hitter. From now on, a nonfielding player is allowed to hit for the pitcher.

1/12/1927. Zack Wheat signs with the Philadelphia A's after being released by the Dodgers. Here he will play the last of his 19 years in the big leagues. Then he'll retire with more than 1,200 RBIs.

1/13/1944. Larry Jaster is born. The Cardinals pitcher threw five shutouts in his rookie year.

1/14/1919. The New York Giants are sold.

1/15/1943. Johnny Mize, the Cardinals slugger, is elected to the Hall of Fame.

1/16/1935. Dizzy Dean is born.
1/16/1970. Against his wishes, St. Louis Cardinal Curt Flood is traded to the Phillies. He sues but loses in court. Flood's case will lead to major changes in baseball contracts.

1/17/1960. Future Giant and Angel Chili Davis is born in Kingston, Jamaica. He's born with the name Charles. He gets the nickname Chili in high school when he shows up with a horrendous haircut.

1/18/1938. Curt Flood, future Cardinals star centerfielder, is born. (See January 16.)

1/19/1945. Stan Musial joins the Navy to fight in World War II. With players enlisting and being drafted, the war will badly drain the major league talent pool.

1/20/1942. Rogers Hornsby is elected to the Hall of Fame. During a great career he was batting champion seven times!

1/21/1957. Mickey Mantle is named the number one professional athlete of the year for 1956. This season the Yankee slugger was MVP in the American League. He led the league in batting average, RBIs, and home runs.

1/22/1959. Ken Williams dies. Williams was a home run slugging outfielder for the St. Louis Browns, a team that sorely needed talent.

1/23/1962. Jackie Robinson was the first black to play in the majors. Today he becomes the first black in the Hall of Fame.

1/24/1939. Eddie Collins, Wee Willie Keeler, and George Sisler are elected to baseball's Hall of Fame.

1/25/1928. Washington lets Tris Speaker go. One of the greatest centerfielders of all time, Speaker will play for one more year after this, with the Philadelphia Athletics.

1/26/1945. Yankee owner sells team for $2.8 million.

1/27/1937. The overflowing Ohio River floods Cincinnati's Crosley Field.

1/28/1891. Bill Doak is born. When the spitball is banned in 1920, this spitballing pitcher will lead a pitcher protest.

1/29/1961. Sports writers elect Max Carey and Billy Hamilton, two super base-stealers, to the Hall of Fame.

1/30/1943. Davey Johnson is born.

1/31/1919. Jackie Robinson is born.
1/31/1947. Nolan Ryan is born.

Jackie Robinson steals home.

2/1/1928. Star infielder Hughie "Ee-Yah" Jennings dies. He was part of an Orioles team that was known for its rough play.

2/2/1936. The Hall of Fame takes in its first five members: Ty Cobb, Babe Ruth, Honus Wagner, Christy Mathewson, and Walter Johnson.

2/2/1954. John Tudor is born.

2/3/1952. Fred Lynn is born.

2/4/1878. Herman Schaefer is born. He will become the only player ever to steal first base. He does it by first stealing second during an attempted double steal. When the double steal fails, he steals back to first to try again.

2/5/1934. Hank Aaron is born.

2/6/1895. Babe Ruth is born.

2/7/1953. Famed reliever Dan Quisenberry is born.

2/7/1957. Carney Lansford, a future Oakland Athletic, is born.

2/8/1921. Connie Mack dies at 93 after the longest pro baseball career ever. He played as a catcher, then managed the Philadelphia Athletics to 3,776 wins (as well as 4,025 losses). He worked in baseball for 67 years!

2/9/1914. Bill Veeck is born. As owner of the often-losing Cleveland Indians, Veeck will become one of baseball's most famous promoters.

2/10/1919. Billy Evans, future ump, is born. He is one of the few umpires to make it into the Hall of Fame.

2/11/1862. John Paciorek is born. At 18, Paciorek will have a great debut in the majors—but he'll never make it into another major league game, thanks to a bad back.

2/12/1926. Future catcher and announcer Joe Garagiola is born.

2/13/1883. "Prince Hal" Chase is born. He will become known for his brilliant fielding and for his shady dealings wiht gamblers.

2/14/1915. Red Barrett is born. For his most famous feat, see August 10, 1944.

2/15/1948. Future L.A. Dodger great Ron Cey is born in Tacoma, Washington.

2/16/1961. The great Dazzy Vance dies. Famous for getting a late start, Vance is 31 years old before he gets his first major league victory.

2/17/1964. White Sox shortstop Luke Appling is elected to the Hall of Fame.

2/18/1938. Manny Mota is born. By 1980, his last year, Mota will have piled up the all-time high in pinch hits: 150.

2/19/1969. Former Chicago star pitcher Guy "Doc" Harris dies. He had 189 career wins.

2/20/1859. Tony Mullane is born. A powerful right-hander, he will become famous for also pitching left-handed, to try to mess up all the lefty hitters he has to face.

2/21/1958. Future Tiger great Alan Trammell is born.

2/22/1918. Famous and colorful A's owner Charlie Finley is born. On one occasion Finley has his players enter the stadium on mules.

2/23/1930. Elston Howard, future Yankee great, is born.

2/24/1874. Honus Wagner is born. The slugger will dominate the National League for 21 years.

2/24/1956. Future Oriole star Eddie Murray is born.

2/25/1919. Monte Irvin is born. He will grow up to be one of the best players in the Negro leagues and then in the majors.

2/26/1887. Grover Cleveland Alexander is born. Alexander will be one of the majors' greatest pitchers, despite a terrible drinking problem. In a famous World Series game, he got a key strikeout while drunk.

2/27/1964. Mickey Mantle agrees to a salary of $100,000 to play for the Yankees. That was a big salary back then. Today, stars of Mantle's caliber make millions.

2/28/1963. Eppa Rixey dies. Rixey was famous for his pitching and for his hot temper. He had a tendency to tear lockers apart!

2/29/1904. Pepper Martin is born in Temple, Oklahoma. Nicknamed the "Wild Horse of the Osage," Martin was known not only for his baseball prowess but also for his love of practical jokes.

Fred Lynn as a college star.

3/1/1969. Mickey Mantle retires.	**3/2/1902.** Moe Berg is born. He will be a ball player, scholar, and U.S. spy. **3/2/1909.** Mel Ott is born. He'll become a famous home-run hitter.	**3/3/1860.** John Montgomery Ward is born. This pitcher invented the intentional walk. (See also June 17, 1880.)	**3/4/1897.** Lefty O'Doul is born. He will grow up to smack a record-breaking 254 hits in one season, tops in the National League.	**3/5/1860.** Sam Thompson is born. This hitter will knock in 166 RBIs in one season.	**3/6/1900.** Lefty Grove is born. He came within one game of setting a record for games won in a row. He was on his way to winning his 17th game in a row. But he was foiled when an outfielder dropped an easy fly ball.	**3/7/1979.** Major league umpires go on strike.
3/8/1930. Babe Ruth's salary ($80,000) outdoes that of the president of the country, Herbert Hoover.	**3/9/1942.** Bert Campaneris is born. **3/9/1965.** Benito Santiago is born.	**3/10/1963.** Pete Rose plays in his first major league game (an exhibition game) and doubles twice.	**3/11/1972.** Zack Wheat dies. Wheat had a lifetime batting average of .317 and batted in more than 1,200 RBIs.	**3/12/1956.** Dale Murphy is born. **3/12/1962.** Darryl Strawberry is born.	**3/13/1886.** Frank "Home Run" Baker is born. (See October 7.) **3/13/1975.** Frank Robinson, the major leagues' first black manager, manages his first major league game.	**3/14/1954.** Hank Aaron plays for the first time in the majors, in an exhibition game. Not surprisingly, he homers. **3/14/1961.** Kirby Puckett is born.
3/15/1946. Bobby Bonds is born. In one of his best seasons, Bonds will be only one short of getting 40 home runs and 40 stolen bases in the same year. The first player who pulls this off is Jose Canseco, the A's sensation, in 1988.	**3/16/1906.** Lloyd Waner is born. He and his brother will become known to Pittsburgh Pirate fans as "Little Poison" and "Big Poison."	**3/17/1919.** "Pistol Pete" Reiser is born. The Dodgers star will play the outfield with great abandon. In fact, his career will be shortened by injuries suffered as he repeatedly crashes into the outfield wall.	**3/18/1953.** Boston's Braves say they're moving—to Milwaukee.	**3/19/1984.** Stan Coveleski dies. In a career that spanned 16 years, the pitcher won 215 games.	**3/20/1973.** The baseball Hall of Fame elects Roberto Clemente, the great Pittsburgh Pirate slugger. Clemente had died in a tragic plane crash just eleven weeks earlier.	**3/21/1883.** Johnny Evers is born. He will be part of the famous double-play combination—Tinker to Evers to Chance. (Joe Tinker played shortstop, Evers covered second, and Frank Chance was at first.)
3/22/1972. Sox trade ace reliever Sparky Lyle to the Yankees. Another bad trade for the Sox (see also January 3). Lyle wins the Cy Young Award in 1978.	**3/23/1863.** Catcher Joe Gunson is born. He is the inventor of the catcher's mitt.	**3/24/1893.** George Sisler is born. His hitting streak record of 41 will last until DiMaggio arrives (see July 17).	**3/25/1920.** Howard Cosell is born.	**3/26/1951.** In an exhibition game, Mickey Mantle clobbers a 660-foot home run—his longest ever.	**3/27/1879.** Miller Huggins is born. He'll become one of baseball's most famous managers.	**3/28/1909.** Pitcher Lon Warneke born. He'll come to be known as the "Arkansas Hummingbird" and come within seven of getting 200 career wins.
3/29/1867. One of the greatest pitchers of all time, Cy Young, is born (see also May 5).	**3/30/1904.** James "Ripper" Collins is born. In one of many great seasons, he "ripped" 35 homers.	**3/31/1868.** Happy Jack Stivetts is born. The star pitcher once duelled the great Cy Young to an 11-inning 0–0 tie. It was the first of a nine-game play-off series in 1892 between Boston and Cleveland.				

Twins outfielder Kirby Puckett, whose stay play earned him a three-year $9 million contract after the '89 season.

APRIL

4/1/1930. Gabby Hartnett, a catcher for the Chicago Cubs, sets a new record for catching towering pop-ups. He snags a ball dropped from the Goodyear Blimp 550 feet over his head, setting a record.

4/1/1939. Phil Niekro is born.

4/2/1945. Don Sutton is born.

4/2/1964. Pete "Inky" Incaviglia is born.

4/3/1974. Cleveland trades teenager Pedro Guerrero to the Dodgers, where he will become a major star.

4/4/1944. Rusty Staub is born. Among other fine stats, Staub will finish his career 10th on the all-time pinch-hit list with exactly 100 pinch hits.

4/4/1956. Tommy Herr is born.

4/5/1951. Rennie Stennett is born. For Stennett's claim to fame, see September 16, 1975.

4/6/1951. Bert Blyleven is born in Zeist, Holland.

4/7/1984. Dwight "Dr. K" Gooden pitches his very first game in the majors. The 19-year-old Mets phenomenon will go on to win the Rookie of the Year award. He wins this first game, too: 3–2 over the Astros.

4/8/1954. Gary Carter is born. Known for his slugging power, the star catcher will play great ball for the Expos, Mets, and Giants.

4/9/1965. The Houston Astros beat the New York Yankees 2–1. Thanks to the Astrodome's roof, this is the first major league game to be played indoors. President Lyndon Johnson, a Texan, was there.

4/10/1971. The first day of baseball for Philadelphia's Veterans Stadium.

4/11/1961. "Yaz," Carl Yastrzemski, goes to the plate for the very first time in what will be a celebrated 23-year career with the Boston Red Sox. Today he strokes a single, the first of 3,419 career hits.

4/12/1962. Pete Richert pitches his first game in the majors and strikes out four batters in one inning. One of the batters gets safely to first when the catcher drops the called third strike. Richert still gets credit for the strike-out.

4/13/1964. Bret Saberhagen, future star pitcher for the Kansas City Royals, is born.

4/14/1942. Pete Rose is born.

4/15/1947. Jackie Robinson plays in his first major league game. He's the first black to play in the majors in 20th century.

4/15/1954. Today marks the Orioles' first game in Baltimore's Memorial Stadium.

4/16/1960. Bob Feller is the only man ever to pitch an opening day no-hitter. Thanks to him, the Indians edged the White Sox 1–0.

4/17/1953. Mickey Mantle wallops the longest *measured* home run ever. He knocks the ball for a 565-foot ride. (Babe Ruth is credited with a 600-footer, but it wasn't measured.)

4/18/1923. Yankee Stadium opens. The Yanks defeat the Red Sox 4–1 behind Babe Ruth's three-run blast. Red Sox fans remember how much they hate the owner for selling Ruth to the Yanks.

4/19/1960. Frank Viola is born.

4/19/1966. The California Angels open play in Anaheim Stadium. They lose to Chicago by a score of 3–1.

4/20/1912. Fenway Park opens. The Red Sox top the Yanks 7–6 after 11 innings.

4/20/1939. Ted Williams plays in his first game.

4/20/1962. Don Mattingly is born.

4/21/1989. Here's a good trivia question: Who hit more home runs for the Braves, Hank Aaron or Dale Murphy? As of today, the answer is Murphy as he hits home run number 336.

4/22/1970. Mets pitcher Tom Seaver sets a record for most strike-outs in a row—he fans 10 straight Padres.

4/22/1982. With today's victory, the season is 14 games old for the Reds. They haven't lost yet (a new record)!

4/23/1921. Warren Spahn is born.

4/23/1962. The Mets start off their terrible first season with a string of losses. It takes until today to notch their first win.

4/24/1964. Sandy Koufax fans 18 Chicago Cubs in one game.

4/25/1884. John "Pop" Lloyd is born. The shortstop first became famous in the Negro leagues.

4/26/1955. Mike Scott is born.

4/26/1961. Roger Maris clouts his first homer of the season. He goes on to hit many more—61, in fact. That breaks Babe Ruth's record, one many said would never be broken.

4/27/1896. Rogers Hornsby is born.

4/27/1916. Enos Slaughter is born.

4/28/1898. A baseball game in Philadelphia is snowed out!

4/28/1988. The Orioles lose their 21st game in a row. It doesn't cheer the team up to learn that this is a new record in the American League.

4/29/1986. Red Sox pitching wizard Roger Clemens sets a new major league record. He whiffs 20 batters in one game.

4/30/1969. Cincinnati's Jim Maloney, pitching against the Astros, throws the first of what turns out to be two no-hitters in a row (see also May 1).

For years, Bob Feller was the youngest pitcher to win 20 games. (Dwight Gooden broke his record.)

237

5/1/1969. Houston pitcher Don Wilson returns Jim Maloney's favor by pitching a no-hitter right back at the Reds (see April 30). See also September 17, for the first time such a feat occurred.

5/2/1939. A sad day in baseball, for it ends Lou Gehrig's famous streak. Until this day, he'd played in 2,130 straight games. Weakened by a rare illness, the "Iron Man" finally had to take himself out of the lineup.

5/3/1904. Red Ruffing is born in Granville, Illinois. In his 22 big league seasons, he will pitch 273 victories.

5/4/1936. Joe DiMaggio, the Yankee great, plays in his first major league game at age 22. His two singles and a triple add to the Yankee's 14–5 slaughter of the St. Louis Browns.

5/4/1982. Gaylord Perry pitches his 300th victory.

5/5/1904. Pitcher Cy Young set many records. With today's no-hitter for the Boston Red Sox, he becomes the only pitcher ever to pitch no-hit ball both before 1900 and after.

5/6/1931. Willie Mays is born.

5/6/1978. Dennis Kinney gives up a grand-slam homer to a pinch hitter. He does it again on June 27, 1978, making him the only pitcher to allow this to happen twice in one season.

5/7/1925. Glenn Wright, playing shortstop for the Pittsburgh Pirates, makes an unassisted triple play.

5/8/1968. Oakland's "Catfish" Hunter pitches a perfect game.

5/9/1960. Tony Gwynn is born.

5/10/1944. Fifteen-year-old Joe Nuxhall makes his first appearance in a game, the youngest player ever in the majors.

5/11/1897. In one game, Duke Farrell, a catcher, throws out eight runners as they try to steal. Not all at once, of course!

5/12/1925. Yogi Berra is born.

5/12/1935. Felipe Alou is born. He is the first of three baseball brothers. (The other two Alous are Jesus and Matty.)

5/13/1929. The first major league game is played in which the players wear numbers on their uniforms.

5/13/1952. Minor leaguer Ron Necciai strikes out all 27 batters in the course of nine innings.

5/14/1972. At age 41, Willie Mays plays his first game as a New York Met. His homer in the fifth inning beats his old team, the San Francisco Giants.

5/15/1953. George Brett is born.

5/16/1928. Billy Martin is born.

5/16/1955. Jack Morris is born.

5/17/1939. For the first time ever, a college baseball game is aired on TV. Using only one camera, NBC shows a game between Columbia and Princeton.

5/18/1937. Brooks Robinson is born.

5/18/1946. Reggie Jackson is born.

5/18/1968. Frank Howard hits his 10th homer in six games.

5/19/1956. Dale Long, the Pirates first baseman, begins his record-breaking streak of games in which he hits at least one home run.

5/20/1946. Future Yankee star Bobby Murcer is born.

5/21/1960. Kent Hrbek is born.

5/22/43. Tommy John is born.

5/22/1956. Dale Long hits a homer in his fourth straight game.

5/22/1962. Home-run master Roger Maris is intentionally walked four times in one game, a record.

5/23/1956. Dale Long homers in his fifth straight game (see May 19).

5/24/1935. The first major league night baseball game is played. Thanks to all the lights, fans in Cincinnati are able to see their Reds beat the Phillies, 2–1.

5/25/1935. Babe Ruth hits the last of his record-shattering total of 714 major league homers.

5/26/1959. Pirates pitcher Harvey Haddix pitches 12—count 'em—12 straight perfect innings. Unbelievably, he winds up losing the game in the 13th, 1–0.

5/27/1945. Dave "Boo" Ferriss and Emmett O'Neill tie the Dean brothers' record for fewest hits given up in a doubleheader. Ferriss allows only one hit, O'Neill only two. (See also September 21.)

5/28/1956. Pittsburgh's Dale Long completes his record-breaking streak. Today marks the eighth straight game in which he hits at least one homer. The streak stops here (see May 29).

5/29/1956. Dale Long has an 0–fer day. He has 0 hits in 4 at-bats, or 0 for 4 (an 0–fer). That ends his streak of eight games in a row with at least one homer.

5/29/1962. Eric Davis is born.

5/30/1922. The Cardinals and the Cubs face each other in a double-header. After the first game, two players are traded. Max Flack starts out for the Cardinals but plays game two for the Cubs. Cliff Heathcote switches to the Cardinals.

5/31/1949. Charley Lupica, a devoted fan, starts sitting on a flagpole. He vows he won't come down until his team, the Cleveland Indians, reaches first place.

A common sight from Billy Martin's stormy career as a manager.

JUNE

6/1/1859. The very first baseball game between two college teams. Amherst *squeaks* past Williams, 66–32!

6/1/1989. Robin Yount, a Milwaukee Brewer, gets a single. In his 16-year career, this is hit number 2,500.

6/2/1959. A huge swarm of gnats stop a game between the White Sox and Orioles. Yuck!

6/3/1932. In one game, in four at-bats in a row, Lou Gehrig hits four homers. No one in the majors had ever done this before.

6/3/1953. Frank Tanana is born.

6/4/1957. Tony Pena is born.

6/5/1874. Jack Chesbro is born. He'll win 41 games in one season while pitching for New York in 1904.

6/6/1962. Wally Joyner is born.

6/7/1947. Thurman Munson is born.

6/7/1950. The Sox set a new scoring high. They belt 29 runs as they maul the hapless St. Louis Browns.

6/8/1968. Los Angeles Dodgers star pitcher Don Drysdale sets a new record for the most scoreless innings pitched in a row. He pitches his 58th straight inning without letting a run in.

6/9/1951. Dave Parker is born.

6/10/1921. Babe Ruth clouts home run number 120. That breaks the record of Gavvy Cravath, and makes Ruth the official Sultan of Swat.

6/10/1954. Andre Dawson is born.

6/11/1938. Johnny Vander Meer throws a no-hitter for the Cincinnati Reds. What's so amazing about that? In his very next game, he does it again (see June 15). No other pitcher has ever pulled off this stunt.

6/12/1974. Little League baseball allows girls to join the boys' teams.

6/12/1981. The start of the second baseball players' strike. This one will last 50 days.

6/13/1973. Montreal Expo Hal Breeden smashes two pinch-hit homers in one day, one in each game of a doubleheader.

6/14/1965. The Reds' Jim Maloney allows no hits for 10 innings against the Mets. But he gives up two hits in the eleventh, and he ends up with a loss.

6/15/1938. Johnny Vander Meer hurls his second no-hitter in a row!

6/15/1956. Lance Parrish is born.

6/15/1958. Wade Boggs is born.

6/16/1881. Louis Pessano "Buttercup" Dickerson bats six times and gets six hits.

6/17/1880. John Montgomery Ward pitches a perfect game. He's only 20 years old, making him the youngest pitcher to achieve perfection in the big leagues.

6/17/1948. Dave Concepcion is born.

6/18/1936. Lou Brock is born.

6/18/1961. Andres Galarraga is born.

6/18/1986. Don Sutton pitches his way to win number 300. Only 18 other pitchers have ever reached that number.

6/19/1846. One of the first baseball games played in the modern style takes place. The New York Club beats the Knickerbockers 23–1. The winning pitcher is fined for yelling at the umpire. The fine? Six cents.

6/20/1915. The St. Louis Browns forget their uniforms for an away game and have to borrow clothes from the other team. They also lose the game. (Compare this with the blunder by the Red Sox on the 26th of this month.)

6/21/1956. Rick Sutcliffe is born.

6/21/1964. Jim Bunning hurls a perfect game, making him the only major league pitcher to throw perfect games in both leagues.

6/22/1903. Carl Hubbell is born.

6/23/1917. Ernie Shore of the Red Sox pitches a perfect game. But he isn't the starting pitcher. Babe Ruth is! Ruth walks the leadoff man, argues with the ump, and gets tossed out of the game. Then Shore gets 27 outs in a row.

6/24/1983. The infamous pine tar incident. Geoge Brett has his home run taken away after a crafty protest by Billy Martin. (See page 163.)

6/25/1819. Abner Doubleday is born.

6/26/1901. The Red Sox have an away game, but they go to the wrong city. They were supposed to play Baltimore. They arrive in Philly.

6/27/1978. Dennis Kinney gives up his second pinch-hit grand slam of the season (see May 6).

6/28/1907. Catcher Branch Rickey lets 13 runners steal bases off him in one game.

6/28/1948. Don Baylor is born.

6/29/1936. Harmon Killebrew is born.

6/30/1959. In a game between Chicago and St. Louis, two baseballs are put in play at the same time! By mistake, the umpire gave the catcher a new ball before the play was over.

Milwaukee Brewers' two-time MVP shortstop, Robin Yount.

239

7/1/1958. When a ball sails into the Chicago bullpen, the pitchers trick the Giants outfielder. They look under the bench for the ball. The outfielder searches too. But the ball actually has rolled on. The batter scores a homer.

7/2/1964. Jose Canseco is born.

7/3/1966. Tony Cloninger of the Atlanta Braves hits two grand slams in one game. He's the only player in the National League ever to slam so grandly. He also pitched the game!

7/4/1976. Tim McCarver hits a grand slam—almost. He passes a teammate on the base paths. He's out!

7/4/1983. No fireworks for the Red Sox on this July 4. Dave Righetti of the Yankees throws a no-hitter.

7/5/1951. Goose Gossage is born.

7/6/1933. The first All-Star Game. The American League All-Stars win 4–2.

7/7/1906. Satchel Paige is born.

7/7/1957. Dan Gladden is born.

7/8/1941. Two outs, bottom of the ninth. Ted Williams is batting for the American League in the All-Star Game, his team down 5–4. It's out of here! Williams's three-run shot gives the AL team the win.

7/9/1946. Pitching for the National League All-Stars, Rip Sewell throws his famous "ephus pitch." This pitch drops down right before the batter swings. Ted Williams knocks the ephus out of the park. The American League wins.

7/10/1934. In only the second major league All-Star Game ever, Giants pitcher Carl Hubbell strikes out five American Leaguers in a row.

7/10/1954. Andre Dawson is born.

7/11/1953. Tony Armas is born.

7/11/1985. Nolan Ryan whiffs Danny Heep of the Mets. It's Ryan's 4,000th strikeout. No other pitcher in major league history has even come close to this pinnacle.

7/12/1962. Hank Aaron and his brother Tommie both homer in the same game. It's one of three times they manage this trick.

7/13/1977. A huge blackout hits New York City. Among other things, the blackout stops a game between the Mets and Cubs, and strands thousands at Shea Stadium.

7/14/1969. Pitcher Joe Niekro out-throws his brother Phil as the Padres beat Atlanta 1–0. Not good for sibling rivalry.

7/15/1952. A Detroit player, Walt Dropo, sets a record for the most hits in a row (without being walked). Today he gets his 12th straight hit!

7/16/1887. Shoeless Joe Jackson is born. A tremendous player, Jackson will suffer a tragic downfall. He takes part in throwing a World Series. The players lose games on purpose and are paid off by gamblers.

7/17/1941. The end of Joe DiMaggio's famous hitting streak. He hit in 56 straight games but doesn't get a hit today.

7/18/1897. Cap Anson gets his 3,000th hit. He's the first baseball player ever to reach this high mark.

7/18/1962. The Minnesota Twins become the first team to hit two grand slams in one inning.

7/19/1909. Neal Ball, Cleveland shortstop, makes an unassisted triple play. He's the first ever to do it. To date, seven have repeated the stunt.

7/20/1973. A Chicago White Sox pitcher named Wilbur Wood starts both games of a doubleheader. He's the most recent pitcher ever to try such a stunt. He doesn't finish either game, however. And he loses both of them.

7/21/1975. The Mets' Joe Torre hits into four straight double plays. A record, but not the kind you want to set!

7/22/1944. Sparky Lyle is born.

7/23/1919. Pee Wee Reese is born.

7/23/1936. Don Drysdale is born.

7/23/1964. Bert "Campy" Campaneris plays in his first major league game for the Kansas City Athletics and hits two homers.

7/24/1968. Hoyt Wilhelm is brought in as a relief pitcher against the Oakland A's. It takes him only six pitches to set down the side—one, two, three. Not only that, it's his 907th pitching outing in the majors, a new record.

7/25/1930. The A's pull off two triple-steals in one game, a record.

7/26/1923. Hoyt Wilhelm is born. (Look back two days—but ahead 45 years—for more information.)

7/27/1906. Leo Durocher is born.

7/28/1875. The first major league no-hitter as Joe Borden of Philadelphia wins 4–0 over Chicago.

7/28/1949. Vida Blue is born.

7/29/1959. Left-handed ace pitcher Toad Ramsey strikes out 16. He strikes out a total of 499 over the season.

7/30/1891. Casey Stengel is born.

7/31/1978. Pete Rose ties Wee Willie Keeler's old National League record for games in a row where he got at least one hit. This is known as "hitting safely" in a game. Rose, like Keeler in 1897, hit safely in 44 straight games.

Rip Sewell shows off the blooper pitch in 1947.

AUGUST

8/1/1972. A record for RBIs by one player over the course of a double-header is set by Nate Colbert. He bangs in 13 runs.	**8/2/1907.** Walter Johnson pitches his first game at age 19. He will go on to pile up more than 400 wins. Who gets the first hit off Johnson today as he begins his 20-year career? Ty Cobb. Cobb bunts his way on.	**8/3/1959.** For the first time the majors hold two All-Star Games. **8/3/1989.** The Cincinnati Reds are red-hot against the Astros. They knock in 14 runs with 16 hits in the *first* inning, a new major league record.	**8/4/1962.** Roger Clemens is born. **8/4/1982.** Joel Youngblood is traded. He plays a day game for the Mets. Tonight he plays for the Expos. He gets hits in both games. A first! **8/4/1985.** Rod Carew gets hit number 3,000.	**8/5/1921.** KDKA, a radio station, does the very first play-by-play broadcast of a major league game. The Pirates beat the Phillies 8–5 with Harold Arlin announcing the action.	**8/6/1930.** A Texas player named Gene "Half-Pint" Rye hits three home runs in one inning—a record.	**8/7/1929.** Don Larsen is born.
8/8/1947. Jose Cruz is born.	**8/9/1981.** The National League wins its 10th All-Star victory in a row. The A.L. won't win again until 1983. **8/9/1988.** Night games have been played for a long time, but never at Wrigley Field—until tonight.	**8/10/1944.** Boston Brave Red Barrett pitches nine innings with only 58 pitches! (The minimum possible is 27 pitches. Why? There are three outs per inning, and you have to throw the ball at least once to each batter.)	**8/11/1936.** Vada Pinson is born, future Reds star. **8/11/1951.** A major league game is shown on TV *in color* for the first time ever. **8/11/1961.** Lefty Warren Spahn wins his 300th game.	**8/12/1880.** Christy Mathewson is born.	**8/13/1988.** The Red Sox beat the Tigers at home in Fenway. It's their 24th home victory in a row, a new American League record.	**8/14/1930.** Earl Weaver is born. **8/14/1954.** Mark "The Bird" Fidrych is born. His star pitching career will be cut short by injury.
8/15/1886. Guy Hecker of the Louisville Eclipse sets a record that still stands today: He scored seven runs in one game.	**8/16/1870.** Fred Goldsmith proves that the curveball really curves. To prove it, he sets up three posts in a straight line and curves a baseball around them.	**8/17/1941.** Boog Powell is born.	**8/18/1934.** Roberto Clemente is born.	**8/19/1909.** The Phillies are rained out for a record 10th straight day. **8/19/1951.** Midget Eddie Gaedel pinch-hits and walks. **8/19/1960.** Ron Darling is born.	**8/20/1944.** Graig Nettles is born. **8/20/1945.** Tommy Brown hits a homer for the Dodgers. At age 17 and in school, Brown is the youngest player to homer in the majors since 1901. **8/20/1960.** Tom Brunansky is born.	**8/21/1951.** The American League passes a height rule to prevent a repeat of the midget pinch-hitter stunt. (See August 19, 1951.)
8/22/1939. Carl "Yaz" Yastrzemski is born. **8/22/1956.** Paul Molitor is born.	**8/23/1957.** Mike Boddicker is born. **8/23/1958.** A Mexican Little League team wins the championship. It's the first time a foreign team has won.	**8/24/1960.** Cal Ripken, Jr., is born.	**8/25/1946.** Rollie Fingers is born. **8/25/1985.** At age 21, Dwight Gooden wins his 20th game of the season. He's the youngest pitcher to win 20 in the majors.	**8/26/1939.** The first TV broadcast of a major league game. The announcer is Red Barber.	**8/27/1951.** Buddy Bell is born. **8/27/1982.** Rickey Henderson "steals" a new record. He safely reaches second with his 119th stolen base.	**8/28/1950.** Ron Guidry is born. His fire-ball pitches will earn him the nickname "Louisiana Lightning."
8/29/1925. Babe Ruth is fined a record-breaking $5,000 for showing up late for warm-ups.	**8/30/1918.** Ted Williams is born. **8/30/1965.** Casey Stengel retires. **8/30/1988.** Pitcher Orel Hersheiser begins his record streak of 59 scoreless innings. The streak will last until September 28.	**8/31/1935.** Frank Robinson is born.				

On April 29, 1986, Red Sox ace Roger Clemens struck out a record 20 against the Mariners.

241

SEPTEMBER

9/1/1900. Hub Pruett is born. This pitcher's only claim to fame will be his startling success against Babe Ruth. He faces him 11 times and strikes him out 10 times.

9/2/1933. "Marvelous" Marv Throneberry is born.

9/2/1955. Shortstop Ernie Banks hits home run number 40, a record for his position. Shortstops are usually known for their great fielding and so-so hitting!

9/3/1901. Iron Man McGinnity pitches a complete doubleheader. He will repeat this trick five times, a record.

9/3/1916. Eddy "The Brat" Stanky is born.

9/4/1916. Christy Mathewson pitches, and wins, his very last game. The future Hall-of-Famer won 373 games and had an overall earned run average of 2.13 (very very low!).

9/5/1923. Hank Hulvey pitches in his one and only major league game for the Philadelphia Athletics. During the game he gives up a homer to Babe Ruth. He's the only man to serve up a homer to Ruth and never pitch again.

9/6/1888. Future spitballer Red Faber is born in Cascade, Iowa.

9/7/1916. The New York Giants beat the Brooklyn Dodgers 4–1. No one knows it yet, but it's the first of a record-breaking 26 straight wins. The streak will last until September 30.

9/8/1916. Wally Schang, a Philadelphia switch-hitter, hits home runs from both sides of the plate in the same game. He's the first to pull off such a feat.

9/8/1954. Don Aase is born.

9/9/1965. Pitcher Sandy Koufax racks up the fourth no-hitter of his career. Only this time he's *perfect.* (In a perfect game, the pitcher gives up no hits, no runs, and *no walks.*)

9/10/1934. Roger Maris is born.

9/10/1974. Lou Brock breaks Maury Wills's base-stealing record with his 105th bit of base-stealing thievery for the season.

9/11/1912. Eddie Collins steals a record-breaking six bases in one game.

9/11/1985. Pete Rose singles, a common event for Rose. In fact, this is his 4,192nd hit. And that breaks Ty Cobb's long-standing record.

9/12/1962. Tom Cheney of the Washington Senators sets a strikeout record. He whiffs 21 Orioles batters over the course of a 16-inning game.

9/13/1883. A one-armed Cleveland pitcher, Hugh Daily, throws a no-hitter.

9/14/1968. Denny McLain, a Detroit Tiger pitching ace, gets his 30th win for the season. He's the first pitcher to get that many wins in one year since Dizzy Dean did it in 1934.

9/15/1969. The Cardinals' Steve Carlton sets a strikeout record. He sets down 19 New York Mets. He also loses the game, 4–3!

9/16/1958. Orel Hershiser is born.

9/16/1959. Tim Raines is born.

9/16/1975. Rennie Stennett of Pittsburgh goes seven for seven, a record.

9/17/1968. Gaylord Perry of the Giants pitches a no-hitter against the Cardinals. Tomorrow the Cardinals will no-hit the Giants. It's the first time in the majors that two teams trade no-hitters back to back. (See May 1.)

9/18/1959. Ryne Sandberg is born.

9/18/1968. Ray Washburn of the Cardinals no-hits the Giants (see September 17).

9/19/1926. Duke Snider is born. He'll grow up to be one of the greatest home-run hitters ever.

9/19/1943. Future Cincinnati star Joe Morgan is born. (See October 22.)

9/20/1988. Wade Boggs gets his 200th hit of the season. It's the sixth year in a row that Boggs has gotten at least 200 hits, and that adds up to a new major league record.

9/21/1934. Two brothers, Dizzy and Paul Dean, set a record for fewest hits given up over the course of a doubleheader. Dizzy pitches a three-hitter. Paul tops that with a no-hitter.

9/22/1960. Vince Coleman is born.

9/22/1968. Cesar Tovar plays all nine positions in one game, repeating "Campy" Campaneris's stunt.

9/23/1908. "Bonehead" Merkle is on first. The batter drives in the winning run from third. So Merkle never touches second. The other team claims that Merkle is out, and the winning run doesn't count. The game has to be replayed.

9/24/1956. Hubie Brooks is born.

9/25/1918. Phil Rizzuto is born.

9/25/1949. Mr. Lupica finally comes down off his flagpole (see May 31, 1949).

9/25/1986. Split-fingered fastballer Mike Scott throws a no-hitter and Houston cops the pennant.

9/26/1908. Cubs pitcher Ed Reulbach pitches back-to-back complete games in a doubleheader. He shuts out his opponents in both games!

9/26/1960. Ted Williams has his last at-bat. The result? A home run.

9/27/1949. Mike Schmidt, the future Phillies powerhouse, is born.

9/27/1973. Nolan Ryan gets his 383rd strikeout for the season, breaking Sandy Koufax's old record.

9/28/1920. Say it isn't so. Eight Chicago White Sox players are charged with taking money from gamblers and losing the World Series on purpose.

9/29/1986. It's the first time brothers face each other as opposing pitchers in the majors. Greg Maddux pitches against older brother, Mike. Greg wins, 8–3.

9/29/1987. Don Mattingly hits his record-setting sixth grand slam of the season.

9/30/1927. Babe Ruth hits his 60th homer of the season! His record will last until 1961, when Roger Maris hits as many homers as the year: 61!

9/30/1984. The Angels' Mike Witt throws a perfect game.

The Phillies Mike Schmidt leaped his way to 10 Gold Glove awards.

10/1/1903. The first game of the first World Series ever.

10/1/1961. Roger Maris sets the new home-run record with his 61st four-bag shot of the season.

10/1/1963. Mark McGwire is born.

10/2/1932. Maury Wills is born.

10/2/1947. Yogi Berra gets the first World Series pinch-hit homer ever.

10/3/1951. Dave Winfield is born. On the same day, Bobby Thompson hits the home run known as "The Shot Heard 'Round the World."

10/3/1954. Dennis Eckersley is born.

10/4/1987. Reggie Jackson has earned the nickname "Mr. October" for his superb postseason play. Today he plays the last game of a great career—in October, of course.

10/5/1941. The Brooklyn Dodger catcher Mickey Owen drops a third strike that would have ended a World Series game. Thanks to the catcher's error, the Yankees go on to win the game and the Series.

10/6/1923. The Boston Braves shortstop, Ernie Padgett, makes one of major league history's eight unassisted triple plays (See October 10 for the only time it's been done in the World Series.)

10/7/1913. "Home Run" Baker wins the first game of this year's World Series. How? He homers, of course.

10/8/1956. Don Larsen pitches a perfect game. In the World Series, no less! No one has ever done this before or since.

10/9/1972. Gene Tenace bats for his first time, and his second time, in a World Series. He homers both times.

10/10/1920. Second baseman Bill Wambsganss manages to make a triple play all by himself—in a World Series game.

10/11/1854. Will White is born. He will become the first ballplayer to wear glasses.

10/12/1936. Tony Kubek is born.

10/12/1962. Sid Fernandez is born.

10/13/1960. Bill Mazeroski slams one of the most famous homers in baseball history in the bottom of the ninth inning of a World Series game. The home run gives the Pirates the Series, as they beat the Yankees.

10/14/1988. Kirk Gibson hits his game-winning pinch-hit homer in the World Series. Gibson is badly injured at the time and can't run. His only hope is to hit the ball out of the park and limp around the bases. That's just what he does.

10/15/1945. Jim Palmer is born.

10/15/1972. Joe Rudi makes his famous, game-saving World Series catch. He jumps high up the outfield wall and snabs the ball backhanded.

10/16/1941. Tim McCarver is born.

10/16/1969. The underdog Mets win the World Series. Stars for the Mets include Tom Seaver, Jerry Koosman, Ron Swoboda, and Tommy Agee.

10/17/1989. An earthquake strikes San Francisco just before game three of the World Series, and shakes the stadium. Luckily no one is hurt. In San Francisco, however, people are killed as a bridge collapses.

10/18/1950. Connie Mack retires, ending the longest career in major league baseball.

10/19/1876. Mordecai Brown is born. He's missing a finger on his pitching hand. But that doesn't stop him from becoming an all-star pitcher.

10/20/1931. Mickey Mantle is born.

10/20/1953. Keith Hernandez is born.

10/21/1975. Carlton Fisk homers in the 12th inning to win today's World Series game for the Boston Red Sox. Fisk's reaction will become famous. He screams at the ball to try to keep it from going foul.

10/22/1975. Joe Morgan singles in the ninth inning of the seventh game of the World Series. Morgan's hit wins the Series for the Reds.

10/23/1884. The first World Series game ever. Providence beats New York 6–0.

10/24/1929. Jim Brosnan, future pitcher and author, is born.

10/25/1923. Bobby Thompson is born.

10/26/1917. Miller Huggins is hired to manage the Yankees. (See March 27.)

10/27/1922. Ralph Kiner is born.

10/28/1959. The Los Angeles Dodgers cap a dramatic comeback. They win the seventh game of the World Series 9–2 and defeat the Yanks.

10/29/1918. Ted Williams is born.

10/29/1959. Jesse Barfield is born.

10/30/1919. The spitball is declared illegal. No, not the kind of spitball kids throw in class. In baseball pitchers rub spit on the ball to make it move differently when they throw it, and to throw off the hitter.

10/31/1900. Cal Hubbard is born. He will make it into both the Baseball Hall of Fame (as an ump) and the Pro Football Hall of Fame (as a lineman).

Catcher Tim McCarver crouched behind the plate for 21 seasons.

11/1/1960. Fernando Valenzuela is born. **11/1/1966.** The first Mens' World Softball Championships begin in Mexico City. The American team will win.	**11/2/1958.** Willie McGee is born. **11/2/1974.** Hank Aaron and Sadaharu Oh, Japan's home-run king, hold a home-run showdown in Tokyo. Aaron edges Oh, 10–9.	**11/3/1918.** Bob Feller is born. **11/3/1951.** Dwight Evans is born.	**11/4/1929.** Jimmy Piersall is born.	**11/5/1869.** Nowadays you won't find major league games going on in November. In the old days, the season calendar was quite different. Today the Cincinnati Reds play their last game of the year.	**11/6/1953.** John Candelaria is born.	**11/7/1928.** No team has a history of making bad trades as famous as that of the Boston Red Sox. Today they send Rogers Hornsby to the Chicago Cubs. Hornsby was hitting only .387 for the Sox.
11/8/1951. Yogi Berra, Yankee catcher, wins the MVP award. Berra is famous for his funny sayings. His most famous: "The game's not over until it's over."	**11/9/1935.** Bob Gibson is born. As a powerful Cardinals pitcher, he will pile up many impressive statistics. On one occasion, he'll throw five shutouts in a row.	**11/10/1955.** Jack Clark is born.	**11/11/1981.** Fernando Valenzuela wins the Cy Young Award for his fantastic pitching. He's the first pitcher to win the award in his rookie year.	**11/12/1956.** Jody Davis is born. **11/12/1961.** Greg Gagne is born.	**11/13/1973.** Reggie Jackson wins the American League MVP honors.	**11/14/1954.** Willie Hernandez is born.
11/15/1920. Harry Frazee sold Babe Ruth to the Yankees earlier this year. Now he trades Waite Hoyt and Wally Schang to the Yanks. Both players will turn into stars as Red Sox fans pull more hair out.	**11/16/1964.** Dwight Gooden is born.	**11/17/1944.** Tom Seaver is born.	**11/18/1888.** "Colby Jack" Coombs is born. Over 14 big league seasons, the pitcher will have a 2.78 earned run average.	**11/19/1921.** Roy Campanella is born. He'll be voted his league's MVP three times.	**11/20/1866.** Judge Kenesaw Mountain Landis, a famous baseball commissioner, is born.	**11/21/1920.** Stan Musial is born.
11/22/1957. Mickey Mantle wins the MVP. For the second time in his career, Ted Williams misses the honor by one point in the voting (see November 27).	**11/23/1940.** Luis Tiant is born.	**11/24/1944.** Baseball commissioner Judge Kenesaw Mountain Landis dies.	**11/25/1914.** Joe DiMaggio is born. **11/25/1951.** Bucky Dent is born.	**11/26/1908.** Lefty Gomez, the Yankee pitcher, is born.	**11/27/1947.** Joe DiMaggio wins the MVP. Ted Williams misses by one point.	**11/28/1979.** Steve Stone, pitcher and poet, signs with Baltimore. He'll win the Cy Young award.
11/29/1923. Minnie Minoso is born.	**11/30/1920.** Because the majors won't allow blacks to play, a pitcher named Rube Foster organizes the Negro National League.					

Minnie Minoso played in five different decades!

DECEMBER

12/1/1948. George Foster is born.	**12/2/1947.** Johnny Bench is born.	**12/3/1968.** The strike zone is made smaller to help batters get more hits. The zone used to go up to a player's shoulders. Now it extends only to his armpits.	**12/4/1868.** Jesse "Crab" Burkett is born. Twice in his career he will bat over .400 for the season (.409 and .410).	**12/5/1973.** The Expos trade Mike Marshall to the Dodgers. The very next year they'll have reason to regret it. Marshall pitches so well for the Dodgers that he wins the Cy Young Award.	**12/6/1957.** Steve Bedrosian is born.	**12/7/1947.** Johnny Bench is born. He'll become one of the most famous catchers of all time.
12/8/1939. Lou Gehrig is voted into the Hall of Fame.	**12/9/1965.** Branch Rickey dies. Among many feats in a long career, Rickey once took over a horrible Pirates team and turned it around. At first they were known as the "Rickeydinks." Then they won the World Series (in 1960).	**12/10/1981.** Shortstop Ozzie Smith is traded to the Cardinals for shortstop Garry Templeton.	**12/11/1959.** Roger Maris is traded to the Yankees.	**12/12/1903.** Three-Finger Brown is traded to the Cubs. (See October 19.)	**12/13/1927.** Last year, Detroit's Heine Manush hit a whopping .378. This year his average falls to .298. That's nothing to sneeze at, but Detroit trades Manush to the Browns. Next season he will hit .378 again, for his new team.	**12/14/1949.** Bill Buckner is born. Through his legs the ball will roll as the Sox face the Mets in the World Series on October 25, 1986. His infamous error keeps the Mets alive.
12/15/1900. The Cincinnati Reds trade Christy Mathewson to the New York Giants. He will go on to win 373 games! (see September 4.)	**12/16/1982.** Mets fans never forgave the team for trading pitching superstar Tom Seaver. Now, with Seaver well past his prime, the Mets get him back.	**12/17/1957.** Bobby Ojeda is born.	**12/18/1886.** Ty Cobb is born.	**12/19/1934.** Al Kaline is born.	**12/20/1881.** Branch Rickey is born. **12/20/1938.** Matty Alou is born.	**12/21/1948.** Dave Kingman is born. **12/21/1952.** Joaquin Andujar is born. **12/21/1960.** Andy Van Slyke is born.
12/22/1944. Steve Carlton is born. **12/22/1948.** Steve Garvey is born.	**12/23/1862.** Connie Mack is born. **12/23/1942.** Jerry Koosman is born.	**12/24/1913.** Louis Sockalexis dies. This former Cleveland player was an American Indian. He gave the Cleveland Indians their name.	**12/25/1958.** Rickey Henderson is born.	**12/26/1947.** Carlton Fisk is born. **12/26/1956.** Ozzie Smith is born. His brilliant fielding will earn him the nickname "Wizard of Oz."	**12/27/1912.** Jim Tobin is born. Pitchers aren't usually known for their hitting ability. But on one occasion this pitcher will hit three home runs in a single game.	**12/28/1900.** Ted Lyons, future Hall of Fame pitcher, is born.
12/29/1888. Asa Brainard, star pitcher, dies. In 1866, Brainard's annual salary was only $1,100.	**12/30/1935.** Sandy Koufax is born.	**12/31/1974.** "Catfish" Hunter is signed by the Yankees for millions. It's the start of the era of free agents.				

Lou Gehrig scoring one of his career 1,888 runs.

FREE STUFF! FREE STUFF! GET YER FREE STUFF HERE!

official and compl... baseball. This nearly 3,000-page, oversized volume includes: the yearly performance of everyone who was ever in the major leagues; a chronological listing of teams and their players ...th complete batting, pitching, and fielding ...tics for each season through 1989; and ...and single-season record holders in every

from the old Negro ...... and authoritative collection of statistics ever p... into one volume makes this 8th Edition the mos... comprehensive and indispensable book on baseball history. 1990. ca. 2600 pages. 8 1/2" x 11". (Macmillan)

ALSO FEATURING 125 NEW BOO...

L et's say a company makes a T-shirt that reads I HAVE BAD BREATH.

The company only makes size extra-large and in an ugly beige color. They're selling the T-shirts for $20 apiece. Are you interested?

No way, you say.

Okay, but how about if the T-shirts are free?

Tell the truth. Don't you suddenly begin to tell yourself things like this: "Well, maybe I could give them out as presents. Maybe I could wear them as pajama tops.... I'll take fifty!"

The fact is that everyone loves to get something for free. And this chapter is full of baseball freebies!

HIDDEN COSTS

As you go through this catalogue, you'll see lots of items (mostly catalogues and other print materials) that you can send away for, free of charge.

Well, not totally free. Most places will at least want you to send a SASE (self-addressed stamped envelope—see page 4) for more SASE instructions). And many companies make you pay "handling charges." That's a little money to pay for the time it takes to *handle* your request.

And, even when you're getting something from a company that doesn't require a SASE, you're still not getting it completely free. If you write to the company, you've spent a stamp. If you call, there's the price of the phone call.

But that kind of talk is for party poopers. Free is free, and it's fun to get.

When you send out letters for free stuff, don't forget to include your return address on the envelope and letter. Print it legibly. And state exactly what you want.

If you send out enough letters and get on enough mailing lists, you can start receiving a steady stream of mail. It's a nice feeling.

There's one more catch to mention. Some free materials take a while to arrive. The best strategy is this: After you send out your letters, forget all about it. Go out and play ball. Then, when your freebies arrive, they'll come as an exciting surprise.

PASS THE PASTA

As any professional athlete can tell you, being in good shape is crucial to playing well. To get in shape, athletes exercise and try to eat right.

For extra energy, some athletes make a point of eating a meal loaded with carbohydrates the evening before the game.

Pasta is one excellent source of carbohydrates. For some free pasta recipes aimed especially at athletes, send a business-size SASE to the following address. Ask for

THE BULL PEN
Q: **What does a team with a wild pitcher have in common with an Almond Joy?**
A: **They both have nuts on the mound.**

the booklet called *Pasta for Athletes.*

The National Macaroni
Institute
P.O. Box 336
Palatine, IL 60067

EATING RIGHT

To be a good athlete, you're going to have to eat more than just noodles. Here's a free booklet with advice on a well-balanced diet, plus recipes, quizzes, and puzzles. It's called *Mr. Peanut's Guide to Nutrition.* Write to:

Standard Brands
Educational Service
P.O. Box 2695
Grand Central Station
New York, NY 10017

FAN CLUBS

In Chapter 2, there's a roundup of some of the major league fan clubs around the league. Some charge a membership fee, but many are free. When you join a fan club, you'll usually receive some gift items, such as a member-ship button, a newsletter, etc.

For example, the Pittsburgh Pirates have the Knothole Gang for kids 14 and under. For a $1 handling charge, you get a free pass to two Pirates games, a membership button, a painter's cap, a

vinyl 6 × 8 baseball card holder, a wooden bat pen, and two issues of the Pirates newsletter.

FREE BASEBALL CAMP BROCHURES

If you're shopping for a baseball camp, you might want to browse through some brochures to see what's out there. You can use the listing in Chapter 4 to receive free brochures and fliers.

FREE BOOK CATALOGUES

Chapter 6 lists some of the many dealers of baseball books. In most cases, you can get a free catalogue if you send a SASE. If you love baseball, these catalogues are fun to browse through, because you'll want everything.

For example, you can get a free catalogue by sending a SASE to:

Don Wade Baseball Books
31702 Campbell
Madison Heights, MI 48071

FREE SAMPLE ISSUES OF BASEBALL MAGAZINES

Your chances of getting a free sample of a big, glossy magazine are not good. These magazines are available on news-stands everywhere. If

you're interested in one copy, they figure you can buy it.

But some of the smaller magazines listed in Chapter 6 will be glad to send out a free sample copy, on request. They want you to get to know the magazine, and subscribe.

There's only one problem. If you really like the magazine, you'll do just that. And the rest of the copies you get won't be free!

Here's one to get you started. *Baseball Card Investment Report* sends out free copies. Write to:

Baseball Card Investment Report
American Card Exchange
125 East Baker, Suite 150
Costa Mesa, CA 92626

FREE BASEBALL NEWSLETTERS

Some of the major league teams publish free newsletters, and so do fans. If you're interested, you can begin receiving large numbers of free baseball newsletters. Most don't come often—they're published five times a year, say. But if you get on enough mailing lists, you'll always be getting a newsletter from someone!

Here's one free baseball

newsletter to get you started. There are more newsletter listings, plus tips on where to look for even more, in Chapter 6.

Here's the Pitch
Mr. W. Lloyd Johnson
205 W. 66th Terrace
Kansas City, MO 64113
(816) 822-1740

FREE BASEBALL MERCHANDISE CATALOGUES

Chapter 9 has listings for makers of all sorts of baseball-related products, from baseball caps to pitching machines. Some of these companies don't sell through mail order. But many of the ones that do will be glad to send you a free catalogue of their baseball goods. See Chapter 9 for more information.

FREE SIGNED PHOTOS OF BASEBALL PLAYERS

Is there a particular player you admire on a major or minor league team? As described in Chapter 10, the team office might very well send you a free photo of the player if you write and ask nicely. They might even get the player to autograph the photo.

FREE ADDRESSES

Speaking of autographs, if you want to get serious about baseball autograph collecting, there are books for sale with addresses for all the major league players. (To find a book like this, use the listings for baseball book catalogues on page 103.) That way, you can write to the players directly and ask for their free signatures. (*Note:* Current players prefer that you write to them in care of their team. And some players may charge a fee for their autograph.)

FREE BASEBALL BOARD GAMES CATALOGUES

Chapter 11 lists a number of companies that sell baseball board games via mail order. Many of them will send you a free brochure or catalogue. For example, for a brochure about the baseball board game Statis-Pro, write or call:

The Avalon Hill Game Company
4517 Hartford Road
Baltimore, MD 21214
(800) 638-9292

FREE COMPUTER GAME CATALOGUES AND NEWSLETTERS

Are you a baseball video game fanatic? The makers of computer games often put out free newsletters. These carry lots of plugs for their games, but they also may have puzzles, game-playing strategy tips, high scores, and other items of interest.

The ads in computer game magazines (such as *Gamepro* and *Video Games and Computer Entertainment,* which you'll find in any large magazine shop) are a good place to look for such newsletters. They also run sweepstakes and other contests for winning free games. Here are a few computer game newsletters to get you started.

Sunsoft Game Time News
Sunsoft
P.O. Box 2390
Libertyville, IL 60198

Taito Times
Taito Software, Inc.
P.O. Box 1439
Bothell, WA 98041-9926

The Fun Club
4948 Highway 169 North
New Hope, MN 55428

FREE T-SHIRTS FOR HIGH SCORERS

After you get all those strategy tips from video game newsletters, you'll probably become a

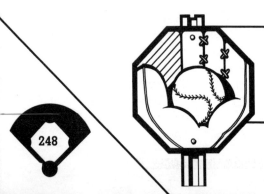

SHORTSTOPS
Yogi Berra, known for his funny quotes, was once asked how he liked school as a kid. His answer? "Closed."

superpro at your home baseball game. You might be able to use your high score to win a free T-shirt.

Gamepro magazine prints high scores each month. The winners get a free Gamepro T-shirt. The contest is for Nintendo, Sega, Genesis, and Atari games. For the rules, see any issue of *Gamepro*. (Alas, it's not free!) (See page 215 for Gamepro's address.)

FREE TRIPS

In addition to free things you can get in the mail, there's a whole other class of free things covered in this catalogue. There are free things you can *do*. For instance, Chapter 3 lists free baseball exhibits and museums. In Chapter 4 you'll find a list of free tours offered by major league stadiums. And Chapter 12 describes free youth league games and free ceremonies at the Baseball Hall of Fame.

TRADING

It's not exactly free (you're not getting something for nothing), but trading is another great way to get baseball stuff without spending money.

The possibilities for trades are limitless. Here are some that are covered in this catalogue: You can trade cards with your friends and dealers (Chapter 10), you can trade in old video games for new ones (see page 215), and you can trade in your duplicate Panini baseball stickers with the sticker company itself (see page 198).

I'LL TRADE YA:
WHEN BASEBALL STARS SWITCH TEAMS

If you're a baseball card collector or a fantasy league player, you've probably traded a player now and then. It's easy. All that changes hands is a small piece of cardboard or a name on a piece of paper.

But when major league owners trade players, the players and their families have to move to a different city. And the fans can lose a star they have rooted for and cared about for years. Still, trades are just part of the business and the game of baseball.

Sometimes players are traded because they're unhappy with their current team. Not only that, a good trade can help both teams, sometimes turning so-so teams into pennant winners. Bad trades can do the reverse. Here's a look at some of the amazing facts about trades in baseball history.

Many superstar players don't start out that way. As rookies, they may be traded away for peanuts. When they go on to become immortal players, the team that first traded the player looks pretty stupid.

Take Cy Young, for example. He became such a famous pitcher that the pitching MVP award is named after him. But when he was a rookie, who knew he would someday become *the* Cy Young? One Ohio team traded him to another for a bunch of clothes!

Cy Young's not the only player to be traded for something other than another player. Ball players have been traded for a plate of beans, two barrels of oysters, a dozen doughnuts, and a box of prunes!

Kansas City traded Roger Maris to the Yankees—another famous mistake. One year later Maris knocked out his record-breaking 61 homers. He won the MVP award twice while playing for the Yanks.

Trades can involve more than two teams at a time. In 1953 and 1977 there were trades that involved four teams!

In his 17-year career, pitcher Bobo Newsom was traded 14 times! (He was traded to the Senators five times!)

Teams don't always trade players. Sometimes they just sell them. In the 1880s, a star player named Mike "King" Kelly was sold by the Chicago White Stockings to Boston for $10,000. He was the first baseball star to be sold in this manner.

In 1920, Red Sox owner Harry Frazee sold the superstar Babe Ruth to the Yankees. A player deal can't get much worse than that.

In 1954, the Yankees and Orioles made a whopper trade involving 17 players, a record for a trade between two teams.

Brooks Robinson is a rarity in the world of trades. In his 22-year career, the Orioles star was *never* traded.

INDEX

W

Y